100 Careers in Film and Television

100 Careers in Film and Television

Tanja L. Crouch

First edition published 2003 by Barron's Educational Series, Inc.
Text © copyright 2003 by Tanja L. Crouch
Text design and cover © copyright 2003 by Barron's Educational Series, Inc.

All inquiries should be addressed to:
Barron's Educational Series, Inc.
250 Wireless Boulevard
Hauppauge, New York 11788
http://www.barronseduc.com

International Standard Book No.: 0-7641-2164-2
Library of Congress Catalog Card No.: 2002028319

Library of Congress Cataloging-in-Publication Data
Crouch, Tanja.
    100 careers in film & television/by Tanja L. Crouch.—1st ed.
        p.   cm.
    Includes index.
    ISBN 0-7641-2164-2
        1. Motion pictures—Vocational guidance.   2. Television—Vocational guidance.
    I. Title: One hundred careers in film and television.   II. Title.

PN1995.9.P75 C76 2002
791.43'023—dc21   2002028319

Printed in the United States of America

9 8 7 6 5 4 3 2 1

CONTENTS

APPENDICES

CONTENTS

PREFACE

Some of my earliest childhood memories are of our family gathering in the living room to watch *The Wizard of Oz, White Christmas, Rear Window*, and other film classics. I fondly remember Friday nights spent at the Granada Theater watching *2001: A Space Odyssey, Funny Girl*, and *Love Story*. Later, when I was a teenager, friends and I spent hot summer nights at the drive-in, watching *American Graffiti, Jaws, Star Wars*, and *The Way We Were* unfold across the enormous screen.

Equally captivating was television. In fifth grade I bought one raffle ticket at my elementary school carnival and won a black and white console television. Since I had won it, and the family already had a color set, I was allowed to put it in my bedroom. For years I reveled in *The Man from U.N.C.L.E., Bonanza*, and *Bewitched*, and fell asleep nightly to Johnny Carson's *Tonight Show*.

Growing up in my small Eastern Oregon hometown, it never occurred to me that people could have a career in the film or television industry. To this day, I don't know why I never thought to investigate who created those environments, lit them, costumed and made-up the actors, directed the action, filmed it, composed music for, and later edited the action, but it didn't cross my mind. Job titles like gaffer, first AD, UPM, and visual effects artist were not only foreign to my ear, but completely out of my realm of understanding.

It was not until several years later, when I was working in Los Angeles as a visual merchandising director over a landmark department store where a pilot for the series *Berrenger's* was shot, that I began to realize there were hundreds of artisans working behind the scenes to create the production I would later view. It was while serving as an in-store technical adviser to the art department that week, and the week following, when the production moved to the then Lorimar lot, that I become intoxicated with the filmmaking process. Over the next few years, I freelanced from time to time, working with the art department on *Knot's Landing* whenever sets involving retail stores were needed. But with no family connections in the business to help me, I was never able to amass the required number of hours in the proper category to gain admission into the union.

If only I had known then what I know now, it might not have taken me another fifteen years to realize that my passion lay in film and television production. While serving as vice president of Barbara Orbison Productions (the Roy Orbison estate), my interest in film and television production was rekindled by working on television specials, documentaries, and a London stage production based on Roy Orbison's life and music. Licensing Orbison's songs and recordings for features such as *For the Love of the Game*, *In Dreams*, *Love Letter*, and *You've Got Mail*, and television series *Ally McBeal*, *Beverly Hills 90210*, and *Felicity*, further fueled my desire to find my niche in filmmaking.

Having never written a script or television treatment, I seized an opportunity to pitch an idea and write the treatment for what later became a two-hour documentary called "This Joint is Jumpin'" that originally aired on Bravo! I remained with the production, serving as a co-producer. It led to the creation of other documentaries, other producing opportunities, and some location work. As I finish this book, I am negotiating salary for work on a major feature film. That job would not have been possible if I had not made a connection with someone working in the industry while writing this book.

Frequently, while researching this book, I found myself wishing I had had a copy of it when I was back in Eastern Oregon. This book is meant as an inspiration and catalyst for anyone considering a career in filmmaking. Whether you are still in high school or contemplating a career change, there is something here for you.

INTRODUCTION

*1*00 *Careers in Film and Television* presents more than one hundred job descriptions and profiles individuals working in those capacities, sharing their perspectives on the business, advice for breaking in and thriving in the industry, and their personal stories of how they found their way into the business and have achieved their current success.

In selecting those profiled, I chose a diverse group of individuals. Some knew they wanted to be filmmakers from the time they were very young, while others made a career change later in life. Some focused on a specific area of interest, others tried several different jobs before discovering their niche. Some had family and friends working in the business, while others knew no one. Most work as independent contractors, but some hold salaried positions working for a studio, a production company, film office, or other related businesses.

Salary information has not been included because this changes periodically and differs greatly between nonunion and union productions, and commercials, television, and features. For a general idea of union salaries, contact the union office of your area of interest (see Appendix I) for information about the current minimum and maximum rates.

Six appendices are included at the back of this book to provide information about film organizations, schools, festivals, directories, and databases with the most up-to-date contact information for studios, production companies, and related businesses, trade magazines, and books about filmmaking. There is also a glossary that defines terms peculiar to the industry.

For those who already know what area of filmmaking their passion lies in, I tried to organize the book in such a way that similar departments, positions, and areas of interest are grouped together in the same chapter. But, as you read the biographies of those profiled in the book, you will discover that depending on the size of the production, and whether it is a feature or television program, commercial or video, job functions sometimes overlap. For those uncertain about their area of interest, and for those wanting to gain a better understanding of the many jobs available in the industry and how they interconnect, I hope you will enjoy reading the book from cover to cover.

In talking with the individuals interviewed for this book, three recurring themes emerged:

1. EDUCATION. While some in this book do not have a college degree, most agreed that a background in filmmaking and a well-rounded knowledge of film history are vital to success. Where that knowledge comes from—whether from a conventional university, college, or film school, or through an internship or self-study—is not as important as the fact that the knowledge is obtained.

It is important to note that some companies require executives to hold a degree. For instance, a bachelor's degree is required for entrance into the agent-training program at William Morris Agency. You may not feel it is necessary to obtain a degree for your particular field, but realize that no one was ever *not* hired for having earned a degree.

Of equal importance is self-education. Study movies, television programs, or commercials; read every book and magazine you can find about the industry. Educate yourself about business trends, technology, and become familiar with the names of important individuals in the industry.

2. PRODUCTION ASSISTANTS, INTERNSHIPS, APPRENTICE-SHIPS. Entry-level positions—PAs, Interns, and Apprentices—are an invaluable way for you to discover how the industry works, to see firsthand how different departments relate to one another, and to allow potential future employers to evaluate your skills and work ethic. Many, many of those profiled in this book began as production assistants, interns, or apprentices. Some of them had already achieved a high level of success in another career, and gave it up for an entry-level industry position where they could learn and then progress. Every production has PAs and everyone needs them.

Understand that entry-level jobs pay little or no money. Think of them as your advanced education in the industry. Whether you have saved money in advance, live at home, or have the backing of a spouse or friend, it is important to have a means of financial support while you pursue your first jobs. Some of those interviewed for this book have suggested having enough money to live on for one full year.

3. NETWORKING IS VITAL. The old adage "It's who you know" is true. Success in the film and television industry is a team effort, and when building your team, you tend to pick the players you know you can work well with. Each person you meet is a potential employer or reference. Treat everyone the way you want to be treated and you will not have to worry about what impression you leave behind.

Constantly put yourself in a position to better your craft and meet others working in the industry: work for little or no money on student and low budget films; be willing to help others with their projects; work at an equipment rental facility; volunteer to work on industry events; find someone who is working in an area you are interested in and offer to serve as an intern or apprentice. In return, you will meet people and they will have a chance to observe your talents and work ethic.

The film and television industry is an exciting and creative business to be a part of. Thus, there are thousands of people competing for the same job you want. Someone has to fill the position and that someone can be you. Prepare yourself by studying the business, history, and technology of filmmaking, arm yourself with skills, and be prepared to start at the bottom. Work hard and passionately, and you will succeed.

CHAPTER

1

WRITERS

Writers write the story. Directors, producers, actors, and studio executives may all have their input, but it is the writers put their pens to paper, so to speak, to give the story its form. They create and write the screenplays, without which there would be no actions to film, no words to record, no emotions to convey; in short, no movie or television program.

Some writers sit alone in a room and write entire screenplays; others, writing for television, may be responsible for creating the plot bible for the entire season and writing or co-writing individual episodes; some writers are hired to rewrite existing screenplays, which can vary from a final polish to a complete overhaul. Others fill even narrower parameters, like punching up existing jokes or writing new ones, or tailoring dialogue to a particular actor's limitations. Some writers adapt their own literary work for the screen; others are hired to adapt existing books.

Many writers specialize in a specific genre, like action/adventure, drama, comedy, or medical- or legal-themed material. Some work solely in television, and may further specialize in made-for-television movies, dramatic series, or sitcoms. A very few writers, like David E. Kelly, somehow manage to do it all.

Regardless of what, where, or why, all writers write.

Three writers of diverse background, experience, and expertise are profiled in this chapter.

JOB TITLE: WRITER/PRODUCER

Job Overview

The writer creates characters and situations, invents dialogue and story line, and rewrites and polishes the treatment or script for production.

A writer/producer often oversees the writing to ensure that what is written can be filmed, weighing such considerations as sound stage availability and budget limitations. "You're responsible as a writer/producer to trim the script down to budget and still keep it interesting," says writer/producer Peter Dunne. "There is a way to write it that is just as colorful and less expensive."

Episodic television writer/producers are responsible for the quality of production, making budgetary choices that balance cost against value. The writer/producer may also assign directors to the different episodes; oversee casting, the hiring of crew, and all aspects of production; and coordinate post-production. They also work with the writing staff.

Special Skills and Education

Write. Hone your craft by immersing yourself in writing spec scripts over and over again. The way to develop your writing skills is to keep writing.

Speaking of attending college or film school, Dunne says, "I think it's great to study, because you find yourself [through] study, but it doesn't guarantee you a job. It doesn't better your chances of getting a job unless you make connections while you're in school. Like studying art, sooner or later you have to go out and make your own paintings. All the studying in the world isn't going to get you your first sale."

Advice for Someone Seeking This Job

Dunne suggests watching a lot of television to determine what type of writing appeals to you most: drama, like *Ed* or the *Gilmore Girls*, something political like *West Wing*, or criminal like *C.S.I: Crime Scene Investigation* or *Law & Order*, and start writing in that genre. "There are so many screenplays available to every person now, at specialty bookstores and online. Go to *scripts.com* and buy some, or visit the WG [Writer's Guild] offices downtown and read scripts. Read episodic pilots. Immerse yourself. The trick to writing and becoming a writer is to write. That's the trick most people avoid. They want to plan around it and educate and theorize and learn about writing theory. Sit down and write, and you learn to write. Just write one screenplay after another, one episodic spec script after another, and keep going. They don't take a long time to write. Keep writing until you can attract an agent, and off you go."

It is a myth that you need to have sold something to get an agent. Dunne says your writing will get you an agent, "then the agent will get you the job, if your writing is any good at all." Check with the Writers Guild to find out when they are hosting events where writers can meet potential agents. Some agencies will accept unsolicited scripts. Ask the Guild for a list of agencies and guidelines.

"You just have to write; get the writing out and be prepared for rejection, because that's a big part of the deal."

Professional Profile: Peter Dunne, Writer, Producer, Line Producer

Filmmaking is the second successful career for Peter Dunne, who was an advertising executive in Manhattan before relocating to the West Coast. Through friends made in the film industry, he met Aaron Spelling socially. Spelling told Dunne that if he ever wanted to get out of advertising and work in the business, to give him a call. One day he did.

Dunne's film career began as a trainee on *Mod Squad*. "As a trainee, I was an observer. I ran errands and was elevated a little bit above a production assistant." Working for Spelling was better than going to film school. "Aaron was very generous and said, 'Why don't you work with this director for a couple of months, then work with this editor for a couple of months, and these writers for a couple of months.' He just groomed me."

At the end of each season, Spelling sat down with each employee for fifteen to twenty private minutes and asked them how they felt about the past year, how they liked their job, and what they wanted to do next. "Many people wanted to move up and he accommodated that. If an editor wanted to direct, he would promise them a directing assignment, but he would also arrange for the editor to observe Aaron's favorite directors on different sets. By the end of the season, that editor would have an opportunity to direct. I wanted to write, so he put me into development. He gave me a choice between grooming me as a producer or a development exec. I wanted to be a development exec first because I thought in order to be a producer, I really had to know a lot more about scripts."

VOICES OF EXPERIENCE

What do you like least about your job?

"I do so many different jobs from season to season (some years I take a job as a line producer and other years as a writing/producer) that I don't dislike any of it. I don't think I would be happy if I had to stick with one thing forever."—Peter Dunne

What do you love most about your job?

"I love writing more than anything else. I also teach at UCLA, and I'm working on a novel and a screenplay. I think writing came first to me in terms of artistic expression because it's a lonely art."—Peter Dunne

Ready for a new challenge, Dunne left his development job at Aaron Spelling Productions to become the head of development for Lorimar Productions. There he developed several projects that included *Eight Is Enough, Helter Skelter,* and *Sybil,* for which he won an Emmy. In addition to development, Dunne often filled the role of writer and/or producer as well. He spent three seasons as a writer and producer on the mega-hit series *Knot's Landing,* followed by nearly two years as supervising producer for *Dallas.*

Another mentor early in Dunne's career was David Jacobs, "especially in the writing field, when I started working with him on *Knot's Landing.* He was very generous. He gave me room to write and let me make mistakes. He framed and put on my wall scenes that could never be shot— they were just too impractical—that he knew I loved, so I would always appreciate them."

CAREER TIPS

★ *"Show business, probably more than any other business, is terribly cruel. You're only as good as your currency today. It doesn't matter if you have a lot of great credits; it really doesn't. It just matters if you have a good idea today. I think the thing you have to keep in mind is that your life can't be about this business; as much as I love it, and as kind as it's been to me (and ugly at times), I can't judge myself as a success or failure in life based on the business. I have to keep other interests: writing, art, family. You have to stay centered as a person, and then success will come."—Peter Dunne*

★ *"You have to be passionate and really love the art of filmmaking; then you'll have fun doing it. That's the bottom line of whether you're a success: if you've actually smiled during the day and you feel good about your work."—Peter Dunne*

In the late 1990s, Dunne wrote and produced *Nowhere Man,* starring Bruce Greenwood. "It was one of the most fun projects for me as a producer and writer. I did the pilot here in town and then shot the series in Portland. We didn't have any stages. That's what made it interesting. We shot on the streets every day, whether it rained or snowed; no matter how hot it was. It was like doing a film every day."

For a time, Dunne reunited with Spelling to serve as supervising producer on *Melrose Place,* and later to write an episode for the series. Then it was off to New Zealand to work on the pilot of the ABC series *McKenna.* In 2001, he worked on the series *That's Life,* starring Ellen Burstyn and Paul Sorvino, and is currently about to launch a series that he wrote and will produce.

In addition to Spelling and Jacobs, Dunne states that he has found many mentors in the business: "guys in craft services, ladies in casting, grips on high; everybody has taught me something and they still do."

JOB TITLES: WRITER; EXECUTIVE STORY EDITOR

Job Overview

For a one-hour episodic television series, the story editor has a number of duties; some specific, some more loosely designed. On *Walker, Texas Ranger*, executive story editor Duke Sandefur worked with other writers, developing and constructing stories before they went to teleplay. Then, he rewrote scripts for production. "Writing for production is a little like cutting crystal in a mudslide," Sandefur explains. "Sometimes, it's a trophy. Other times, you wind up with broken glass and mud.

"There are a lot of practical concerns that arise before and during production that call for rapid rewrites on-the-fly. A little rainstorm or an injured actor can cause a sequence to be totally reconstructed in a matter of hours. Personally, I love that kind of work. It's fast and exciting and entails the same kind of deadlines one finds in newspaper journalism. I work best under pressure."

Special Skills

"It's worth noting," says Sandefur, "there are two skills one needs for writing prose that one does not need for writing screenplay: spelling and punctuation. There are machines that spell for you. That part's taken care of. And as to punctuation, the most important thing is to write the way people speak. People generally do not punctuate or spell very well when they speak. Listen to some of David Mamet's dialogue and tell me how it should be punctuated on paper. Good luck! As far as education . . . read a book on screenwriting, any book. Pick one; they all contain the basic formats and conventions of screenplay. It also helps to take a class, because it will force you to write and you can't learn this stuff without actually writing. Talking about writing doesn't get it done. You don't have to go to college and major in film and television to write a screenplay. Many successful professional writers I know started off doing something quite different. My 10-year-old son says he wants to be a writer. I told him to learn how to build bridges first."

Advice for Someone Seeking This Job

"Write," says Sandefur. "Secondly, don't stop writing. Lastly, finish each thing you start. If you don't finish, it doesn't count. It's like sailing halfway across the Atlantic. Glub! It's like playing 17 holes of golf. It's like drinking three beers out of a six-pack. If you build a house without a roof, it still won't hold water. Just finish, no matter what. Then go on to the next thing. But finish! Get some produced scripts. Some scripts have been published and are available in bookstores. I think you can even buy scripts on eBay. Read them. Copy a format or a style you like. If you can't think of anyone to copy at first, find a script by William Goldman. Goldman is a screenwriter's screenwriter."

Professional Profile: Duke Sandefur, Writer

"When I was about five years old, I was watching *Bonanza* with my father in the basement. He was a dentist at the time in Indiana. I can't quote him, but he ventured that he could probably write that show. Next thing I know, we're moving to Hollywood. And damned if he didn't wind up writing a lot of *Bonanza* episodes (and decades of television material since). He took a screenwriting class at Hollywood High School and was off to the races."

The elder Sandefur's first gig was the result of persistence. "He wrote a story for *Bonanza* and gave it to the story editor (I believe that was John Hawkins's title at the time) at the Paramount gate. John was the first to arrive every day and the last to leave some days. He considered my father a nuisance at first, but read the material. After several exchanges in the early morning hours—my dad handing in revised material and John giving him notes—John finally invited my father inside and bought a story. John taught my father a lot . . . and later, taught me a lot. He was a great man.

"We eventually settled in Studio City, almost in the shadow of Universal Studios. From the beginning, I read what my father wrote. I learned the craft and conventions of screenplay from a man who was also learning. His primary life advice for me at the time was: 'Do whatever you want to do, but I won't support you if you choose dentistry.'

"I went to a few colleges and majored in everything from physics to 'undeclared' before I settled on television and film. In hindsight, I should have majored in anything else. Technologies such as nonlinear digital editing have made much of my formal education mostly obsolete.

"One of my early writing classes required writing a teleplay. I figured that if I were going to write a teleplay, I was absolutely going to try to sell [it]. So, I picked a target . . . There was a series getting underway called *Spider-Man* and I had a passing acquaintance with two guys on the show: Bob Janes and Ron Satlof. I wrote an episode in about five days and handed it in to my instructor. I also got a copy to Bob Janes . . . I sold the episode. I failed the class. Go figure."

Over the next few years, Sandefur studied at "some of your better colleges in Southern California" and worked as a freelance writer, before accepting his first staff job in the series *Enos*. "Every job is a milestone. Jobs are few and writers are many, and it's getting more and more competitive, especially in one-hour episodic. When I began, television was dominated by one-hour dramas. It was relatively easy to get a pitch meeting. With the advent of half-hour comedy and reality programming, the number of one-hour dramas has been greatly reduced and it's not such an open market.

"If I had to pick one job that meant the most . . . I'd have to say it was an episode I did for *Little House on the Prairie: A New Beginning*. At the time, I was pretty young and I'd sort of given up on writing as a career. But there was a true story from my life that I wanted to tell and it fit with *Little House*. Don Balluck [*Little House* executive story consultant], a good friend and a great writer who has since passed away, was open to a pitch, so I told him my story. In short order, I had an assignment and wrote the script. It turned out to be a very rewarding experience and helped refocus my energies. I never looked back after that."

With a renewed interest in screenwriting, Sandefur worked on a number of television shows, picking up odd episodes here and there, rewriting or polishing existing material, and creating screenplays of his own. He worked regularly on *The Rockford Files*, *Mickey Spillane's Mike Hammer*, and other series. He served as script consultant on the crime drama *Dark Justice*, writing ten episodes himself and co-writing a two-hour movie.

He served as executive story editor on the high action series *Soldier of Fortune, Inc.*, producer Jerry Bruckheimer's first venture into television. "Working for Jerry Bruckheimer was a lot of fun because he demanded big action. *Soldier of*

VOICES OF EXPERIENCE

What do you like least about your job?

"Beginning. 'Fade In:' is the hardest thing to write. The blank page is potentially one's best friend, but also an enemy to be feared."—Duke Sandefur

What do you love most about your job?

"Finishing. 'Fade out' is the easiest and most rewarding thing to write. Finishing is where the satisfaction is.

"Wait . . . suddenly I'm thinking of lots of things I love about my work. The flexible hours (often called 'unemployment' or the preferred 'hiatus') are great. As a freelancer, I don't clock in, I don't hit a key without my morning coffee, and if I feel a compelling need to go fishing, I do. Staff work is more rewarding in this regard because it's task oriented. You get to finish a lot more often."—Duke Sandefur

Fortune is notable because it gave me the largest explosion I ever got. They blew up an old sewage treatment plant—it was spectacular."

CAREER TIPS

★ *"My father told me very early: 'Don't tell me what you want to be— tell me what you want to do!'" With that advice in mind, Sandefur tells people, "I write."*

★ *"It's important— no, it's critical—to listen to people speak. Like fingerprints, there are no two speech patterns that are the same. Characters should always have a unique voice of their own, and it helps immensely to be able to remember bits of speech from life. Stealing from yourself, from your memories, is a huge part of writing, especially in dialogue. Dar Williams wrote it in a song: '. . . stealing from myself, it's what I do . . .'"*
—Duke Sandefur

★ *[Finishing a script is] "like gestating a baby, then throwing it to wolves. If one is on staff, then one plays the role of the wolf too."*—Duke Sandefur

After the show was cancelled he returned to freelance writing, then served as executive story editor for the final season of *Walker, Texas Ranger,* and resumed work on speculative scripts and other freelance work.

"If I had to list all the people who have helped me or contributed to my career in one way or another, we'd need another forum and much more space. But I'd be remiss if I didn't mention John Hawkins, a mentor to my mentors. He was a very skilled and unselfish writer and I miss him very much. I learned an awful lot from him about writing and life.

"I don't know that I ever wanted to be a writer. The craft was something I learned, partly by exposure and osmosis. To be truthful, writing chose me more than the other way around. I did it because I knew how to do it and I knew one could make a pretty good living at it. Finally, in the last few years, I've come to love it. I really wouldn't want to do anything else."

JOB TITLE: SCREENWRITER, WRITER

Job Overview

The screenwriter creates the characters, devises the plot, invents the dialogue, and writes the screenplay.

Special Skills

Screenwriter Beth Szymkowski discovered that her experience as a journalist not only enhanced her writing and editing skills, but also introduced her to diverse people, stories, and voices. It taught her to accept criticism without being discouraged or offended, and to use it as a tool to improve her writing.

Advice for Someone Seeking This Job

Sometimes Szymkowski wishes she had realized that she wanted to be a screenwriter when she was still in high school, so she could have gone on to film school, but doubts that she would be the writer she is today if she had not taken a circuitous path. That pathway provides the depth of life experience that her writing draws upon.

Professional Profile: Beth Szymkowski, Screenwriter

When Beth Szymkowski discovered screenwriting, she found her passion. A Philadelphia native, she initially studied computer science at Duke University before switching majors and earning a bachelor's degree in English. She went on to get a masters degree in teaching in 1992, but then discovered she did not want to teach. For a time she worked in retail, and then took an internship at a weekly newspaper in Durham, North Carolina. "I always knew I wanted to be a writer, ever since I was little. I liked writing short stories . . . When I got out of college it seemed too much of a stretch. I was too scared, basically. I wanted to get a job where I had security."

The internship led to a job with *The Sanford Herald*, a small daily newspaper in Sanford, North Carolina. Newly married to up-and-coming cinematographer Clark Mathis, the couple decided to relocate to Southern California in 1994,

VOICES OF EXPERIENCE

What do you like least about your job?

"What I like least is the uncertainty of it all; the feeling that I'm working hard, but that it might not come to anything. It's not like going to school to be a nurse and you become one. You could write and still not get the big payoff at the end."—Beth Szymkowski

What do you love most about your job?

"I like the writing process. I like being able to make up stories—that's what I love the most about it. I can sit down, blink, and ten hours have passed because I get so involved with the characters and what I'm writing."—Beth Szymkowski

so that her husband could further pursue film work. There, Szymkoski found work as a reporter for *The San Bernardino Sun.* "I liked reporting, but it wasn't entirely satisfying to me." She sometimes found herself frustrated that the people in the stories she reported on were not giving her the quotes she envisioned. Seeing an ad for a screenwriting class, she enrolled and from the first day discovered that she loved it. She wrote her first screenplay while continuing to work at the newspaper.

CAREER TIPS

★ *"There is a really good web site: www. moviebytes.com, that has a link to contests."* —Beth Szymkowski

★ *"Always be improving."*—Beth Szymkowski

When her husband's career began to take off, the couple decided to move closer to Los Angeles, and Szymkowski quit her job to devote her energy to screenwriting. Initially she thought she would pursue television sitcom writing, and even performed standup comedy in clubs, trying to network and improve her skills. At the same time, she finished a second screenplay and entered it in most of the major screenwriting contests. Although she did not win, she was a finalist for the Walt Disney Writing Fellowship and the Chesterfield Writer's Film Project, and a quarter finalist in the Nicholl Fellowships in Screenwriting competition.

Szymkowski won the Carl Sautter Memorial Screenwriting Competition, which got her screenplay into the hands of a producer and led to a meeting at Imagine Entertainment. She is currently working on an idea for them that potentially will be presented to Universal for funding. Although she did not win the Set in Philadelphia Screenwriting Contest, one of the judges, screenwriter Stephen J. Rivele, felt she should have. He referred her to an agent and is interested in turning her screenplay into a sitcom.

Since devoting herself to screenwriting, Szymkowski has completed several writing classes at American Film Institute (AFI), UCLA, and other extension courses. She also participates in a screenwriting group.

"I am very happy I've come upon [screenwriting] as what I want to do with my life. Now, I'm at the point where if this doesn't work out, I don't know what I would do. I can't imagine doing something else."

● ● ● ●

CHAPTER

2

PRODUCERS AND
THE PRODUCTION OFFICE

In the broadest sense, it is the producer who makes a film happen. The producer finds the story, gets the money to finance the production, and helps put together the pool of actors and artisans who will bring the story to life. Once the project is set up, the producer troubleshoots problems and keeps the project on track throughout all its phases, until the finished product is released.

Some producers are dealmakers, specializing in the business aspects and hiring out the actual production responsibilities to others. Other producers love the creative aspects of filmmaking and remain actively involved throughout the process. Then there are writer/producers who are sometimes given a producer credit in lieu of a salary increase.

Responsibilities of a producer vary from project to project, and a title may denote one set of responsibilities in film, another set in television, and yet another for commercials and music videos.

The production staff is charged with the hands-on, nuts and bolts responsibility of getting the project made. A huge project may require multiple people to split the responsibilities of a single position, while one person will fill several positions on a small project. Generally, the production staff consists of:

- Unit Production Manager (UPM): oversee budgets, negotiate contracts, strike deals, hire crew, and handle the mountain of paperwork thus generated.

- Production Supervisor: assist the UPM with office responsibilities.

- Production Office Coordinator: the office manager.

- Assistant Production Office Coordinator: assigned duties by the Production Office Coordinator; frequently charged with travel and transportation arrangements.

- Production Secretary: frequently charged with communicating information and scheduling.

- Office Production Assistant: a resourceful gofer.

- Accounting Staff: track budgets, pay bills, and handle payroll.

This chapter is divided into three sections: Producers, Production Office, and Physical Production Facility Management.

PRODUCERS

JOB TITLE: EXECUTIVE PRODUCER, FEATURE FILMS

Job Overview

The executive producer is ultimately responsible for getting the production made. Duties include hiring the above-the-line personnel and crew, overseeing the budget, and making key decisions involving the production.

"There are a lot of titles that get thrown around," says executive producer Alan Blomquist. "I've been called a co-producer, an executive producer, and sometimes the line producer. In television, I would be called the producer and the person who created the show would be called the executive producer. In features, it seems to be the opposite: the person who sells the concept to the studio and raises the money is called the producer, and the person they hire to actually make the movie is called the executive producer.

"In layman's parlance, I'm the general contractor," he adds. "I build the house. The screenwriter is the architect, the producer is the developer who raises the money, and I'm the guy that they give the money and the architect's plans to and ask: 'How much is it going to cost? How long is it going to take? How many people do we have to hire?' I make sure they don't buy too much lumber, and that the permits from the building inspector are signed off before the roof goes on. I'm literally the realizer."

"Once the deal has been set for the movie," explains executive producer Neil Machlis, "the studio hires me and I hire everybody else. Then away we go."

Special Skills

An executive producer must be a good businessperson, a leader, and have strong people skills. "It's a people business," says Machlis. "You have to be able to get along with people. You have to be able to see what makes people tick. You also need an understanding of decision making, and be able to think on your feet and make the right decision when things are tough." Executive producers must also be creative problem solvers. For *Cider House Rules*, Blomquist explains, "I had to learn about apple farming and how to keep the apples on the trees longer than they normally stay, because we needed to film late in the season."

Advice for Someone Seeking This Job

Blomquist suggests getting on set as a production assistant or intern and observing what everyone does, then determine what you want to do and map your path. "If you want to be a costume designer, design things and go and work on smaller movies as a designer. If you want to be a prop person, work only in the art department." Once you know what it is you want to do, commit to work only in that area. Too many people take jobs in areas they are not interested in, just to make money. Before long, they get typecast in the role of a production assistant or grip, when what they really want to do is produce or direct. "They wake up and it's three or four years later and they are a fill-in-the-blank, because that's what they get identified as."

"Get on a set. Observe. Then take what you've learned and put it into practice. Go schedule a movie, even if it is in the abstract. Get a script and break it down into a production board. There are computer programs for all of this stuff that will help, but they don't do the thinking for you. *You* have to think. You can't shoot nights and then [shoot] the next day, because the crew can't finish at 6 A.M. and start back at 7 A.M. So, if you go from nights to day, you're going to lose an entire shooting day. You have to shoot Friday night into Saturday so people have the weekend to turn around, and you can start [shooting] days again on Monday."

Unless you have enough money to finance a production yourself, you will not start out as a producer. Get on set as a production assistant and strive to get in the director's guild so you can work as an assistant director (AD), then make the leap into producing. Or go into locations and work into production management, then into producing.

"Do anything you can to learn as much as you can about all different facets of the filmmaking process," says Machlis. "Experience as much as you can and make sure you have great people skills."

"You're interviewing for a job everyday you're working," says executive producer Duncan Henderson. "What you really want to do is make sure that whoever you're working for feels that they would hire you again or would recommend you."

Professional Profile: Alan C. Blomquist, Executive Producer

Growing up in Boston, the son of a fire chief father and a nurse mother, Alan Blomquist knew nothing about the movie business. His only early view of the industry came when he was 15 and worked as a caddy on the golf course where Norman Jewison was directing Steve McQueen in a scene from *The Thomas Crown Affair*.

He attended the University of Michigan, with plans to become a chemical engineer, but discovered he hated engineering school and dropped out. He then enrolled in pre-med for a semester, then dropped out again to spend time figuring out what career he really wanted to pursue. "I always liked going to movies, but I didn't know anything about making them." For laughs, he enrolled in an 8mm film class at night, while working days as a carpenter, building and remodeling houses, and discovered he loved making movies.

He returned to school and earned a bachelor's degree in general studies with an emphasis in film. He continued to work as a carpenter in the Ann Arbor area until his partner decided to return to school, forcing Blomquist to make a decision about his future. "I decided it was time to either get serious about the building business or, if I was going to go to Hollywood, I should go." In 1977, he sold the business, packed up his belongings, and moved to Los Angeles, not knowing a soul.

His first job was selling tickets at a revival movie theater, where he could see movies for free. He was able to get work as a carpenter on movie sets, but realized very quickly that the job was far removed from the action. "They never see the actors or the director or the camera. They build the sets, and then the actors, director, and camera come in and film while they're gone; then they come back and take the set down."

To get on set, Blomquist worked as a grip on nonunion and low budget productions. "If you had any ambition and smarts, it was easy to move up, because there were a lot of people that just sort of showed up. So very quickly I became the key grip."

The job afforded Blomquist the opportunity to survey the business. Initially, he determined that he wanted to be an assistant director, "because they were the one that ran the set. That seemed like a really fun place to be, in the center of a hurricane." Ultimately, he realized that he wanted to produce.

With no financial burdens, no relationship commitments, and the minimal living expense of a low rent house shared with two other grips, Blomquist felt free to take the first step toward becoming an assistant director: stop working as a grip. For the next year and a half, he supported himself through carpentry while trying to find an assistant director job. "Eventually I got somebody to hire me for free . . . they were exploiting me for my labor and I was exploiting them for the opportunity."

Blomquist researched contracts from the various guilds and unions, then learned the job of an AD while doing it. "I got a copy of all the contracts—IATSE, SAG, DGA, whatever—and read them with a highlighter pen. I studied them like I was taking a class. I learned all the rules and then went out and tried to put them into practice, knowing what I knew about how a set ran. I made a lot of mistakes, but I got one job. Then somebody recommended me and I got a second job . . . So my résumé says, 'assistant director; assistant director; additional experience: key grip; key grip; key grip.' Over time, the grip work fell off the résumé and I only had assistant director [credits]."

He next set his sights on becoming a production manager, initially working on nonunion pictures. In 1980, on the recommendation of crew members he had previously worked with, Blomquist received a call asking him to take over a picture called *Breach of Contract*, then shooting in San Francisco. The previous production manager had been fired and they had been unable to find a replacement. The catch was that Blomquist would have to join the

VOICES OF EXPERIENCE

What do you like least about your job?

"What I like least are the time demands, in terms of my family; having to go on location is really hard. Also, there is an ego factor in this business that sometimes gets to be a little much."—Alan Blomquist

What do you love most about your job?

"What I like most is that it's constantly changing. I never do the same thing twice. While the structure is the same, every movie is different." When Blomquist produced Of Mice and Men, *he recalls, "I had to learn how to grow a crop of wheat, because it was a centerpiece of the movie. I ended up growing winter wheat in the summer. When I did* Everybody's All American, *I had to learn all about college football and how to shoot in front of 80,000 fans in a real football stadium . . . Every movie I do has some kind of challenge, or many challenges. I love that."—Alan Blomquist*

"I also really like the social aspect of it, trying to put a team together; a family that can coexist for six weeks, six months, or a year, with each person doing their job in concert with other people."—Alan Blomquist

vious production manager had been fired and they had been unable to find a replacement. The catch was that Blomquist would have to join the

Directors Guild of America (DGA), something he had been trying to do for three or four years. "They have a test every year for their training program. Twenty-five hundred people apply and twenty-five get picked. Being a white male, I never qualified. I was desperate to get into the Directors Guild."

Blomquist arrived in San Francisco to discover that the picture's $750,000 budget was already spent, but filming was only halfway finished. "I had to figure out how to get the movie done with whatever money they were still raising, and get them to the finish line."

Once he was admitted to the director's guild, Blomquist was informed that he needed to work 400 days outside of Los Angeles to get on the roster. He earned the required days during the next year and a half, working on whatever projects he could find. Once the specified time was completed, he worked on a variety of television and low budget productions, until a friend called to ask for his assistance on the PBS movie *Lone Star Kid*. One of the ADs on the picture had worked for Taylor Hackford on *An Officer and a Gentleman*, and recommended Blomquist for a low budget film called *La Bamba*.

La Bamba was made for $6 million and earned more than $60 million, its success propelling Blomquist to another level in his career. When it wrapped, he worked on the series *Sledgehammer* and other projects, until Hackford was ready to begin production on the $25 million picture *Everybody's All American*. For it, Blomquist was asked to co-produce, and serve as both line producer and production manager.

"It was a huge leap. I was in really, really deep water. In those times you either sink or swim, and I happened to swim." Blomquist called on a friend who was also a production manager, who talked him through the budget. "I had worked on a low budget movie, so the budget was maybe twenty pages long. On a $25 million movie the budget was 120 pages. Everything was inflated. I was completely adrift. He sat me down and explained, 'It's all the same categories. There are more entries, because there are more people and there is more money to spend, but it's the same process.' You're building an apartment building instead of a single family house.

"Basically, I reinvented myself two or three times. The biggest reinvention was from being a grip to assistant director to becoming a production manager. Then going from production manager to producer were two big leaps. One was sort of by my own sheer force of will, and the other one because Taylor Hackford saw something in me and gave me an opportunity when he didn't have to. He could have hired somebody who had lots of experience and credits. Instead, he said, 'This is the guy I want to do it,' and Warner Brothers went along."

With two successful big films under his belt, Blomquist's career continued from one feature to another, including *Of Mice and Men*, *Vanishing Point*, and *What Dreams May Come*.

"On *What Dreams May Come*, there was a ship graveyard scene written into the script. While location scouting one day, we saw this scrapped aircraft carrier belonging to the U.S. Navy that had been mothballed and left sitting at a pier in San Francisco for twenty years. It had been decommissioned and was rusted and rotting in place." After discovering who owned the ship, Blomquist was eventually able to persuade the various agencies involved to allow him access. "We built a huge set around the aircraft carrier that basically cost us nothing. The set cost some money, but the aircraft carrier was free. Those are the kinds of things that are grist for my mill. I just love it."

Blomquist's association with director Lasse Hallstrom began on *What's Eating Gilbert Grape*, and continued on to *The Cider House Rules* and *Chocolat*. Having just completed nearly a year on location, working on *Chocolat*, he chose to turn down *Shipping News* in order to spend more time with his family.

CAREER TIPS

★ *"You can't look in the want ads for a job in the film industry. It's all about referrals, recommendations, and word of mouth."–Alan Blomquist*

★ *"This is a very competitive business. It's a very unforgiving business, but it's also a very wide open business. Anybody can be anything . . . if you're smart, enterprising, and tenacious. But, you have to have a sense of what the job is. You have to have a sense of your own skills. And, you have to have a social aspect. The best technician in the world, who can't get along with people, is going to get hired less than somebody who is less skilled, [but] knows how to get along and schmooze people."–Alan Blomquist*

★ *"Each time you work on a freelance basis, you have 50 to 100 people who become your agents."–Alan Blomquist*

"For *Gilbert Grape*, we actually burned down a house. In the movie, the woman dies and they set the house on fire as a funeral pyre." They considered building a set to burn down, or creating the effect in post, until Blomquist found the perfect house. "It was 150 years old, one of those places in Texas that you drive by and it looks like a haunted house with no window glass, because kids have broken it over the years." Long since abandoned, the farmer who owned the house thought it too expensive to tear down, so he farmed around it. He agreed to sell the house for $5,000 and allow the production to burn it down, if they would agree to haul the remnants away. "That was a huge saving to us, because anything we constructed would have cost a lot more—and it looked great in the movie. That's ultimately what it's about. I have two jobs: the budget and the art. My job is about art meeting commerce."

Between working on hired jobs, Blomquist works on projects he has created, optioned, or read about. Those include shooting a "Blue Collar Comedy Tour," similar to *The Original Kings of Comedy*, but with redneck comics such as Jeff Foxworthy. "Mostly I'm a gun for hire. Other people sell their ideas and hire me to realize them."

VOICES OF EXPERIENCE

What do you like least about your job?

"It's all consuming. There is no amount of time that you can put into it that if you could put another hour in, it wouldn't be incrementally better. You can truly work twenty-four hours a day."
—Duncan Henderson

What do you love most about your job?

"What I definitely love most is the fact that it's different all the time. The two things that I love about it is every time you take on a project, it's different. There are new things to find out. Secondly, I find it fun to work with the new people you come in contact with. Like on this picture [Master and Commander], it's about the British Navy, circa 1805, so we have technical advisers, people who are shipwrights and cannon experts. To live in that world for a year and a half is a really interesting thing for me. I'm sort of eclectic in my interests, so the motion picture business fits that perfectly because one year you're doing Harry Potter and the next year you're doing a naval story, and the next year you're doing something set in the future."—Duncan Henderson

Professional Profile: Duncan Henderson, Executive Producer

"I grew up in the shadow of MGM," says Duncan Henderson, "but I never considered working in the motion picture business." Instead, he pursued finance, earning a bachelor's degree in economics from UCLA and a master's in finance from USC, and then became a successful stockbroker. At age 29, he decided he did not want to spend the rest of his life working in the financial world and determined to make a career change. Having always loved movies, he began investigating filmmaking. Discovering the assistant director's training program offered through the DGA, he applied.

"You come in as a trainee. For me that was a huge cut in salary—I think I worked for $120 a week—if I hadn't been able to save up money in my previous occupation, it would have been impossible . . . I looked at it as they were giving me a stipend to be educated."

The training program afforded Henderson an opportunity to attend seminars to hear experts in the field speak, and to gain actual hands-on experience working on film and television productions. "You were assigned to shows and it was the luck of the draw that I got to work for some really, really good people. Afterwards, those people went on to work elsewhere and they wanted to hire me because they felt I'd done a good job."

An early career break came working as second assistant director under William Beasley on *American Gigolo*. "I consider Bill one of the great assistant directors. He was a good teacher and a good friend." As Beasley went from show to show, he hired Henderson to work with him on *Halloween II, Staying Alive, The Star Chamber, Racing with the Moon,* and *The Man with One Red Shoe*. When it came time for Henderson to make the leap from second to first AD in the early 1980s, it was through the recommendation of Beasley.

CAREER TIPS

"This is a business where you are trying to get the most out of the people you're working with. One way you do that is by your example: you're willing to work hard and so they're willing to work hard. Also, you have to actually know about and respect the jobs other people do so you understand what their problems are . . . It's really trying to inspire people to do their very best work."—Duncan Henderson

Producer James Brubaker was another champion of Henderson's career early on and became influential in his moving up from trainee to second AD, to first AD, and then to production manager. "The real hard thing in this business is to make a change from one category to the next. You have to have somebody willing to say, 'I think he could do this job.' . . . Jim thought I had potential and kept moving me up." Henderson worked with Brubaker on several pictures including *Staying Alive, Rhinestone,* and *Cobra*.

Racing with the Moon's unit production manager (UPM) Art Levinson was another person who recognized Henderson's potential early on. "When I was a brand new second, Art would give me the budgets to go over so I could learn that part of the business. He was very helpful to me."

By the mid-1980s, Henderson was working as a unit production manager, associate producer, and line producer. In the late 1980s, he served as UPM and associate producer of *Dead Poets Society*, directed by

Peter Weir, and went on to work with him as a co-producer of *Green Card*, and executive producer of *Master and Commander*. He has executive produced two Wolfgang Petersen films, *Outbreak* and *The Perfect Storm*, and two Chris Columbus pictures, *Home Alone 2: Lost in New York* and *Harry Potter and the Sorcerer's Stone*.

Professional Profile: Neil Machlis, Executive Producer

New York native Neil Machlis was working toward his master's degree in investment finance at American University in Washington, D.C., when he first discovered filmmaking. A visit to brother-in-law Roger Rothstein on the set of *Paper Lion* facilitated Machlis working on the film during semester break. He learned the business from the ground up, starting as a production assistant, making photocopies and running errands.

After returning to Washington, Machlis looked up production companies in the *Yellow Pages* and found a small film company that specialized in industrial shorts and political commercial spots. Again, he accepted an entry-level job serving as a production assistant. "I would go in every day and do whatever needed to be done: I did some negative matching, I swept floors, I ran errands, I took film to the lab. I did everything."

His first location job was covering the 1968 Democratic Convention, held in Chicago. "Being in Chicago as a part of history was terrific. We were filming senators on a newsreel-type system. The senators would then send the film back to their home state television stations."

VOICES OF EXPERIENCE

What do you like least about your job?

"Sometimes the days can be very long."
—Neil Machlis

What do you love most about your job?

"I love dealing with people. I love taking a script and trying to figure out how to make it all happen. Every movie is a puzzle. Part of the enjoyment of it is trying to get all the pieces together to make it right."
—Neil Machlis

Education was put on hold when Machlis was called up to active duty in the National Guard. Once released, he returned to New York to pursue filmmaking as a career. At the time, the Directors Guild was starting a training program. He took the admission test and was one of ten accepted out of approximately 1500 applicants.

Machlis almost immediately began working as a trainee, often hired by Rothstein, who was then a production manager. "I was lucky to have him. He taught me a lot about the business. He was very well-respected in this field." Machlis moved up to second AD, and then to unit production manager.

He relocated from New York to California in 1976. "There were some big union problems in New York and the business really slowed down. There was a large movement of personnel [from] New York to California, because the work originated there." His first big feature after the move was *Grease.* "That was such a successful film; a good movie to have on your résumé."

★ *"You have to work hard . . . You need to persevere. You need to have good contacts and you need to be lucky as well."—Neil Machlis*

Machlis progressed from unit production manager to associate producer, and by the late 1980s, he was executive producing some the screen's most successful films, such as: *Planes, Trains & Automobiles; Postcards from the Edge; Wolf; I.Q.; The Birdcage; Primary Colors; Bedazzled; Dr. Dolittle 2;* and *The First $20 Million.*

"I worked on six movies with Mike Nichols, so I had the benefit of working with some great talents along the way." Machlis is currently executive producing *The First $20 Million Is Always the Hardest.*

JOB TITLE: LINE PRODUCER

Job Overview

Answering to the production's producer, the line producer is responsible for supervising the budget; hiring the below-the-line crew; overseeing the production, from the daily operations on set through postproduction; and working with the director to execute his vision for the production.

Special Skills

A line producer must be able to manage a budget, and possess the people skills to work with and motivate a variety of personalities. Line producers also must be good listeners and be flexible.

While scouting locations for *Avalon,* the director and producer determined that a particular scene needed to be shot on a sunny day. The day the company arrived at that location, it was pouring down rain. So line producer Peter Giuliano packed up the company, equipment, and trucks and got everyone moving to another location. He and the DP were in a car preparing to leave, when they received a call on the walkie-talkie from the producer and director, saying they had decided to shoot the scene in winter, meaning they would shoot in the rain and make it appear it was winter. Giuliano needed to bring the whole company back.

"I did a U-turn in the car. The DP [Allen Daviau] turned to me and said, 'Today you'll earn your entire salary from the movie.' I brought the company back. People were pissed off . . . You can either be really rigid and say, 'The company has moved,' or you can go with it and understand that it's part of the creative process. You have to remain flexible at all times to accomplish things that are not planned for."

Advice for Someone Seeking This Job

"Work for free," says Giuliano. "Understand that it's going to be long hours. You have to really want it, because it's very difficult. Most jobs work a 40-hour week—we work an 80- or 90- or 100-hour week. It's a shock to a lot of young people."

Professional Profile: Peter Giuliano, Line Producer

Peter Giuliano did not plan on a career in filmmaking. The opportunity presented itself because he owned a van. He was living in Manhattan, working odd jobs, when he was approached to pick up film equipment for a small independent film company. The catch was he had to arrive after hours to avoid trouble with the teamsters. Soon he was working with the company on numerous industrials, documentaries, and commercials, eventually creating commercial parodies for the first two seasons of *Saturday Night Live*. "It was just a director and me, so I did everything: I was the camera assistant, the production manager, production assistant, sometimes the sound person, whatever was needed."

Giuliano produced commercials for a time, but realized he preferred the assistant director role. His first break into television series work came when producer Kenneth Utt hired him as first AD on the one-hour police drama *Baker's Dozen*. Utt became a mentor, and the two remained close throughout Giuliano's career.

His first small feature as an AD was *The Prowler*. "It was a spin-off of a *Friday the 13th* type film. I also ended up being the killer . . . Farley Granger was supposed to be the killer, but he couldn't be there all the time. I fit his wardrobe, so they just had him there for the parts where his face showed. When his face was covered, when he was doing all the killing, I did the work."

Ghostbusters provided the lucky break that changed Giuliano's career. "I was working on a movie of the week and the producer got sick. The guy who took over refused to hire me because he didn't know me, even though I was already on the job. I was really depressed, sitting at home. The AD on *Ghostbusters* was fired and they needed somebody right away, somebody in New York. I was literally the only first AD not working in New York at the time. It was just luck that I got the job. And, it changed everything." At the time, *Ghostbusters* was the biggest film ever to shoot in New York, both logistically and in terms of crew size. The film's success changed people's perception of Giuliano, and brought him many more opportunities.

Having successfully worked with director Ivan Reitman on *Ghostbusters*, Giuliano was hired back to first AD other Reitman pictures, including *Legal Eagles, Twins, Ghostbusters II, Kindergarten Cop,* and *Dave.*

VOICES OF EXPERIENCE

What do you like least about your job?

"I like the budget the least amount."
—Peter Giuliano

What do you love most about your job?

"The part I like the most is the filming part—and solving problems. You come in at 7:00 and there is a problem you have to overcome: an actress or actor that didn't show up; it's raining and it wasn't supposed to be; a director can't figure out how to do a shot and you help him; or the set burnt to the ground and you have to figure out how to shoot something else that day— it's the problem solving part that I like most."—Peter Giuliano

Giuliano moved to Los Angeles in the mid-1980s, where another important break came when he landed the first AD job on *Avalon,* directed by Barry Levinson. Hitting it off with Levinson, he served as first AD on *Bugsy,* was upped to first AD/co-producer on *Toys,* and was then promoted to line producer on *Jimmy Hollywood, Disclosure, Sleepers,* and *Sphere.*

In 1994, Giuliano relocated to Missouri, and spent his time off between productions there. Looking for a new creative challenge, he accepted an offer from a friend to produce a television pilot called *The Force.* Discovering that he enjoyed the format's ever-changing opportunities to solve problems, he went on to work on the series *Bull,* and then *Thieves.*

While working on *Thieves,* Giuliano had a premonition that he should be working on a production about three different crime fighters with different powers. After *Thieves* was cancelled, he was offered another pilot. "It was a really good script, but something bugged me about it. A week later, I got a call about another show, called *Birds of Prey*. It's about three women: one who has psychic powers, one who has physical powers, and one who has all the brain power. It was like my premonition." Giuliano called the studio and made arrangements to switch projects. After *Birds of Prey* was picked up, he remained on as producer of the series.

CAREER TIPS

★ *Peter Giuliano attributes his success to "being able to catch your mistakes before anybody else does."*

JOB TITLE: PRODUCER—TELEVISION

Job Overview

There are different types of producers, and responsibilities may vary from project to project. The producer oversees a project from beginning to end and may be involved in any or all of the following responsibilities: finding, acquiring, and developing material; securing financing; hiring the director, talent, and key crew members; supervising the project through postproduction and release.

Special Skills

In addition to knowledge of filmmaking and contacts within the industry, a producer must have the ability to work successfully with a variety of personalities, be highly organized, and be able to motivate others.

Advice for Someone Seeking This Job

Start out as a PA, secretary, or assistant for a production company or producer to learn the business and make contacts. In looking for a job, "Be persistent," suggests producer Anne Grace. Don't just send in a resume and expect someone to call you—call them. "You have to keep calling. That's the one thing that impresses me. Whenever I hire somebody, I'm going to hire the person that has called for the last six months. You have to have a certain amount of eagerness to be a PA. If you're sincere and you can convey to people that you are serious, someone will give you a chance."

Professional Profile: Anne Grace, Senior Producer, Scene Three Media Works

From an early age, Anne Grace knew that she wanted to be a producer. The best friend of a child actor whose father was a writer/director for Disney, Grace was raised around the film industry. "Our families were close—I pretty much grew up on the Disney lot." After high school she attended University of San Diego for two years, then transferred to Cal State Northridge, where she earned a bachelor's degree in radio and television broadcasting.

During her last semester of college, Grace took an internship at Landsburg, working on *That's Incredible*. "They had this huge library that two women ran. They needed interns to come in and find stories for them. I would stay late, above and beyond, and they would ask me to come in on shoot days and help the script supervisor. I did that on my own." The company had no paying positions available when Grace graduated, so she took a job working for a record promoter, but stayed in touch with her Landsburg connections. When production for *Science Times* began staffing up, she was offered a job as production secretary series.

Shortly after Joan Barnett joined the Landsburg company, Grace was recommended and hired as her assistant. "She was vice president of movies and miniseries for NBC for four years under Brandon Tarticoff, and then her contract was up. Joan was the first female vice president at a network. I started working for her and it was the greatest thing of my career. She taught me everything. Not only would she develop scripts, but she would executive produce them and I would work with her on them." Over the next several years, Grace gained experience working on a variety of projects, including the *Kennedy* miniseries with Martin Sheen, *Adam* with Adam Walsh, *Parent Trap II*, and the series *Bluegrass*.

Newly married, Grace relocated to Nashville with her husband in the late 1980s, leaving the Landsburg company after seven years.

VOICES OF EXPERIENCE

What do you like least about your job?

"What I hate about the business is that everything is needed now . . . You never have enough time when you're shooting, and then the delivery time is tight. That is the hate part of it, but I love that too because it is like total adrenaline." —Anne Grace

What do you love most about your job?

"I love the unpredictability. Every job is different—you've always got a different hurdle to jump over." —Anne Grace

Upon arriving in Nashville, contacts at the William Morris Agency and Creative Artists Agency (CAA) introduced her around town. One person she met was Kitty Moon, who would later offer her an opportunity with Scene Three Media Works. Before Grace could settle into a new job, her friends at Landsburg called to offer her three months' work on two movies and a television pilot they were shooting in South Carolina. "It was a six day week, 18 hour day life," she recalls. By the time Grace returned to Nashville, she was burnt out on filmmaking and stayed home for a few months before accepting work at a nonprofit organization.

CAREER TIPS

★ *"Stay until you're the last one in the office. Be eager and listen to what is going on around you. Ask questions. People generally respond in a positive way to hard work and enthusiasm. Do things above and beyond your job description."*
–Anne Grace

★ *"Surround yourself with people who are good at what they do and look for mentors who are willing to share their knowledge and experience with you."*
–Anne Grace

A few months later, she received a phone call from Kitty Moon, leading to an interview with partner Marc Ball. "The timing couldn't have been better, because I was ready to get back in the business. I came in and met with Marc for three hours." Grace joined Scene Three in 1990 and has been with the company for just over a decade. During that time she has produced numerous music videos, commercials, and television projects, including the series *CeCe's Place* starring CeCe Winans, an Emmy-nominated campaign for Nashville Public Television, "Tracy Lawrence: In the Round," a one hour special for CMT/TNN, and the CBS special "A Day in the Life of Country Music."

JOB TITLE: EXECUTIVE PRODUCER— COMMERCIALS

Job Overview

Oversee all aspects of production, including hiring, working with and developing directors, giving creative input, and interfacing with the client. As the owner of a commercial production company, Stuart Wilson also manages all business operations.

Special Skills

A basic knowledge of filmmaking and the ability to hire and work with directors appropriate for each job. Wilson also considers perseverance to be an important trait for a potential producer: "Always believing in what you can do and sticking to it."

Advice for Someone Seeking This Job

"If you want to be a producer you should probably go to film school," says Wilson, "but you don't necessarily have to graduate. Just get the basics down, and find work as a PA or an assistant from the day you enter film school. You should work for free if you have to and do anything you can to work on a production. If somebody says they have a spec job—a free job—just do it; anything you can to get experience. If you want to be a producer, start as a PA, become a coordinator, a production manager, and a producer. Work your [butt] off and push constantly. Ask for opportunities and don't be afraid to take any offer that comes."

Professional Profile: Stuart Wilson, Executive Producer and Owner of Right Brain Films

You might say that Stuart Wilson got into the television commercial business because Harvey Weinstein was always late ordering dinner. Wilson was injured on the job while working as a terminal superintendent for an oil company. While he recuperated, he tried to decide upon a new career while managing a nonprofit beach and tennis club on Martha's Vineyard where Weinstein was a member.

"You had to call in your dinner order by a certain time so the chef could go shopping. Harvey always called in late, so I would have to go to the chef." The two became friendly and Weinstein suggested Wilson should look into television or film. Subsequently, he introduced him to a few people after Wilson relocated to Los Angeles.

His first industry job was as an assistant to a producer of reality programming, eventually developing and working

VOICES OF EXPERIENCE

What do you like least about your job?

"What I like least is managing the company; the day-to-day business operations."–Stuart Wilson

What do you love most about your job?

"What I like most is that I have the freedom to pursue projects that I want to do. I also like developing and working with the directors, and having input creatively into how they approach each project."–Stuart Wilson

as a PA on *Amazing Love Stories*. When the show lost its funding, Wilson landed a job as a PA on the television movie *Long Shadows*. When *Amazing Love Stories* got picked up, he returned as a coordinator.

CAREER TIPS

★ *"Commit your life to the work. Make it everything that you do, so that your personal life doesn't exist. The only life that you have is production, because otherwise it's not going to happen. You have to absolutely commit 110% to it and in the end it pays off really well."—Stuart Wilson*

★ *"Relationships are very important. Meet everybody you can and maintain relationships forever. Everybody is an opportunity. You never know when somebody that was a PA is going to be in a position to help you. I don't ever step on anybody."* —Stuart Wilson

Wilson connected with some music video makers and worked as a PA on a Prince video. On the shoot he met some craft services people and began working craft services on various commercials, films, and television programs when not working as a PA or coordinator. He worked again with Prince on a multimedia rock opera, beginning as a PA and moving up to stage manager.

Realizing he did not want to PA—"I was older and had been an executive at a company. To go back and PA was really demeaning and demoralizing"—Wilson combined his skills in business and cooking to form Ala Carte Craft Services, one of the first to offer cappuccino and smoothies. "We really took craft services to a whole different level, doing it very high end." The company catered to music video and commercial productions, which have more money to spend.

When not providing craft services, Wilson continued to work as a coordinator on various projects. Along the way he produced a commercial for Mattel, which led to another 75 commercials. While working on *Masked Rider* for Saban, he was approached to start up a commercial production company. With two partners, Wilson formed Right Brain Films in 1995. One partner quit after three months and the other left the business two years later, leaving Wilson as sole owner of the company.

"We didn't have letterhead, we didn't have business cards, and we didn't have labels. Yet right out of the gate we landed a $250,000 Petco job." On his own, Wilson has grown the company from jobs averaging $50,000 to 60,000, to projects in the $250,000 to $750,000 bracket, by producing commercials for N. Saatchi & Saatchi (Toyota), Campbel-Ewald, Grey (Kaiser Permanente), and J. Walter Thompson (Ford Motor Company). Wilson is currently developing a new division of his company to produce independent feature films.

One of Wilson's keys to success was his commitment. Once he decided he wanted to be a producer, he refused to accept any work as a PA or coordinator and closed his craft services company. "It was very difficult financially because through the craft services company, I was making $10,000 to $15,000 a month. It allowed me to finance the production company. It was difficult because it meant I had to stand only on my ability to produce and land jobs. But at some point you have to jump off and say, 'I'm a producer.' This is what I am, period."

JOB TITLE: PRODUCER—COMMERICALS

Job Overview

The producer manages the total project, balancing the client's needs and the director's vision. Responsible for devising a financial plan and ensuring that the production is completed on time and within the specified budget, the producer is involved in casting, hiring the crew, overseeing postproduction and all other mechanics of the project.

Special Skills

A commercial producer must be organized, possess the ability to devise a realistic budget, and bring the production in within cost, have an overall understanding of the filmmaking process, and have contacts within the industry. "The more educated you are and the more knowledge you have, the more you bring to the profession," says producer Jane Raimondi. "There are many people that have a wide variety of majors and backgrounds: English, math, engineering, or history. All of those things lend themselves to the film industry. You don't have to have a film education, but an education, in itself, is really valuable."

Advice for Someone Seeking This Job

"Everybody shares the commonality of being a production assistant," says Raimondi. "Most people I talk to who are assistant directors or producers, directors, gaffers, key grips, people in really good positions, started out as PAs. There is nothing wrong with that. Take a starting position, get your foot in the door, and then you can prove yourself and move up. You will move up if you prove yourself. The good are separated from the bad pretty easily . . . The main thing is just love it with such a passion that you're willing to do anything to get started; dive in and go for it. Call on people. Be persistent. We get résumés every day of the week and you can kind of tell the people that just have a little something; some spark above the others. It's really a nice persistence that they have. A passion."

Professional Profile: Jane Raimondi, Producer and Co-Owner, Raimondi Films

Jane Raimondi was 33 years old when she discovered her love for filmmaking and got into the business. She had earned a bachelor's degree in sociology and worked a variety of jobs—on Capitol Hill, as a social worker, and for a magazine—but none of them sparked her passion. On the verge of divorce, Raimondi's therapist asked her: "What would you like to do if you could do anything at all?"

What do you like least about your job?

"What I like least, at this stage, is how all-encompassing it is. We just shot last Saturday, and spent this past Saturday and Sunday working. We worked for 13 days straight. That's hard, sometimes. It overwhelms you, particularly in a small company. We haven't had a two-week vacation in probably ten years. It's a tough business in the sense that you're always working. I'm at the point where I'd like to have a little more time off."—Jane Raimondi

What do you love most about your job?

"The thing I love most is probably the joy of seeing something finished that you produced and worked on from the very small germ of an idea. That's a big satisfaction. There are a million little ones: when the director or client gives you a challenge and everyone says, 'I don't know if that's possible,' and you're able to actually see it through and achieve it."—Jane Raimondi

"Nobody had ever asked me that question. I said, 'What I want to do is not really possible . . . I've always thought I would love to work in film. I love movies. I find it interesting. But you can't really earn a living at that, particularly living in Washington, D.C.'"

Two days after the conversation, Raimondi was riding the bus to work and looked up to see an advertising card for Corcoran College of Art & Design, offering classes in art, painting, photography, and filmmaking. "It was a revelation. I got to work and called them immediately. They were starting a beginning filmmaking course. It was every night from six to nine, five days a week. At the end of my day, I'd go take this course and I was in heaven. I couldn't wait for 6:00 to come."

One of a very small group of students, Raimondi learned the basics of filmmaking by working on Super-8 student films. When the course ended, she signed up for an intermediate class, the only other filmmaking course the college offered. "I was in love."

Separating from her husband, Raimondi moved into a small studio apartment, quit her job, and began looking for work in the film industry. She telephoned every motion picture production company in the telephone book and offered to work for free to gain experience. "I had squirreled away enough money to live on for six months, which at that time was $5,000. I was not going to be living extravagantly!"

She began to pick up production assistant work. "I was 33 and I was schlepping coffee for 22-year-old directors. I didn't care. I would have done anything." Over a short period of time Raimondi worked up to jobs that paid, filling a wide range of positions, from props and wardrobe, to assistant camera-

> **CAREER TIPS**
>
> ★ *Have enough money saved up that you can afford to work for free as an intern or production assistant until you can gain enough experience and contacts to land paying jobs.*
>
> *"Don't give up."—Jane Raimondi*

man. "Washington [D.C.] is not compartmentalized like it is in L.A. . . . which was great, because you got a much better overall view of the industry. People are amazed that I can step in and run a Nagra, for instance, or load a 16mm magazine in a very short amount of time.

"There is not a big filmmaking community in Washington [D.C.]. A lot of the work is documentaries, but I was amazed at how many companies were out there and how many people were actually making a living in the film business."

She continued to build a résumé working on various documentaries and commercials. While attending a seminar hosted by Eastman Kodak in 1980, she met director Paul Raimondi, who later became her husband and partner in Raimondi Films.

Initially, the pair produced industrial films and documentaries, traveling all over the world to shoot, but later changed their emphasis to commercials. "Doing documentaries got too physically exhausting to continue. You're in a foreign country with sixteen cases of equipment, no bellman, no skycap, just two of you [hauling] stuff around."

To expand their client base, they began sending Paul's director's reel to Los Angeles production companies, eventually signing with one for representation on the West Coast. After two years, the pair had built up enough contacts to open an office of Raimondi Films in Los Angeles, closing down their Washington, D.C., operations a year later.

One project Jane Raimondi is particularly proud of producing are "The Los Angeles Times" trailers that run on 2,200 movie screens throughout Southern California. "About ten years ago, Paul came up with the idea of filming people in the film industry for the ads. They are little minute pieces on the less well-known parts of the industry. We didn't want to do directors, producers, writers, or actors, people that everyone knows." Having completed about 25 so far, the ads have become a staple with moviegoers.

In the mid-1990s the Raimondis formed an alliance with two other filmmakers, enabling Jane to produce the independent film *Crosscut*, which aired on Cinemax, HBO, and Showtime.

JOB TITLE: PRODUCER—MUSIC VIDEOS, COMMERCIALS, AND INDEPENDENT FILMS

Job Overview

A music video producer is charged with marshaling all of the physical and financial resources necessary to realize the director's creative vision. They meet with record label executives, managers, and artists to pitch the talent and ideas of the director(s) they represent, devise a budget for the project, hire crew and talent, and oversee all operational aspects of the video production.

Special Skills

Producers must have a basic knowledge of filmmaking, the ability to hire and motivate crew members, and possess sufficient accounting skills to devise an appropriate budget and bring the production to completion within it.

Advice for Someone Seeking This Job

If you want to work in the film industry, producer Clarke Gallivan suggests going to a major film school in California. "Then you're connected with other people in the industry. Whether someone wants to be a director, sound person, or a producer, you need to learn the craft. Each position in each department requires a specific set of skills. Focus on learning the craft. It's like playing in an orchestra: you have to know your part and have respect for all the other parts." Once you've gained some basic knowledge, begin looking for opportunities to serve as a production assistant. Try to find a producer who needs an assistant and volunteer to work for free so you can learn from that individual and gain some experience. "If you're going to be a producer, you have to work your way up from the bottom."

Professional Profile: Clarke Gallivan, Producer and Partner, Ruckus Film

Although she enjoyed taking film study courses in college, Clarke Gallivan had never considered filmmaking as a career. It wasn't until after she had earned a degree in political science that she began to have second thoughts about going on to law school. Undecided about what to do next, she returned home to Nashville in the mid-1970s and took a job assisting a photographer who often worked with the music industry. The photographer introduced Gallivan to several filmmakers, who hired her to shoot production stills of their projects. Through this experience she discovered that she had more interest in film work than in still photography.

VOICES OF EXPERIENCE

What do you like least about your job?

"The most frustrating part of being a music video maker is that in all other aspects of filmmaking, even commercials, the film itself is considered creative content. Many [record] label people view video as a necessary evil. They see the song as the creative content and the video is seen as a lesser adjunct for selling the artist and selling the song."—Clarke Gallivan

What do you love most about your job?

"What I like best of all is being involved in making something that touches people, and is also entertaining. Film is a very, very powerful medium. It is a huge thrill to be associated with making something that people respond to. That's why I do it. Plus, it's a team sport. You get to put together a great team and work with some amazing people."—Clarke Gallivan

She began finding jobs as a production assistant on commercials and anything else she could get as a way to learn the business. She later apprenticed as a film editor under directors Jim May and Coke Sams. For the next several years, Gallivan worked as an editor of commercials, documentaries, television shows, and movies. When country artists began making music videos in the early 1980s, she found herself editing them by the dozen. Growing tired of sitting alone in a darkened editing room, she began directing videos as well. Later, inspired by the work of another video filmmaker, she decided she could be more creatively effective as a producer, and from that point focused her career in that direction.

★ *"I try to surround myself with people who are better and smarter than I am. I'm a pretty good team builder. I like to delegate to people who are experts at what they do."—Clarke Gallivan*

★ *"My lawyer always says, 'There is no such thing as entertainment emergency. Is anyone spurting blood? Is the ambulance coming? If not, then it's not an emergency.' Because there is so much money involved in making anything that has to do with film, when something goes wrong, it feels like an emergency. I think we have to keep our heads about what we're really doing."*
—Clarke Gallivan

In 1985, Gallivan became a partner with May and Sams in Studio Productions. The firm's video client roster ranged from Aerosmith to Johnny Cash. They branched out into developing projects for Disney, HBO, and Paramount and continued to produce commercials.

With Coke co-writing and directing and May behind the camera, Gallivan produced the 1997 independent film *Existo*, which won numerous awards at film festivals around the world. The company recently joined forces with Honest Images to form Ruckus Film, to develop and produce a wide spectrum of projects, including programming for cable and network television, feature films, music videos, and commercials.

PRODUCTION OFFICE

JOB TITLE: UNIT PRODUCTION MANAGER (UPM)

Job Overview

The unit production manager assists in formulating the budget for a production and then manages it. The UPM's duties include hiring the crew and negotiating their contracts on behalf of the production, striking deals for equipment, reviewing contracts, authorizing payroll, arranging travel, issuing and approving purchase orders, and overseeing the production staff.

Special Skills

A UPM must possess strong people skills to negotiate with, manage, and motivate a diverse group of personalities. Organization and the ability to administer a budget are necessities. "I think anyone can do my job technically," says UPM Donna Bloom. "What makes me good at it are my people skills. I can talk to people and I'm fair. I do not have a temper. I don't think I have ever yelled at anyone in my life. I worked for some pretty awful people and I learned from them how I never wanted to be. I knew if I became a production manager, I was not going to be that kind of person. I choose to follow the path of people I thought were great."

Advice for Someone Seeking This Job

"You have to believe you can do it," says Bloom. "Do all the home-work you can. Touch base with people. Take any job. Never be a quitter. If you're starting out in this business, you're going to eat a lot of crow. You have got to pay your dues . . . People at the top are still paying their dues. Don't be in a hurry to do it. Take your time and enjoy it as you're on your way. You have to be humble, and be assertive, without being aggressive. You have to talk to people and make it known what you want, but in a nice way."

Professional Profile: Donna E. Bloom, Unit Production Manager

Originally from New York, Donna Bloom's family moved to Italy when she was ten. After a year of college overseas, she returned to America in her early twenties to study at Emerson College in Boston. There she earned a bachelor's degree in broadcast journalism, planning to become a foreign correspondent. Returning to Europe, she landed a job making documentaries for the Italian television network. "I was the jack-of-all-trades. I was the production manager, the location manager, and interpreter. You did everything."

Unable to get papers to work overseas, Bloom returned to the United States in the early 1980s and took a job working at *Good Morning America*. One day she realized that what she really wanted to do was make movies, and quit her job.

Through her sister Julie, who was working as a production assistant, Bloom met several crew members. A couple of days later, one of the crew members called to ask if Julie were available to work on *Tootsie*. Donna answered the call and advised them her sister was working on another picture. "Well, what are you doing?" he asked. "That's how I started making movies: working as a production assistant on *Tootsie* at the Russian Tea Room for two days."

What do you like least about your job?

"What I don't like is the deal making with the crew, because there is often a feeling of me versus them, which is exactly what I don't like, because I am them. I have to be faithful to a budget and fair to the people that I'm hiring."—Donna Bloom

What do you love most about your job?

"What I love most is the feeling of camaraderie in putting together a movie, a group of people that work well together. I love the sense of accomplishment when I walk on the set that first day and everything is in place and it's like, 'Wow. Here we go. Let's make a movie!'"

Bloom continued to serve as a production assistant for a time, then as an assistant to a producer on *Falling in Love*, before segueing into location assistant, scout, and then manager. Her first big feature to location manage was *When Harry Met Sally*, a job she landed thanks to writer Nora Ephron.

"I had worked on *Cookie*, a film that Nora Ephron wrote. I met Nora—she is very pro-women getting ahead in this business—and she was always cordial to me, but I didn't know she even knew my name. She went on to write *When Harry Met Sally*. She was talking to Rob Reiner and he said, 'We'll be shooting in New York, so I need a location manager.' She said, 'I know the person.'"

When one of the film's producers called, Bloom thought it was a joke. "I was unemployed. I had quit *The Equalizer* and was sitting at home thinking, 'Well, let's see if the phone rings,' and this man called me up and said, 'I'm Rob Reiner's producer. Would you be interested in meeting with me to be the location manager for Rob's next movie?' I thought it was a joke; I thought somebody is really playing a nasty joke on me." Hired for the job, it was the beginning of a long relationship with Castle Rock.

For the next nine years Bloom continued to work as a location manager on films such as *State of Grace, The Super, This Is My Life*, and *Mr. Wonderful*.

The leap from location manager to production manager came on the Castle Rock film *North*. "The same man who gave me my first job as a location manager gave me the New York portion of *North*—Jeff Stott. He's been my mentor. I have had two mentors: Jeff, and Steve Nicolaides, who was the production manager on *When Harry Met Sally*. They were the two men who offered me that first job."

When Nicolaides stepped up to produce his first film, another Castle Rock picture entitled *Little Big League*, he asked Bloom to manage the production. Feeling secure in her transition to production manger, she decided to relocate to Los Angeles in the mid-1990s, but still kept her home in New York. "I would not have moved out to L.A. to become a location manager. You need to know the lay of the land, every nook and cranny of the city and everybody who runs the city."

Over the next few years she worked on several films, including *One Fine Day*, *The Postman*, *Anywhere But Here*, *Hearts in Atlantis*, *Swimfan*, and is currently working on another movie for Castle Rock.

"My whole career has been a highlight. I've met wonderful people along the way and worked with some really wonderful producers, directors, and actors. We get to do things normal people don't get to do: everything from closing the Brooklyn Bridge to flying helicopters into Canada. You get to do and experience things that are just wonderful."

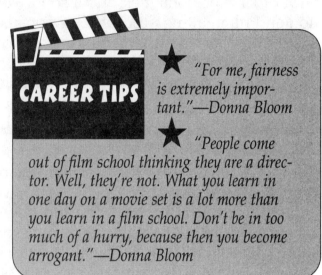

CAREER TIPS

★ *"For me, fairness is extremely important."—Donna Bloom*

★ *"People come out of film school thinking they are a director. Well, they're not. What you learn in one day on a movie set is a lot more than you learn in a film school. Don't be in too much of a hurry, because then you become arrogant."—Donna Bloom*

PHYSICAL PRODUCTION FACILITY MANAGEMENT

JOB TITLE: PRODUCTION EXECUTIVE, PRESIDENT

Job Overview

As president of Rialto Production Group, Tim Clawson manages the overall company operations and vision. "When customers sign on to what we do, I am the key person they are involved with."

Rialto is a physical production department for hire. Traditionally, studios maintained their own physical production departments, but today many films are financed outside the studio system, leaving production companies and producers without production support. "Many companies don't want to carry additional overhead and bring on a staff when they really only need them going into production. It's an economical way for companies and producers to be able to have all the vital necessities of physical production handled for them at a fraction of what it would cost them to maintain that staff full time."

Special Skills

Production executives must possess leadership skills, the ability to work with diverse personalities, and a solid working knowledge of the production and filmmaking process. Clawson also credits his success to having experience working in different media: feature films, commercials, videos, and television. "Each of those has what I call their own etiquette. Each is different in terms of how they are administrated . . . I understand the etiquette of each type of project because I have a solid knowledge of the production process, and am able to apply what works in one area to another."

Learn the craft of filmmaking. Get your hands on a camera and shoot film. "You have to run film through the camera and make mistakes; have things come in and out of focus. You have to learn to edit things together, and see how things don't work and how they do work. Whether it's film school, with friends, or an internship, you have to get your hands on some basic equipment. It doesn't matter if it's film or video. You can learn about the filmmaking process even shooting a little DVD camera and editing on an Apple computer. It's also important to understand the film process—what happens when light hits film, what happens when film runs through a processor—understanding the basics of filmmaking from all aspects. There is no substitute for getting your hands on equipment and doing it.

"You don't necessarily have to get a degree. It's what you learn at the school that means everything. If you're a person that isn't great at school, you might find it easier to take an internship someplace or work for a lighting and rental company. Go to work for a theater company. Anything where you can get your hands on equipment and you're able to work with lighting, scenery, editing, or with cameras. You've got to get that experience. I was good at school, so school was a good structure for me. Film school worked for me because the structure of school worked for me."

Advice for Someone Seeking This Job

"It's a combination of who you know, and being in the right place at the right time," says Clawson, "which can sound really demoralizing to somebody who doesn't know anybody in the business and is sitting in their apartment thinking, 'How do I find that right place and right time?' You've got to learn to network. It's important because there aren't formal ways of getting jobs. There are job boards, but none of them mean anything. Even though the irony is that I've gotten two jobs in my career—which were both significant—by answering ads in *Daily Variety*, believe me: that's total, total, total luck. You have to find ways of seeking out people who need help. I was fortunate enough to find them. To work in this business you have to find ways of finding people who are looking for help.

"People would come to me at Propaganda all the time, which was a big, busy production company, and ask, 'What's the best way to get in here?' I would say, 'Sit at the cappuccino bar,' because suddenly a job would get awarded and a producer would be in need of a PA. The regular guy wasn't answering back and you're sitting there—you might get the chance. It's horrible to tell people, because you can't just hang out at companies, but it's an example of a way of saying, 'Try to seek out those who need help and network the best you can.' Try to be persistent without being too much of a pain for people. Immerse yourself in areas where the activity is going on that you want to work in. If you find yourself in the middle of the country, where absolutely no film production is going on, you have two choices: you can see what the local television stations are doing, or if that's not an opportunity, then you've got to go where the work its—you've got to go to Hollywood or New York or someplace where there is some activity; someplace where you can be in the right place at the right time."

Professional Profile: Tim Clawson, President, Rialto Production Group

"I have always been a big movie fan," states Tim Clawson. "It probably goes back to when I was in high school. I went to the movies every weekend and saw everything that came out, and I studied the old movies. I really enjoyed film.

Growing up in Southern California, he had ample opportunities to be exposed to the film business and industry icons like the Hollywood sign, Grauman's Chinese Theater, and the many studio lots. As soon as he was 16, Clawson frequently drove an hour north to Hollywood, just to drive past them all, reinforcing his desire to be part of the business.

He began making Super-8 movies at an early age. Junior and senior high school brought many more opportunities to study filmmaking and work on student projects. Clawson went on to study film at Orange Coast College and then transferred to University of California Los Angeles (UCLA). Both schools had excellent programs where he learned the nuts and bolts of filmmaking.

Upon graduation, he created a résumé outlining his student film work and the various screenplays he had written. Then came his first timely break. "There are two ways people get into our business. One way is: you know somebody; the other way is: you get really lucky. I fell into the 'I got really lucky' category." Seeing an ad in *Daily Variety* announcing a project in development, Clawson sent off a résumé, thinking they might need help. "Funny enough, I got a phone call from the director. He said, 'We need somebody to come in and write a synopsis of the project so that we can raise money. We have a screenwriter, but he's off writing the script and we don't want to slow him down.'"

Clawson went in and met with director Elliot Hong, who pitched him the story for *They Call Me Bruce?* The film was built around the act of popular Korean comedian Johnny Yune. Clawson took copious notes and came back with a treatment a few days later. "I walked in the office and Johnny was there with the director and a couple of other assistants. It was a really weird vibe; like someone had died." The screenwriter had delivered the first thirty pages of the script and they were terrible. The group was about to scrap the idea. "I'm sitting there and all of a sudden they ask, 'What's he got?' I said, 'Well, I have the synopsis, but it doesn't sound like you need it.'" Reading the synopsis reinvigorated their desire to make the film. The development team simply needed to find a good screenwriter. That is when they turned to Clawson.

With Clawson hired to write the screenplay, Yune brought in his joke writer, David Randolph, and some of his comedian friends for inspiration. "We created characters around their acts. It was a hilarious time." Money was raised and the film was made

VOICES OF EXPERIENCE

What do you like least about your job?

"What I like least about what I do is that there are times when certain people's agendas are different than what others' are, and it creates a conflict there doesn't need to be in the actual production of the film. You try to create an open dialogue and line of communication. Everybody is trying to make the best film they can make, but when people take it on their own how to get that done and almost act maverick-ly about doing it, that's when it gets to be not so much fun."—Tim Clawson

What do you love most about your job?

"What I love most about my job is actually solving the problem. I use problems in a positive way, meaning every film and script has its idiosyncrasies about how you need to shoot it in order to tell the story. You add on top of that issues that come with the cast that are involved, and issues that come with the director, then how much funding is available to make the project. You take all those things and boil them in the pot, and try to figure out how to make the film and solve all those issues so that none of them conflict with each other. That's the challenge. It's really exciting, figuring that out."—Tim Clawson

for $2.2 million dollars (a lot of money for an independent film at the time). In addition to writing, Clawson also served as assistant director and postproduction supervisor. He was just 21 at the time. He went on to write a couple more scripts for Hong, but they were unable to get money to make them. Clawson continued to write screenplays, thinking it was his calling.

His next lucky break came from answering another *Daily Variety* ad. London-based music video company Limelight was expanding into the United States and needed a production manager. When Clawson was offered the job, he was promised that he would have down time between projects to write or work on other projects. "I thought it was a great idea for me to make a little money and continue to write. From the day I joined them, I didn't have a day off for the next five years." Then in the heyday of music videos, the company was responsible for producing many landmark productions such as Peter Gabriel's "Sledge Hammer," Aha's "Take On Me," Dire Strait's "Money for Nothing," and many of Madonna's and Prince's early videos.

Clawson next went to work as head of production for Propaganda Films-Hollywood,

CAREER TIPS

★ *"In film production, there is nothing that can replace experience. That's what I used to call 'mileage.'"*—Tim Clawson

★ *"There's a great quote I've seen attributed to a number of different people, but I'll attribute it to Earl Weaver, the manager of the Baltimore Orioles. He said, 'It's what you learn after you know it all that counts.' I think that applies to physical production. Just when you think you know it all, you're in a place where you really start to learn. I still learn something every day about the business and how it works. Keeping that kind of attitude and an open mind towards what I do, helped me take on whatever challenges come my way."*—Tim Clawson

★ *"The business tends to be fairly informal, but I don't think anyone should let that fool them. You should still approach everything as a professional and give 110%. Even though you see people showing up to work in shorts, T-shirts, and sneakers, it doesn't mean that they are casual about their work. Anything you are asked to do, as menial as it might be, do it 110%. Because what tends to happen in our business is: those who do well for others get the opportunities."*—Tim Clawson

★ *"Keep your head down, work hard, keep your ears open, and learn as much as you possibly can; never stop learning, and never stop listening. When you don't know something, ask. Most people love to talk about what they know. If you ever ask a question and they get grumpy with you, there is only one of two reasons why: you've asked them at the wrong time, or that person doesn't know the answer and they're intimidated by your question."*—Tim Clawson

remaining with the company for eleven years. At the time of his hiring, Propaganda had produced many videos, but had just begun entering the commercial market, and had produced only one or two low budget features. During the period of Clawson's employment, the company was involved with numerous commercials and videos, and between thirty and forty television shows and feature films, including *Being John Malkovich, Candyman, The Game, Kalifornia, Nurse Betty, Ruby,* and *Sleepers.*

The company was eventually sold to Seagram, and Clawson relocated to New York City to become president of Shooting Gallery Productions. Shooting Gallery had a big postproduction infrastructure and strong relationships with independent filmmakers, and was looking for a way to exploit those relationships and build commercial and music video divisions. Clawson was charged with the expansion. Under his leadership the company also managed production for film companies coming into the city to shoot New York segments. Unfortunately, the company folded six months after he arrived. Clawson remained in New York for a few more months as president of Lot 47 Productions. When production business suddenly dried up in the aftermath of September 11, 2001, he returned to Los Angeles.

In January 2002, Clawson was appointed president of the newly formed Rialto Production Group.

CHAPTER
3

DIRECTORS AND ASSISTANT DIRECTORS

The making of a film, like the construction of an automobile, is a collaborative effort. The writer designs the vehicle, the producer gets it built, and the director drives it. It is he who chooses the route, steers the actors and technicians to the destination, and determines what type of journey the audience will experience.

Precisely what a director does varies according to his personal style, and whether the project is for feature film, television, commercial, or music video. In any case, it is the director's vision that the audience sees onscreen. He may be assisted in this effort by the following:

- First Assistant Director: handle logistical and technical aspects so that the director can concentrate on the creative aspects.

- Second Assistant Director: assist the 1st AD.

- Second Second Assistant Director: assist the 2nd AD.

- Second Unit Director: direct the filming of stunts and/or secondary locations.

JOB TITLE: DIRECTOR

Job Overview

The director is responsible for interpreting the script and bringing his, or the producer's, creative vision to the screen. Usually the primary artistic and creative force behind the production, the director guides the actors' performances to achieve that vision.

Writer/director Patrick Read Johnson explains, "The director is the guy the producer hires to drive the tanks into battle for him; to take all of the assembled team and corral them, cheerlead them, cajole them, work with them, and drive them like a herd, to extract from them their best work."

"A director is a storyteller," says director Mel Damski. "He interprets stories. He visualizes them and magically creates images, words, music, and tells a story the best way possible."

Advice for Someone Seeking This Job

One of Johnson's messages in his film *5-25-77* is that it doesn't matter if you're from a small town with no contacts in the film industry—you can make it, just like he did. "It's not unattainable. The only thing that keeps you back is the belief that you can't get there. But you can get there from here. It's doable.

"An old producer gave me this advice once, when I was 18 years old and had just arrived in California. He said, 'Are you willing to wait until you're 25 to be a director?' (I was 18 at the time.) I said, 'Sure.' And he goes '35?' I said, 'Yeah.' '45?' 'Yes.' '55?' 'Absolutely.' '65?' I said, 'I'm willing to wait until I'm 75.' And he goes, 'You might just make it.'

"What he meant was, if you think it would be sort of fun to try out being a director or producer or actor—any of the arts—forget it. It's not for you. You can't just see if it will be fun. If you can't *not* do it; if you can't find a way to see yourself doing anything else, if you can't sleep at night because you want so badly to do it, if all you think about and read about and talk about and want to be around is film information, if that stimuli is all that drives you, then you just might make it if you're willing to stop at almost nothing to do it. Then you've got to say to yourself, 'How far am I willing to go?' Are you willing to jump in your car with $200 in your pocket and drive across the country, end up with no money in your pocket and take any job you can? Are you willing to sleep on floors for two years and go get the second meal and the pizzas for the crew late at night? Are you willing to do all those things? If you are, you might make it. If you're not willing, if you even hesitate, forget it. This is good advice. This will save you years of heartache, because it is always a struggle.

"It's a struggle from the day you start, until the day you get knocked down, to the day you start again. I've been up and down and up and down. I've been in the industry professionally for twenty years—I've wanted to be in the industry since I was nine. I've been very rich and I've been very poor. I've been very successful and had total failures. I've been beaten up, and given accolades, then torn apart. The only reason I can still do it, and still smile about it and enjoy it, is that I can't *not* do it. I would persuade anyone who isn't willing to get extremely dirty and extremely tired and extremely frustrated and extremely beat-up for art, to just walk away."

Professional Profile: Patrick Read Johnson, Writer, Director, Producer

About halfway through watching the movie *2001: A Space Odyssey*, Patrick Read Johnson decided he wanted to be a filmmaker. He was only six at the time. "My father had been waiting forever for this movie to come out. He had read a few tidbits in *Time* magazine and was absolutely riveted." The family dressed up and drove to downtown Wadsworth, Illinois, population 750, to view the Kubrick epic at the local movie theater.

"Within the first few frames, I was just riveted." Although he fell asleep before the movie ended, he recalls, "I did know halfway through that I needed to know how they did what I was seeing. I was fascinated by the visual nature, the manipulation of images to make me see things I thought were impossible." As he was carried out of the theater nearly asleep, he turned to his parents and said, "I'm gonna direct movies when I grow up."

From that time on, Johnson was fascinated with movies, particularly with discovering how various effects were created. He read everything he could find about the process, including a book on the making of *2001*. By the age of nine, while his father was at work, he was stealing his Super-8 camera and making movies. "I'd run outside and set fire to my model air-planes and blow up armies of GI Joes, trying to imitate my favorite effects."

In his teen years, he once tried to create weightlessness on film by sus-pending his little brother from the garage ceiling with piano wire. In the midst of shooting, he received a phone call from a friend. Forgetting his brother was still suspended in mid-air, he dashed out to meet the friend. "He hung there for another four hours and fell asleep."

In high school Johnson studied theater, but his heart was set on film-making. Constantly searching for reading material about film, he discov-ered *American Cinematographer* magazine. Each month he poured over the pages, reading how the effects for his favorite films were created and dreaming of going to Hollywood to meet some of his visual effects heroes. One day he came home from school to discover his mother holding one of his *American Cinematographer* magazines while carrying on an animated telephone conversation. Finding a phone number on the masthead, she had telephoned the magazine's editor, Herb Lightman, and convinced him to not only introduce her son to his hero, Douglas Trumbull, but to allow the 15-year-old to tag along with him for a week while he interviewed filmmakers.

Johnson was met at the airport by friends of his mother, and each day was dropped off at the American Society of Cinematographer's clubhouse in Hollywood, where he would meet Lightman. "He showed me pictures of the old brilliant cinematographers and equipment. Then he said, 'Let's start going on our adventures.' I met Bill Abbot, who did the effects for *Tora! Tora! Tora!* and many other movies, and the grand master of effects, Linwood Dunn, who started on *King Kong* and did *It's a Mad, Mad, Mad, Mad World*, all the way up to the original *Star Trek* TV series. He is just a genius." An early inventor of visual effects, Linwood became a mentor for Johnson and the two remained lifelong friends.

As much as it thrilled him to meet these legendary filmmakers, Johnson's heart was set on meeting Douglas Trumball. "That was the whole reason for this trip—because I'd seen his work on *2001*. I had to meet him." Finally, with the week passing rapidly, Lightman called to say, "Tomorrow we're going down to the set of a movie called *Close Encounters of the Third Kind*. It's the next film for this young director Steven Spielberg, who did *Jaws*. Doug is working on the film."

"We go down to the visual effects stage in Marina Del Ray, a building known as Future General, Doug's company at the time. We walked in and it was just magic." Everywhere, it seemed, were FX people working on various visual effects. One of the first things to catch Johnson's eye was a big, black-draped stage with a giant Plexiglas aquarium. Using a layer of fresh water over a layer of saline solution, the look of cumulus clouds was being created by pumping white shoe polish between the layers and letting it float over the layer of salt water. Using fiber optic probes, different colored lights were fired to create the effect of UFOs hiding in the clouds. Fascinated by what he was seeing, Johnson hardly noticed the man dressed in jeans and a T-shirt, sneakers, and a ball cap, who sat down beside him and offered a can of Coke, then yelled "Cut!"

"The lights come on and everyone looks at me like I said it. I said, 'No, no' and I point to this guy sitting next to me. That's when I notice two very important things: his baseball cap says *Jaws* and his face is Steven Spielberg." He tells them to set the shot up again and turns to me and says, 'You're Pat, right?' My jaw is hanging open and I say, "Yeah . . . ." And he says, 'I'm Steven.' I go, 'I know.' He gets up and says, 'Herb told me you guys were coming. Come on and I'll show you around.'"

For the next couple of hours, Spielberg gave Johnson and Lightman a personally guided tour of the effects facility. "He's showing us the miniatures, the storyboards, the matt painting department, and talking about the design of the mothership and where he got his inspiration. I didn't really understand the full measure of what a director was yet. To me, Steven Spielberg was more of an executive. I didn't realize he was responsible for how this all looks and feels. Remember, I'm a 15-year-old kid from Wadsworth, Illinois. I don't know any better at this point. So while he's talking, I'm torn by this feeling that maybe while I'm listening to this very intelligent craft guy talk about this movie, I'm missing the chance to meet Doug Trumbull."

While Spielberg and Lightman continued to talk about details of the film, Johnson wandered off in search of Trumbull. "Behind this one curtain there are all these guys building models and working on the mothership. Greg Jein, Ken Swenson, and Dave Jones—all these heroes of mine in the model making world, just sitting around having their Cokes, eating junk food, and working on the mothership." The group invited Johnson to come sit with them while he asked a multitude of questions. Soon he was invited to help them attach fiber optics to the mothership. "I'm always searching for the ones I did."

While wondering if he will ever get to meet Doug Trumbull, a door suddenly blasts open and a big burly guy comes charging in, obviously in a hurry and not in a good mood. "Herb goes, 'Hey Doug, how ya doin'?' And he's like, 'Fine, fine. I've got some fire to put out.' He's walking along pointing at things, still moving fast, and Herb is running along trying to catch up and not knock over models. Herb says, 'Doug, this is the young man I told you about whose big dream it has been to come out to California and meet you.' Doug turns and he goes, 'Hey,' and he turns away

VOICES OF EXPERIENCE

What do you like least about your job?

"What I like least about it are the overriding economic concerns. It's not like we should take someone's money and go off and spend it any way we like, without regard to having to pay that money back. There are legitimate concerns, but unfortunately there seems to be a dearth of executive and studio personnel who truly, truly understand the filmmaking process, the actual creative end. Rather than admit they don't necessarily know what's going on and look like fools, they'd rather act like they know it all and start making decisions, just to be seen making decisions."—Patrick Read Johnson

What do you love most about your job?

"What I like most is the opportunity to work with a lot of incredibly talented people: everybody from the camera team to the art team, the costume designer, prop, makeup, and visual effects people, and actors—really talented actors. I have really had golden opportunities, so far, to work with some amazing actors: some who are Academy Award winners and some who have never acted a day in their life, and both have been rewarding. Getting together with a whole bunch of creative people and essentially putting on a play is as much fun as I can imagine."—Patrick Read Johnson

and walks off, leaving me standing there. You can see the camera just pulling away and this little doe-eyed kid going, 'Oh . . . Hi . . . ' That was the last I saw of Doug. I thought, 'Okay, I can go home.'"

With one day remaining, Lightman suggested that Johnson might want to take in some of the tourist attractions since he wasn't sure the film he was covering that day would be very exciting. "He said, 'The name is pretty silly; it's called *Star Wars*.'" Having come out to see all he could of filmmaking, Johnson decided to tag along. "We pull into this industrial building parking lot where the Death Star is laid out before us—I don't even know what the Death Star is yet. Then I notice this giant, two-story hot tub. In it were all these long-haired guys smoking cigarettes and racing radio-controlled cars around the parking lot. We walk in the place and cool our heels in the waiting room. It was one of those bad industrial waiting rooms with a couple of couches and some copies of *Daily Variety* on the table. On the back wall that leads to the stage is a Mylar teaser poster for *Star Wars*. All it said was 'Coming to your galaxy this summer.'" Apparently behind schedule, beneath the tag line someone had written "Or maybe next summer" and then on a piece of masking tape below that someone wrote, "Or maybe the summer after that," and so on.

"I thought, 'These guys are having fun!' Then suddenly this titanic man—he had to be seven feet tall—comes bounding out of his office and says, 'I'm John Dykstra. Come on in and let me show you some stuff.'" Everywhere were prototypes and models for X-Wings, the Blockade Runner, Landspeeder, TIE Fighters, and the Death Star. "They are all made out of dragster model kits like I used in my own model building. I recognize every single part. It was really amazing."

Before the tour is over, Dykstra shows them the Millennium Falcon, then takes them to an upstairs area to view some of the film footage. "It was this black tarped-off area with these ratty old couches, old popcorn on the floor, and a big steam-powered projector that looks like it will smudge any film that goes through it. He turns on the projector and Herb and I are thinking, 'This guy is nuts.' The first thing we see is the Star Destroyer going overhead. No sound, no music, just the Star Destroyer, and tears sprang from my eyes. Herb and I are mesmerized, staring at this. We look at each other and Herb just starts writing—fast. With that first shot I realize I'm about to see something unbelievable.

"I got on my little Eastern Airlines flight and went back to Wadsworth, Illinois, population 750. I had to figure out how I was going to spend the rest of my life in that town (Hollywood) now that I'd seen all of this. It was just incredible; it was life changing." Back in school, Johnson tried to explain to his classmates what he'd experienced, and that this incredible movie called *Star Wars* would be opening on May 25, 1977.

His senior year, Johnson loaded up on classes so he could graduate early. He went directly to Illinois State University for a semester, before packing up in 1980 and moving to Los Angeles with the intention of going to USC Film School. "I had $200 in my pocket when I left. By the time I got to L.A., I had about $20 left."

Armed with sketches, drawings, and spaceship models he had created, Johnson knocked on the door of Brick Price Movie Miniatures and said, "Hi. I just moved from Illinois and I need a job." Asked if he could drive in addition to building models, he answered "Yes" and was told to get a time card. "I started working that day." Starting out as a gofer, he moved up to model making, and then supervisor on some projects. He remained there for two years, working on commercials, industrial displays, and models for NASA and The Smithsonian Institute, all the while writing screenplays.

One night at a "mid-level Hollywood party," he was introduced to producer Cassius Weathersby, who was looking for medium-to-low budget movie projects to develop at 20th Century Fox. An introduction was made and Johnson was asked to pitch some of his ideas. "I pitched him this sort of alien on earth story." Weatherby loved the idea and made an appointment for Johnson to pitch the idea to Richard Berger, then president of production, and to story editor David Madden. The idea was so well received that "they sort of yanked me by the shirt collar and dragged me down the hall to Sherry Lansing and said, 'Do that again.' I basically acted out the movie. I was standing up and moving around and playing all the parts. I got about five minutes to pitch and she said, 'I don't know what this is, but I like it. Let's do it.'"

At 19, Johnson had landed a deal with a major studio and started to work on the script for his science fiction film. Three drafts later, the studio was sold and Johnson was back building models at Brick Price. "I ate some crow." He later worked for Mark Stetson and ShowScan, progressing to visual effects supervisor. Along the way he sold a few more scripts, and the desire to direct grew more intense after directing the second unit for *Dead Heat*. After seven years, Johnson had grown weary of model making and channeled his energies into a project called *Martians!!!*, which he co-wrote with friend Scott Lawrence Alexander, and hoped to direct.

The pair loaded the "wacky" film with special effects and determined that, using contacts such as FX friends Scott Ressler and John Knoll (then at ILM working on *The Abyss*), they could make a film with a $10 million look for $2 million. Friend and producer Jason Clark (*Stuart Little*) introduced the pair to a development executive for a Yugoslavian businessman who agreed to give them $1.75 million. Releasing the film was the best offer they were going to get, so they took the deal. "It was one of those 'we don't know that it's impossible so we're going to get it done' type movies. And we did. It would never be a diamond, but when we finished, it was a flawed, but fun, little ruby."

Johnson assumed the film would go direct to video, but that he would have something to show which he had directed. Word about the film spread through the Hollywood community, making its way to Steven Spielberg's ear. "He called my representative and asked for a copy of the movie. A couple hours later I got a call saying, 'You're going over to meet with Kathy Kennedy, Frank Marshall, and Steven tomorrow. They want to pick up your movie for Disney to distribute. They loved it—Steven loved it!'"

CAREER TIPS

⭐ *Johnson credits his success to perseverance. "In the words of Winston Churchill, 'Never, never, never, never, never give up.' The minute you give up, the minute your spirit is broken by all that can be thrown at you in Hollywood, you'll never get up again. They won't let you—or you might not let yourself. So you just can't give up."—Patrick Read Johnson*

⭐ *"If you hit a wall or miss an opportunity, or you've blown a relationship or you've made the wrong turn in any step in the making of a film, that doesn't mean you're a bad human being, or that you're an incapable director or actor or artist or writer or whatever. You have to simply say, 'Okay, that didn't work. I'm a rat in a maze and I've learned that that direction gets me shocked. Now I'm going to move in this direction.' That's the only thing you can do if you're going to survive in Hollywood. Good luck to us all."—Patrick Read Johnson*

It would be the first time Johnson had seen Spielberg since their meeting on the set of *Close Encounters*. "Even though Steven was very gracious and told me to come see him if I ever got out to L.A., I never wanted to be one of those people that just sort of showed up on the set . . . I wanted to show him what I could do when I was ready." Spielberg championed the film to Jeffrey Katzenberg at Touchstone, and convinced him to buy the film. Then, for the next several months, executives at Disney set out to recut and reshape the film, eventually destroying its gem-like qualities, and releasing it as *Spaced Invaders*. The film was into profit the first weekend of release and went on to make several times over its cost in profit.

At the same time, both Disney and Universal became interested in Johnson's script *Starsailor* and both were courting him. "Jeffrey Katzenberg was very honest and said, 'We'd like to make *Starsailor*, but it will take a lot of development,'" while Universal said they loved the script and were essentially promising a green light on it and other projects. "I made the mistake a lot of young filmmakers make and played one side against the other. I finally ended up at Universal with a huge deal and nice offices, great computer equipment, and a screening area. I made them pay for me to be there, which, of course, I ultimately had to pay for when all those expenses were charged to my project later."

While at Universal, Johnson began developing *Dragonheart*, a film he wanted to direct. Although she was more interested in *Starsailor*, Raffaella De Laurentiis sent Johnson off to the family's hotel in Bora Bora to eat, drink, and work on the script for *Dragonheart*. Returning to the States, he realized he needed help and partnered up with Chuck Pogue (*The Fly*). Together, they came up with a script that Universal green-lighted, and Johnson was off to scout locations in Spain with Laurentiis.

Every agency in Hollywood, including Johnson's representatives at CAA, championed the project and sent over top stars to vie for roles. Johnson had conceived of Draco, the dragon, with Sean Connery in mind. "Sean had read the script and expressed interest in doing the role." Liam Neeson was his choice for the knight. The Henson Creature Shop would build the dragon. But it was not to be. When he delivered test footage of the dragon, Universal misinterpreted it as representative of the quality level of the film Johnson would direct. "I was getting in a lot of fights with Universal." The studio was comfortable with Johnson being the director of a $2 million movie. Making the jump to a $20 million movie overnight made studio executives nervous. Eventually, Universal took away the directorship of *Dragonheart* and gave it to someone else.

In an effort to make up some of the loss, Universal offered Johnson a film entitled *The Day Before Midnight*, which was later developed into the ground. It was time to move on. At about the same time, he received a call from John Hughes, asking if he was interested in *Dennis the Menace*. After Johnson had finished *Spaced Invaders*, Hughes brought him a serious project called *Reach the Rock*. At the time, Johnson did not feel that he was ready for such a dramatic piece and passed on the project. Hired to direct *Dennis*, he relocated to Chicago and started "designing it, casting it, and getting locations going." When his vision for the film strayed too far from Hughes's concept, Johnson was replaced as director.

As a concession, Warner Bros., the studio behind *Dennis*, gave Johnson offices and he started developing *Speed Racer*, which ultimately never got off the ground. Nearly a year to the day after *Dennis the Menace*, Hughes called Johnson and offered him *Baby's Day Out*. Although it was not an ideal project for his talents and passion, he took the job. "Remember, at this point I'd only directed one $2 million dollar picture, and this had a budget of $50 million." Having to make numerous compromises, the film never achieved Johnson's vision of what it could be, but it did get made with him as the director.

"While *Baby's Day Out* was in postproduction, I was flying to San Francisco, to Skywalker Ranch, to work on the mix. On the flight I saw a movie called *Cool Runnings*. I remember being sent that script early in my heyday of being the newly discovered fair-haired boy and thinking 'This is never going to be a movie.'" Noting that the film was produced by Dawn Steele, he telephoned manager Melinda Jason when the flight landed and asked her to tell Steele that he was a fan of the movie. Three hours later, Steele called him with an invitation to lunch when he came to L.A.

Over lunch, Steele told Johnson that she wanted to work with him. An hour later she sent him a script entitled *A Brief Moment in the Life of Angus Bethune*, which later became *Angus*. At first he shied away from the project, but Steele was relentless and finally he agreed to direct the project. Again, studio executives imposed changes to his vision for the film. "It was a challenging experience, but one I'm ultimately proud of."

Post *Angus*, Johnson continued to develop projects and write. Then came a call from David Madden, president of production for Fox TV movies, asking him to take over a project called *When Good Ghouls Go Bad*. "He said 'You're going to have to completely rewrite it and you'll have to go to Australia to make it. You'll only have $3 million and so many days . . . but it will be you and I creatively producing it.' I said, 'You got me.'

"Now I'm working on *5-25-77*, which is the story of a young kid from Wadsworth, Illinois, who got to see *Star Wars* and *Close Encounters* before anybody else . . . it's *American Graffiti* on the night that *Star Wars* came out. It's about finding the courage to take a step that no one believed I could take. It's very heartfelt." Carrie Fisher is slated to play Johnson's mom. Truth is sometimes better than fiction.

Special Skills

Mel Damski says a director must be good at "using the camera to tell the story, talking to actors, interpreting the script, and understanding what the important story points are." A director also must be able to get along with people and inspire them to work as a team.

Advice for Someone Seeking This Job

"My first advice is to read, read, read," says Damski. "I think that's the best education you can get. Be as aware of the world around you as possible. Directing is about storytelling and understanding human nature.

You have to be a keen observer of human behavior; that's very important. You've got to have what I call a bullshit meter, so that when somebody is giving a line reading and it rings false, you have to A) know it rings false; and B) know how to communicate with the actor to find the truth and interpretation. I think it helps to be a participating member of the human race. (By the way, there are people with none of these qualities who are very successful filmmakers. They are dictatorial, self-centered, and narcissistic.)

"I think the best way to become a director is through screenwriting. That's the easiest because you can do it on your own . . . Many directors come from cinematography, from acting, and from the stage. There are a lot of different ways to approach it. The important thing is you've got to understand the story. If people go into directing thinking it's all about getting sexy shots and clever angles, they are going to miss the boat.

"Because movies are so expensive to make, you have to establish credibility so that someone will hire you. That's a hard thing to do when you're young. That's an important part of the process: to somehow establish credibility. The easiest way to do that would be to write a terrific script, then show people a short film so that you can demonstrate that you can direct your own script."

Professional Profile: Mel Damski, Director

Although filmmaking was a second career for director Mel Damski, he has always been a storyteller. In high school and college he served as sports editor for his schools' newspapers. A linebacker, he earned a football scholarship to Colgate University, where he majored in English literature. After graduation he landed a job as a sportswriter, but soon found the profession limiting and moved to general assignment reporting for the New York based paper *Newsday*. "The problem with sports is you've got to write so many column inches, even if it's a really boring game you're covering. Whereas when you're a general assignment reporter, you don't write unless there is a story."

VOICES OF EXPERIENCE

What do you like least about your job?

"I think that the most difficult part of my job is when egos obstruct the creative process."
—Mel Damski

What do you love most about your job?

"I like the creative rush. I like making things up, interpreting, and having my own unique vision . . . The most important thing in my life is to be able to create something."
—Mel Damski

Still feeling unfulfilled as an assignment reporter, Damski considered becoming a film critic. "I went to the University of Denver, taught journalism as a graduate teaching assistant, and studied film in their mass communications program. I thought I would return to New York as a film critic." Damski soon realized he loved making movies much more than writing about them. He applied to the American Film Institute (AFI) and was fortunate to be one of ten directors admitted into the program that year.

"It was an awakening. It was so fascinating to study movies. To watch them over and over, forwards and backwards, in slow motion, and realize all of the decisions that went into making a film. I was excited by that.

"The program at AFI was very good because I studied the best film-makers in the world and a lot of them came to speak to us. I sat at the feet of [Bernardo] Bertolucci and [Steven] Spielberg, and Fritz Lang. It enabled me to take a very high view of filmmaking. It's very important to have a point of view and bring something to the table, my own unique vision of the material."

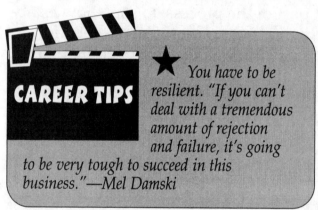

CAREER TIPS

★ *You have to be resilient. "If you can't deal with a tremendous amount of rejection and failure, it's going to be very tough to succeed in this business."—Mel Damski*

During his time at AFI, Damski was accepted into another program that afforded him the opportunity to serve as an apprentice to Stanley Kramer on the film *Oklahoma Crude*. "I was with Stanley every day throughout preproduction and the production of the film. I learned a tremendous amount about the practical aspects of how movies are made, what all the people on set do and their responsibilities. That helped me a lot when I made my AFI film."

For his AFI project, Damski adapted the short story "The Lost Phoebe" by Theodore Dreiser into a half hour 16mm color film. "It was about a man whose wife died and he can't accept the fact that she's dead. He goes around to the neighbors asking where she is. It's how the community deals with him." Through the film, Damski attracted the attention of an agent, who immediately secured work for him, directing an episode of *Barnaby Jones*. The job enabled him to join the Directors Guild (DGA). The difficult part was coming up with the $2,500 initiation fee. Between that and taxes, he actually lost money on that first job.

Soon after, Damski got the chance to direct an episode of *Lou Grant*, where his unique storytelling vision earned him further opportunities and recognition. "I shot three minutes of dialogue in one take. In those days, they never did that; the camera just went from one character to another." After seeing Damski's first round of dailies, the producers hired him to direct several more episodes. His work also earned him his first Emmy nomination and an invitation to direct an episode of the hit series *M*A*S*H*.

Damski has refused to allow himself to be typecast as a director of any one particular genre by working on a wide spectrum of films like *Mischief* and *Yellowbeard*, and television series such as *Ally McBeal, American Gothic, Any Day Now, Boston Public, Charmed, Chicago Hope, Early Edition, Lois & Clark: The New Adventures of Superman, Picket Fences,* and *The Practice.* "I've tried to constantly mix it up. My feeling is if you stand in one place, they will nail your feet to the floor."

JOB TITLE: FIRST ASSISTANT DIRECTOR, 1ST AD, OR ASSISTANT DIRECTOR

Job Overview

Frequently, the assistant director's first task is to break down the script and create a shooting schedule, estimating how many shooting days will be required at the various locations. This is reviewed with the director and/or producer, and adjustments are made based on their input and budget restraints. Throughout production, the first AD oversees scheduling and generating of call sheets, supervises the crew, sets up shots, and conducts run-throughs, coordinates and sets the background actors, and assists the director in every way possible to keep the production running smoothly.

In addition to his duties as assistant director, Arthur Anderson also co-produces films directed by John Woo. In that capacity, he is involved in the creative process almost from the moment of Woo's decision to work on a picture. For *Windtalkers*, Woo, the second unit director, and Anderson used toy soldiers on a board to work out action sequences, before bringing in a storyboard artist to illustrate the action they wanted to create. Next, Anderson typed up their ideas into script form and gave it to the writers, so that they understood what Woo was looking for in a particular sequence and could incorporate that action into the script.

Special Skills

The first AD must understand the entire filmmaking process and the role of each department. ADs should be excellent communicators, organized and thorough, and have the ability to manage and motivate people.

Anderson suggests reading the book *The Film Director's Team* by Alain Silver and Elizabeth Ward.

Advice for Someone Seeking This Job

To get hired on a production you need to know someone, which can be a daunting task for someone with no contacts in the industry. Volunteer to work on student films and nonunion projects so you can meet people, and hopefully impress someone with your work ethic. Save up money and be prepared that once you start looking for entry-level work, you may have to live for the first six months on little or no salary.

Most first assistants begin their careers as a production assistant. "The greatest thing about being a PA when you start out is that you don't have a lot of responsibility and you get to see everything that goes on. Pay attention to what all the people are doing on set." Anderson attributes his advancement to the fact that he looked to be a hole-filler: "When I saw something that wasn't being done, I would volunteer to do it. I would listen to the ADs, to what was going on, and be there to help them."

For anyone considering a job in the film industry, Anderson's advice is: "If you don't really have a passion to make films, don't do this. It's very stressful, in terms of the insecurity of having periods of unemployment. When you're working as a first AD on a big action film, you usually work 16 hours a day and your weekends are consumed with getting ready for the next week's adventure. It's hard on your family . . ."

Professional Profile: Arthur Anderson, Assistant Director/Co-Producer

Born and raised in the Bible Belt, Arthur Anderson attributes the source of his success to his strong spiritual upbringing and belief. During his senior year of high school, he prayed frequently to discover his mission in life. One day, while driving a tractor plowing fields, an inspiration told him, "I want you to go to Hollywood to make films." He laughed at the idea, knowing he had no Hollywood contacts and no money to pay for film school, but a series of events over the next few years would point him in that direction.

Growing up in rural Charleston, South Carolina, Anderson often used his imagination to entertain himself. When he was five, his parents got a television set and he saw his first movie on that little screen. He first became interested in making films after his father bought an 8mm camera to photograph Christmas and other family events. "I would take the 8mm camera into the kitchen and shoot stop action, a frame at a time, of potatoes fighting each other."

In 1974, he entered the University of South Carolina, majoring in acting and performing standup comedy on the side. He quickly determined, "if I wanted to eat three meals a day in South Carolina, this was not going to cut it," so he changed his major to finance and management—a field that would later prove useful to him when he became an assistant director and producer.

He spent his summer breaks in Myrtle Beach, a tourist hot spot that swelled from about 10,000 residents in the winter to more than 100,000 in the summer. He began producing comedy commercial spots for local nightclubs with a college friend who worked at WTGO

VOICES OF EXPERIENCE

What do you like least about your job?

"One of my least favorite things is that it is an insecure business. You don't have a regular job where you know all year long you're going to be working . . . Once a job is over, you really never know where your next job is coming from."—Arthur Anderson

What do you love most about your job?

"What I really love is, it is magic making films . . . I think of a motion picture as a director's painting on moving canvas. The brushes he uses to paint his images on that canvas are his cast and crew. It's my job to manage those paintbrushes. That's what I like most about it."—Arthur Anderson

Radio, after the station signed off for the evening. When they returned to school in the fall, they took samples of their spots to advertising agencies and immediately started getting calls to create additional comedy spots. With his friend employed at a Columbia radio station, they again went in after the station signed off the air at night and cut the spots until they could afford to build their own studio.

By their senior year, Anderson and his friend had their own studio and had built a busy radio commercial production business. When a client asked if they also did television spots, the pair said, "No problem." Having never before shot a commercial, Anderson ran out and bought a book on 16mm filmmaking and put himself through a crash-learning course. They enlisted the aid of another friend who was interested in filmmaking, got a camera, and learned on the job. Taking a microphone into the parking lot, they created their own special effects sound library by recording screeching cars and noises. By Christmas time, Anderson and partner Rick Page had landed a huge account, and their radio and commercial production company was thriving. But driving back to school after the holiday, Page died in a car wreck. With half of the company's creative talent gone, Anderson struggled to keep the business going while carrying a nineteen-hour course load.

Reading that production for a film called *The Double McGuffin* was coming to Charleston, Anderson's mother alerted him to the news, supplying a phone number she found in the newspaper. He connected with the extra casting director and landed a job assisting her, then went on to serve as a set production assistant.

Through connections he made on *McGuffin*, Anderson went on to work as a production assistant on *The Brink's Job*, which lead to *Willie and Phil* and *Urban Cowboy*. In 1979 he decided to relocate to Los Angeles. Having worked almost nonstop for the previous four years, he had already amassed more than 700 production days, allowing him to join the Directors Guild.

Anderson's first job as second assistant director was on the Oliver Stone directed picture, *The Hand*. Over the next few years, he continued to work as a second AD on a variety of features and television series. He met his wife, a former casting director, on a film set. They married in 1982 and had a daughter in 1985, after which Anderson focused on working as a first AD on television series, allowing him to stay in town until she was older. In the mid-1990s, he returned to features, working as an AD on *Beverly Hills Cop III* with director John Landis.

Through friends Barrie Osborne and Marty Ewing, whom Anderson had met on previous productions, he was introduced to John Woo in 1996. Hitting it off, the two began a successful working relationship on the movie *Face/Off*, which continued onto *Mission: Impossible II*, and *Wind Talkers*.

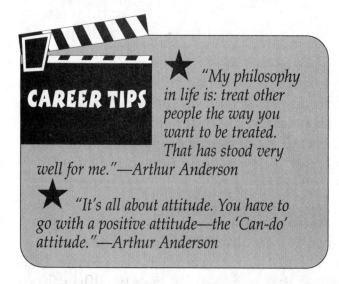

★ *"My philosophy in life is: treat other people the way you want to be treated. That has stood very well for me."*—Arthur Anderson

★ *"It's all about attitude. You have to go with a positive attitude—the 'Can-do' attitude."*—Arthur Anderson

"John is one of the humblest and [most] creative guys you could ever want to work with. He's got a great heart . . . We have the same belief of making good moral films that tell a story.

"He listens to a lot of music. You could take one of John's movies and remove the dialogue, put music to the picture, and still understand the story."

Between working on features, Anderson returns to television, where he has worked on *The Client*, *Pasadena*, and *Birds of Prey*. He is currently working with Woo on *Men of Destiny*.

When asked what he credits his success to, he says, "Faith in God. I'm a pretty average person. My vertical relationship with God is the most important thing . . . God, family, and work; I never let those three things get out of proportion."

JOB TITLE: ACTION UNIT DIRECTOR OR SECOND UNIT DIRECTOR

Job Overview

The action unit director is charged with directing the action sequences of a film. Following discussion with the director to gain a clear understanding of what he wants to achieve, the action unit director works closely with the stunt coordinator to safely choreograph the stunt. The action unit director then guides the performers and cinematographer through capturing the sequence on film.

For instance, in the James Bond film *Tomorrow Never Dies*, Vic Armstrong directed four major sequences, including the opening scene with the speedboat, and a ski sequence with flying parachutes. In *Charlie's Angels*, he directed the helicopter scenes, a racetrack sequence, and all of the fights.

"We go out and shoot quite difficult stuff. It's a whole different technology of telling a story through action, keeping it interesting, and not getting repetitive. Also, putting your main artists into it safely." In Armstrong's case, he often serves as both stunt coordinator and action unit director.

Special Skills

"You have to have a specific ability and then utilize that ability," says Armstrong. "Don't come into the business as a jack-of-all-trades and expect somebody to use you."

Advice for Someone Seeking This Job

Action unit directors must have first-hand knowledge of what is required to safely achieve a stunt. Thus, most are former stunt people and stunt coordinators. It is also important to have a strong background in filmmaking. Coming up through the ranks as an assistant director is another route.

Professional Profile: Vic Armstrong, Director, Action Unit Director, Stunt Coordinator

"I realized I wanted to be a stuntman when I was eight or nine years old," says Vic Armstrong. "My dad was training racehorses for a very, very famous actor called Richard Todd, who was the highest paid actor of his era in the '50s." Todd played the title roles in *The Story of Robin Hood and His Merrie Men* and *Rob Roy, the Highland Rogue*, and starred in classics like *Dorian Gray, The Longest Day*, and *The Virgin Queen*. "Every weekend he'd come down with women covered in furs and jewels, in top cars, and smelling of aftershave. I thought, 'Wow, what an elegant gentleman.' He'd tell us stories about films he'd just been to or had been working on. We'd see pictures of him at premieres."

Armstrong frequented the cinema to take in Todd's latest film, usually an action adventure. "I'd come home and get my pony out, and charge along and throw myself off. It drove my dad mad. He believed you should never get off a horse unless it threw you off."

At age 14, Armstrong's main ambition was to race as a steeplechase jockey. Too tall to ride professionally, he competed as an amateur for many years, even riding some of Richard Todd's racehorses. In his late teens, he met a stuntman who wanted to borrow a horse for a film. The next day, Armstrong was asked to ride it. He made his film debut as Gregory Peck's stunt double in *Arabesque*, parlaying that experience into doubling for the actor in three more films.

Armstrong was the only young stuntman working in England at the time. "All the others were ex-commandos from the war or what have you; middle-age people. I built up a huge portfolio of work very, very quickly." Vain, mature actors sometimes chose the much younger Armstrong as their stunt double over an older stuntman.

In 1966, just a year into his career as a stuntman, Armstrong got the opportunity that would impact his career for the next 35 years: he was hired to work on the James Bond movie *You Only Live Twice*. "I was on a picture in Switzerland with [Gregory] Peck. Bad weather forced them to cancel the movie." He returned to England and telephoned to chat with a friend—the stuntman whom he had beaten out for the role in the Peck film. Unable to accept work on the Bond picture because he was already signed on to *2001: A Space Odyssey*, the friend suggested that Armstrong call and get the spot. "I met with Bob Simmons, Dickey Graydon, and George Leach, who is now my father-in-law, and got the job. It was awe-inspiring: this huge set, this massive film. It was all mind-blowing for a young stuntman."

More Bond films followed: *On Her Majesty's Secret Service, Live and Let Die, Never Say Never Again, Tomorrow Never Dies*, and Armstrong's latest project, *Bond 20*, a.k.a. *Die Another Day*. "I'm very, very proud of my input on the Bond movies."

After only a few years working as a stuntman, Armstrong had earned a reputation for his precision and talent with complicated stunts. While working on *Figures in a Landscape* in Spain, the stunt coordinator left the project to work on another picture, and Armstrong was promoted to the position. "I became a stunt coordinator, which is much more creative, because you devise the stunts: A) you work out what the stunt will be; and B) you then break it down and work out how it's going to be achieved. Let's say you've got somebody jumping off a 200-foot building. We know you can't do it for real, but want it to look as though they jumped off and landed in the back of a pickup truck, for instance. We would devise all the methods that you would need to safely visually transport somebody from the top of the building to the bottom, to get in the truck, and drive away."

VOICES OF EXPERIENCE

What do you like least about your job?

"What I hate about it most is the unfairness of life and the bullshit."
—Vic Armstrong

What do you love most about your job?

"I love the creativeness. I thoroughly enjoy carrying out a sequence that people go, 'Wow, I really enjoyed that motorcycle chase in Tomorrow Never Dies.' *Or, 'I really enjoyed the stunts with the girls in* Charlie's Angels.' *'The battle on* Henry V *looked so realistic.' I love the creativity of actually telling a story on film."*—Vic Armstrong

He worked steadily on *A Touch of Class, A Bridge Too Far, Young Winston,* and the first two *Superman* movies, in which he also doubled for Christopher Reeve and met future wife, stuntwoman Wendy Leach. By the late '70s, he was second unit director on the Bette Davis movie *Watcher in the Woods.*

His resemblance to and friendship with Harrison Ford, established on the film *Raiders of the Lost Ark,* earned Armstrong the opportunity to double for Ford and stunt coordinate on *Indiana Jones and the Temple of Doom* and *Indiana Jones and the Last Crusade.* He also served as a stunt double for Ford on *Witness, The Mosquito Coast, Frantic, Working Girl, Regarding Henry,* and *Patriot Games.*

Armstrong's work on the Indiana Jones movies impressed George Lucas, earning him work on all three seasons of the television series *Young Indiana Jones.* He made his directorial debut on the second season premiere, *The Young Indiana Jones Chronicles.* The following year, he directed the internationally successful *Joshua Tree.*

In 2001, Armstrong was awarded a Technical Achievement Award from the Academy of Motion Picture Arts and Sciences, for the refinement and application of the Fan Descender to the film industry. Considered a standard of the industry, the Fan Descender provides a means for significantly increasing safety of very high stunt falls. The system permits falls to be made under controlled deceleration, with a highly predictable stopping point and without limitation of camera angles.

Armstrong has worked with some of the world's most well-respected directors, such as Sir Richard Attenborough, Michael Cimino, Roland Joffe, Irvin Kershner, Ridley Scott, and Steven Spielberg, amassing an impressive body of work that includes: *Air America, An American Werewolf in London, Black Beauty, Blade Runner, Captain Correlli's Mandolin, Charlie's Angels, Dune, Empire of the Sun, Entrapment, Johnny Mnemonic, The Last Action Hero, Legend, Quills, Rambo III, Star Wars: Episode VI—Return of the Jedi, Shadow Conspiracy, Starship Troopers, Terminator 2,* and *Total Recall,* to name just a few.

"I'm proud of my reputation, I must say. I'm still friends with all of the people I started off with, which is nice. (Early mentor, actor Richard Todd, recently visited Armstrong on the set of *Bond 20*.) I enjoy the whole [process] of filmmaking and am proud to be part of that. When I look back at my credit list, I go 'Wow!'"

JOB TITLE: SECOND ASSISTANT DIRECTOR, 2ND AD, OR KEY SECOND ASSISTANT

Job Overview

The second AD disseminates information to the entire crew, such as setting call times and making up call sheets; notifying actors and crew of what scenes are scheduled to be shot, and when; and assisting the assistant director in his duties as needed.

"Everything goes through the key second AD," explains second AD Eric Tignini. "If something is not on set, the first AD is going to hear about it; so *you* hear more about the problems than you do about the things that are good: 'Why didn't we bring so-and-so in earlier?' (Because you told me to bring them in at this time!) You're the middleman. You have to be thick-skinned. It's a strange position. A lot of people have said that the key second is the hardest job on the set. You put in the longest hours of anyone. You're the first one there and the last one to leave."

The second AD is also responsible for setting background. "Take a scene from *The Godfather*, where Al Pacino is talking to James Caan at the wedding. Behind them are 300 to 400 people dancing, partying, eating, and having a good time: young and old, men, women, and children are running around in tuxedos and dresses. Our job is to place those people in the frame and give them direction of what do to in the scene. It's the only part of our job that people see on screen."

Special Skills

The second AD must be a good listener and communicator. "Keep things simple when you communicate and try to treat everyone with respect," says Tignini, "whether they are the highest paid actor on the show or the lowest paid crew member. You just try to give everyone respect. Most of the time you'll find out that people are very good at their jobs and know exactly what you need. You just tell them where you're shooting and when. You have to be something of a diplomat on the set. You listen to a lot of people's problems. You have to stay calm, be clear and polite."

Advice for Someone Seeking This Job

One way to become a second AD is to first serve as a production assistant. "It's one of the best ways to get into the business," says Tignini. "If you are applying for a job, I wouldn't even bother lying about your experience." Some students fresh out of film school make the mistake of trying to present themselves as jacks-of-all-trades, proficient as a camera operator, a key grip, in set dressing, and any other position. "People will realize right away that you're not good at any of those things. Jobs on films are very specific; you specialize in your field. As a production assistant, you are allowed to see how all the different departments work. Then you can choose where you wish to stay as a production assistant and become an AD, or branch off and get into a specialized field. Your eagerness and personality will get you the work."

Professional Profile: Eric Tignini, Second AD

From the time he was a youngster, Eric Tignini knew he wanted to be a filmmaker. Born in New York, his family moved to Arizona when he was 10. There, he began making movies with his parents' Super-8 camera. "We made three-minute rip off versions of other movies, like *Planet of the Apes*. It would be a few kids in the neighborhood and me, wearing werewolf and monkey hats, chasing whoever we deemed to be Charlton Heston. It always ended with kids wrestling on the ground, but we thought they were spectacular."

What do you like least about your job?

"What I like least is that the second AD has to deal with every single department. It's the flip side of the coin. Sometimes it's really wonderful and other times it's a complete pain, because it can be very taxing. You have to switch gears so quickly. One minute the grips are saying, 'We can't put the crane here for this reason . . .' You listen to them complain for a few minutes. You really can't help them, you have to let them sort of work it out themselves, but you listen to them. You turn around and there is a makeup person coming up complaining about something, or an actor asking, 'Why did you bring me in early?' At times you feel like a really high-paid concierge."—Eric Tignini

What do you love most about your job?

"What I love most about my job is that every day is different. Every day is a different challenge. I remember working on Forrest Gump; it was really interesting. The first half of the day we would be shooting something that took place in an army barracks, the mid-to-late '60s period, and in the second half of the day, it would be 1974 and we would be on a disco set. It was something different every day. It's not like being in an office. I like that."—Eric Tignini

"Another thing I like about being the second AD is you communicate with every single person on the crew. You have to go to every department and let them know what we're going to do tomorrow. I like meeting all the different people. The film business is made up of really diverse types of people. I don't know too many jobs where you have the costume department working side by side with the big burly grips for a common purpose."—Eric Tignini

After graduating high school in 1980, Tignini majored in film at San Francisco State, earning a bachelor's degree in 1984. "Film school opened my eyes to world cinema, documentaries and classic films that I would not have been exposed to, things that I reference today. It was amazing to see where some of our filmmaking masters get their influences from."

Knowing no one in the film industry, Tignini was lucky to land a job on a feature right out of film school. Discovering that the Coen brothers were planning to shoot a film called *Raising Arizona* in Scottsdale, he contacted the production company and landed a job as a production assistant. "I'd seen their first movie, *Blood Simple*. I really liked that movie and thought, 'This really speaks to my sensibilities.' I pursued getting on the film.

"[*Raising Arizona*] was my first film and turned out to be a really lucky break. It was low budget enough where I was able to be up close to see a lot of things happening. It had a wacky script and wild characters. It also had, at the time, very inventive camera work. It had babies, animals, explosions; it was everything. It was like a cartoon come to life for someone right out of film school."

Tignini cut a deal to be paid $250 a week. Unfortunately, the production alternated between shooting five days a week, then six days a week, while Tignini's salary remained the same. "I was young and wide-eyed. I would pick the boys [the Coen brothers] up in the morning and drive them to the set, then stay with them all through the dailies afterward. I was putting in 16 to 17 hour days, every day. It was in many ways like film school."

When the picture wrapped, Tignini moved to Los Angeles and landed work as a PA through connections he had made on *Raising Arizona*. "You build your reputation on word-of-mouth: people recommending you.

"I remember being very excited about my first big location job. They flew me out to Pittsburgh to do a movie called *Dominick and Eugene*." Tignini continued as a production assistant on numerous productions, including 13 episodes of *The Highwayman* television series, which got him into the Directors Guild. Although hired as a production assistant, the duties of the second second AD were often delegated to him. "Someone dropped a dime on the company, that they were using a production assistant in an AD's capacity. A representative from the Directors Guild came to the set and said, 'Either fire this kid and bring in a real AD, or pay a small fine and we'll upgrade the guy.' So they upgraded me. What I didn't realize was, I had to complete 400 days outside of Los Angeles in order to work back in Los Angeles as an AD, which is a long and complicated rule of the DGA. It was torturous. It was very, very daunting to get those 400 days, but it happened."

One of Tignini's career highlights was working on *Forrest Gump*. "It was literally different every day because of the character's journey. We would be duplicating part of the Vietnam war for a couple of weeks, and then off doing a running sequence across the country. We filmed a protest march at the Washington Monument with 2,500 background dressed like hippies; we got to take over the whole reflecting pool area at the Monument. We filmed outside the White House.

"I was brought in to help coordinate the military for the Vietnam sequence. I went with military adviser Dale Dye (who also worked on *Private Ryan* and *Platoon*) and the actors to train for four days and nights out in swamps, dressed in full army gear. We ate rations and slept in holes that we dug. We had our own little boot camp. It was fascinating and educational; it was an adventure.

"It was also interesting to watch how Robert Zemeckis worked. It was a big script, with big sequences where Forrest would move through a crowd and pass Abby Hoffman and somehow wind up onstage in front of 25,000 people. It was interesting to see how Zemeckis shot it. He's really smart. He'd find a really creative, but economical way to shoot.

It was basically one shot. He'd always focus on Forrest and follow him, whatever Forrest did, wherever he went. When Forrest sees something, the audience sees it too."

After *Forrest Gump,* Tignini went on to work on *Terminal Velocity, Nine Months, Mulholland Falls, Phenomenon,* and *Desperate Measures.* In 1997, he worked on *City of Angels.* "We created traffic jams in Los Angeles which was, in and of itself, fun. We were shooting things from an angel's perspective, which means we would shoot way up high atop billboards and on top of skyscrapers. We'd shoot over and down from them onto the city. It took a lot of planning and preparation, but at the end of the day, it was really fun. It takes the audience somewhere they haven't seen."

Work on features such as *The In Crowd* and *America's Sweethearts* followed, along with offers to serve as first AD beginning with the television series *Tenacious D.* Between jobs, with partners David Elton and Thomas Johnston, Tignini wrote, produced, and directed *Jerome.*

CAREER TIPS

★ *"Wear comfortable shoes. You will be on your feet all day long. I remember my first day on the job was an unusually short day. It was 12 hours. After standing on my feet for 12 hours, I remember saying, 'Gosh, that was a long day.' A guy turns to me and says, 'Long? That was a short day! Wait until you see tomorrow.'"—Eric Tignini*

★ *"The thing you learn really quickly is just what a small community the film industry is. I think any of us could walk onto another film, and nine times out of ten they would know somebody working on the picture. It's a very, very small community of people who are out there working, which is why word-of-mouth and recommendations go a long way. People know very quickly who's working on what. Or if something bad happens, you know right away; it spreads quickly."—Eric Tignini*

"That's my passion. I make my money working on big Hollywood productions, but my passion lies in smaller independent film with personal stories." More than ten years in the making, the film was released in 1999. That success came after writing four screenplays that were all rejected. Tired of trying to guess what Hollywood executives were looking for, the partners wrote the type of movie they would want to see. "To our surprise, it was the screenplay that people responded to. People tapped into the story, and we were able to raise financing for it. It was very low budget."

Written during short stretches between working on features, *Jerome* was shot under the same time constraints. "We'd take three months off to shoot, go back to work, then come back to edit. It took a long time. From the time we wrote it until we had it in the can took about three years." After a successful tour of film festivals, the picture played on the Sundance Channel and Showtime.

JOB TITLE: SECOND SECOND ASSISTANT DIRECTOR, SECOND 2ND AD

Job Overview

In general terms, the second second AD serves as an assistant to the second AD. Often they are responsible for setting the background. Other times they may run the first team, meaning that they communicate daily schedule adjustments and other information to the cast.

JOB TITLE: VIDEO DIRECTOR, MUSIC VIDEO DIRECTOR, OR DIRECTOR

Job Overview

The music video director is responsible for the visual presentation of the artist's music on film, from devising the concept and pitching the idea to the record label and artist, to directing the shoot and editing the video.

Special Skills

Video directors must possess filmmaking experience, creativity, imagination, and have a friendly personality and strong communication skills.

Advice for Someone Seeking This Job

"There is no easy route," says director Steven Goldmann. "You can make a music video while you're in film school, and be looked down on by your peers who want to make movies, or you can realize it's a great way to make little movies and just get some experience. Find a friend's band and shoot them; try to make something that looks like a video. Then start meeting with video companies. The hardest part of getting someone to give you a shot in the professional world is that you really have to show people that you've shot someone singing. Singers want to know how you're going to portray them. Find a local band and practice shooting them and build a reel."

Professional Profile: Steven Goldmann, Director and Co-Owner, The Collective

Most of Steven Goldman's early life in Canada revolved around film and music, from the television commercials he acted in as a child, to the mobile sound system he operated as a teenage disc jockey. The proceeds from both financed his entry into the film school at New York University. During a summer job working at the United Nations for UNICEF, he began directing and editing short instructional films. Through contacts made at the time, he landed work as an assistant manager on some episodes of *Tales of the Dark Side*, and as an apprentice editor on *Home of the Brave: A Film by Laurie Anderson*. Following work for an editing facility on a series of toy commercials, he was hired by an advertising agency to direct projects for Milton Bradley, Franklin Mint, and others.

VOICES OF EXPERIENCE

What do you like least about your job?

"The hardest part, over the long haul, is that it's hard to grow and stay fresh."
—Steven Goldmann

What do you love most about your job?

"I love what I do. I love coming up with ideas. I love reading and writing. I love people, so I love that my job allows me to be around a lot of people. I love being on the set. I love editing; I love being in the editing room and seeing it all come together. I've got a job that allows every side of my personality to shine."—Steven Goldmann

It took several false starts, but Goldman finally landed a job as a director at a startup video production company. After doing some pop and country projects, he began to make a name for himself as a director of heavy metal bands. When the demand for that music declined, so did the demand for his services, until all he could find was the occasional job editing television commercials. "It was one of those crazy tailspins that life can take. I was practically out of work. It was a very low point in my career," recalls Goldmann. Then a series of phone calls turned his career around.

The first call came from a New York company that had seen his work and wanted to hire him as a director. When he got to the firm's office, he received another telephone call from a Montreal production company that wanted to represent him. Minutes later, he got a third call from Cynthia Biederman, a former colleague who was now working at Scene Three, a Nashville-based film production company. Biederman had a project she wanted him to direct. The year that started without much promise ended with Goldman being named Country Music Television's

Director of the Year for Michelle Wright's "Take it Like a Man" video. After that, his career took off.

Over the next few years, Goldmann divided his time among New York, Montreal, and Nashville, building a reputation as one of the most creative and sought-after directors of music videos and music spe-

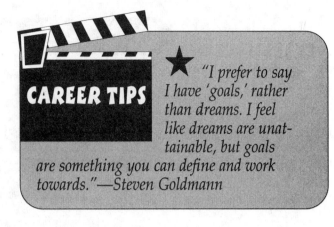

CAREER TIPS

★ *"I prefer to say I have 'goals,' rather than dreams. I feel like dreams are unattainable, but goals are something you can define and work towards."—Steven Goldmann*

cials. When an offer came to direct the television music series *The Road*, Goldmann moved his family to Nashville to join the newly opened office of High Five.

Goldmann continued to direct videos, mostly produced by Biederman, and in 1996 joined with her and fellow director Thom Oliphant to form a production company called The Collective. Since that time, he has won numerous awards in both the United States and Canada, including the CMA Music Video of the Year award for Kathy Mattea's "455 Rocket" in 1997 and Faith Hill's "This Kiss" in 1998, as well as twice being named CMT's Video Director of the Year. In 1999, Goldman opened a second office in Canada. To date, he has well over 100 videos to his credit that include acclaimed work with artists like Alan Jackson, Martina McBride, Shania Twain, and Tricia Yearwood.

●●●●

CHAPTER
4
LOCATIONS AND TRANSPORTATION

Gone are the days when a project was constructed and filmed entirely on a studio soundstage. Today's production budgets require that suitable existing locations be found as settings, and transportation arranged for the actors, crew, and equipment to get there.

The location manager finds locations that fit the needs of the script, director, and budget; negotiates usage with the owner; obtains the proper permits and variances; and smooths out the inevitable problems. Scouts are sometimes used for the legwork of photographing the prospective locations. A large production may require multiple location managers and scouts.

The transportation department is in charge of just that: getting people and equipment where they need to be, when they need to be there. Office staff members handle vehicle purchase and rental, dispatching of personnel, contracts and paperwork, and accounting. Drivers handle the actual transport.

This chapter is divided into two sections: Locations and Transportation Department.

LOCATIONS

JOB TITLE: LOCATION MANAGER

Job Overview

Location managers are responsible for finding potential shooting locations and arranging for permission to shoot in those locations, including obtaining the necessary city and state permits and licenses. Additionally, they may oversee any location scouts used to do the legwork of finding and photographing potential sites.

Special Skills

Successful location managers are tenacious problem solvers. They must listen well, follow instructions, and be able to negotiate with people. "The ability to listen to what others have to say and having a good sense of humor has helped me," says former location manager Charlie Baxter. "I'm pretty easygoing."

Advice for Someone Seeking This Job

Baxter suggests working as a production assistant as the best way to begin your career in filmmaking. "Start in a position that allows you to see what other people do." Offer to work for the location manager for free, so that you can learn firsthand what they do, then work your way up the ranks. "It's a hard business to get into if you don't live in L.A. or New York, and it's a hard business to get into if you *do* live in L.A. or New York. You just have to go out and try and hook up with people. It's all about personalities. If you get along well with people and they like your attitude and your energy, they'll recognize that."

Professional Profile: Charlie Baxter, Production Manager, New Dominion Pictures, and former Location Manager

A Virginia native, Charles Baxter earned a bachelor of fine arts degree in theater from Virginia Commonwealth University in Richmond. "My plan was to work in theater, regional and national theaters, as an actor and ultimately as a director."

While auditioning as an extra for the television miniseries *Kennedy*, Baxter was offered a job that changed the course of his career plan.

"I had just gotten out of college and went down to this big audition for extras. It was in a high school gymnasium. There were about 3,000 people there." Seated in the bleachers were a few members of the production crew: the location manager, production manager, and publicist. They asked Baxter what he was doing at the audition, and that if he really wanted work, to give them his name and telephone number. He later received a call offering him work as a production assistant.

"I hadn't really thought about film until I took that job. I was making $25 bucks a day and no per diem." Toward the end of the first week, he was sent to Washington, D.C., with the rest of the production. There he shared a hotel room with two other crew members, still making only $25 a day. Filming returned to Richmond for another month, and then went on to West Palm Beach, Florida. Baxter was again asked to go along. The offer paid for airfare and hotel accommodations, but included neither a wage increase nor per diem. He took it. The final location was in New York and although Baxter was invited to continue working on the film, the budget would not allow him a hotel room. Fortunately, he had made friends with crew members who lived in the city and they offered him a place to stay. "It was a great experience. I didn't make any money, but I got to see all the different jobs available. I was smitten by the time I returned to Richmond. I let it be known to other production companies that this was a business I wanted to be in."

Baxter found work as a production assistant with several local production companies. About nine months passed, and the same location manager who had hired him for *Kennedy* called to offer him an assistant location manager position on *The Murder of Mary Phagen* miniseries.

Baxter continued to make connections, establishing a reputation for being dependable and hard working, while he scouted locations for local production companies. He was hired as assistant location manager when the NBC miniseries *Gore Vidal's Lincoln* came to Richmond. Three weeks into the shoot, the location manager was let go and Baxter was offered the job.

"Trying to be a location manager outside of New York or L.A. is a catch-22 in a major way. Nobody is going to hire you if you don't have experience, and how are you going to get experience if nobody is ever going to hire you? They took a chance."

As production on *Lincoln* wound down, one of the show's producers offered him the job of location manager for the Disney Channel's *Goodbye, Miss 4th of July*, shooting in Tennessee. When that show wrapped, Baxter returned to Richmond to serve as location manager on the television movie *My Name Is Bill W*, starring James Woods and James Garner. Three-quarters of the way through production, Baxter had a near fatal car accident. "It was four blocks from my house at 8:30 in the morning on March 11th. I was reaching over my seat taking notes while talking on the cell phone and ran a traffic light. A city bus T-boned me."

Rushed to the hospital with collapsed lungs, broken ribs, a fractured pelvis, a concussion, a damaged aorta, and other injuries, he was given a one percent chance of survival. On the eighth day after the accident, the film was coincidently scheduled to film at a location near the hospital. Garner and Woods came to visit Baxter and a walkie-talkie was brought to his room so the crew could talk with him.

Baxter was released from the hospital just ten days after the accident. A month later he received a telephone call from British film producer Bernard Williams, offering him the location manager job on *Navy Seals*. Another Williams-produced film, *What About Bob?*, followed.

"*Navy Seals* was one of the greatest experiences I ever had. We built all of the sets in the interior of a National Guard

VOICES OF EXPERIENCE

What do you like least about your job?

"*Probably my least favorite thing is that it's a lot of hours, a lot of changes, and a lot of stress in trying to rectify all the changes. It's all-consuming.*"—Charlie Baxter

What do you love most about your job?

"*I like the creative aspect. I like being able to give my opinion on how and why something will work. I like the collaboration between people trying to make something happen. I like meeting new people. I like the satisfaction of not just finding a location, but actually making it happen.*"—Charlie Baxter

Armory in Roanoke, Virginia. We had carefully laid down this sub floor and laid everything down on top of it because . . . it had a traditional gymnasium floor. On the last day, at the end of the shoot, everything was done; everything was over and everybody was happy." One of the crew members dragged a genie lift across the floor, gouging a furrow that cost the production $50,000 to replace the floor. "Those are the little things you get to deal with. You think it's all over and guess what? The floor is ruined. Everybody is gone and you've got to call the insurance people and deal with it. It's a headache."

Baxter went on to work on *True Colors*, the series pilot for *The Monroes*, and features *Major Pane*, *First Kid*, and *Hush*. For *Hush*, he scouted locations from Georgia to Rhode Island looking for the right setting. "I was on the road forever. They finally settled on a house near Charlottesville . . . When we looked at it, it was so magical and beautiful in the middle of nowhere . . . [By the time the production began filming, it was] summer, one of those years where the 17-year locusts come out. We were ready to start filming and all of a sudden there was this incredible noise of these locusts; it was deafening. Everyone was looking at me, asking 'Can you go out there and exterminate them?' I'm like, 'Yeah. Billions of locusts?'"

For the film *Virus*, Baxter was charged with moving a 600,000-foot ship that no longer had an engine from one shipyard to another to have work done on it. "The construction crew would come in from L.A. I found a space for them: some hangars and a dock in Newport News. We were ready to go and I get a phone call from the producer saying, 'We're going to have to bail out and regroup. We have to take three or four months off, but we want you to stay on. I ended up moving the ship to a shipyard in Norfolk and spent three months having work done on it to get it up to safety and speed so we could film on it. Then I kept hauling it around to different docks."

Baxter went on to turn a small Tennessee town near Brushy Mountain Correctional Complex into a coal mining community for *October Sky*. His challenge for *The Replacements* was to not only find and negotiate use of a football stadium for shooting, but two additional football fields for actors to practice on. "It wasn't as easy as you might think, because high schools and colleges were getting ready to practice."

CAREER TIPS

★ *"I don't get wound up and I never accept 'No'—I just don't accept it. There has got to be a way to make whatever it is happen. I don't give up. I find a way and am willing to negotiate."*
—Charlie Baxter

★ *"Compromise and don't take things too seriously. Many of the people I know, the stress absolutely fries them. You have to find a way to not take it all too seriously. Don't let the pressure that the production company and other parties are applying become insurmountable. Focus and let common sense be your guide, and you'll probably find out it's not as bad as you thought it was."*—Charlie Baxter

His next film was *Hannibal*, directed by Ridley Scott. "That was probably the best experience I have had so far in my career of filming, without a doubt. Ridley is so smart and creative and funny. He's a gentleman. It's an absolute pleasure to work with the guy—but talk about stress." When Scott had initially scouted Washington D.C.'s Union Station, it contained a carousel. When the time came to shoot, the carousel was gone and Baxter had to locate another one and have it re-erected in the same spot. "Then I find out that Sue, the Tyrannosaurus Rex from the Chicago Museum, is going to be erected in the main hall.

I have to call and tell Ridley there is going to be a dinosaur in the hall. We adjusted."

He was finishing up work on *Hannibal* when he was offered the location manager position on *Hearts in Atlantis*. "They asked me to come replace someone. It was a hard show. We took over a community in the small town of Stanton, Virginia. We had 13 homes at an intersection up on the hill. We needed to be there for weeks. Because of the type of lighting and how they were going to control the shade, they wanted the power lines dropped or turned off so that there was no chance of the guys operating the big condors getting an electrical shock." It proved too time consuming to turn the power off and on each day, so the only solution was to shut the power down for two weeks. "Which meant I had to bring in and wire each house to a commercial silenced generator." Then, someone had to deal with making sure the generators didn't run out of fuel.

After *Hearts* wrapped, Baxter accepted the position of production manager for New Dominion Pictures. The company produces television programming such as *The FBI Files*, *The New Detectives*, and *Special Forces: Untold Stories*, for Discovery, The Learning Channel, and other cable outlets. Baxter's next step will undoubtedly be producing.

JOB TITLE: LOCATION SCOUT

Job Overview

A location scout is an individual who finds potential shooting locations, photographs them, and obtains the owner's permission to shoot there.

TRANSPORTATION DEPARTMENT

JOB TITLE: TRANSPORTATION COORDINATOR

Job Overview

The transportation coordinator is the head of the transportation department and is responsible for obtaining and managing all vehicles associated with a production, including big trucks, trailers for the makeup, hair, lighting, camera, and wardrobe departments, dressing room trailers, honey wagons, personal trailers for the director, stars, and others, picture cars, and all rental cars for cast and crew. The coordinator also hires and manages the transportation captain and drivers. "Transportation is an art," says transportation coordinator Bob Foster. "It's the art of putting big trucks in little spaces."

Special Skills

A commercial driver's license and experience driving big trucks are necessary. Union productions require drivers to be members of the Teamster's union.

Expanded Job Description

Prior to being put on payroll for an upcoming television series, Foster will have already arranged for rental cars for the production staff. His first day on payroll, he sets up his work space within the production office and meets the various crew members he will be working with. His next tasks are to read the script and take notes of picture cars and other vehicle needs, then obtain a list of locations and acclimate himself to them, making note of potential concerns. For instance, the production plans to film while traveling down a particular road. Foster's job is to point out that a certain bridge along the road has an 11-foot clearance, but all the trucks are 13 feet tall.

When a production is produced by DreamWorks, which requires that all drivers pass a drug test before being hired, Foster is responsible for making certain that testing is completed.

Before the rental vehicles are assigned out, he ensures that a purchase order has been processed for each and that each is insured. "Whether I get a piece of equipment from Georgia, Florida, or wherever, before that vehicle leaves to come to me, it has to have insurance on it." Next, Foster makes a list of the trucks and trailers required by each department, from property to makeup, camera to wardrobe. He must also determine trailer requirements for individual cast members, some being predetermined by contractual obligation.

Foster then concentrates on acquiring the needed equipment and hiring drivers. In the course of making these arrangements, he will go with the location manager to scout various locations. "They will be looking for me to tell them whether we can park all the trucks in a particular lot or if we need more room." He also goes out with various tech scouts to determine where the generator and lighting will be set up, and checks out the proposed camera angles to ensure that the vehicles will be parked out of camera range, yet remain easily accessible.

Throughout the production, Foster oversees the transportation department, ensuring equipment and drivers are where they should be, when they should be. "Being a driver, you're the first one on set and generally the last one to leave. If the crew call is 7:00, that means the actors probably have to be there at 6:00 for hair and makeup. Which means the hair and makeup people probably have to be there at 5:30 to get ready for the actors. We have to be there prior to that to get the trailer set up. If it's hot outside, we have to get it cool inside. If it's cold outside, we have to get it warm inside, so that everybody is comfortable when they come in. We make sure all the lights are working and the generators are up and running. At the end of the day we have to take it down, move it, and get ready for the next day."

Generally, Foster begins prepping a production three weeks in advance of filming, and concludes between two to five weeks after filming has wrapped. In addition to making sure that all vehicles are returned, he may also have to oversee the repainting and/or restoration of a picture car to its original condition.

Advice for Someone Seeking This Job

"Transportation is not just carrying a pretty actress down the street in a blue Lincoln Town Car. You're always the first person on set and the last person to leave. You have to be in the Teamster's union to drive on movies, in most cases. Try to come in as a PA in the transportation department or an intern, and see what goes on and work your way up. I don't hire anybody who does not have a commercial driver's license. I recommend you get a commercial driver's license and then decide what you want to do. If you want to learn how to drive a big truck and you've never driven one before, I recommend going to a reputable trucking company or driving school to learn. If you want to be a generator operator, get with a vending company that specializes in production equipment and learn. All generator operators have to pull cable before they become operators. Learn from the ground floor up. I like my people, men or women, to be able to drive everything that we have. If you're on the set and you have some type of situation where you need to move something in a hurry, anybody can do it."

Contact rental houses and volunteer to intern so you can learn the equipment. They will train you and when the equipment goes out, you may be the person they send with it.

What do you like least about your job?

"The thing I like least is having to deal with budgets. I don't like it when you come onto a production and they say, 'Here is what you've got to work with,' and then they tell you they need 10 trailers, but the budget has just got room for five. That's the thing I like least: working on a budget."—Bob Foster

What do you love most about your job?

"I love the people. I have always been a people person—I've never met a stranger. I like working with people from all different walks of life and different parts of the country. I like talking with them and learning something from them. I love the camaraderie of being with people."—Bob Foster

Professional Profile: Bob Foster, Transportation Coordinator

Bob Foster never considered that his experience driving big trucks and pulling trailers while in the military, in construction, and as a volunteer fireman, coupled with his knowledge of law and the people skills gained as a police officer, along with a love of automobiles and a passion for collecting antique cars, would be ideal skills for becoming a transportation coordinator for feature films and television.

He discovered the potential for working in the film industry when a friend asked him to help move some trailers for a production. Later, the friend called on Foster to go to North Carolina and work on the film *Love Field*. He was assigned to drive for actress Michelle Pfeiffer for 16 weeks. "She is just a down-home sweetheart; a very, very nice girl," he recalls. Upon completion of that assignment, he was offered another driving job on a production shooting in Richmond. He worked his way up to co-captain while driving on a production filming in Georgia, returning to Virginia as a full captain on the made-for-television movie *Miss Rose White*, all within his first year working in the business.

Offers continued to "snowball" with television work, and on films such as *My Cousin Vinny* and *The Jackal*, for which he served as transportation captain. Before long, Foster was being hired as transportation coordinator. His work on *Girl, Interrupted*, which shot in

CAREER TIPS

★ *"Be yourself and treat other people like you would want to be treated."—Bob Foster*

★ *"When I go to work for a producer or a unit production manager, my main objective is I want them to hire me on the next project. I want them to want me to come work for them again."—Bob Foster*

Pennsylvania, earned him a referral from the state film office to work on *Lucky Numbers*. His résumé also includes the features *The Contender*, *Hannibal*, *Hearts in Atlantis*, and the series *DC*.

JOB TITLE: TRANSPORTATION CAPTAIN

Job Overview

The captain assists the transportation coordinator in the leasing and insuring of all production vehicles, hiring the drivers, and generally overseeing the drivers and vehicles while on set.

JOB TITLE: TRANSPORTATION OFFICE COORDINATOR OR TRANSPORTATION ACCOUNTANT

Job Overview

The transportation office coordinator is responsible for every piece of accounting paperwork for the transportation department, including purchase orders, check requests, and driver time cards. The office coordinator reports to the transportation coordinator, and generally works in the production office.

Special Skills

Organized, detail-oriented, personable, and problem solving skills are all attributes that make for a good transportation office coordinator. "I think being a people person has helped me," says coordinator Kris Golashesky. "A lot of times people will forgive your mistakes because they like you. If you have a good demeanor and are good with people, it takes you to another level."

Advice for Someone Seeking This Job

Although the film industry is tough to get into, Golashesky suggests, "The best thing that anyone can do is contact their local or state film office and volunteer your time to the office of a production company. There are lots of opportunities once you get in, but you have to wait your turn to get there. Nobody starts out as a producer."

VOICES OF EXPERIENCE

What do you like least about your job?

"What I like least of all is that you are confined to four walls. When people ask the question, 'Was such and such piece of equipment at such and such location?' I would have no clue. I'm only a messenger of the information that is provided to me."—Kris Golashesky

What do you love most about your job?

"What I love most is that two and two equals four. You're pretty regimented. All the purchase orders and everything lines up, and at the end of the shoot the accountants hug you."—Kris Golashesky

Professional Profile: Kris Golashesky, Transportation Office Coordinator and Location Scout

After the sports marketing firm that employed Kris Golashesky for 10 years folded, she took a position in events planning with Special Olympics, but soon discovered the job was less about events and more about fundraising. Through a friend she became familiar with opportunities in film and television production and decided to make a career change.

Hired as transportation office coordinator on the feature *Girl, Interrupted,* Golashesky learned the tasks quickly. She went on to work in the same capacity on *The Contender.*

Having become friendly with the staff at the Virginia Film Office, they hired her to do some location scouting for them, leading to work for location manager Charlie Baxter on the film *The Replacements.*

She went on to work on *Lucky Numbers,* serving as a personal assistant (driver) for actress Lisa Kudrow. After *Lucky Numbers,* she went to work on the film *Hannibal.* In addition to being the transportation office coordinator on the picture, she also worked for Charlie Baxter as a location scout.

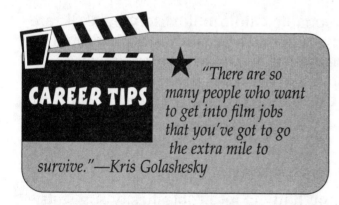

CAREER TIPS *"There are so many people who want to get into film jobs that you've got to go the extra mile to survive."*—Kris Golashesky

"The director, Ridley Scott, had a keen eye for what he wanted and the location manager was concerned at not being able to find exactly what he was looking for. I went out for a month, shooting various locations in and outside the city of Richmond, knocking on a lot of doors and asking a lot of people I had never met before if I could come in their house and take photographs. I had to find Clarissa Starling's apartment, the cottage, and a chemistry laboratory."

Golasheskey followed up with the film *Hearts in Atlantis*, and is currently at work in the transportation department of the series pilot *DC*.

JOB TITLE: GENERATOR OPERATOR, GENNY OPERATOR

Job Overview

The generator operator ensures that the generator is functioning at the proper cycle and voltage to keep the lights on the set lit, handles basic maintenance of the diesel engine that powers the generator, and drives the vehicle that carries it. (Note: an electrician may sometimes be called upon to run the generator.) Typically, a generator is used for location shooting where there are insufficient quantities or no electricity available.

Special Skills

Genny operators must be mechanically inclined, possess the ability to handle minor repairs of diesel engines, be a member of the Teamster's union, and have the skill to maneuver large tractor-trailers through congested areas. "Driving a tractor-trailer in cities is not the easiest thing to do, especially the ones we use, with a generator mounted on it," says genny operator Bobby Jones. "They look like a normal truck, but the tractor is usually longer than a normal truck, extended out to have enough room to carry all the equipment we need."

Advice for Someone Seeking This Job

Working for a rental house that provides vehicles and equipment for productions is one way to land a job driving for a film company. The experience also affords you an opportunity to learn about lighting equipment and other gear the company provides. If you already have a commercial driver's license and experience driving trucks, contact transportation captains and let them know you are available.

VOICES OF EXPERIENCE

What do you like least about your job?

"My least favorite thing is the hours we work, especially when we're working all nights. Sometimes on night shoots you work all night for two or three weeks at a time. You're not conditioned to stay up all night and sleep during the day. That's my least favorite thing."—Bobby Jones

What do you love most about your job?

"I just enjoy the work itself. I have never worked in an office atmosphere and I don't like being inside a building continuously. I like being outdoors. Most of our work is on location and a lot of it is out of town. I like that we get to go to a lot of places that normal people wouldn't. I like to see what goes on behind the scenes."—Bobby Jones

Professional Profile: Bobby Jones, Generator Operator

Eleven years ago, Bobby Jones discovered that his driving skills could be directed toward a career in film and television.

He learned to drive trucks right out of high school and honed his skills driving for a logging contractor, maneuvering a tractor-trailer through the woods. He went on to work in construction, building houses and sometimes driving trucks.

The girlfriend of a former schoolmate introduced Jones to filmmaking when she employed him to assist her with wrangling animals for various productions. When the school friend got into transportation, he employed Jones to drive the truck that pulled the hair and makeup trailer. He gave up construction soon afterward to devote himself to driving for film and television productions.

At the time Jones began driving, Virginia was a "right to work" state and did not require him to be a Teamster. As more production came into the state, it eventually became necessary for him to join the union. He learned to run a generator from watching the genny operators of the productions he worked on.

CAREER TIPS

★ *Once on set, pay attention to what others do and if the opportunity presents itself, learn new skills from those working on set. Jones was working as a driver when he learned to run a generator.*

Jones's first full time film work was the television movie *My Name Is Bill W.*, starring James Woods and James Garner. Work on *Love Field, The Contender, Kingpin, Beverly Hills Ninja, Hearts in Atlantis*, and many features and television series followed.

JOB TITLE: DRIVER, TRANSPORTATION DEPARTMENT

Job Overview

A driver is any person who drives a vehicle leased by the production, from a big rig and trailer to the cars assigned to individual actors. Generally, drivers are required to have a commercial driver's license. Union productions require drivers to also be a member of the Teamster's union.

JOB TITLE: CAMERA CAR OPERATOR AND PICTURE CAR COORDINATOR

Job Overview

The camera car operator drives the camera car or process trailer.

"The camera car is a specially designed vehicle, usually built on a pickup truck chassis. It looks like a large director's set on wheels," explains coordinator Gary Duncan, "due to all the aluminum pipe, known as speed rail, and camera plates and mounts. The purpose is so you can mount a camera anywhere onto the camera car. The camera operator, the director of photography, the camera assistant, and the director can ride on the vehicle while operating the camera and looking at video monitors to make sure they are capturing the actual moving shot they need. If you're following a kid on a skateboard or a person on horseback, the camera car moves down the street alongside. The camera car driver is responsible for maintaining the speed that the kid on the skateboard is maintaining, so that the camera operator can keep the camera focused on the kid without a lot of forward or backward movement in the frame. That is called free running: the camera car is moving and your subject is moving. You try to stay in a tandem speed, as if you are attached."

The camera car is also equipped with a tow bar to pull the picture car behind, so that the camera can look directly into the car and film the talent as though they are driving. "The actors do their dialogue with the background moving, as if it were an actual car driving down the road."

The process trailer is a flatbed trailer pulled behind the camera car, and carries the picture car the talent is riding in. It enables the camera crew to shoot directly into the front window of the car. "A good example of this is *Driving Miss Daisy* or *Thelma and Louise*. Those two movies made extensive use of picture cars sitting on the process trailer and being towed by the camera car."

A picture car is any vehicle that will appear on film. The picture car coordinator locates, arranges for, and supplies camera and picture cars, which can be classic cars, vintage cars, period correct cars, special interest cars, stunt cars, or any other requested vehicle.

Special Skills

Excellent driving ability and quick reflexes are a necessity.

Advice for Someone Seeking This Job

If you have a collection of cars that you want to rent to movies, photograph them, and send a copy of the prints with a letter of introduction to companies that provide picture cars. If you want to be a camera car operator, contact companies who already provide vehicles and apply to work for them. Working for an existing company will afford you the opportunity to see how the industry works and to make contacts, before venturing out on your own.

Professional Profile: Gary Duncan, Picture Car Coordinator/Camera Car Operator

"I never really chose this profession; I fell into it," says Georgia native Gary Duncan. The owner of an automotive body shop, Duncan repaired wrecked cars and provided special fabrication work on race cars. "In the mid-70s, Georgia was becoming a hot spot for location filming. [For *Smokey and the Bandit*], I was approached to paint and repair the stock cars they damaged during the day of filming. I rebuilt them overnight so they could be used again the next day.

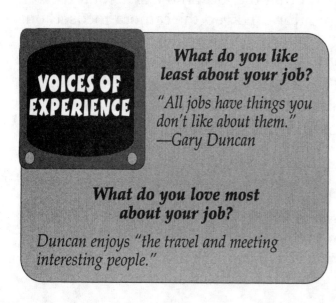

VOICES OF EXPERIENCE

What do you like least about your job?

"All jobs have things you don't like about them."
—Gary Duncan

What do you love most about your job?

Duncan enjoys *"the travel and meeting interesting people."*

"They had that gold and black TransAm. There were five of them. One was the beauty car, the car that you saw Burt Reynolds and Sally Field in for their close-ups. It looked spotless and immaculate. The rest of them were stunt cars and they had various degrees of roll cages on them, just like a race car . . . Instead of having 50 cars, you have five that have various types of rigging for the stunts, and then you keep rebuilding them as you go through the show. Economically, it's more feasible to rebuild five than it is to have 50 and dispose of them as you crash them."

Next, Duncan's shop was selected as one of numerous shops that built and repaired cars for *The Dukes of Hazzard* television series. With those two credits to his name, more and more offers came in.

At the time, camera cars were not available in the South and were shipped in from the West Coast. Together with a person he met on the set, Duncan decided to build a camera car and try to rent it to the many productions coming to the area. Finding success in renting, they built another one and another one. Along the way, he also

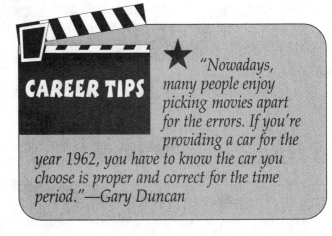

CAREER TIPS

★ *"Nowadays, many people enjoy picking movies apart for the errors. If you're providing a car for the year 1962, you have to know the car you choose is proper and correct for the time period."*—Gary Duncan

began providing picture cars for feature films such as *The Big Chill*, *Witness*, *When Harry Met Sally*, *Patriot Games*, *Forest Gump*, *Inspector Gadget*, and *Hannibal*. He has served as picture car coordinator on *Striking Distance*, *A Time to Kill*, and *Hearts in Atlantis*, to name a few.

"I'm fortunate that this industry has been very good to me financially. I've enjoyed it and met a lot of great people that I would never have met, had it not been for the film business."

● ● ● ●

CHAPTER 5

ART DEPARTMENT

Remove the actors from the set, and everything else you see falls under the direction of the Art Department. Responsibilities vary according to the size and scope of a production, with smaller projects requiring that one person fill several positions. Those positions include:

- Production Designer: conceptualize and design the project's total look.

- Art Director: oversee the conversion of artistic vision into physical reality.

- Assistant Art Director: more than just an assistant, the assistant art director is assigned responsibility for various areas of the art director's duties.

- Set Designer: give design input and draft the plans used to build the set.

- Art Department Coordinator: manages the art department office and budgets.

- Model Builder: build scale models of sets for approval prior to construction.

- Construction Coordinator: oversee the carpenters who actually build the set.

- Set Decorator: create and/or locate all the furnishings necessary to dress the set.

- Leadman: manage the set dressers.

- Set Dressers/Swing Gang: move, place, pack, and store the set furnishings.

- On-Set Dresser: maintain continuity of the set during filming.

- Shopper: do the legwork of finding the props or furniture items the Set Decorator needs.

- Propmaster: find and maintain those props that the actors will handle.

- Prop Man: distribute and collect the hand props to the actors for each scene.

- Propmaker: create or alter those props that cannot be rented or purchased.

- Storyboard Artist: convert the director's, art director's, or production designer's vision into a sequence of sketches that guide the rest of the crew to achieving a cohesive presentation.

- Greensman (Nursery): provide, place, and maintain real or artificial plants and flowers.

- Food Stylist: provide any food or drink that will be used or shown during a scene.

JOB TITLE: PRODUCTION DESIGNER

Job Overview

The production designer is responsible for the visual design of the settings where the screenplay will exist. After meeting with the producer and director to determine their goals and get a feel for their expectations, the designer devises an appropriate concept within budgetary parameters. The designer presents sketches and/or models of his proposed design to the producer and director, and once it is approved, hires the craftsmen to construct the set, purchases furniture and props, and oversees the realization of the design.

Special Skills

A production designer must possess creativity and basic design skills, as well as being a good communicator, able to explain what they visualize and how it is to be accomplished. Many production designers have studied architecture and environmental design, or theatrical set design.

Advice for Someone Seeking This Job

Many production managers begin their careers working on commercials or small independent films where union membership is not required. Most begin as a production assistant or assistant to the art director to gain on-set experience. Volunteer to art direct or design student or low budget films to gain some practical experience, build your résumé, and make contacts for future projects. Contact production designers whose work you admire and volunteer to work for free so that you can observe them. If you're working as a production assistant on a project, offer to help the art department after your own work is completed.

VOICES OF EXPERIENCE

What do you like least about your job?

"What I don't like is when you run into people who hire you, but they don't really respect what you do—they're a control freak personality—they hire you to do a job and then they want to tell you [how to design everything], what colors they want . . . they bring in tear sheets and say, 'I just want it to look like this.' They don't understand that you have to have a concept that encompasses the overall look of the movie, versus just a fragmented portion. What I don't like about my job is when you run into people that don't know their job."—Carlos Barbosa

What do you love most about your job?

"I love the fact that it's always different. It's a learning experience with every project: you could go from the year 1750 to the year 3030, to the present time, depending on the job and the subject matter. You're constantly discovering and challenged to come up with new worlds."—Carlos Barbosa

"My advice is to become an intern on a production," says production designer Carlos Barbosa. "An internship is like a scholarship—you don't get paid, but at the same time, you're learning film [without paying tuition]." Through an internship you are gaining practical experience while you learn and making contacts for future work.

Professional Profile: Carlos Barbosa, Production Designer

"I have always been fascinated with the worlds created on television and film," says Carlos Barbosa. "I always admired it but never really pursued it." Instead, the Columbian native studied another passion: architecture. He graduated with a bachelor's degree of architecture from Tulane University in 1982 and worked in firms located in New Orleans, Los Angeles, New York, and Connecticut.

By the late 1980s, Barbosa says he "was very disillusioned with the endless amount of unpleasant paperwork, permits, codes, and city officials" involved in getting one project off the ground. "You work on a project for a year and it doesn't get built—that was very frustrating."

One day he was talking with his partner in a small Connecticut firm, after having recently finished all the projects they were contracted for. "I just had this realization. I said, 'I'm going to Los Angeles and get into the movies.' My friend

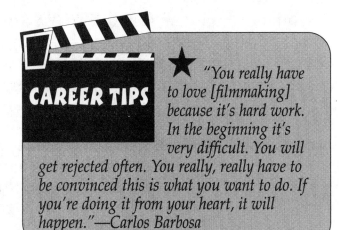

CAREER TIPS

★ *"You really have to love [filmmaking] because it's hard work. In the beginning it's very difficult. You will get rejected often. You really, really have to be convinced this is what you want to do. If you're doing it from your heart, it will happen."—Carlos Barbosa*

started to laugh—I didn't know anybody working in the movies." Undaunted, Barbosa got up and started packing. Within three days he had shipped all his belongings west and set out driving cross-country.

His first break came when he stopped in Nevada to see a house he and his former partner had designed. The homeowners were excited for Barbosa to meet their neighbors, a couple that loved the home's architecture. As it turned out, she was a former soap opera actress and he was a retired costume designer. When they discovered Barbosa was on his way to Hollywood to try and get work in the movies, they immediately made calls on his behalf.

A meeting with one of the producers at IRS Media led to his first job, as construction coordinator on a movie called *Shakes the Clown*. Through connections make on that film he was offered the job of art director on *Lonely Hearts*. After that, he began picking up production design jobs on lower budget projects, steadily building his portfolio of work.

When not working on features or television programs, he honed his designer skills for commercials, including spots for Burger King, Coca-Cola, Durasoft Contact Lenses, Isuzu, 7-Eleven, and Sony.

Production designing the television series *Moloney* enabled him to join the union, which opened up many more opportunities for work. Designing on a permanent installation for Euro Disney's Tomorrow Land garnered a recommendation for the art director job on the 1998 remake of *Psycho*—"My first big studio movie." It was an important break in Barbosa's career in terms of recognition.

He went on to production design the pilot for the series *Action*. "It was very smart; hilariously funny. But it was an inside joke of Hollywood and how production companies work. It was Hollywood poking fun of itself—it didn't do well in middle-America."

Another important step in Barbosa's career was designing *Presence of Mind*, starring Harvey Keitel and Lauren Bacall. It introduced his work to the Spanish film industry, bringing offers to work on other Spanish films.

Through his connection with Don Reo, one of the producers of *Action*, he was hired as production designer for the series *My Wife and Kids*. He went on to design the pilot for the series *24*, which earned him a "best production design" award from the production designer's guild.

Barbosa followed that up with work on the series *Fastlane* and *C.S.I.: Miami*.

Professional Profile: Jeff Mann, Production Designer

"I never anticipated being involved in film—ever," states Jeff Mann, whose mother is a successful costume designer. "My parents were divorced. My little brother and I spent a lot of time on our own because of my mother's choice of career. She was consumed by it, so we had a bit of resentment." Consequently, Mann steered away from the film industry, instead becoming a mechanic, working on automobiles and boats.

VOICES OF EXPERIENCE

What do you like least about your job?

"Dealing with money and budgets is probably what I most dislike; trying to put a price tag on aesthetics."
—*Jeff Mann*

What do you love most about your job?

"What I love most is getting people excited about things that they had never thought of before and converting them to my vision. The second greatest thing is working with the group of people in my department. On any project, it's a long time commitment: 18 hours a day for nine months straight, or more. You hope and pray when you start a show that you're going to be with people you want to be with for a long time."
—*Jeff Mann*

One day, a friend working in the business telephoned with the offer of a weekend job paying $300 a day, cash. Mann accepted. Slowly, calls came in offering other video and commercial work, until he realized that he could make more money working in film than as a mechanic. Mann decided it was time for a career change.

From the beginning, he was assigned to the art department. Working on videos gave Mann experience in assisting with special effects, driving a truck, gripping, set design and construction, and more. "On music videos and commercials you do everything . . . It's not that way in movies; it's very compartmentalized and unionized."

His first feature work came on the 1992 film *Kalifornia*. Friend Michael White was production designer and offered Mann the art direction gig. The film proved pivotal to his career and personal life, introducing him to both director Dominic Sena and his future wife, who was serving as the film's production coordinator.

Over the next six years, Mann honed his skills working on commercials with talented directors like Jonathan Glazer and Sena, with whom he worked on a 90-second Nike spot that aired during the Super Bowl. When Sena was later tapped to direct the Jerry Bruckheimer feature *Gone in Sixty Seconds*, starring Nicholas Cage and Angelina Jolie, he campaigned for Mann to be hired as production designer. "Dom went in and lobbied for me. To Jerry's credit, he likes to take people from commercials and give them an opportunity." It was only Mann's second big feature, and his first as production designer.

Mann again teamed with Sena on *Swordfish*. The film's ending, where a helicopter picks up the bus, was not in the script. That was Mann's idea. "Dom embraced the idea . . . we pitched it to the studio and they loved it, but the implications were huge from financial and labor standpoints." Although the film was already in production, the studio agreed to the additional expense.

His next picture, *Showtime*, was with director Michael Dey, whom Mann had first worked with on commercials. Then came *Terminator 3: Rise of the Machines*, due out in 2003. Producer Colin Wilson initially planned to hire Kirk Petruccelli for the film. Discovering that he was unavailable, Wilson telephoned agent Jonathan Furie, who also represents Mann, for a recommendation. Vying for the job against the top production designers in the business, Mann went in and showed his book and commercial reel, and left a copy of *Swordfish*. On the way home from the meeting, his agent called to say he'd landed the job.

CAREER TIPS

★ *"Be honest."*—Jeff Mann

★ *"Don't try to climb so fast that you put people off, that you're looking to jump rungs. Put 100% into whatever you're asked to do."*—Jeff Mann

★ *"Know what everybody does—try your hand at what everybody does, so that when you suggest something, you know what the implications are of what you're presenting, what it means for the people who have to facilitate what you're offering up."*—Jeff Mann

JOB TITLE: PRODUCTION DESIGNER, COMMERCIALS

Job Overview

The production designer is responsible for the visual design of the settings where action will be filmed.

Production designer Ernest Roth spends time researching concepts and discussing them with his illustrator, who puts on paper what Roth visualizes in his head. The illustrator begins by making rough sketches, gradually revising and refining them until they accurately depict what Roth envisions. The finished drawings are presented to the producer and director to ensure they have a clear idea of the designer's vision. Any requested adjustments are made, the design is approved, and production begins. Later, the illustrations are used as reference guides to ensure that the craftsmen accurately understand what they are constructing.

Special Skills

Production designers must be skilled environmental designers and have an understanding of filmmaking. An environmental design major, Roth says, "You really have to love architecture, interior design, and art in general. I think you have to have the ability to control how people see something when they come into a space . . . The way I arrange things, I can take your eye from right to left or left to right, or up to down, just by the color and texture and the way things are angled."

Advice for Someone Seeking This Job

Some production designers come up through the ranks of the art department. Others find a working production designer and offer to serve as a production assistant or to work for free to learn the business. Studying interior design, architecture, or scenic design will provide an opportunity to learn design skills and build a portfolio before attempting to find a job.

Professional Profile: Ernest Roth, Production Designer

Ernie Roth knew he wanted to be an architect from the time he was in grade school. Growing up in Olympia, Washington, he was the kid who painted pinstripes on all his friend's bicycles. "I always had a little leaning toward artistic things." He began taking art classes in junior high school, quickly realizing that he had a talent for it and could earn an "A" with little effort.

After a tour of duty in the military, Roth enrolled at California College of Arts and Crafts in 1969. Although he held down three part-time jobs while attending school, he finished in three and a half years with a 3.75 GPA. He accepted the offer of a high-paying job at a space-planning firm in Los Angeles, but left after five months to work for a smaller firm where he had more control over the projects he designed. While working there he became acquainted with socialite Diana Murphy, who designed interiors for her multimillionaire friends. Roth and Murphy became partners in Diana Murphy Designs, and over the next eight years worked on a variety of projects, from designing the interiors of a Leer jet, to entire homes in Beverly Hills, Palm Springs, and Catalina.

Eventually looking for a career change, Roth was steered toward art direction by two friends who worked in the film business. With design portfolio in hand, he began making the rounds of advertising and production houses. His first job was designing a jockey's room for a Shasta Diet Cola commercial, directed by photographer-turned-director Sid Avery. After confessing to the prop master that he had never designed a set before, the two went to Santa Anita Race Track for research. When shooting began, Roth didn't speak to anyone on set for fear they would discover he knew nothing about the business. What he lacked in actual set experience he more than made up for in design ability. His manner and design sense impressed Avery, who continued to work with Roth over the next few years on commercials for Chrysler, Lincoln, and Sunbeam.

During his initial transition from interior design to art direction, Roth worked nights as an illustrator, making electrical ink drawings of airplanes, to keep his days free to pursue work. Introduced to another ad agency through a first assistant director he had worked with, Roth landed a 7-Up commercial and a commission to redesign the agency's offices. Since that time, he has worked on several hundred commercials.

"I had always avoided features, because I wanted to have more of a home life. At the time, in features you would wind up going away on a

VOICES OF EXPERIENCE

What do you like least about your job?

"The thing I don't like about the business is the politics . . . It's the plague of the business."—Ernest Roth

What do you love most about your job?

Besides someone calling to offer him a job, Roth loves the variety of his work. "You're designing an ice field with igloos or you're doing a space station. You never know what you're going to be doing."—Ernest Roth

location for six or seven months. I didn't want to do that. But one of the directors I worked with doing commercials wanted to switch to features and asked me to work on a job with him." The director was Farhad Mann and the film was science fiction flick *Lawnmower Man 2: Beyond Cyberspace.*

Approached to design for television movies, Roth turned the work down after discovering how low the budgets were. "If I can't do something that is really a quality product, I'm not interested." Although his résumé includes a few pilots, the independent film *Anacardium,* and the live-action sequences at the beginning of *The Tigger Movie*, Roth's emphasis remains in commercials. His clients have included: American Airlines, Betty Crocker, Energizer, Head & Shoulders, McDonald's, Nissan, Radio Shack, and Toyota.

JOB TITLE: ART DIRECTOR

Job Overview

"I facilitate the designer's vision," says art director David Lazan. "I'm in charge of managing the art department, [including] budgets and crew—when it comes to set designers, graphic designers, illustrators; communicating with the construction coordinator; going over budgets, schedules, what we need to do both in sets and location; and meet with the different departments: effects, props, and onward . . . to talk about logistics. It's both a design and management position."

Special Skills

Art directors must possess strong managerial skills, be organized, communicate well, and have the ability to administer a budget. A background in design, architecture, art, drafting, and illustration is also an asset.

Advice for Someone Seeking This Job

If you want to be an art director, Lazan suggests studying theatrical design, architecture or industrial design, as well as lighting and filmmaking. Once you have some basic skills, volunteer to work on student, music video, commercial, or nonunion productions. Contact set designers, art directors, or production designers, and offer to apprentice or serve as a production assistant for the art department. Get into a position to observe and make contacts for future work.

Professional Profile: David Lazan, Art Director

The son of a director of photography, David Lazan grew up around the film business. Instead of following in his father's footsteps, his goal was to become a doctor. For two years he studied psychobiology at UCLA before realizing he was on the wrong career path. He decided to instead pursue his artistic inclinations and transferred to Arizona State, where he earned a bachelor's degree in architecture and industrial design.

Lazan returned to Los Angeles in 1989 with the intention of earning money to finish his design portfolio. At the time, his father was working on a Spanish children's television series. Lazan interviewed for an assistant art director position with the show and was hired on.

His early exposure to the film industry had come through cameramen, grips, and gaffers. The design aspect of filmmaking that he discovered in the art department had never occurred to him. Lazan realized he enjoyed the work and that he was good at it, and went on to assistant art director for the movie *The Linguini Incident*. During filming, he connected with production designer Marcia Hinds, who hired him to work with her on *Paradise*.

After gaining some experience art directing commercials, Lazan landed his first feature as an art director on the film *Candyman*. The production designer, Jane Ann Stewart, later hired him to art direct the series *Love, Cheat & Steal*. His association with production designer Howard Cumming yielded work on the television movie *Indictment:*

VOICES OF EXPERIENCE

What do you like least about your job?

"I dislike the disorganization of the decision making process. It could be more efficient. Also, going job to job is very difficult. You're a salesman your whole life. You're selling yourself on a new job every time. You're an independent contractor, so you're always looking for a new job."—David Lazan

What do you love most about your job?

"I love that every job is different: new people, new situations, new designs, and new problems to solve."—David Lazan

CAREER TIPS

★ *"It's important to me to work with people I like and respect, because you work so closely with them. You want to learn from them, but it's also up to you to learn, meaning you don't rely on everyone else for your experience and knowledge. You have to go and get it by asking questions, figuring things out, and researching."—David Lazan*

The McMartin Trial and on features *The Usual Suspects, The Next Best Thing,* and *What's the Worst Thing That Can Happen.*

An association with another production designer begun on *The Replacement Killers,* directed by Antoine Fuqua, continued on to *Teaching Mrs. Tingle, American Beauty,* and *Training Day,* which was also directed by Fuqua. Lazan is currently in Hawaii at work on another Fuqua-directed film, *Hostile Rescue* (working title).

JOB TITLE: SET DESIGNER

Job Overview

Working under the direction of the production designer or art director, the set designer creates working drawings of assigned sets or props. "It may be as simple as measuring an existing location and having it drawn up, then turned into a model for studying, or sketching sets from scratch to be constructed on a soundstage," says set designer Todd Chernawsky

Special Skills

Set designers must possess good illustration or drafting skills, be flexible and creative, and have the ability to communicate well.

Advice for Someone Seeking This Job

No matter what industry job you aspire to, Chernawsky suggests learning all you can about the craft of filmmaking. It is important to have strong drafting and illustration skills before beginning the job search. Work on student films, commercials, and music videos to gain experience and make contacts. Let people know of your desire to work in the art department for a feature film or television series.

"Many people's first jobs find them," says Chernawsky. "You'll offer to help someone on a project and they will hire you for their next one, or you impress someone else who is also helping out and they hire or recommend you for a job. It's all about networking."

Professional Profile: Todd Chernawsky, Set Designer

Although he had been interested in films from the time he was a young boy, it was while walking home from the theater after seeing *Raiders of the Lost Ark* that Todd Chernawsky first considered making them. Midway through his college studies in architecture, industrial design, art/design history, and painting, the idea of a career in filmmaking began to resurface. After providing art direction for some small short films, he realized it was something he wanted to pursue. Chernawsky received a bachelor's degree in fine arts from University of Alberta, then went on to earn a master of fine arts in production design from the American Film Institute in 1996.

While at AFI, Chernawsky acted as production designer on eight short films. The first two and a half years following graduation were spent working on a variety of projects, serving as an electrician, grip, carpenter, and scenic painter, "just to learn more about how production worked and how the set ran. It really gave me a sense of every aspect of how films are made."

Chernawsky then began to focus his energy toward art direction, taking on only those types of jobs. He worked on television commercials, network campaigns, and bumpers. As his name and reputation got around, he was offered work as a set designer on *Sphere*, working on several interiors and details for the underwater laboratory.

Under the direction of production designer Michael White, Chernawsky went to work on *Armageddon*. "I took care of the interior of the space shuttle and a variety of props." White hired him again to design the set of his next film, *Inspector Gadget*. "I ended up focusing a lot of my time on the gadget mobile and a variety of gadgets for Gadget himself. It was at this point that I realized I was doing a fair amount of drawings specifically for the special effects department, which became useful down the road, as far as my understanding of how the special effects department works."

VOICES OF EXPERIENCE

What do you like least about your job?

"The thing I like least is the hours. Regardless of whether it's a low budget or big budget film, the days are very, very long. Personal and social life definitely come in second when you're in the middle of production."—Todd Chernawsky

What do you love most about your job?

"Whether it's a period film, contemporary, or science fiction, you're constantly looking to create new worlds. That's probably the thing I enjoy most."—Todd Chernawsky

After *Inspector Gadget* wrapped, Chernawsky went to Toronto as production designer of the independent movie *Ginger Snap*, which had a successful run on the film festival circuit. Returning to Los Angeles, he worked on James Cameron's IMAX project *Mars*, before landing the job of set designer on *Planet of the Apes*. Although Chernawsky worked primarily with set decorator Rosemary Brandenburg, detailing items of the spaceship, he also met production designer Rick Heinrichs and had an opportunity to work closely with him.

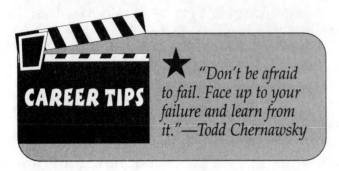

★ *"Don't be afraid to fail. Face up to your failure and learn from it."—Todd Chernawsky*

Chernawsky worked as the set designer on another James Cameron IMAX project titled *Ghosts of the Abyss*, and picked up some work as an illustrator on *Company Man*. He next worked as the production designer for the television movie *100 Days in the Jungle*, shot in Central America. There he had to hire a local crew to realize his vision for the film, which wrapped just before Christmas 2001. He had only been back in the States a few weeks when he was hired to design the set of *The Hulk*, another film with production designer Rick Heinrichs.

JOB TITLE: ART DEPARTMENT COORDINATOR

Job Overview

Working under the direction of the production designer and/or art director, the art department coordinator manages the department office. The coordinator is responsible for tracking the department's budget; negotiating usage and obtaining legal clearances for products and artwork appearing on screen; researching products, periods, and other information; ordering samples and other materials; and dispersing information for the production designer and art director.

Special Skills

A production coordinator must be detail oriented, able to multi-task, have excellent verbal and written communication skills, be a people person, have the ability to negotiate, and be a problem solver.

Advice for Someone Seeking This Job

Most production coordinators begin their career as production assistants, whether specifically assigned to the art department or not, and work their way up. "When you start out as a PA, the best advice I could give is: Move your ass!" says coordinator Laura DeRosa. "When somebody asks you to do something, you get up and you do it right then. Be very anal about what you do and get it done quickly, nicely, and neatly . . . Try to learn by asking questions and making an effort to help the coordinator as best you can."

Professional Profile: Laura DeRosa, Art Department Coordinator

While managing entertainment industry hangout The Hollywood Athletic Club, Laura DeRosa became intrigued by the possibility of working in the film business. "We hosted all the big Castle Rock parties . . . [and] a lot of photo shoots. It was a Hollywood hot spot." In time, she began to wonder if there was a job in the industry that might be right for her.

Shortly after a friend took a job working on a film, she telephoned to alert DeRosa that an

VOICES OF EXPERIENCE

What do you like least about your job?

"I don't like filing, but I normally have an assistant do that. The only thing I don't like is filing."—Laura DeRosa

What do you love most about your job?

"What I like most is getting involved to the point where I become an important part of the art department. I love making sure everything gets done. I love tracking the money. I love doing the research. I love finding or getting things that are impossible."

For the movie Bounce, *production designer David Wasco wanted Vespa Scooters for the film, but the company had already refused to allow their logo to be used in the film* Austin Powers. *Undaunted by that fact, DeRosa contacted the Italian-based company and not only persuaded them to sign off on the use of their name and logo, but negotiated the use of two classic model Vespas for free. "Getting something that nobody else has been able to get—I love that."—Laura DeRosa*

office down the hall was looking for a production assistant for the pilot of the television series *Fame L.A.* DeRosa'a initial response quickly changed from "I'm not going to make any money. I'm going to make half what I'm making now," to "I'm going to do it."

From production assistant on *Fame L.A.*, De Rosa made the jump to art department coordinator when she was recommended for the television movie *Virtual Obsession*. Soon after it wrapped, she landed her first feature, *The Breaks*. From that point on, she worked continuously as an art department production coordinator, moving from one feature to another, including *The Bachelor* and *Bounce*, and as construction buyer on *Mulholland Drive*.

While working on *Waking Up in Reno*, De Rosa impressed set decorator Jay Hart enough that when he went on to do *Swordfish* with production

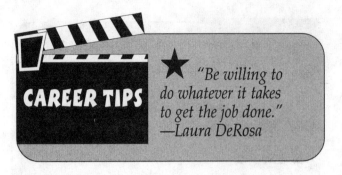

designer Jeff Mann, DeRosa was recommended for the coordinator position. Already at work on *Dude, Where's My Car?*, she had to turn down the offer. But Mann remembered the recommendation and when he was hired to design *Showtime*, he again offered her the coordinator position. Having just wrapped *Legally Blonde*, she accepted. The working relationship with Mann continued with the film *The Antoine Fisher Story*.

Three days after the show wrapped, Jay Hart, who was art directing *Hostile Rescue* (working title), hired her as art department coordinator. Unfortunately, the production shut down for a time. Just after receiving the news that the show had gone down, DeRosa telephoned a friend to share the fact that she was out of work and needed to find a job. Fifteen minutes later, Jeff Mann called offering her the coordinator job on *Terminator 3: Rise of the Machines*.

JOB TITLE: ART DEPARTMENT SWING OR SWING GANG

Job Overview

Swing gang members, under the direction of the lead man, are responsible for moving furniture, accessories, pictures, props, and various objects used for set decorations, on and off the set.

Special Skills

Swing crew members must be physically able to lift and carry furniture and other heavy objects. They should be willing to take direction and have the ability to get along with people of varied personalities and temperaments.

Advice for Someone Seeking This Job

"Meet as many people as you can and stay friendly with all of them," says Brian Erzen, who works in the art department. "Much of getting work in this business is meeting people and their taking a chance with you. When you meet someone, ask if you can give them a call. If they say 'Yes,' call every two weeks for the rest of your life.

"I never turn down jobs, no matter what it is; even if it's at the last minute, I still do it.

"Take any opportunities that are given to you—even working for free, to gain experience and contacts."

Professional Profile: Brian Erzen, Art Department Production Assistant, Art Department Swing, Set Dresser

Although he was uncertain about what career to pursue, Brian Erzen knew he "wanted to work in the entertainment industry." A Connecticut native who studied communication at Middletown Community College, he was intrigued by the visual aspect of movies, television shows, and some music videos.

After his best friend moved to California at the end of 1998, Erzen set a goal to do the same by the following August. "It was a weird pipe dream—I had never been to California, but I knew I had to go." A few months later the friend phoned to say he was sharing a place in Venice and they were looking for an additional roommate. Erzen committed to be there in six weeks.

VOICES OF EXPERIENCE

What do you like least about your job?

"What I like least is the politics. I don't have nepotism working for me, so that sometimes makes it tough to land jobs . . . It can sometimes be difficult having someone with less experience tell you what to do. You just have to learn to grin and bear it."—Brian Erzen

What do you love most about your job?

"I love the creativity. You solve problems and you're thinking on your feet."—Brian Erzen

"The key thing I did was ship all of my stuff to California—30 boxes of clothes, CDs, DVDs, my computer, sound system, everything—to my friend in Venice. I sold off a lot of my furniture and gave other pieces away. Then I threw myself a going away party!" With a friend, Erzen drove cross-country to California.

"It was extremely difficult when I first came to California," he says. "I had a job set up and it fell through." Undaunted, Erzen obtained a copy of the *LA 411* [411 Publishing, published yearly] directory and called every postproduction house in Venice and Santa Monica, eventually landing an internship. After three weeks, he was hired full time: 9 to 5, Monday to Friday, for $300 a week.

Slowly, Erzen began to meet people and was hired as a production assistant. He also worked as an extra. "I'd never been on set. Working as an extra was the easiest way to get on set and see what really goes on. I talked with everyone on the crew and eventually landed more work as a production assistant." Called upon to help paint, hang something on a wall, or bring in a piece of furniture, he was introduced to the art department.

Erzen continued to network, landing better and better jobs. While working at a postproduction facility, he was sent to deliver a package to a downtown Los Angeles address. There he inquired at the production office if they needed a production assistant for the following day. Instead, he learned they needed someone for that evening. "I got four days' work. Sixteen hour days, all night long, blocking off a section of downtown LA for a Backstreet Boys video shoot. That is how I get a lot of my work—creating an opportunity."

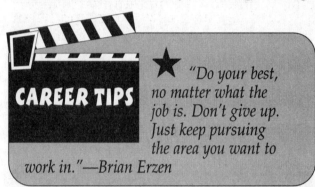

CAREER TIPS

"Do your best, no matter what the job is. Don't give up. Just keep pursuing the area you want to work in."—Brian Erzen

Erzen sees each job as an opportunity to learn more about the craft of filmmaking and to make new contacts that might lead to his next job. He gained experience working swing, in the art department, on commercials for Kraft, SlimFast, Mastercard, and other products. He has also worked on videos for Destiny's Child, Jessica Simpson, and Genuine; he helped build a set for the opening ceremony of the 2002 Olympics, and on the film *A Piece of My Heart*.

JOB TITLE: ON SET DRESSER

Job Overview

The on set dresser maintains the integrity of the set for the set dressing and property departments. If a cup is moved or a piece of furniture is rearranged, the on set dresser is responsible for putting them back in their original places to maintain the continuity of the shot. Often, the on set dresser will take Polaroids or digital pictures to aid in this process.

Special Skills

On set dressers must be physically able to lift and carry furniture and heavy objects. "For my particular position, you need muscle," says set dresser Diana Richardson. "To move up in the ranks, education in design and period pieces would be helpful. An understanding of characters in the script is also an asset. To dress a set, one would have to interpret the character: what the individual wants, likes, dislikes. Is this person neat or messy? Does this person have a collection? If so, of what?"

Advice for Someone Seeking This Job

"I think the best tip I can give to anyone interested in working in the industry is to grab the local entertainment guide," says Richardson. "Here in California it is *The Hollywood Reporter* and *Variety*. On Wednesdays, they have a listing of productions in prep, work, and post. Contact these places until you land a job. Work and learn. Read as much as you can and listen to others. This is an industry of 'who you know'—so know as many [people] as possible."

"Like anything, you have to be persistent . . . It is a very word-of-mouth industry. Persistence is the key. Individuals will commonly start as a PA, then move towards the department desired."

Professional Profile: Diana C. Richardson, On Set Dresser, Set Dresser, Assistant Props

Growing up in Southern California, Diana Richardson was surrounded by the film and television industry. Her earliest taste of her future career came during high school, working with theater stagehands.

She landed her first job in film serving as an extra, working deferred (meaning that her salary was credited, rather than paid out; the idea is that if the film makes a certain amount of money or gets a theatrical release, depending upon the contract, the actors will then be paid). There is an industry saying that "Everyone works deferred once."

VOICES OF EXPERIENCE

What do you like least about your job?

"*Sometimes the pay doesn't seem to be enough for the amount and type of work demanded. 'Splits' or all-nighters are my number one complaint. Splits are where we start at 3 P.M. and work until 3 A.M., and you can guess about the all-nighters.*"—Diana Richardson

What do you love most about your job?

"*I like the hubbub. I was drawn to the art and prop departments because it is the kind of person I am—just as a photographer would be drawn to the camera, or a [person] to act.*"—Diana Richardson

During the shoot, she seized the opportunity to observe the various crew members and different departments. Her first crew job was as an art department PA for a low budget film. "The pay was ridiculous: $30 a day for 14 hours, but I was young and energetic. I was also very excited about working on a film." Although she earned little money, she gained valuable experience that enabled her to land other work.

Drawn to the art and prop departments, Richardson continued to work off and on throughout the 1990s. "I quit a couple of times to work in an office, but I always came back." Some of Richardson's credits include: *American Pie II, Nuk'em High II* and *III, Slow Burn, Shock 'em Dead,* and *Time Force.*

JOB TITLE: PROP MASTER, PROPERTY MASTER

Job Overview

The prop master is responsible for obtaining and maintaining all portable objects used in the production, such as a book, dish, glass of water, or a desktop computer.

Prop master Rick Toone points out there are added responsibilities for prop masters working in commercials. "If there is cereal in the cupboards, you set the cereal box so the brand name is seen. Whatever the product is, you're responsible for making it look good."

Special Skills

In addition to having an understanding of camera lenses to know how a shot is framed and a knowledge of the filmmaking process, Rick Toone says, "Working in props, you have to be a jack-of-all-trades; the handyman who has a sense of style and knows what looks good in the frame and what doesn't. Nowadays you need to know a lot about graphics. You need to have a general decorating sense of color, style, and texture."

Advice for Someone Seeking This Job

"Landing a first job is hard," says Toone. "You have to have been on the set doing something else. You don't start out being a prop master. You assist or work in the art department. The best way to become a prop master is working your way in through the art department. Start as a PA or become a swing guy. You need to have a sense of what it takes to get the job done, as well as seeing what it is. There are a lot of things the art department does that you have to understand how to do. Once the camera rolls, the set is yours. If they've hung the drapes a certain way, you've got to understand the various ways of doing that, because invariably the director wants to lower them three inches or pull them back. You've got to solve the problem without rerigging the whole thing."

Professional Profile: Rick Toone, Prop Master

Rick Toone planned to be a rock and roll lighting designer, until he discovered property work. The Virginia native earned a bachelor's degree in technical theater from the Virginia Commonwealth University, then found work doing lighting design with a Baltimore theatrical lighting company. After a couple of years, he decided that to further advance his career, he needed to relocate to New York or Los Angeles. He picked the latter.

Through friends working in the film industry, Toone found employment as a carpenter on a couple of movies. Connections made on set led to work as a lead man in set dressing for the television movie *Love & War*, and six films for Cannon. Over the next couple of years he worked on a variety of projects, eventually drifting toward props. "I realized I lifted too many refrigerators and couches and worked longer hours for less money than the prop guys."

In conjunction with an art director who worked steadily in commercials, Toone and another man handled set dressing and props on her projects. "The three of us would kind of do everything," affording him an opportunity to gain more set experience and make contacts.

Through a production designer he had worked with on several commercials, Toone's first job as prop master was on the film *Pontiac Moon*. Prop master gigs continued to come in, bringing work on such well-known commercial campaigns as the Jerry Seinfeld spots for American Express and the first series of Got Milk? "I did a lot of AT&T and Federal Express stuff."

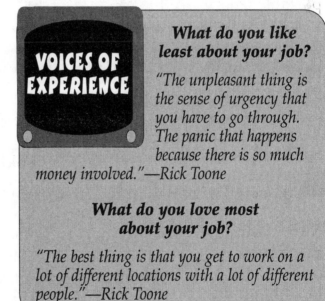

VOICES OF EXPERIENCE

What do you like least about your job?

"The unpleasant thing is the sense of urgency that you have to go through. The panic that happens because there is so much money involved."—Rick Toone

What do you love most about your job?

"The best thing is that you get to work on a lot of different locations with a lot of different people."—Rick Toone

When the Oxygen network started up, Toone decided to try out working in television. "I was intrigued because they used the same crew to shoot six shows; I was propping all six at the same time. We did a show in the morning, one show after lunch, and one show in the late afternoon. We just moved the cameras around the stage. The quality of the work wasn't very good and the money wasn't great, but the people were nice and fun. It was a way to work eight hours a day and see my kids." After a year, the programs went on hiatus for four months, then returned and did another short run of shows, before production moved to New York.

CAREER TIPS

★ "Pay attention to everything around you at all times." —Rick Toone

Toone returned to commercials, working with some of the biggest feature directors, such as Ridley Scott, on Nike and other spots. Even with contacts that would enable him to transition into feature films, Toone elected to focus on commercials.

"If you do three movies a year, two of them are out of town, so you're gone from your family. The divorce rate is very high in features. Then you can have eight or nine months off because a project gets pushed back or it falls through. To me it's more of a roller coaster ride than commercials."

JOB TITLE: PROP ASSISTANT, ASSISTANT PROPS, OR PROPERTY ASSISTANT

Job Overview

The prop assistant, under the direction of the prop master, is in charge of all props used throughout the production. Some productions may designate an outside props person to purchase props, and an inside props person to oversee their placement, use, and maintenance on set.

"On a feature, it is very clear what your rank and file is," says prop person Jason Ivey, "but on a commercial, waters get a little muddy. You may be in the prop department and end up doing special effects, like smoke or snow. You may be the entire art department, in which case you rely a lot on production to help you move large pieces of furniture."

"If you're doing property on a feature, it can be stressful, making sure everything is right. You have to stay true to what the person would really use and make sure the environment matches the script. If a glass is half full or a light wasn't on, you have to make sure it is the same when they reshoot the scene."

Special Skills

Individuals working in the property department must be physically able to lift and carry furniture and other heavy objects. They should possess the ability to remember the details of an environment, and have strong people skills.

Advice for Someone Seeking This Job

"I think anybody who wants to get into the film industry at any level should begin by working as a production assistant," says Ivey. "Unless you're working on getting your days for DGA [Directors Guild Association membership], I suggest they don't PA on features. On a feature you learn how to tell people not to cross through the frame, how to get coffee, and how to hand out call sheets. Instead, get on a commercial or smaller film, where you'll learn more about what every department does. You can't learn about film from any book or any film school; the reality is you learn by fire. You learn by making mistakes—and in the film industry you're not allowed many mistakes."

Professional Profile:
Jason A. Ivey, Prop Assistant, Prop Master, Set Dresser, Art Director

Jason Ivey was living in Charlottesville, Virginia, focusing on a career in the music industry, when a friend referred him for a production assistant (PA) job working on a Herb Ritz and Bill Haden commercial for Bank One. At the time, his only qualifications were that he knew the area and was a warm body. The job changed his life. "It was the best time I ever had. It seemed like we could do the impossible."

VOICES OF EXPERIENCE

What do you like least about your job?

"What I like the least about props is that there is a lot of pressure. There are so many details to get correct. When you look at a scene and the glass is half full, and then it becomes a quarter full, and no one has been drinking out of it, that's your snafu."—Jason Ivey

What do you love most about your job?

"I love the diversity of people and experiences making movies. You pinch yourself sometimes and say, 'I can't believe I'm getting paid to do this.' I also like the fact that my day is never the same—ever."—Jason Ivey

Quickly addicted to the idea of working in film and television, Ivey made contacts on that first gig that led to additional PA work. "You just need one person on your team: a good production manager, production coordinator, or second AD—someone who will hire you." With growing experience and contacts, he relocated to Washington, D.C., and continued to PA, but set his sights on working in the art department.

He worked on commercials, television programs, and whatever project he could network himself on set for, steadily moving into props assistant and set dressing. Eventually, a friend sponsored him for union membership.

★ *"Be prepared to eliminate all your future plans. Working in the film industry, particularly freelance, you can't really have a planned social life. If someone calls, nine times out of ten you better take that work or they won't call you again. You have to be willing and open to work any time, anywhere, any hours, and do just about anything, within reason."* —Jason Ivey

CAREER TIPS

★ *"Listen! [When you listen], you learn how things actually work, in terms of money and other aspects of the business."* —Jason Ivey

Ivey's first big feature was *Random Hearts*, serving as key swing in set dressing. Over time, his career has gravitated toward props assistant, prop master, and art direction. His résumé has grown to include work on features such as *Election, Book of Shadows: Blair Witch 2, Hollow Man, The Replacements, Rules of Engagement, Hannibal, Along Came a Spider,* and *Gods and Generals*, and television series including *The Agency, America's Most Wanted, The District,* and *The West Wing*, and numerous commercials.

JOB TITLE: STORYBOARD ARTIST

Job Overview

Working under the direction of the producer, director, or production designer, the storyboard artist illustrates a sequence of scenes to help everyone involved in the production grasp the same visual image. The storyboard artist may also be called upon to sketch the production designer's ideas for various sets and locations. "A storyboard is very similar to drawing a comic strip or book," says artist Mike Harris. "You take a sequence of events and make them visually exciting."

"There are two kinds of storyboards. The first is what I would call a presentation storyboard. This is generally quite finished and quite slick. It may even be in color. It is to either sell the concept to the client or, in the case of a movie, to sell the concept to the people who are banking the project. The second type of storyboard is what I call a production storyboard—so that everyone on the crew is on the same page—and is less finished." It may be no more than a rough pencil sketch.

Special Skills

A storyboard artist must be skilled in both quick sketching and in creating more detailed, finished drawings. Communication and people skills are essential to understanding the client's vision and being able to draw it clearly. "It's important as a storyboard artist to find out exactly, or as close as possible, what the client wants," says Harris. "You have to draw them out with questions: 'What is the character looking at? What is his problem in this scene? Is he puzzled, or angry? What's happening?' You have to ask questions so that you can get it down on paper and everybody will understand."

Advice for Someone Seeking This Job

To work full time as a storyboard artist, you most likely will need to move to Los Angeles or New York, where the majority of film and television production originates. To obtain work, you must have a portfolio that demonstrates your abilities. To build a portfolio, Harris suggests taking a film or television script and storyboard a few scenes. "Do them in black and white, and maybe one in color. Make sure you draw them by hand. This is a visual business. You've got to have something to show people."

Professional Profile: Mike Harris, Storyboard Artist

Mike Harris studied commercial art and graphic design in his native England. After completing a four-year program, he found work at an advertising agency where his design skills were an asset. "I was one of the youngest people at the agency, but because I could draw, I was being used by the senior people to lay out their television commercials."

Harris honed his skills working at several London advertising agencies before taking a job as a newspaper artist. Before computers became common-

VOICES OF EXPERIENCE

What do you like least about your job?

"What I don't like is the fact that what you create is never seen by the public. It's not like drawing a comic strip that is going to be printed in the newspaper, or doing a painting that will go in a gallery. As a general rule, it's very rare for anyone outside of the production crew to ever see what you've spent hours and hours doing."—Mike Harris

What do you love most about your job?

"I love being deeply involved in the creative process. Usually a director and I will talk about the project. Sometimes I'm able to add things that he or she has never thought of. Together, we can create the look of a movie, a television commercial, a music video, an industrial—whatever. I love being involved right from the beginning."—Mike Harris

place, he designed local ads by hand and did some cartooning for the paper. Having built a strong portfolio of work, he relocated to New York City in the late 1970s. "At the time, I thought it would be pretty easy for someone like me to get a really hot-shot job in a New York advertising agency—wrong!"

While continuing to pursue advertising work, Harris took a job at a newspaper in Poughkeepsie, selling classified ads, "until I got a real job. The bad news was I found I was pretty good at it." He quickly rose to top salesman and then to sales manager, traveling around the country to the company's regional newspapers. Transferred to Nashville, he realized he had had enough of ad sales and quit.

Recognizing Nashville's substantial television production community, Harris began promoting himself as a freelance illustrator, cartoonist, and storyboard artist. "You have to be a bit of P. T. Barnum to sell yourself. I sent out promotional material at least four times a year."

With few storyboard artists in the city, firms were knocking on Harris's door almost immediately to sketch storyboards for commercials such as "NFL: It's a Way of Life" and "Cows in the Coffee" for Purity Dairy; opening titles for the television series *Spin City*; and videos for many of country music's top artists, including Garth Brooks.

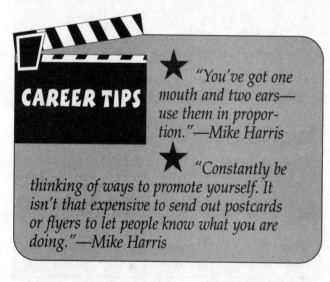

CAREER TIPS

★ *"You've got one mouth and two ears—use them in proportion."—Mike Harris*

★ *"Constantly be thinking of ways to promote yourself. It isn't that expensive to send out postcards or flyers to let people know what you are doing."—Mike Harris*

"Garth is a very interesting guy to work with in that he has very specific ideas about what he wants. On one occasion we were walking around the outside of a church with a pad in hand. He kept pointing out things to me that he wanted to think about. For instance, looking at the front of the church through a car windshield . . . Most recently, Garth did a music video and tied in a television commercial for Dr. Pepper. I was involved from the very beginning. The director, Jonathan Small, and I spent two hours or so before I even put pencil to pad, just listening to the music and trying to imagine what we could do visually. I was able to come up with several little pieces which were incorporated into the shoot."

To supplement his income between storyboard jobs, Harris uses his drawing talents to create cartoons and illustrations for newspapers and magazines. "It's amazing how you can parlay your skills into other things."

●●●●

CHAPTER

6

CAMERA DEPARTMENT

The cinematographer is responsible for creating and capturing the overall photographic impression of a film. As head of the camera department, responsible for hiring the camera crew, the cinematographer oversees the camera operator, first assistant cameraman or focus puller, second assistant cameraman, and the film loader. On large productions, the camera crew might also include a camera department assistant or PA. Depending on the director's needs, a steadicam operator may join the crew for a few days or the duration of the production.

> ## JOB TITLE: CINEMATOGRAPHER OR DIRECTOR OF PHOTOGRAPHY (DP)

Job Overview

During preproduction, the cinematographer meets with the director to discuss his overall vision for the film, and the specific needs of individual scenes. Based upon these discussions, the cinematographer selects the necessary cameras, equipment, and film stocks, and preps the lighting and grip departments for anticipated needs.

Throughout production, the cinematographer determines how each scene will be lighted; what filters, lenses, and film stock will be used; the position and movement of the camera; and composes each shot of the picture to achieve the look he envisions.

The cinematographer works closely with the processing labs to make certain the film is developed correctly, preserving the colors and moods he has created, and supervises the transfer of image from film to tape to ensure quality control.

Special Skills

Cinematographers must possess a good photographic eye and know how to light a scene properly to achieve their vision. They must be good technicians, with an understanding of cameras, lenses, and film stocks. "You have to have the technology down," says cinematographer Allen Daviau. "You have to have it at your fingertips so that you don't even think about it."

Richard Crudo, another cinematographer, agrees. "Study as hard as you can," he says. "The technology is evolving constantly; it never stays still. More so than ever before, the technology changes every week."

"Study film," Crudo adds. "You've got to go back and look at old films; look at the work of the masters. It's never been easier. You can go down to Blockbuster and get practically any movie that has ever been made. Take it home and look at it back and forth. Study the work of great directors and cinematographers. Break it down. Understand why you like that and why this works and that doesn't work. You have to be relentless.

"Look at light in your real life, in your house, in your car, on the street at daytime and nighttime; in the bank, in the supermarket, in a restaurant—you have to look at light. You have to see how light creates feelings. It's a thought process that goes on constantly if you're engaged in it."

Crudo says that these technical skills can be learned, but what sets the best cinematographers apart from others is their innate taste. "Taste, and application of technical facility. It is an art form. We all use the same cameras and lenses, film stocks, and laboratories, but if you take one scene and have 100 people shoot it, it's going to have 100 different looks . . . some will innately be better."

"This is the world's most collaborative art form," says cinematographer Clark Mathis. He discovered his people skills an asset for "being able to assert my own creative ideas in a nonthreatening way."

"The most important skill that you need to be successful in the film business is to be able to play well with others," says cinematographer John Schwartzman. "It's probably the single most important thing."

Daviau echoes the charge that "The most important thing is how you deal with other people. Getting their trust and becoming their partner in what they're doing. That, to me, is what is really gratifying about film. Your colleagues are so important . . . One of the most wonderful things is simply the appreciation of the variety of people there are in this world and that they all can work together for some amazing results."

"The next skill is that you bring yourself to the job," says Schwartzman. "Bring whatever it is that you have to offer that makes you unique. It doesn't help the world for somebody to be able to copy John Schwartzman's work. What is important is that you bring your own sense of authorship to what you do."

Advice for Someone Seeking This Job

"Everybody comes to filmmaking by a different route," says Crudo, "which makes it so interesting, but you have to study and apply yourself constantly. It's not an easy thing to do, so you have to have a certain amount of passion just to get through the process. You need to make personal connections with people that are in the industry, so that they will help you get work. Learn from them. Learn something new every time you're on a set, regardless of whether you're a production assistant or on the camera crew.

"I came up through the system as an assistant," Crudo says, "so I have a certain bias toward that route. When I was an assistant, I worked with some of the best cinematographers in the world and that was an education that you couldn't afford to pay for . . . Many young people get out of school and want to start at the top as a cinematographer. It doesn't quite work that way. People forget that on every set the cinematographer is going to be the most experienced person there, almost without exception. You are much better served to start out as an assistant, work up to operator, and learn the job from the inside out. Otherwise, you shortchange yourself."

According to Crudo, you must be tenacious to succeed as a cinematographer. "Tenacity, more than anything—more than anything: tenacity. I really do mean that. I cannot emphasize enough to people how difficult a pursuit this is. Unless you're born in it or touched by a silver spoon, it is an incredibly, incredibly difficult pursuit to get the work and keep the work going. The opportunities are fleeting and it's a capricious process. In many ways, it doesn't have anything to do with you personally or your abilities. It's a very capricious process, the way jobs will come to you, and there is no rhyme or reason."

"Contact people whose work you admire and ask their advice," says Daviau. "Come and watch them on the set. Come and be an intern when you can. Work a lot for free. You need to find allies . . . It's what I call the art of being persistent without being a pest."

"Try to support yourself and just go out and shoot," advises Mathis. "In the absence of having trucks full of lighting and actors, when your resources are limited, take still photographs. Pick a movie whose visual style you like and try to emulate a few frames. I used to pause the VCR on certain frames and try to diagram what I thought the lighting was, then set it up with the crudest household lamps.

"Take stills on slide film so you can project them, much like the environment that a movie is shown in. I have filing cabinets full of slides and ring binders of scrawled notes. It goes back to my scientific background; it was almost like an experiment for me, trying to dissect what was going on . . . Only after mastering the craft aspect, getting to where exposure, lens selection, and lighting ratios are second nature, can you turn your attention towards the more emotional and artistic side. A simple analogy is learning where the keys on the typewriter are. You spend a couple of weeks learning and then one day you realize you're not thinking about where you're putting your fingers, you're thinking about what you're writing. That's what it has to be."

Although Mathis did not move up through the camera department to become a cinematographer, he points out the advantage of that route as "being able to watch other cinematographers work." The down side is that it not only takes longer to become a cinematographer, but that many find it difficult, if not impossible, to make the leap. "I have seen so many career assistants try to make the next leap and they have not gotten any practice. An assistant does not prepare you because you're attending to completely different duties."

"If you want to be a cinematographer," says Schwartzman, "find a way to shoot as much film as you possibly can, whether it's film or video . . . Obviously, if you want to get into the film business you have got to be in either Los Angeles, New York, Austin, Texas, or Wilmington, North Carolina—places where they make movies . . . If you're enthusiastic, people will respond to that. Perseverance pays off in this business."

Professional Profile: Richard Crudo, ASC, Cinematographer

"The cinematographer is the director's closest collaborator. You help him turn what's on the page into reality."—Richard Crudo

"I always loved movies as a kid growing up, but it never dawned on me that people actually do this for a living," recalls Richard Crudo. A gifted baseball player, he caught the eye of a Red Sox scout while still in high school, but elected to attend St. John's University instead of pursuing a sports career.

Unable to decide on a major, an instructor who was also a director/producer/writer, helped Crudo discover his passion for filmmaking. "He needed some bodies to help out on a commercial job he was doing one day. I went and helped and got attached to the camera department. That was my first exposure to it. I was enamored. It immediately sparked my passion."

Crudo immediately began pursuing filmmaking as a career, working on student and nonunion films while going to school. Having no friends or family in the business, the relationships he made early on were essential to his being able to obtain work and experience. After completing his bachelor's degree in communications in 1979, he went on to earn a master's degree in film from Columbia College in 1981. He served as an assistant cameraman for two to three years before he was admitted into the union.

VOICES OF EXPERIENCE

What do you like least about your job?

"What I like least is the time off between jobs."
—Richard Crudo

What do you love most about your job?

"What I like most is the job; doing the work. The job itself is fantastic. It's always different, stimulating, and exciting. The people you work with are always fun, always interesting. It's never twice the same. No matter how long you've been working, there is always something new to learn."—Richard Crudo

For 12 years, Crudo worked in New York as an assistant cameraman on numerous features, including *Broadway Danny Rose, Field of Dreams, Ghostbusters II, The Money Pit, The Purple Rose of Cairo,* and *Raising Arizona.* Moving up to camera operator, he spent only a couple more years in that capacity before making the leap to cinematographer. Along the way, he gained experience shooting whenever he could, working on student and nonunion films, "whatever I could get my hands on. I shot tons of things, going back to day one as an assistant, just trying to learn. The only way to learn is to film, film, film."

A film called *Federal Hill*, directed by friend Michael Corrente, proved to be a break in Crudo's career as a cinematographer. "We'd known each other for quite a few years. He'd been trying to get this thing up on its legs for no money. Finally, he scraped the money together." Corrente, a native of Rhode Island, where the picture was shot, garnered immense support from the community. Shooting with 35mm black and white film, and calling in favors from people Crudo had developed relationships with at Panavision, Kodak, and the DuArt laboratory in New York, enabled the filmmakers to put the film in the can for $80,000. The picture's critical success brought notice to Crudo's work, legitimizing his status as a cinematographer in the eyes of the industry.

In 1991, Crudo relocated to Los Angeles, where opportunities were more abundant. "If you want to shoot and be a cinematographer, you have to be tremendously connected. I wasn't." Over the next few years he worked on a variety of projects, including the 1997 film *Music From Another Room*, written and directed by Charlie Peters. "It remains my

favorite movie. Charlie is one of the best directors I've ever worked with. He and I spent a lot of time prepping that movie, and consequently we were very well prepared. Charlie is the type of director that doesn't know or care which end of the camera you look through. He's really smart and a great communicator. He doesn't need to know technology and lenses. The director needs to know how to communicate what it is they want to get out of the scene, and Charlie was really good at that. I had a good understanding of Charlie and the script. Together, we came up with a very good plan for the movie. It's the closest I have ever come to putting on the screen exactly what the director and I intended to do. Not necessarily in a virtuoso photographic sense, but in the sense of servicing the story. It was an enormously rewarding experience and remains very close to my heart."

While Peters was editing the film, Orion Pictures, who owned the project, was bought by MGM. The new studio released the picture with no advertising, promotion, or support.

The first of Crudo's films to achieve commercial success was *American Pie*, directed by brothers Chris and Paul Weitz. "I love them dearly. *American Pie* was shot for Universal, very much under the radar for not a lot of money. It was a short schedule, with first-time directors. It became a minor cultural phenomenon and an overwhelming success. It's one of those movies that could last forever because it's a timeless theme."

Since the late 1990s, Crudo has taught filmmaking courses at UCLA Extension, Cal-State Northridge, and American Film Institute (AFI), on the rare occasions when he is not working on a film. Although he has done a number of commercials and some television work—and if the right series came along, he wouldn't say no—Crudo has always been primarily drawn to feature films, his first love. "Features offer more of a challenge in almost every way; they allow you to develop a closer relationship to the material; you take more care with images.

"I've been a lucky guy, in that this has never seemed like work to me. The hours and conditions can be brutal. You can be working 16 to 18 hours a day for months and months and months on end, in all kinds of horrible climatic conditions. It's physically demanding in many ways, but it's never seemed like work. My feeling is: whatever they pay me when I'm working is money for the time off in between jobs. The work is always a pleasure."

Professional Profile: Allen Daviau, ASC, Cinematographer

"The cinematographer is there to put the director's dream on the screen."—Allen Daviau, ASC

It is almost unfathomable that despite five Academy Award nominations for best achievement in cinematography, Allen Daviau had to fight for more than a decade to be admitted into the union, but he did.

Raised in Southern California, Daviau does not remember a time when he didn't love movies. "My parents were moviegoers. We had a neighborhood theater, The Baldwin, right down the street from us, so I went to movies from the time I was an infant." When he was six, his father bought a black and white television and Daviau reveled in studying the older movies broadcast at the time.

His fascination with film continued to grow. In high school he became acquainted with students who were into foreign, old, and silent films. "I just became a student of [film]. I really love film history." He began "gate crashing" the many movie and television studios in the area to get a look at production. At the time, live television was the norm and Daviau was intrigued by it. He was just 16 when he determined that "the director of photography is the best job in the world."

Daviau graduated in 1960 and briefly attended Loyola University, but his heart was not in schoolwork. Instead, he preferred working in camera stores and labs, devoting his off time and energy to making films. Determined to become a cinematographer from the start, he purchased a 16mm camera to start shooting. "I used the idea that the kid who owns the football gets to play quarterback." Over the next few years he worked for free on several student projects, including one for director Nick Frangakis, who went on to work on educational films and employed Daviau to shoot them.

In the mid-60s, he freelanced for KHJ Radio making rock and roll promotional films. The work evolved into a television series called *Boss City*. Meeting with the show's producer, Daviau showed the promos made for KHJ and the film he shot for Frandokis to land the job as cinematographer. While continuing to work at a camera store, he shot and edited three or four films for *Boss City* each week.

When the show ended, Daviau began working on commercials and low budget features, connecting with Peter Deyell on a short film that never came to fruition. When Deyell discovered that friend Ralph Burris was putting up money to finance a 35mm short called *Slipstream* for up-and-coming director Steven Spielberg, he recommended Daviau for the job. Spielberg and Burris arranged to meet Daviau at the Sherman Grinberg film library, where they viewed some of his rock and roll promo films. Feeling he did not have enough 35mm experience, Daviau suggested they hire French cinematographer Serge Haigner instead, and use him as the B camera operator.

The film's theme was bicycle racing and was to be shot entirely outdoors in just two days. Unfortunately, the weather conspired against the project, which quickly ran out of time and money. *Slipstream* remains unfinished. "It was heartbreaking. You could see it then; you just had to meet Steven Spielberg and you knew exactly what was going to happen."

A year later, when Spielberg was preparing to direct another short called *Amblin'*, he invited Daviau to shoot it. "We shot that film in 10 glorious days in 1968." When Spielberg showed the completed film to executives at Universal, they signed him immediately. Attempts were made to sign Daviau as well, but the union blocked his admission into the cinematographer's guild.

"It was a slow year in the industry . . . Somebody may have pushed a little too hard because years later, I found out that my file got red flagged at the union, which means 'he never gets in!'" Daviau took the high road and assured Spielberg he would get in the union through one of the commercial houses he worked for. But it was 10 more years before he was admitted.

Spielberg went on to work on *Jaws*, and Daviau returned to work on educationals, industrials, documentaries, and commercials. "I stayed in touch with [Spielberg]. We would see movies and talk. While he was doing *Jaws*, I talked to him every Sunday. He was going through hell because again, the weather was working against him."

Daviau went on to amass a large body of work, but was still unable to get into the union. In 1975, he filed a class action lawsuit on behalf of all cinematographers, and asked Spielberg to sign the petition. Even after the suit was settled, it took an additional two years of submitting paperwork and pay stubs, which more than once mysteriously disappeared, before Daviau finally gained admittance into the union in 1979. Not long after, Spielberg called upon him to shoot some additional scenes for *Close Encounters of the Third Kind*.

In the spring of 1980, Daviau shot his first union film, a made for television movie called *The Boy Who Drank Too Much*, with director Jerrold Freedman, whom he had previously met on a documentary. When Freedman's first cameraman asked to be released from the picture

VOICES OF EXPERIENCE

What do you like least about your job?

"What I like least are the compromises. But, you have to be a good compromiser to make movies. You have to know what is really valuable. Every second you're on a motion picture set, you're making decisions about what is most valuable to you at this given moment. You may have to give up something that was really important to you three weeks ago because something else has become more important . . . The schedule and the budget sometimes force you into a compromise . . . You make decisions second by second, and then you live with those decisions forever . . . You have to sacrifice some things to get others."—Allen Daviau, ASC

What do you love most about your job?

"Steven Spielberg said something along the lines of, 'I'm paid to dream' . . . I love harnessing a complex technology in the service of art, in that you make art using a lot of technologies."—Allen Daviau, ASC

because he had gotten feature work, Freedman acquiesced and offered the job to Daviau. "[Jerry] took me into Mary Tyler Moore Enterprises and said, 'You've never heard of this guy, but don't worry; he'll do a great job or I'll kill him.'" Daviau went on to work on other television projects before landing the feature film *Harry Tracy, Desperado*.

Shortly after getting into the union, Daviau had signed with Randy Herron at the Herb Tobias agency. When Spielberg wrapped *Jaws* and began preproduction on *E.T., the Extra-Terrestrial*, producer Kathy Kennedy telephoned Herron looking for possible cinematographers for the film. Daviau was suggested.

Herron wanted Spielberg to see some of Daviau's recent work that weekend, and set out on a crusade to get his hands on the footage. With *Harry Tracy* still in editing, *The Boy Who Drank Too Much* was selected. When Herron called the studio to get a 35mm print, he was informed that it was still in New York. "Randy proceeded to call a friend at CBS, a gal who owed him one . . . Breaking a lot of rules, she went to the vault, got the air print, and snuck it out to him in the parking lot." Herron next had to take the footage to a film house to have it put on reels and into a carrying case, before personally delivering it to Spielberg's home on Sunday afternoon. (Daviau is still represented by the same agency, now known as Skouras Agency.)

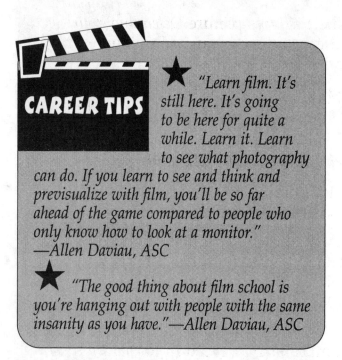

CAREER TIPS

★ *"Learn film. It's still here. It's going to be here for quite a while. Learn it. Learn to see what photography can do. If you learn to see and think and previsualize with film, you'll be so far ahead of the game compared to people who only know how to look at a monitor."* —*Allen Daviau, ASC*

★ *"The good thing about film school is you're hanging out with people with the same insanity as you have."* —*Allen Daviau, ASC*

That evening, Daviau received a call at home from Spielberg, inviting him to come read the script. Daviau received his first Oscar nomination for his work on *E.T.*

Over the next few years, Daviau went on to shoot two segments of *Twilight Zone: The Movie* (one of which was directed by Spielberg), reunited with Jerrold Freedman for the film *Legs*, then on to *The Falcon and the Snowman* with John Schlesinger, and the California unit for Spielberg's *Indiana Jones and the Temple of Doom*.

A friend introduced Daviau to the book *The Color Purple*. "I remember reading it on the plane back from New York. I thought it was a remarkable book . . . " Spielberg directed the film with Daviau as cinematographer, earning him a second Oscar nomination.

Two years later, Daviau earned a third nomination for cinematography on *Empire of the Sun*, also directed by Spielberg. "I remember the first day of shooting. We were in Shanghai . . . I remember standing and looking down at 5,000 extras milling around and saying to myself, 'I'm really glad to be here, because they're not going to make many more of these.' Today, those extras would be digital."

The success of *Empire* was followed by the Barry Levinson directed *Avalon*. Daviau had met Mark Johnson and Barry Levinson during the shooting of *The Color Purple*, when they came to North Carolina to show

Spielberg a cut of *Young Sherlock Holmes*. Johnson later suggested Daviau to Levinson for *Avalon*.

"I had to meet with him and talk about multiple cameras . . . before he would give me the script. Then, I took the script home and went, 'Wow.'" For certain flashback sequences, Davaiu worked out a stretch printing technique. "You shoot in silent film speed, which was 16 frames a second, and then you take it and print every other frame twice. That gives you 24 frames. That's how silent films are updated for showing at sound speed. You've seen this many, many times, but you don't see it very often in color. I did tests and showed them to Barry and he bought it immediately." Daviau earned a fourth Oscar nod for his work on the film.

He went on to work on the Albert Brooks picture *Defending Your Life*, then reunited with Levinson for *Bugsy*, which brought Daviau yet another Academy Award nomination.

Over the next decade he added *Fearless, Congo, The Astronaut's Wife, The Translater, Sweet,* and *Hearts in Atlantis* to his résumé.

Professional Profile: Clark Mathis, ASC, Cinematographer

"My job is to collaborate with the director in developing a visual look for the film and carrying it out," says Clark Mathis.

Filmmaking was not part of Clark Mathis's original career plan. "I was sort of destined for a life of science," he says. Both his parents worked for NASA and several relatives were in science and engineering. In preparation to enter the family business, Mathis studied science and mathematics throughout high school.

His first inclinations toward filmmaking surfaced in his senior year, when home video equipment became readily available. "I was enamored with it instantly. My friends and I made the most superficial photo plays and movies." Instead of writing a term paper about Captain John Smith and colonial customs, he was allowed to make a video about the subject. "By the time I finished shooting and editing it on the crudest interfaces, I spent probably 10 to 20 times more hours doing it than if I'd just sat down and written a paper. And I couldn't have been happier. I realized for the first time I had found something that when I was doing it, I completely lost track of time." Although he loved the idea of filmmaking, he still only considered it a hobby.

Mathis entered a magnet school program outside his high school, to study science and physics. "One of the requirements of that program was that I intern with someone in the general professional community." Most students interned with a scientist; many went to NASA. "Having just had an amazing experience getting out of a paper by doing a video, but at the same time frustrated by the crudeness of my tools, I had an idea to use the leverage of this science program to get me into ABC, which had an affiliate in Norfolk, Virginia."

Since nothing in the program literature stated he had to study with a scientist, the school reluctantly agreed to let Mathis intern at ABC. "That was the catalyst for the rest of my career, because I got in with professional people and was able to learn all about cameras and editing equipment."

After school, each day of his senior year, he made the hour and a half round trip from his high school to the television station. While the college communications students interning at the station were relegated to answering phones and making photocopies, Mathis asserted himself, looking for opportunities to learn and get his hands on equipment. His investment of time paid off when the chief editor became gravely ill and was out for one week. Mathis was promoted to editor of the local nightly news, at just 17 years old.

He was accepted into the engineering and physics program at Duke University and scored high enough on certain tests to allow him to take a semester off, while still receiving credit for his first semester's work. He stayed on at the station as an editor, but after his 10-hour shift was over, he would go out for another six hours with the cameramen on their evening assignments. Initially he hauled batteries, heavy cases, and fetched coffee, but eventually the crew taught him how to shoot. "Only after spending hardcore time at the news station did I realize that shooting was the aspect that appealed to me most."

Come January, Mathis entered Duke full time and "for the next two years pretended I was going to have a career in engineering." He returned to the television station during summer vacations and in his junior year transferred out of engineering and into art history.

VOICES OF EXPERIENCE

What do you like least about your job?

"I don't like the long hours or the high probability that a job will take me away from my family."—Clark Mathis

What do you love most about your job?

"I love telling a story in a purely visual sense; in a way that compliments the words, but enhances them beyond any point that they would be if they were simply spoken. I like taking the audience on an experiential ride. I love photography and I love making images that aren't just beautiful, but really stir someone's emotions."—Clark Mathis

Mathis took a semester off to work on Sean Penn's directorial debut film, *The Indian Runner*. "Thom Mount, one of the producers, has roots in Durham. He came to speak at the University and I asserted myself as someone who was really interested in a career in the film business. He allowed me to come and be a film loader/second assistant cameraperson on the movie . . . That was my first taste of Hollywood filmmaking."

In his senior year he met producer Bill Hayes, a Duke alumnus, who had landed a series for the Discovery Channel called *The Operation* and would be shooting in the area. Mathis submitted his résumé and was hired as cinematographer. While working on the show, he managed to finish school, earning a bachelor's degree in art history in 1992. He stayed on with the series for another year.

In 1994, Mathis relocated to Southern California and took work shooting segments for *Entertainment Tonight*, while looking for feature and series work. He submitted his résumé and reel *en masse* to independent productions, and for the next couple of years worked for free or for little money to gain more celluloid experience. "I had done some 16mm and video, but I hadn't done a lot of 35mm production." During that time he also cold-called agents.

"I didn't want to go the assistant cameraperson route because having a taste of that during *Indian Runner*, I realized that I wasn't good at it. Having been a cinematographer, I found myself on the set just stopping and watching what Tony Richmond was doing, much to the chagrin of the other assistants I was supposed to be supporting and helping . . . While [working as an assistant] would have meant the most immediate financial stability, my wife and I decided to just eat peanut butter sandwiches and live in a 20 × 20 apartment in Burbank and try to tough it out."

By 1997, Mathis had garnered enough credits to resume cold-calling agents, connecting with one who was looking to diversify her client roster to include cinematographers. She submitted his reel to Tollin Robbins Productions and secured him work on three one-hour youth programs

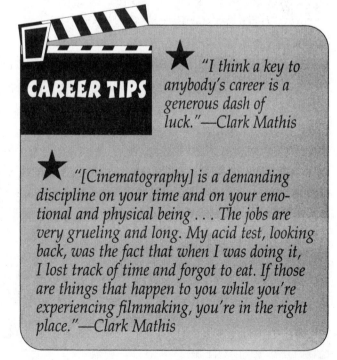

CAREER TIPS

★ *"I think a key to anybody's career is a generous dash of luck."*—Clark Mathis

★ *"[Cinematography] is a demanding discipline on your time and on your emotional and physical being . . . The jobs are very grueling and long. My acid test, looking back, was the fact that when I was doing it, I lost track of time and forgot to eat. If those are things that happen to you while you're experiencing filmmaking, you're in the right place."*—Clark Mathis

called *Sports Theater*. Through the experience, Mathis developed a relationship with Brian Robbins, which led to work on the Nickelodeon series *Cousin Skeeter* and later, the pilot for *Popular*.

Mathis's first big studio feature, *Ready to Rumble*, was also due to Robbins. "Each step of the way, Brian gave me a chance to work on bigger and bigger projects with more mature subject matter. He really went to bat for me with the studio. They were understandably reluctant to let a 29-year-old guy with just television and independent film credits do a $30 million studio movie."

Ready to Rumble wrapped just as pilot season was starting. Mathis quickly found himself directing two pilots and then picking up the series *The Fugitive*. The show was cancelled after one season and he went on to shoot the pilot for *Birds of Prey*, directed by Robbins.

"One thing I'm particularly proud of in the pilot [for *Birds of Prey*] was that I attempted to pay homage to one of my idols, Gregg Toland, who did *Citizen Kane* and *The Grapes of Wrath*. As opposed to doing very shallow focus photography that a lot of folks are doing, I pitched to Brian, the director, and the studio about doing it with a wide angle and lots of depth of field, almost theatrical tableaus and compositions . . . "

In the summer of 2002, Mathis returned to features, shooting *The Perfect Score*.

"I have been very, very lucky, and cannot overstate the fact that I have been very lucky to meet people who are interested in giving me a chance . . . I used to read about guys like Allen Daviau and dream of the day when I could do this for a living."

Professional Profile: John Schwartzman, CSA, Cinematographer

"The cinematographer is responsible for translating the written word to film images."—John Schwartzman, CSA

Like most successful filmmakers, John Schwartzman parlayed his relationships in the industry into opportunities that launched his career as a cinematographer. The method he used to achieve success translates to anyone starting out; the difference is that his contacts were Francis Ford Coppola, George Lucas, and friends Michael Bay, Michael Lehmann, and Gary Ross.

"I grew up around the film business. My best friend's father [Lawrence Turman] was the producer of *The Graduate*. He had offices at Warner Brothers. He or his secretary would pick us up from school and take us to Warner Brothers, where we would do our homework at his office and run around and elude the studio security . . . It was kind of my playground as a kid."

From the beginning, Schwartzman's parents supported his artistic interests in painting, drawing, and photography, even helping him build a darkroom and equipping him with supplies.

His father was an entertainment attorney whose clients included prominent producers and directors such as Stanley Kubrick and William Friedkin. From a young age, Schwartzman became familiar with these great filmmakers in the casual setting of his family's home. When he was 16, he spent a summer working as a gofer for Hal Ashby. "He used to edit movies at his house in the Malibu Colony. I remember he showed *Coming Home* at his house. I was probably one of the first to see it all put together."

Although Schwartzman's father approved of a career in filmmaking, he insisted that his son go to college and earn a degree, to ensure he had "something to fall back on." Following his father's advice, he earned a bachelor's degree in economics from the University of Colorado and planned to go on to law school. Prior to graduation, he participated in a program for photographers called "Semester at Sea," sailing around the world on a freighter equipped with a darkroom, stopping at exotic ports of call. "Photography became a real means for me to express myself. On that trip, I really got into photography and began to understand it on a

VOICES OF EXPERIENCE

What do you like least about your job?

*"The thing that I like least about the job is the hours. Because filmmaking has become so expensive it requires a huge commitment in terms of time. The idea of a 40-hour week in which you can get home at night and go out to dinner with your friends is something that does not exist in the film business. On a typical movie I work on, in a five-day week I will put in somewhere between 70 and 80 hours. If you do the math, that is between 15 and 17 hours a day. It is all consuming. You don't see your family much. You have to have the kind of friends that understand, when you're working on a film, you're probably not going to call them back right away. If I could change anything, it would be that we work more days and less hours, instead of longer hours and less days. But, it's the economics of filmmaking."
—John Schwartzman*

What do you love most about your job?

"What I love most about my job is my office changes every day. One day my office may be the beach and the next day it may be the 35th floor of an office building. How great is that? There is this constant newness to the job. The other thing I love is, how many people can get up in the morning on a rainy day and say, 'When I go to work today, I'm going to make it sunny'? Or on a sunny day, say, 'I'm going to make it rain outside the windows.' It is a lot of fun. It's so creative."—John Schwartzman

graphic level." When not taking pictures or developing them, he read books and studied about light, exposure, and composition, then applied what he learned to make his photographs better. When he returned to school, he did not yet know that he wanted to be a cinematographer, but had decided that if he were going on to graduate school, he should attend the USC film school.

When he was 16, Schwartzman's parents divorced and his father married actress Talia Shire, making Francis Ford Coppola his uncle. "So I hit up my uncle, who is a wonderful guy, for a letter of recommendation to film school and he said, 'No.'" Explaining that he received thousands of requests from friends of his own and friends of the family, Coppola had determined to say no to all of them. Undeterred, Schwartzman later found another way to get a letter of recommendation from Coppola, and one from George Lucas as well.

During the 1981 Thanksgiving holiday, Schwartzman was one of the many family and friends who celebrated at Coppola's home and vineyard in Napa Valley. "Thanksgiving evening, George Lucas was there . . . George and Francis were bragging about what great Risk players they were. So around 11:00 at night, we sat down to play a game and made a friendly wager: If I lost, I would be their slave for the next four days. If I beat them, they would write me a letter of recommendation to film school." Around 3:30 in the morning, Schwartzman won.

Although he possessed a high GPA and test scores in his own right, the letters from Lucas and Coppola earned him a personal welcome call from the dean of the university. But after partnering with director Phil Joanou to make *The Last Chance Dance* and breaking too many of the film school's rules, he was asked to leave. Even though the film was banned by USC and Schwartzman was given a failing mark in cinematography, *The Last Chance Dance* won national recognition and received that year's Focus Award (now called Student Academy Award) for cinematography.

In the mid-1980s, "behind the scenes" video press kits for feature films were becoming a popular way for cable outlets like HBO and Showtime to fill the 15 or 20 minute gaps between when one program ended and the next started on the hour or the half hour. Supplying this type of programming were former USC students Les Mayfield and George Zaloom. When Schwartzman left USC, they immediately tapped him to shoot the specials. Just 25 years old, he was making $500 a day as a working cinematographer. By living modestly, he could support himself on a few days' work and continue his education by seeing movies, going to museums, and reading books.

To supplement his income, Schwartzman often worked as an electrician on various productions. "I knew I was going to be a cinematographer, but the world didn't know it yet . . . I felt whatever I could do to either be on a set or get a camera to my eye, whether shooting Betacam or film, was an opportunity I was not going to miss."

Schwartzman's first feature film came as a direct result of the student film *The Last Chance Dance* and doing a freebie for someone who said, "If I ever get a job, I'm going to pay you back." Screenwriter Richard Martini wanted to direct, but Columbia, where he was signed, denied him the opportunity. Finally, he decided to put up $10,000 of his own money to make a short film he had written and would direct. Impressed with *The Last Chance Dance* cinematography, he contacted Schwartzman to shoot the project. Although he could not afford to pay, Martini promised that if he ever got to direct a film, he would hire Schwartzman to shoot it. Schwartzman accepted and rallied friends from film school to assist. Six months later, Martini called to say that he was slated to direct *You Can't Hurry Love* and offered him the job of cinematographer.

For the next two years, Schwartzman picked up work on "slasher" movies, using them as vehicles to further develop his skills as a cinematographer. When he realized that he was becoming typecast as a cinematographer of really bad movies, he consciously began looking for ways to transition his career into working on better films. Reading that legendary cinematographer Vittorio Storaro was coming to America to shoot *Tucker: The Man and His Dream* for Francis Ford Coppola, Schwartzman determined to find a way to intern for him. "His work is so extraordinarily beautiful and sophisticated. He is a very brilliant guy . . . I needed to understand why Vittorio Storaro's movies looked better than everybody else's. He's using the same camera, the same lights, and the same film as everybody else. Why does his work look so much better?"

Using his experience making video press kits for other features, Schwartzman convinced one of the film's producers, George Lucas, to hire him as a documentarian for the making of *Tucker*. "As a crew member on the movie, I was getting paid to be in San Francisco while they made the movie, and getting to hang out with my idol, Vittorio Storaro. Needless to say, I spent a lot more time talking to Vittorio than I did shooting behind the scenes footage. But it was a wonderful experience to be mentored by a master. He was very gracious and took a lot of time explaining to me why he was doing certain things. It was about emotion; it wasn't about technique. To understand that where you put the camera or the choices you make is how the audience relates to the story that is being told. It was a wonderful four months for me."

Upon returning to Los Angeles, Schwartzman's friend since elementary school, Michael Bay, was preparing to direct his film school thesis project and asked Schwartzman to shoot it. The day after Bay graduated, he was signed to Propaganda Films: a young, hip, burgeoning production company. Bay and another young director named David Fincher were making names for themselves directing cutting edge music videos, and both used Schwartzman to shoot them. Soon advertising agencies were clamoring for the hip filmmakers to direct and shoot their commercials.

> **CAREER TIPS**
>
> ★ *"Part of my job as a cinematographer is to keep the attitude on the set positive. When you find out that lunch is a half hour late because the cook screwed up and everybody is hungry—we've been working in the rain and we're cold and all we want is to take a break—that's when you start to hear grumbling. What you try to do is keep everybody focused . . . That's part of my job—sometimes it's a lot of my job."* —John Schwartzman
>
> ★ *"Listen to your subconscious, because your subconscious knows a lot."* —John Schwartzman

For a couple of years in the late 1980s, Schwartzman was working 200 days a year. Every week, he would scout locations on Monday, prep, and shoot Thursday through Saturday, and start all over again on Monday. At just 28 years old, Schwartzman was earning a couple hundred thousand dollars a year and was one of the hottest commercial cinematographers in the business.

Contacted by a company who wanted to reinvent the image of director Jeremiah Chechik, Schwartzman was hired to shoot commercials for him. When Chechik was later hired to direct the feature *Benny and Joon*, he turned to Schwartzman to film it. "The last movie I had shot was *Red Surf*, a low budget genre movie . . . *Benny and Joon* had a real story; I loved the script." In 1991, he went to Seattle to shoot the project. The union came in during filming and organized the crew. Schwartzman and the film loader, being the only two nonunion crew members, paid their $5,000 admission fee and were added to the union roster.

When Schwartzman returned to Los Angeles, he married and made the commitment to work on movies only on alternate years, spending the intervening years making commercials, so that he could build and maintain a personal life. "I just didn't want to be the guy who went from location to location, living out of hotel rooms . . . The nice thing about commercials is you can pick and choose your schedule . . . On a movie, you can't even go to the dentist or the doctor. As a cinematographer you cannot be sick. Unless you have a 105 fever, you're there, wrapped up in a blanket, sitting in a chair, shivering. You don't get a day off, because they can't make the movie without you."

The next feature was *Airheads*, directed by college friend Michael Lehmann. Between feature films, Schwartzman continued to work on commercials, often with Michael Bay. When Bay directed his first feature, *Bad Boys*, he asked his friend to shoot it. Schwartzman graciously declined, opting to stay in Los Angeles to spend time with his father, who was battling cancer.

The success of *Bad Boys* earned Bay the opportunity to direct *The Rock*, and Schwartzman was hired to shoot it. "For my career, *The Rock* was like getting fired out of a cannon. I had done respected films, but nothing that would be considered flashy, in terms of visibility . . . I am very thankful that Michael gave me the opportunity to do *The Rock*, because that suddenly put me in a whole new category. Suddenly I had done a movie that was the number one movie of the summer in terms of box office."

Conspiracy Theory with Richard Donner came next, followed by *Armageddon* with Michael Bay, whom he would later work with on the epic *Pearl Harbor*. In between the two pictures, he shot *Edtv*, for director Ron Howard.

"On *Edtv*, we shot the film and the video simultaneously. That was the deal I made with Ron . . . I knew it was going to make my job a lot harder, but I also thought it was going to give the film a certain amount of energy. I was excited about working with Ron Howard. He is a very good director."

Schwartzman's favorite film is also his most recent work: *The Rookie*. "I was so happy with the way the movie turned out." In discussing shots with director John Lee Hancock, Schwartzman pointed out, "If we shoot baseball late in the afternoon with the sun low and all those long shadows, it will be beautiful, but it's going to be false. Look at all these baseball fields . . . the grass is dead, the ground is rock hard, and there are kids out there playing baseball. This is what it is: it's those bleachy skies and it's hotter than hell. That's what we need to shoot.

"As a cinematographer, I think right now, *The Rookie* was the culmination of my life's experience. I think it's the best work that I've ever done. It's not the most beautiful—I would say *Pearl Harbor* may be the most beautiful, photographically—but I think *The Rookie* has the most photographic truth in it of anything I've ever done . . . The director, John Lee Hancock, to date in my career, is the most talented director I've work with. He is amazing. He's got a great sense about storytelling and he brought so much to the table."

At the request of President Bush, arrangements were made for a special screening of *The Rookie* at The White House. Schwartzman became the first cinematographer invited to attend such an event.

He is currently prepping a film based on Laura Hillenbrand's best-seller, *Seabiscuit: An American Legend*. Gary Ross, another friend since high school, will direct the film.

An especially inspiring aspect of Schwartzman's career is that he has managed to succeed in a business that requires excruciatingly long hours and travel to sometimes primitive locations, all the while dealing with the fact that he is a type one diabetic. "I'm the guy who travels with food and insulin everywhere he goes, but I never let that stand in my way . . . I love what I do, and although I may not always do it as well as somebody else, I try my hardest. I always give 100%.

"There is a line in *The Rookie*, when Dennis Quaid's character says, 'You know what we get to do today? We get to play baseball!' I can certainly relate to that."

JOB TITLE: CAMERA OPERATOR

Job Overview

Under the direction of the director of photography, the camera operator composes and frames the shot, and operates the motion picture camera. On smaller productions and commercials, it is not uncommon for the director of photography to also operate the camera.

Special Skills

Knowledge of cameras and lenses, light-meter readings, staging, lighting, composition, optics, and special effects is a must. Art or film schools are good preparation for anyone desiring to become a camera operator or cinematographer. Practical experience may be gained working at a motion picture camera rental company. Communication skills are also important.

Advice for Someone Seeking This Job

Serving as a production assistant is one way to gain some practical set experience and make contacts for future work. Another way to break into the business is by working for a motion picture camera rental company, where you will have an opportunity to learn about the equipment and meet camera crew members currently working on productions. Volunteer to work for free on student films and nonunion productions, music videos or commercials. In the beginning, do whatever you can to get on set where you can learn more about cameras and make contacts.

Professional Profile: Daniel L. Turrett,
Camera Operator and Cinematographer

Growing up near New York City afforded Daniel Turrett an opportunity to be exposed to rich artistic achievements. From an early age, his parents took him to museums, the ballet, and other dance events, the symphony, theater, and movies. The film *Citizen Kane* made a lasting impression on the future filmmaker.

"I remember the first time I saw *Citizen Kane*: I was home sick with the measles . . . I was so taken by it, by the cinematography. That was the first time I realized how powerful movies could be. That interesting stories could be told." A few years later, in a high school humanities class, Turrett was again exposed to the film, and from that point on he began to view "cinema as an art," and began considering it as a career.

He majored in fine arts at Long Island University and learned the basic craft of filmmaking. Summers were spent working summer stock at different theaters across the country, where he built sets, was involved in lighting, and learned the craft of production design, at one point considering it as a career. Working at The Brunswick Music Theater afforded him an opportunity to work alongside actors and craftsmen from Yale University Repertory Company and Drama School. Through the experience, he gained a better understanding of how to use lighting to create moods and help tell a story, an important skill he would later apply to filmmaking.

Studying filmmaking masters like Bernardo Bertolucci and Jean-Luc Godard, and other French and Italian directors, was a motivating factor in his decision to become a filmmaker. The work of avant-garde filmmakers Stan Brakhage, Ed Emshwiller, Michael Snow, and others further solidified his desire.

"*Hallelujah the Hills, Relativity, Dance, Branches*—I saw these movies and I was so taken by them. The movement of avant-garde filmmaking just drove me toward wanting to be a filmmaker."

Having made the decision to become a cameraman, after graduation he began the arduous task of finding a job, committing himself to only taking work in the film industry. "I spent a whole summer jobless, going into New York City daily and walking around with a guidebook to help me locate production companies that made TV commercials, films, and such." Having no experience to list on a résumé, he instead left each with a letter of introduction. His diligence eventually paid off and he landed a job at The Camera Mart, one of the largest motion picture camera and equipment rental companies in New York at that time.

Working as a technician, Turrett learned about the equipment while preparing it for production companies to rent. After two years, he received a job offer from prominent photographer and commercial DP

VOICES OF EXPERIENCE

What do you like least about your job?

"I hate the politics, the political stuff that has nothing to do with making movies."
—Daniel Turrett

What do you love most about your job?

"I love the creative moment—being in the moment on the set."—Daniel Turrett

Amir Hamid to work as a staff camera assistant at his production company, Focus Films. There, Turrett had an opportunity to work with a number of illustrious commercial directors/DPs including Fred Peterman, Henry Sandbank, and Alan Dennis, to name a few. It proved an excellent training for the future cameraman. A year and a half later, he felt prepared to go out on his own as a freelance camera assistant.

To supplement his income, he taught filmmaking courses at the School of Visual Arts, initially as a substitute and eventually moving into a full time staff position for a year. Not only was it an opportunity for him to give back to the industry he was becoming part of, the preparation for teaching broadened his knowledge and further solidified his burgeoning passion for filmmaking.

For the next few years he worked on small films and numerous television commercials with directors from New York, Los Angeles, and London, most notably Elbert Budin. Best known for developing lighting styles and techniques used to photograph food, Budin was a major influence on many top cinematographers, including Turrett.

Over time, he found work as a director of photography, filming television spots for political campaigns, while continuing to serve as an assistant on feature films.

His next major career break was working with famous English cinematographer Brian West, first as an assistant, and later promoted to camera operator, on several films including *Jackknife* and *84 Charing Cross Road*. West became and remains a mentor.

"Brian and I have been close a lot of my career. Even though he's retired, I still talk to him. He was a big influence on my career, teaching me not only about cinematography, but about the business of filmmaking, and about life in general."

After a decade on the East Coast, Turrett relocated to Los Angeles. Almost immediately, he landed work as a camera operator on several commercials. Another break came when well-respected filmmaker Vic Armstrong (best known for his work on action films such as *Gangs of New York, Charlie's Angels, The World Is Not Enough,* and *Tomorrow Never Dies*) was sufficiently impressed by Turrett's experience with West to hire him as second unit director of photography for *Universal Soldier.*

"I went to Arizona for a month and photographed the second unit—amazing action footage. Vic and I became friends on that film. He has been very helpful and a big influence on my career." Later, when Armstrong prepared to direct *Joshua Tree,* he again hired Turrett as cinematographer. The pair worked together a third time on *Starship Troopers* with Armstrong serving as second unit director and Turrett as second unit director of photography.

Over the past decade, Turrett has worked as a camera operator or cinematographer on numerous feature films, including *American Buffalo, American Pie, Bad Girls, Volcano,* and *The X-Files,* and made for television movies *And the Beat Goes On: The Sonny and Cher Story, The Late Shift,* and *Running Delilah.*

CAREER TIPS

★ *"Anybody who thinks they want to become a cameraman ought to be very sure of it and focused. It's very, very competitive, so you need to be serious about it. Seize all opportunities to go to seminars and shoot on their own. Get a video camera, an old Super-8, or a camera of any kind, and go out and shoot film."—Daniel Turrett*

★ *"Be prepared: study films and know film history, as well as knowing lenses. I'm always disturbed when I meet young kids who want to be filmmakers and they have no film history background. It's disarming to mention classic movies that we all know, and they have never heard of them. It is an important part of the process to know the history of film and to be familiar with the work of other filmmakers."—Daniel Turrett*

He also served as second unit director of photography for the critically acclaimed television series *The Fugitive,* which was principally shot in Seattle. Turrett was charged with filming all the location photography in places like New York, Philadelphia, Atlantic City, New Orleans, Phoenix, and San Francisco. When the series ended, he worked on a television movie for Disney, was immediately hired as second unit director of photography for the series *That's Life,* and went on to work on the pilot for *Birds of Prey.*

JOB TITLE: STEADICAM OPERATOR

Job Overview

The Steadicam is a portable camera system that attaches to the body of the operator, and is generally used to smoothly capture shots that other cameras cannot, such as going up and down stairs or through narrow hallways. As designated by the director and cinematographer, the Steadicam operator composes and executes shots using this camera system.

Special Skills

Although it is not necessary to be large in stature, a Steadicam operator must be physically fit and a skilled camera operator, able to carry the weight of the Steadicam while climbing, running, or moving about the set, while composing shots and capturing the desired action on film.

Advice for Someone Seeking This Job

If you are seriously considering a camera operator job, operator David Emmerichs says you need to move to New York, Los Angeles, or another city where movies are made. If you have an interest in being a Steadicam operator, it is essential that you first go to a camera rental house or a trade show and try one on.

"Initially it hurts. There are a lot of people who physically cannot do it . . . There are workshops where you can go and for two or three days learn from some of the better operators. Put it on and see if it's something you want to pursue." Attending a workshop is also a good place to make connections with people who may be able to help you find work. Contact other operators and ask them if you can assist them or watch them work. Get a job at a camera rental house where you can meet people working in the industry. Volunteer to shoot student, low budget, or music videos for free, so you can gain experience using the equipment.

Professional Profile: David Emmerichs, Steadicam Operator and Camera Operator

Inspired by the movie *Star Wars*, David Emmerichs decided at the age of 10 that he wanted to be a filmmaker. He started making Super-8 movies with his friends, and when they weren't available he made animated films. After high school, he left his home in Milwaukee to attend Tisch School of the Arts at New York University. Captivated by special effects and animation, he initially thought that was the area he would pursue. But in his first year, he discovered that he enjoyed shooting other people's movies.

"I loved running around and moving the camera. I didn't even know what a Steadicam looked like, but I knew the concept existed." When Emmerichs first tried on a Steadicam at a New York trade show in 1986, "It was love at first sight."

In his freshman year, he contacted Steadicam operator Ted Churchill to learn more about the gear and job function. "He took me under his wing as an apprentice and started teaching me how to use the equipment. He took me on jobs. I started learning the ropes from his assistants: how to thread cameras and be a focus puller. He taught me how to do shots. I was learning throughout the last three years I was at NYU." Another mentor was Steadicam operator Jim Moru, who would later recommend Emmerichs for his first feature.

During his senior year, Emmerichs bought a used, nonfunctioning Steadicam. His mentor, Churchill, "had enough spare bits to sort of slap it together and make it work. I put up little home-made advertisements, with a very serious picture of me wearing the Steadicam, and stuck them up all over the school: 'Willing to work on serious student films for free.'"

Emmerichs' first paid job was an industrial film for Brown University, which came through a recommendation from Churchill. Before graduating with a bachelor's degree in fine arts, and for the three years following, Emmerichs honed his skills working on student films and music videos. His first feature was *Hangin' with the Homeboys.* "It was my first big chance. When I showed up, they saw that I was just a kid and didn't want to let me shoot anything. I sort of sat on the bench for most of the night, until they finally came to a shot they couldn't figure out

VOICES OF EXPERIENCE

What do you like least about your job?

"The thing I like the least about my job is that sometimes the politics get in the way. And, I sweat a lot."—David Emmerichs

What do you love most about your job?

"The things that I like best about my job are the places I get to go, the people I get to work with, and the things I get to do. For instance, on Armageddon, *I was on the space shuttle launching pad a few days before the ship was in orbit . . . running around in the temples in Cambodia [for* Lara Croft: Tomb Raider] . . . *As a civilian, where else do you get to do that kind of stuff?"*—David Emmerichs

another way to do. So they gave me a shot at it. It went really well and after that I shot most of the movie."

In 1991, Emmerichs relocated from New York to Los Angeles. Much of his initial work was filming rap videos. He worked on the critically acclaimed feature film *Joshua Tree*, followed by two low budget horror films. "I thought of them as Steadicam boot camp. We'd go somewhere, strap the steadicam on, and work all day for five weeks straight, then collapse. I learned a lot." He worked on various television programs, then, through the recommendation of Jim Muro, landed his first feature, *Cool Running*, in 1993. He joined the union just prior to shooting the film.

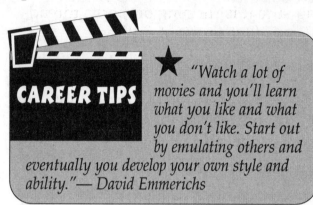

★ *"Watch a lot of movies and you'll learn what you like and what you don't like. Start out by emulating others and eventually you develop your own style and ability."— David Emmerichs*

Having wanted to work with Industrial Light and Magic since he first saw *Star Wars* as a child, Emmerichs finally realized that aspiration on a job shooting a Volkswagen commercial. His next career highlight came working with director David Fincher on *Se7en*. From that point on, Emmerichs continued to work on blockbuster features, such as *Nixon, The Fan, Con Air,* and *Alien: Resurrection*, taking commercial jobs in between. While shooting an ad for Snapple, he met director Michael Bay, and went on to work with him on *Armageddon*.

Edtv came next, followed by his first feature job as an "A" camera operator on *The Green Mile*, working with cinematographer David Tattersall. Emmerichs first worked with Tattersall on the straight to video release *Theodore Rex*, which lead to their reteaming on *Con Air* and *The Green Mile*, followed a couple years later with Emmerichs as camera operator on *The Majestic*.

Con Air director Simon West recommended Emmerichs to cinematographer Peter Menzies, Jr. as a replacement Steadicam operator on *The General's Daughter*, when the original operator had to leave the film a week before it wrapped. Impressed with Emmerichs's work, Menzies hired him as his operator on *Bless the Child, Lara Croft: Tomb Raider,* and for a few weeks on *Spider-Man*. "Peter taught me a lot. He was tough on me and as a result made me a much better operator."

Emmerichs's next film is another Michael Bay directed picture: *Bad Boys 2*.

JOB TITLE: FIRST ASSISTANT CAMERAMAN, ASSISTANT CAMERAMAN, OR FIRST ASSISTANT CAMERA OPERATOR

Job Overview

"The first assistant cameraman is in charge of running the department in terms of ordering cameras and equipment needed, checking in the equipment, setting it up, and making sure it is running properly, threading the camera, and maintaining it," says first assistant Anthony Cappello. "But our primary function is to pull focus."

"Pulling focus" is the act of focusing the camera lens. The first assistant works closely with the camera operator, ensuring that each shot is in focus. "They are in charge of setting the aperture on the lens, the zoom, or focus—the person who is actually touching and operating the focus during the shot," explains assistant cameraman Mark Walpole. They also oversee the second assistant camera operator and film loader. On small shoots, where there is only one assistant, they perform the duties of both assistants and the loader.

Special Skills

The first camera assistant must have a well-rounded knowledge of cameras, lenses, and light-meter readings. Additionally, Coppello credits his passion for the job as being an important part of his success. "You have to have a good attitude; you have to be passionate about what you're doing."

"I think the best thing about my education at NYU was that all the other schools pamper their students. At NYU, the first thing they said to you was, 'Why are you going to film school? There are no jobs out there. Everything is going to video. You guys are ridiculous.' I thought, 'I'm paying you $10,000 a year; aren't you supposed to teach me?' But it made you very independent and very resilient. You had to fight to get the classes you wanted; you had to sleep overnight to register for the classes. I didn't understand it then, but it taught me some of the persistence that this business requires. You're going to get turned down a lot. It's not an easy business to get in and there is a lot of rejection, but if you stick it out, the people that work in this business, *work* in this business."

Advice for Someone Seeking This Job

"Ninety percent of the people in this business start out as production assistants," says Cappello. "Basically, you are a gofer and you do whatever you have to do: get coffee, wrangle chairs, whatever they need you to do. All shows have them and all shows need them. You get paid a flat salary. You meet a lot of people. That's how you start."

Working as a PA affords an opportunity to see what each person's role on set is and to better determine what career path you want to follow. "PA to see how the whole process works. Watch and figure out what you want to do."

Another inroad to the camera department can be through working at an equipment rental house. "Go in and offer to help them on preps—which are the two-week period before a feature—that's where you learn what we need.

"If you want to be in camera, learn about it. Get books. Read. Understand it. Get set experience—you get set experience by working as a PA."

Professional Profile: A. Anthony Cappello, First Assistant Camera

"I got into the business because I love motion pictures," states Anthony Cappello. "I think movies have a lot to say. It's a great way to communicate to a large audience."

Cappello also had a love for still photography. The New York native attended Rochester Institute of Technology (RIT), possibly the best still photography school in the country. Pressured by his parents to take business classes, he changed his emphasis to motion picture photography and enrolled in film school at New York University (NYU). "I thought it was more specialized and less competitive—silly me."

Before graduating in 1984, he served an internship at Silvercup Studios. Through the internship he made contacts that led to becoming a production assistant and then a location assistant. With no relatives in the business and no contacts within the camera union, he realized early on that it would be difficult to become a cinematographer. Initially, he told no one he wanted to work in the camera department and instead used the opportunity to be on set to watch and learn.

When *The Equalizer* television series began crewing up, a producer offered Cappello the job of location manager, with the promise of making him the production manager by mid-season. "It was an unbelievable offer." Knowing this might lead him further away from his goal of getting into the camera department, Cappello turned down the job, confessing that he had been trying for four years to get into the camera union. Then he asked if he could work as a camera production assistant instead. The producer sent him to the first camera assistant for approval.

"I went to the first assistant and said, 'I know nobody in this business. I can't get in the union. This is my break. If you let me, I won't touch anything. I'll get you coffee; whatever you want." The assistant agreed and Cappello was hired as the camera PA, earning $300 a week. "That was my big break. For six months, I touched no equipment. I watched and basically got them food. And, I was happy to do it." Eventually he was allowed to slate camera reports and fetch lenses.

When he went for his third interview with the union just to get an application, cinematographer Geoffrey Erb called and told them to give Cappello an application. After passing the written and practical tests, and paying a $4,000 entrance fee, he was admitted into the union in 1987.

An added benefit to his season on *The Equalizer* was making contacts that lead to future jobs. The show often used multiple cameras and rotated the multiple assistants weekly. Consequently, Cappello met numerous potential future employers. He used the opportunity to demonstrate his dependability and willingness to work hard. "Once I was in the union, I let those people know and I started getting hired."

His first union feature was *Running on Empty*, directed by Sidney Lumet. "I couldn't believe I was doing a show with the guy who directed *Dog Day Afternoon* and a thousand other wonderful films." He continued to work as a second assistant on features such as *Cadillac Man*, *Married to the Mob*, and *Jacob's Ladder*.

A friend recommended Cappello for a commercial job working for cinematographer John Schwartzman. Cappello mentioned his growing desire to relocate west, and Schwartzman told him to call if he came out. The summer

VOICES OF EXPERIENCE

What do you like least about your job?

"My least favorite things are egos and politics in the business."
—Anthony Cappello

What do you love most about your job?

"I like that it's different all the time," says Cappello. He also loves that the job affords him an opportunity to experience a variety of careers. "We work in a library sometimes, so I get to see what a librarian does. We work in a law office and I get to see what the lawyers do. We work in a hospital and you learn about the medical profession. You get a little taste of everyone's job."—Anthony Cappello

before moving, Cappello went out to L.A. and worked on several commercials and music videos with Schwartzman. While there, he networked into an offer to work as first assistant on the pilot for *Beverly Hills 90210*. "I didn't take it because it was a nonunion gig for a flat rate. That show went on for seven years. That opportunity would never have happened

CAREER TIPS

★ *"You have to channel what you want to do early on in your career because you get pigeon-holed very easily . . . You start in an area, you do a good job, people like you, and you get rehired in that position—you get hired, and you get hired, and you get hired. It's a bigger show and a bigger director and a bigger actor. You just keep getting better jobs, and before you know it, time flies and it's seven years, and you're in a profession that you never wanted. You've got to channel yourself in the direction you want to be: If you want to do feature films, get into feature films; if you want to do commercials, do commercials; if you want to do TV, do TV; and if you want to do camera-work, try to get your way into camera early on."—Anthony Cappello*

★ *"While you're working as a production assistant, befriend everybody. Never have attitude—never have attitude and you'll never piss anybody off. Everyone will like you and when you need a break, when you need a favor—which everyone does—someone will give it to you."—Anthony Cappello*

in New York. So I realized I had to come out."

In 1992, he relocated to Los Angeles and found work immediately. Hooking up with cinematographer Mac Ahlberg, he worked on three features: *Innocent Blood*, *My Boyfriend's Back*, and *Striking Distance*. Ahlberg promoted him to first assistant for the television movie *The Late Shift*, followed by the feature *A Very Brady Sequel*.

Volcano was the next big break for Cappello. "It was my first big budget feature. A DP I had never worked with, Theo van de Sande, gave me an opportunity to first. He is the director of photography that I have worked with the longest. I've done eight features with Theo." Those credits include: *Blade*, *Cruel Intentions*, *Double Take*, *High Crimes*, and the television film *Tuesdays with Morrie*.

In between, Cappello worked on three Barry Levinson films: *Disclosure*, *Liberty Heights*, and *Bandits*, and the television series pilot *Birds of Prey*. He is currently working on the Adam Sandler picture *Anger Management*.

JOB TITLE: SECOND ASSISTANT CAMERAMAN, ASSISTANT CAMERAMAN, OR SECOND ASSISTANT CAMERA OPERATOR

Job Overview

The second assistant cameraman orders and maintains the camera equipment, ensures it is on set when needed, marks the actors' positions during rehearsals, and slates each take. The second is also responsible for camera crew paperwork, such as camera and film inventory lists and time sheets. Additionally, on some shoots, the second assistant also performs the duties of the film loader.

"The second assistant is my direct assistant," explains first assistant cameraman Anthony Cappello. "He helps me. He brings me the magazine; he does the camera reports, the slate, and takes care of all the paperwork involved with identifying scenes for the editors."

Specials Skills Required

Camera assistants need a working knowledge of motion picture cameras and equipment. "Some real world common sense is necessary," says assistant cameraman Mark Walpole. "People skills are very important—it takes skill to negotiate, sort of twist people's arm to get more money and still maintain a friendly working relationship so they call you again."

Advice for Someone Seeking This Job

Although a college education is not required, Mark Walpole says, "It definitely helped me because it gave me a good educational basis and I made a lot of contacts."

"Go to a school and study the field you are interested in; then start contacting people that do what you would like to do, one step up. If you want to be a second assistant cameraman, you find a film directory and start calling all the first assistant camera people in the town where you want to live and let them know you're interested in working with them."

Professional Profile: Mark Walpole, Assistant Cameraman

Intrigued by making movies from the time he was a teenager, Virginia native Mark Walpole enrolled in a vocational video production course while still in high school. After graduation, he attended Valencia Community College in Orlando, Florida.

VOICES OF EXPERIENCE

What do you like least about your job?

"The schedule is rough—it's great money, but you do work very long hours. Fourteen to eighteen hour days are typical. You're home very little. It's hard on a personal level, having any continuity in your life." —Mark Walpole

What do you love most about your job?

"I like my work because it is completely different every single day: a different location, a different group of people, a different time schedule, and different scenarios. No two jobs are the same."—Mark Walpole

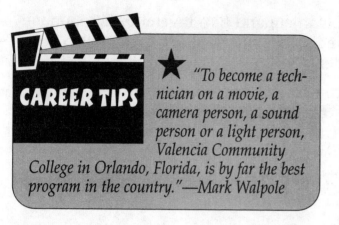

CAREER TIPS

★ *"To become a technician on a movie, a camera person, a sound person or a light person, Valencia Community College in Orlando, Florida, is by far the best program in the country."—Mark Walpole*

An important part of the school's curriculum is working with independent producers who utilize students to fill crew positions. "All the students are crew members. They don't hold the key positions, like director or cinematographer—all the high-end positions are held by paid professionals from New York and Los Angeles. The second, third, fourth, and fifth people down the ladder, stringing the cable from the microphones and moving ladders, are students."

When Walpole graduated in 1997 with an associate of sciences degree, he had already built a résumé of work experience and made many industry contacts. He began working regularly almost immediately and soon joined the union for camera assistants. Early breaks came working on television commercials and music videos for artists Shania Twain, Christina Aguilera, and others.

During the past three years, Walpole has worked as a second camera assistant on several feature films, including *Collateral Damage, Minority Report, Spy Game, The Sum of All Fears, We Were Solders,* and as a camera assistant on *Along Came a Spider, Hannibal, Tuck Everlasting,* and the IMAX film *Ultimate X.* He frequently works on the television series *The West Wing.*

"You start at the bottom and work your way up through the camera department: the lowest position is film loader, then you work your way up to second, and then first, and then to cinematographer," explains Walpole. "I want to be a cinematographer."

JOB TITLE: FILM LOADER

Job Overview

The main job of the film loader is to load film into camera magazines in a darkroom. Loaders maintain accurate film inventories and assist the camera crew.

"Essentially," says film loader/second assistant cameraman Mike Gentile, "my job encompasses just about anything that makes life easier for my camera crew. When I'm not dealing with film issues, I may be found changing filters or lenses, ordering equipment, slating the cameras, setting marks for the talent, maintaining time cards for the camera crew, and even getting their breakfast when they can't step away.

"This is not a desk job. The job can be physically demanding. You'll work 12 to 16 hours a day, sometimes under unpleasant circumstances (rain, snow, smoke, whatever . . .). Sometimes you may be employed for months on end; sometimes you'll be unemployed for months on end. This is the nature of the beast, and most people in the industry experience this on one level or another."

Special Skills

"While I always recommend a college education," say Gentile, "it's not really necessary for most careers in the film industry. In my opinion, the best skills for a career in film are: 1) People skills and networking. You have to know a lot of people in order to work on a regular basis. And, more importantly, they have to like you and your work skills and habits; 2) You have to successfully adapt to an ever-changing, unstable lifestyle."

Advice for Someone Seeking This Job

"Film school doesn't hurt, but don't get cocky," says Mike Gentile. "Most people on a film set don't care where you went to school; school doesn't prepare you for working on a film set and the rules of set etiquette (how to properly handle equipment, procedures, etc.). If you can, try to get a job at a camera rental house or at least visit them periodically. You can meet a lot of ACs (assistant cameramen—your future bosses!) there and learn a lot about the equipment."

Professional Profile: Mike Gentile, Film Loader, 2nd Camera Assistant

Mike Gentile grew up in Somerville, Massachusetts, and attended Emerson College in Boston, planning to become a television news reporter/ anchor. "Once I began taking

VOICES OF EXPERIENCE

What do you like least about your job?

"The lifestyle can frequently be unstable and even problematic . . . This type of erratic work schedule can also affect your personal relationships, usually in a bad way."—Mike Gentile

What do you love most about your job?

"As goofy as it may seem, one of my greatest rewards has been watching my name scroll by on the big screen of a movie theater. For that moment, all the hard work seems worthwhile."—Mike Gentile

broadcast journalism courses, I realized that I hated it. Instead, I became a television production major and found my niche."

Gentile gained experience as a utility crew members for sporting events and spent a semester interning at MTV Networks in Los Angeles. After graduation, he spent a year working in the Boston area as an audio-visual technician.

Returning to Los Angeles, he paid his dues, as they say, over the next two and a half years, working as a runner and production assistant on various productions, such as *Nothing to Lose* and *Batman and Robin*.

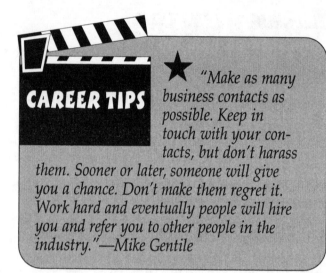

CAREER TIPS

★ *"Make as many business contacts as possible. Keep in touch with your contacts, but don't harass them. Sooner or later, someone will give you a chance. Don't make them regret it. Work hard and eventually people will hire you and refer you to other people in the industry."*—Mike Gentile

"Eventually," Gentile says, "I made some great contacts, people who mentored me and ultimately helped me get into the camera union on the visual effects unit of *Contact*." His next break was working on the pyrotechnics unit for *Starship Troopers* and on the sitcom *The Gregory Hines Show*.

"I was very fortunate. Although it took several years to establish a strong contact base, I am finally enjoying the results of my networking techniques. I have been working as a film loader and second assistant cameraman over the last five years."

In that time, Gentile has amassed an impressive résumé, working on features such as *American Beauty, Eye of the Beholder*, and *What Women Want*; television series *Gideon's Crossing* and *Once and Again*; and commercials for Old Navy, Radio Shack, and Taco Bell.

● ● ● ●

CHAPTER
7
LIGHTING AND GRIPS

Although their jobs overlap to the point that even they sometimes have difficulty explaining their duties, lighting and grip departments perform distinctly different functions. The grip department sets up all of the lighting and equipment needed to film a scene. The gaffers then move in to set and focus the lights, and power the equipment.

Positions within the lighting or electrical department include:

- Gaffer (Chief Electrician): head of the lighting department; light the set to the cinematographer's specification.

- Electrical Best Boy or Second Electric: the gaffer's chief assistant and foreman of the lighting crew; responsible for all electrical hook-ups.

- Lamp Operator or Electrician: place, focus, and maintain the lights.

Larger productions may require a splinter crew, consisting of a Rigging Gaffer, Rigging Best Boy, Rigging Electric or Riggers, that work parallel with the electrical department, handling electrical distribution, running power and cabling, and setting the broad strokes of the lighting on set in advance of the shooting crew.

Positions within the grip department include:

- Key Grip: head of the grip department, with the dual role of supporting the lighting and camera departments; they rig lights, move cameras, dollies, and cranes, and other equipment.

- Best Boy Grip: the key grip's chief assistant and the foreman of the grip crew. Responsible for all equipment and supplies.

- Dolly Grip: move the dolly or crane that supports the camera.

- Grip or Rigger: lift, move, and install lights, camera dolly track, and move other lighting and camera equipment.

LIGHTING DEPARTMENT

JOB TITLE: GAFFER, CHIEF LIGHTING TECHNICIAN

Job Overview

As head of the electrical department, the gaffer is responsible for designing and executing the lighting for a production. "My job is to light the set to the taste of the director of photography and to help make good decisions in helping tell the story with the use of lighting and natural factors," explains gaffer Dwight Campbell.

Special Skills

A gaffer must understand the language of filmmaking and pay attention to details. He must be a problem-solver and have the ability to communicate well, not only with the director and cinematographer, but also when disseminating information to his crew. "I can't stress how important communication is when you're meeting with the director, production designer, or director of photography," says gaffer Russell Caldwell. "If I don't understand, I ask questions until I do."

A gaffer must have a well-rounded knowledge of the filmmaking process. To light a scene properly, he must understand photography and film processing.

Advice for Someone Seeking This Job

Most gaffers begin as grips, work into the job of key grip or best boy grip, then into electrical best boy, or directly into the role of gaffer. "Take any job you can get on a film project," says Campbell. "Work day in and day out and find out what intrigues you the most. Learn everyone's job. Learn what interests you and then pursue it.

"I used to volunteer on AFI, USC, and UCLA films. I worked on projects for no money." Even after he was already working as a key grip on successful features, Campbell continued to work on student or low budget projects for free whenever he was between projects, just to gain more experience and make new contacts. "Every day you help make a film, you meet 40 or 50 new people. All of those people are going to be looking for work tomorrow. All of a sudden you're networking, making a way into the working community of filmmakers. They're all trying to climb the ladder. You help them tell their story and they're going to remember how you helped them out. It's going to help you move up the ladder faster. Film is a collaborative art form."

"If a person specifically wants to be a gaffer," says Caldwell, "he or she should first get in the field and work as an electrician and do some rigging. You have to understand the concept of power and lighting. Find somebody who is willing to teach you. There are a lot of older gaffers who are willing to go for coffee and sit down and talk about their career, what interested them in lighting, and points to remember. A lot of cameramen wouldn't mind doing that also. Make friends with people at lighting rental houses and learn the equipment. There is always new equipment coming out—try to stay on the cutting edge."

Watch a lot of movies [and notice the lighting used]," adds Caldwell. "There will be a time when somebody is going to refer to a classic [film] in terms of the look they want. Persevere. Don't give up. There is going to be a break, a recommendation. If someone comes with a great attitude, even though they may not be the most experienced, the attitude is going to make them fly."

Professional Profile: Russell Caldwell, Gaffer

Although he is a second-generation gaffer, Russell Caldwell did not immediately follow his father into the business. Instead, the New York native studied music at a junior college in Florida, intending to be a jazz guitarist. On the road with a band, he relocated to Los Angeles, where his father was already working, and decided to make a career change. "At the time, it was all about the money for me. I realized I could make more money in film."

Through a friend of his father, Caldwell was hired as a spotlight operator on the series *Don Kirshner's Rock Concert*. It took four or five months to accumulate his 90 days of work, enabling him to join the union. Soon he was being dispatched to jobs at MGM, Paramount, Universal, and Warner Brothers. Early on, he

VOICES OF EXPERIENCE

What do you like least about your job?

"What I like least is the politics. That's a whole other chapter."
—Russell Caldwell

What do you love most about your job?

"What I love most is when we get to have the set. The cameraman and I decide how we want a certain scene to look. We've discussed it, the rigging crew has put the lights in place for us, and now we have a little bit of time to create."—Russell Caldwell

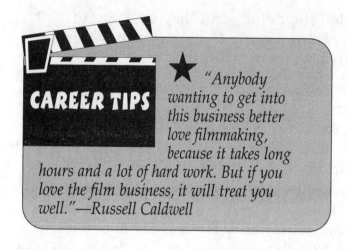

★ *"Anybody wanting to get into this business better love filmmaking, because it takes long hours and a lot of hard work. But if you love the film business, it will treat you well."—Russell Caldwell*

CAREER TIPS

landed electrician work on features *1941* and *The Black Hole*, then the series *B.J. and the Bear*, and the pilot for *Magnum P.I.*

"I met some people that were involved in studio tape; they were doing video shows, so I did some of those." While working on a made-for-television movie, he was promoted to best boy by default when the regular person was out sick.

Caldwell returned to New York in the mid-1980s. While working on *Big*, he connected with brothers John and Jerry DeBlau, which proved to be an important step in his career. At the time, John was working as a gaffer and Jerry as a best boy (later moving up to gaffer as well) on most of the big features coming to New York.

"They were so busy. They would be getting calls to do two or three pictures at a time, so they began splitting the crew; half went with John and the other half with Jerry. When more calls came in, they split up more and that left room for me to work my way up to best boy and gaffer." With the DeBlaus, Caldwell worked on about a dozen films, including *Goodfellas*, *Regarding Henry*, *Glengarry Glen Ross*, *Scent of a Woman*, and *The Cowboy Way*.

"It was on *Regarding Henry* that I moved up to gaffer. Jerry's father was ill, so there was a period of a few weeks where he was spending time with him. I got to work with the famous Italian cameraman Giuseppe Rotunno. He was marvelous to work with, so passionate and artistic. I learned so much during those couple of weeks working with him. I couldn't get that experience any other way than being there."

On the recommendation of John DeBlau, Caldwell was hired to gaff the New York portion of Rob Reiner's film *North*. Shortly afterward, he moved back to Los Angeles. For a time he struggled, working nonunion jobs, until he was able to accumulate enough days to get back into the union. "You have to be scrappy. You have to be on the phone all the time or meeting people. Spend time in rental houses and try to find leads."

Eventually, Caldwell picked up episodic television work—"Which is fantastic training, because you have to move very fast and still maintain a good look,"—and features such as *Eraser*, *Selena*, and *Murder at 1600*. Through a cameraman he met in New York, Caldwell got work on *Erin Brockovich*. "That was one of the best experiences I've had, because of the way Steven Soderbergh operates. He's a class act. Everything is organized and so prepared."

Caldwell's latest projects include *Simone* and *Just Married*. He cites the people he has worked with over the years as the key to his success: "I can't stress this enough: most of the work comes from relationships."

Professional Profile: Dwight Campbell, Gaffer

Dwight Campbell grew up in the suburbs of Detroit and became interested in filmmaking while in high school. "When I made my first film, I realized that writing a paper had very little impact, as opposed to making a film that lived on for years past the paper. It lived on in its own virtual reality forever. Once I realized that making a film was a statement, a process, and a collaborative medium that had life beyond the day, I realized that I wanted to make movies."

Majoring in film at the University of Michigan, Campbell had an opportunity to work on student films. He worked on documentaries and other projects for the National Endowment for the Arts while in college. After graduating in 1978, he spent 18 months working for the oldest daily newspaper in the country, *The Alexandria Gazette*, designing and selling advertising space. "I realized that if I wanted to make movies, I needed to understand the advertising of films and the publications that help promote them."

Leaving the newspaper, he relocated to Los Angeles to enter the producing and camera program at the American Film Institute. Like most film students, he worked on a variety of student films, filling whatever crew post was needed. Upon graduating in June 1981, he was one of the few students to walk out of the program and two or three days later be working on a feature: "*William the Conqueror:* a female-directed, low budget film. I was a general grip or electrician."

Campbell was drawn to lighting early on in his career. "What led me to lighting was wanting to tell a story dramatically; knowing from working with different directors that lighting was the most dramatic way to have an impact on telling the story. You can create a way of elongating the day. You can punctuate a story with lighting. You can change a rainy day into a sunny day; you can make a gloomy day bright. You can make a picture colorful or monochromatic. You can make it a period movie, a contemporary film, or futuristic. You can make it soft, you can make it gentle, or you can make it harsh or crisp. You can make it look so natural that you don't see the moviemaking. It's just a beautiful picture that draws you in."

During his first year out of film school, Campbell struggled to make ends meet. He picked up whatever work he could find, from student films where he gained experience and contacts, but made no money, to commercials. To supplement his income, he also served as the art director of a magazine published by Maureen Reagan. After about a year, he landed grip work on director Gregory Nava's film *El Norte,* affording the opportunity to work near director of photography James Glennon, whose work earned him an Academy Award nomination for cinematography. Campbell went on to work on the Oscar nominated short *Tales of Meeting & Parting*, directed by Lesli Linka Glatter and shot by Jack Wallner. "Then my career just skyrocketed.

"I went off and did *Runaway Train* for Cannon, as a key grip. Director Andrei Konchalavsky was nominated for an Academy Award." By 1985, Campbell had moved up from key grip to regularly working as a gaffer. "I began to get larger and larger films, and then I hooked up with a cameraman by the name of Mikael Salomon and did eight features with him. His career took off and he took me with him. Once you're attached to a prominent cameraman, you're riding on the top of all the waves. Mikael is now a very successful director."

VOICES OF EXPERIENCE

What do you like least about your job?

"What I hate most is being told how to light a scene before they've figured out how they are going to tell the story with the camera, or the dramatic action. They've missed the point of how to make the scene look better and more glamorous. It's about trying to have a seamless image that tells a story that's dramatically appropriate for the scene."—Dwight Campbell

What do you love most about your job?

"What I love most is the flexibility of the job, to be constantly changing and to have creative input in many, many different layers and ways."—Dwight Campbell

Campbell's association with Salomon began on the film *The Man Who Broke 1,000 Chains* and continued through several blockbusters, including *Torch Song Trilogy, Zelly and Me, The Abyss, Always, Arachnophobia, Backdraft, Far and Away*, and *Alien[3]*.

"The best compliment I could ever have is to have someone say, 'I never realized it was a movie I was watching; it looked so realistic.' To give an example of that, I have an uncle who used to be a pilot in World War II. He flew an A-26 plane, which was basically a small bomber. After World War II they made them into firebomb planes to drop fire retardant. That's what we used for Steven Spielberg's film *Always*. When I told my uncle that none of the actors ever left the ground and that all the footage was shot in processed photography, he couldn't believe it. We created the illusion that John Goodman, Richard Dreyfuss, and Holly

Hunter were flying planes, but they were on the stage the whole time. With processed photography, we projected images behind the planes, the actors, and on a screen in front of the plane that reflected into the windscreen of the plane, and created an illusion of reality. When you looked in the plane and saw Richard Dreyfuss or Brad Johnson flying the plane, you saw a reflection on the windscreen that was flipped in reverse."

Initially, Spielberg had doubts about using processed photography to create the illusions needed for the film. He had consulted friend George Lucas and was considering using blue or green screen. But cinematographer Mikael Salomon, with the aid of Campbell's lighting skills, filmed a test for Spielberg and proved they could create a believable effect using the technique.

"The beauty of processed photography is that whatever you shoot is what you get the next day. You see your $10 or $20 million actor doing his performance live with all the elements in a completed piece of film that you can use for your movie, as opposed to a blue or green screen, or other optical, that you have to finish in post. Three or four weeks or a month down the road, you don't have what you need in post and you have a very expensive reshoot. Even though it's expensive up front, it's very cost-effective, saving thousands of dollars in post costs—and you know you have it in the can."

CAREER TIPS

★ "I've always said that if the story is not good, we shouldn't do it. You're only going to get recognized on a project where the script and the acting and the directing works. It could be the most beautiful movie in the world, but if the story does not meet the major demands of a dramatic film, it's just going to be passed; you're not going to get any recognition."
—Dwight Campbell

★ "I would suggest reading The Five C's of Cinematography: Motion Picture Filming Techniques [by Joseph V. Mascelli, Siman-James Press, June 1998] because I think you need to understand filmmaking. The next thing I would suggest is studying all the great painting masters. Learn how they controlled the light within the paintings they've done and try to figure out how you can do as well or better when you make a film. If you walk through a museum, look at the most beautiful paintings on the walls and select one that you'd like to recreate. That's the daily challenge of a gaffer: how do you create on film the look you see in front of you? How do you control that look on film stock? If they can create it in a two-dimensional canvas, then you should be able to create it on a film plate. Anyone can shoot an image for the moment. It's how you sculpt that image with lighting to deliver consistency over a half-day or a full day that matters."—Dwight Campbell

He continued to work steadily throughout the 1990s, serving as a gaffer *on Super Mario Bros., The Three Musketeers, The Shadow, Hard Rain, Girl's Night, Out of Sight, The Adventures of Rocky & Bullwinkle,* on the IMAX 3-D movie *Cirque de Soleil: Journey of Man,* and on the television series *L.A. Doctors.* It was there he met writer/director Gary Fleder, leading to work on the Fleder-directed feature *Imposter.* "He's a very talented director and a very good writer."

Campbell reteamed with cinematographer James Glennon on director Alexander Payne's film *About Schmidt.* "It stars Jack Nicholson. It's very stylized, a great looking film. Alexander is an incredible writer/director/filmmaker with clear visions of what he wants to create. And, it's always fun to work with a cameraman that you've worked with before. Jim [Glennon] includes everyone in the filmmaking process."

He recently finished working on *Haunted Lighthouse* and is gearing up for another picture.

JOB TITLE: RIGGING GAFFER

Job Overview

"The rigging gaffer executes the gaffer's vision," explains gaffer Jay Kemp. "He'll often go on the preliminary scouting and figure out what the needs are, then plan accordingly. He usually has a truck, a best boy, and crew of people that leapfrog with the shooting crew from location to location. It makes sense economically because the shooting crew can come in, all the power is laid out, and the broad strokes are in place. Then the gaffer and cinematographer can come in, finesse the lighting, and be ready to shoot in much quicker time. The lighting takes longer than probably any other part of the lighting process, so it's important to have a lot of it laid in advance."

Special Skills

In addition to filmmaking and lighting skills, gaffers must have strong leadership qualities, enabling them to hire, manage, and motivate their department.

Advice for Someone Seeking This Job

Due to the number of productions shooting outside Los Angeles and New York, Kemp feels it is easier to break into the business in markets outside those industry hubs, such as Virginia. "If a film is coming to your area, and you have a little experience, you stand a pretty good chance of getting on it . . . Kids can come right out of school, or working at a rental house, and hop right onto a major motion picture." Due to escalating costs, the production budget may only allow the gaffer to bring his best boy, and hire the balance of his crew locally.

"As for getting your first opportunity, I think working at a rental house is not a bad idea . . . or working with a rigging crew. It tends to be more manual labor, but you get a good behind-the-scenes view. You learn the equipment and the basics of electricity at a slower, non-production pace. I think it's important that guys rig a few times before they actually get thrown on the set, where the pace is much more frantic.

"There are so many avenues for getting lighting work. If there are commercial houses in your area, try them. Do corporate industrial films, whatever you can find to get your hands on equipment."

Professional Profile: Jay Kemp, Gaffer and Rigging Gaffer

There might have been another lawyer in the world if Jay Kemp had not discovered filmmaking. The Virginia native was entrenched in a liberal arts/pre-law curriculum at James Madison University until opting to spend the first semester of his fourth year abroad. "I went to London and studied art, architecture, theater, and history. It opened my eyes to a lot of different possibilities." Returning to the States, he began looking into other programs at James Madison.

VOICES OF EXPERIENCE

What do you like least about your job?

"What I like least is what the job can do to a family. I've been very fortunate that my family understands what I do. The fact that I'll go for six months of working 70 to 90 hours a weeks, and then go for two months and not work. It can be a real emotional and financial roller coaster. But, at this point, I wouldn't have it any other way. It's kind of a love/hate relationship."
—Jay Kemp

What do you love most about your job?

Kemp enjoys the fact that his job forces him to adapt to new situations, lighting challenges, and diverse personalities. "It's never stagnant."—Jay Kemp

"At the time, they had a quality communications/arts department. One of the directions you could go within that was television and film. I decided to pursue that." Kemp graduated in 1984 with a bachelor's degree in communications/arts, with an emphasis in film and television.

His minor in general social science was the result of all the political science and sociology courses he had taken before changing career paths.

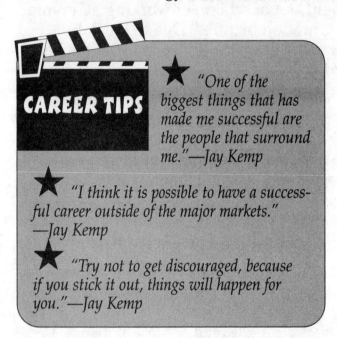

CAREER TIPS

★ *"One of the biggest things that has made me successful are the people that surround me."—Jay Kemp*

★ *"I think it is possible to have a successful career outside of the major markets."—Jay Kemp*

★ *"Try not to get discouraged, because if you stick it out, things will happen for you."—Jay Kemp*

Kemp immediately took a job working in set construction at De Laurentiis Studios in Wilmington, North Carolina, just to get his foot in the industry door. In less than six months he worked on three different films. During that time, he also picked up work on nonunion projects, often in the lighting department. A half-year spent working as a cameraman at a Richmond television station convinced Kemp that this was not a career path he was interested in continuing. Instead he pursued freelance work, serving as a grip, electrician, and dolly grip on commercials and industrials. "Someone recognized I had an aptitude for gripping electric, and that's where I landed."

Just a couple years out of college, Kemp was hired as an electrician/lamp operator on the NBC miniseries Gore Vidal's *Lincoln*. His work on the film impressed gaffer Joey Clayton, who would later hire Kemp for several more television projects.

After being hired in the late 1980s as an electrician on the film *Crazy People*, Kemp focused primarily on electrician work on features, including *True Colors*, *What About Bob?*, *Fried Green Tomatoes*, *Dave*, *Washington Square*, and *The Jackal*. By the early 1990s, he was working regularly as a best boy electrician or rigging gaffer, on films such as *Arlington Road* and *Trading Mom*, followed by *Murder at 1600*, *Hush*, *Cherry Falls*, *Along Came a Spider*, *Hearts in Atlantis*, and *Gods & Generals*. Beginning in the mid-1990s, Kemp was also being hired as a gaffer on features such as *First Kid*, *Blair Witch 2*, *The Contender*, and *Mickey*, and the television series *D.C.*

When not working on feature projects, Kemp studies cameras, lenses, and filtration to hone his skills as a director of photography, with plans to shoot small independent projects.

GRIP DEPARTMENT

JOB TITLE: KEY GRIP

Job Overview

"The cinematographer has a key grip and a gaffer," says key grip Bob Munoz. "Between the two of them, they realize his lighting vision. Grips also take care of moving walls and set construction. If you hit a location and the cameraman wants a light up on the 23rd floor of a building, we figure out how to do that. We also handle all the camera movements."

"The key grip is the head of the grip department," explains key grip Russell Senato. "The grips take their instruction from the director of photography. We mount, rig, and operate all the machines the cameras go on: dollies, jibs, etc. Whether a camera is mounted on a car or a helicopter, the grips usually do the rigging. We also work very closely with the electrician—the gaffer. We rig any lighting that needs to be rigged. We bend, shape, and texture the light with flags. We mainly work with the camera department and the electricians—with the lighting and cameras, but we also support the other departments. Basically, we do anything that needs to be done—if a bridge needs to be built across a stream, and it's doable, we'll put a bridge across the stream."

Special Skills

The strength to lift and carry equipment, carpentry skills, electrical experience, and mechanical aptitude are assets to working as a grip. "You have to know how to use your hands," says Munoz. "Listen and learn. Pay attention. That's the biggest thing I can say: pay attention . . . There are so many people in the business that never get any further, and I think it's because they're just here for a paycheck. They're not really interested in learning the craft."

"Get a book called *The Grip Book* by Michael G. Uva," suggests Russell Senato. "He is a famous full time grip in California. The book shows you all the equipment and gives you the basics."

Advice for Someone Seeking This Job

To be successful as a key grip, Munoz says you must live near Los Angeles or New York, where most of the work originates. "It's hard to pick up a job over the phone. If you really want to do this, go to Hollywood and meet as many people as you can. Go to all the different studios and put your name in. Do whatever it takes."

A job as a production assistant or day player is a good way to get on the set, see what grips do, and make contacts that might lead to a future job. "Call the film commission in your state and tell them your interests," suggests Senato. "They might be able to help you. They know what films are coming into the state and who is looking for interns."

With under two years of experience, Senato says, "I walked up to a key grip doing a scout on a movie. He didn't know me. I saw them moving stuff and started helping them. After a time I told them, 'I'm a grip trying to get on a movie.' He told me to report next Thursday and I was hired."

VOICES OF EXPERIENCE

What do you like least about your job?

"What I like least is driving to work every day—but, if I'm out of town I don't have to drive."—Bob Munoz

What do you love most about your job?

"What I like most is that I don't have to do the same thing every day."—Bob Munoz

Professional Profile: Bob Munoz, Key Grip

"I've got about 29 years in the business," say Bob Munoz, "and gripping is the only thing I've ever done, besides being a stagehand. I just can't imagine doing anything else."

A native of Tucson, Arizona, Munoz's father was a projectionist and a member of IATSE. Through his father's connections, Munoz began working as a stagehand while still in high school. After one semester of college, he realized it wasn't his forte and moved to Los Angeles in 1973 to look for film work.

Munoz found work at Universal Studios, on a crew constructing sets for television series, and remained there for four years. "They had so many TV shows. You went from one stage to another, setting up stuff for the production company to use the next day."

CAREER TIPS

★ When you land a job, listen and learn from those working around you.

Introduced by a friend to key grip Gene Kearney, Munoz got a job on *The Baltimore Bullet* that launched his career in features. He worked as a key grip under Kearney on more than a dozen films during the next decade, including *E.T. the Extra-Terrestrial*, *Twilight Zone: The Movie*, *Ghostbusters*, *The Color Purple*, *Legal Eagles*, and *Alien Nation*.

Munoz had planned to best boy under Kearney on *Die Hard II*. While waiting for production to begin, Kearney flew to Chicago to finish *Flatliners*, and was unavailable when *Die Hard II* got the green light. Munoz interviewed with cinematographer Oliver Wood and got the key grip job instead. He continued to key grip on features such as *Bill & Ted's Bogus Journey*, *Terminal Velocity*, and his personal favorite, *Chaplin*. "It was my favorite because [we] were surrounded with incredibly talented people. The director, Sir Richard Attenborough, is such a class act. Sven Nykvist, the cameraman, is a legend. It was such a relaxed atmosphere."

In the mid-1990s, Munoz reunited with Kearney, who was serving as dolly grip, on *Mr. Holland's Opus*. "That was one of the fun-est times I had on a picture. It was summertime and my whole family came up to Portland, Oregon, where we were shooting on location . . . It was a very pleasant experience because Stephen Herek is a great, great director."

Munoz has continued to key grip on features, adding *2 Days in the Valley*, *Lethal Weapon 4*, *House on Haunted Hill*, and *Collateral Damage* to his credits. "I never had any aspirations to be a key. I loved being a best boy, but I have become fond of being the key grip. After all those years of being the last one to leave—the one to shut the doors on the truck—I kind of like that as the key, when they call it a wrap, I just leave."

Professional Profile: Russell Senato, Key Grip

"I didn't start doing film work until I was 28 or 29," recalls Russell Senato. An upstate New York native, he moved south to Virginia after

VOICES OF EXPERIENCE

What do you like least about your job?

For Senato it's a toss-up: "Either the fact that we sometimes have to work in the most adverse weather conditions [while the crew may have moved indoors to shoot, the grips might have to remain outside in rain or snow to rig the next shot] or playing politics with producers and different departments, instead of just being able to do the job. That's probably my least favorite part: the whole politics thing."—Russell Senato

What do you love most about your job?

"I just love being on the set. I love filmmaking, being part of a project. I really like all the people you meet—that is one of the best things about it. I also enjoy rigging the cameras; it's like being a kid, getting to rig and tinker with equipment. That's probably the most fun thing for me: rigging the cameras."—Russell Senato

high school. There he taught himself to run sound for concerts. "I was a high rigger for years on concert tours, setting up all the outdoor staging." Over time, he purchased equipment piece by piece, building his own sound reinforcement company.

He was introduced to film production when a friend asked him to help out with some commercials he was working on. "I got hooked real quick." Senato went on to work on *Navy Seals* as a day player, assisting the grips and electricians. Working on a big feature with a gigantic crew, he says, "I was not star struck, but work struck. I loved it immediately.

CAREER TIPS

★ Senato says success comes from "downright hard work and perseverance. I talked my way into several jobs because I didn't have the experience. Once I was there, I just busted butt, paid attention, listened, asked questions at the appropriate times, and didn't joke around too much."—Russell Senato

★ "Do what your boss tells you to do. You may have your own ideas, but it doesn't matter. When you get to the point where you're making decisions, then you can use your ideas."—Russell Senato

★ "Try to learn everyone else's craft while trying to learn your own. Pay attention to what is going on, on set. Not just in the grip department, but watch what the set dressers are doing and watch what the electricians are doing and the camera department. You'll see how it all fits together. Get set-savvy. Learn how you should conduct yourself on the set: your attitude, where you should be at the right time (not standing in a doorway or sitting on a set of steps where people are trying to carry equipment up and down). Pay attention and do your job and make sure you're not hindering anyone else from doing their job."—Russell Senato

"After *Navy Seals* I started trying to get on whatever I could. I was persistent. I went and talked to people, even though I was green. They liked my attitude and I promised them I'd be a hard worker." Low budget films followed, some paying only a $50 flat fee for a 16-hour day, but he took the work to gain experience. "I did what I had to do and worked my way up the ladder."

While working in Virginia, Senato connected with some key grips based out of California. An offer of work lured him west when the grips returned home. He gripped and dollied on several movies, always returning to Virginia between projects.

Initially leaning toward becoming an electrician, Senato switch-hit between the lighting and grip departments for a time before discovering that his interests lay more in gripping. Like he had done earlier while working sound, he began purchasing equipment and formed his own company:

Cloud 9 Cranes and Camera Supports. "I own a 40-foot truck—it's a rolling workshop of all kinds of rigging equipment."

Today, Senato's résumé includes work on *Conspiracy Theory, Dave, G.I. Jane, The Jackal, Minority Report,* and *Toy Soldiers.* He has also worked on *The West Wing* since the first season, on location shoots in the Washington, D.C., area.

"I love my job. It can be frustrating sometimes, but I certainly love doing what I'm doing."

●●●●

CHAPTER 8

HAIR, MAKEUP, AND COSTUMES

The proper hairstyle, makeup, and costume help actors to establish their character. This is especially true in a historical setting, where the structure of an authentic period costume may determine how the actor walks, sits, and gestures, and a wig or hairstyle may determine his posture and carriage.

Actors of sufficient rank may request their own hairstylist, makeup artist, or costumer as part of the contract negotiation. On smaller projects, such as a commercial, video, or independent film, the duties of hairstylist and makeup artist are often combined. Epic productions may require teams of stylists and artists to cope with the large number of extras. Positions generally include:

MAKEUP DEPARTMENT

- Key Makeup Artist (Head of the makeup department): design the makeup for each character in each scene and apply or oversee application of makeup on principle actors.

- Makeup Artist: do the actual work of applying makeup to the actors.

- Assistant Makeup Artist: perform lesser tasks, such as applying body makeup.

- Makeup Effects Artist: specializing in the design, fabrication, and application of special makeup effects, such as prosthetics and animatronics.

HAIR DEPARTMENT

- Key Hairstylist (Head of the hair department): determine the hairstyle for each character in each scene and style or oversee hair work for principle actors.

- Hairstylist: do the actual work of coloring and/or styling the actors' hair or wig.

- Assistant Hairstylist: perform lesser tasks, such as shampooing.

COSTUME OR WARDROBE DEPARTMENT

- Costume Designer: determine the costumes for each character in each scene.

- Wardrobe Supervisor: hire wardrobe staff and oversee realization of designer's vision; keep track of costumes on set; supervise the costumers; depending upon size of production, may also perform functions of the set costumer in maintaining continuity.

- Key Costumer: reports to wardrobe supervisor; care and maintenance of lead or principle actors' wardrobe; oversee set costumers.

- Costumer or Set Costumer: maintain and care for costumes on set; help actors dress.

- Wardrobe Production Assistant: an entry-level position; duties vary, from running errands to assisting extras with costumes.

JOB TITLE: MAKEUP ARTIST OR SPECIAL EFFECTS ARTIST

Job Overview

"There are a lot of categories of makeup artists," explains special makeup effects artist Justin Raleigh. "What I do for film and television is everything from beauty makeup to application of prosthetics, and everything in between: being able to make someone look bald, hair work (like beards or other facial hair—a hairstylist does the wigs), injury makeup, and character makeup. A special effects makeup artist actually designs and builds the prosthetics, creates the creatures and any other mechanical type of thing, as well."

Education and Special Skills

"I suggest taking art classes," says Raleigh. "Take illustration and take sculpting classes. Take color theory. Also, go to a makeup school. A lot of makeup artists have gone through cosmetology school. If you're going more into special makeup effects, I suggest chemistry and psychology. Since you're working with actors all the time, you need to understand them."

Advice for Someone Seeking This Job

If you want to be a makeup artist, Raleigh suggests buying books by makeup artists and studying films and television shows, then begin working with whatever products you can get your hands on and learn by trial and error. "I think that is one of the best ways to learn. You're able to think on your feet when you've gone through all the mistakes and come up with the right answer." He suggests that attending one of the many film and television makeup schools is beneficial.

"From the beginning, start building your portfolio. Take photos of everything you do and replace them with better photos as your craft improves. Take student film jobs or whatever, just to build a résumé."

Once you're ready to look for a job, he says, "Start banging on people's doors and constantly cold-calling places. A lot of times you'll send out a résumé and never get an answer, but I feel if you can back it up with a phone call, more times than not you'll get an interview. If you can get the interview, you'll get the job if you have a good personality."

VOICES OF EXPERIENCE

What do you like least about your job?

"Not having a set schedule, and all the hours you put in, in a day."
—Justin Raleigh

What do you love most about your job?

"What I love most is that it is constantly changing; you're never doing the same thing. Even if you've done something similar, it's always different because each person you work on is different."—Justin Raleigh

Professional Profile: Justin Raleigh, Special Effects Makeup Artist

From a very young age, Justin Raleigh knew he wanted to be a special effects makeup artist. In high school, the Louisiana native got a job doing beauty makeup for a portrait studio. "I had never done beauty makeup before— I wanted to do special effects—but that was the one job [where] I could at least get a start doing makeup."

He relocated to Big Bear, California, and along the way briefly considered becoming a doctor specializing in forensic pathology. Seeing a magazine ad for a makeup artist, a friend convinced him to apply. Hired as an apprentice, he moved to Southern California and worked for free for six months, gaining experience and making contacts.

Soon after, Raleigh landed paying jobs on television series *Dawson's Creek*, *The Drew Carry Show*, and *Good Morning America* in 1997 to 1998, followed by a steady stream of features including *Castaway*, *The Hollow Man*, *Nutty Professor 2: The Klumps*, *The Sixth Day*, *Bedazzled*, *Spider-Man*, and *Pearl Harbor*.

CAREER TIPS

★ One of Raleigh's tips for success is to keep pounding on doors and cold-calling. He keeps track of companies and the individuals he has spoken to on his computer, so he can easily remember whom he called when, and what they spoke about.

★ "Try to be nice to everyone. Some people are very standoffish in this industry. I try to be as social as possible. I am also always very prompt."—Justin Raleigh

★ "I studied every aspect of this industry. I know other people's jobs, like lighting techs; it makes you more versatile."—Justin Raleigh

Recommended by a friend, Raleigh was hired at Stan Winston Studio, where he worked on television programs and features like *Jurassic Park III* and *Artificial Intelligence: AI*.

He received a Local 706 "Best Special Makeup Effects" guild award nomination for Jon Voight's Howard Cosell makeup in *Ali*, along with Nick Marra, who designed the makeup and helped Raleigh manufacture the prosthetics, and artist Mark Gabarino, who did the application. Raleigh has also served as a makeup instructor at Joe Blasco Makeup Center West.

JOB TITLE: MAKEUP ARTIST, HAIR AND WARDROBE SYLIST

Job Overview

Makeup artists are responsible for designing and applying the cosmetics and prosthetics worn by on-camera talent. "Makeup is necessary to render true skin tones and bring features forward for correct imaging in the final product (photos, video, live broadcast, movies, etc.)," says media makeup artist, hair and wardrobe stylist, Suzanne Patterson.

Special Skills

"A strong working knowledge of advanced color theory, lighting principles, film stocks, and camera formats," is essential for a makeup artist, according to Patterson. "You also need knowledge in makeup principles as applied to these elements, and that includes skin tones, application techniques, cosmetic chemistry, product knowledge for proper selection, and the right tools to do the job. It is helpful to know about postproduction techniques as well. For students, take classes in school such as art (for color theory and composition), and any video or stage production classes (for camera format and lighting techniques). Oftentimes in high schools or colleges, they offer a stage makeup class, and I strongly recommend that experience. You will have a chance to study facial anatomy and work in three-dimensional makeup, a very important concept and skill to have."

A Typical Workday

On a typical shooting day, Patterson is on the set 20 minutes before call time to set up her materials in the trailer or room designated for the makeup department. "Arriving early gives me a chance to get the kit laid out according to my script breakdown (requirements) and charts I have prepared for that day's shooting schedule (principle actors, secondary characters, etc., and the makeup requirements for each)."

Depending on the number of talent to be made up, Patterson may have a second to assist her. "I think of my seconds as more of co-equals, working with me as a team, not just assistants doing powder puff mechanic work. I pick people who have a high degree of ethics, have the skills to duplicate continuity efficiently, can work quickly and independently without oversight but in line with the key, can think on their feet, and solve problems out of their kits." Patterson works closely with the hair and wardrobe departments to ensure that the talent is ready and on time for their scenes.

Throughout the day, makeup must be maintained to ensure continuity. Polaroid photographs are taken for reference. "If there are any makeup changes or effects scheduled, then we also take care of that. When filming wraps for the day, we take the talent back to the makeup room and remove the makeup and/or effects makeup from their faces, and bring the skin back to prefoundation status. Next, we clean up the room in prep for the next day's shoot. Then back to the hotel (if on location) or home, where I look over the next day's crew schedule, shot sheet, and script requirements and charts."

Advice for Someone Seeking This Job

"Finish high school FIRST! Get that diploma!" says Patterson. "Hopefully, you will have had a chance to dabble in art and stage or video production classes in high school. Take a stage makeup course in college or community arts class. Get grounded in color theory because all elements in production, from makeup, set design, and wardrobe, to camera, film or tape, and lighting, are based on both subtractive and additive color theory, and the lighting is the interactive medium. You must understand gray value scale.

"One can opt to go to a formal makeup-specific school that is oriented to our industry, but above all, practice your art and skill once you acquire it, and keep a brush busy in your hand. Develop diverse skills.

"Check your ego at the door and develop good interpersonal skills and business practices. Eighty percent of success in this business is about public relations, and the rest is talent and skill. Good people skills will get your foot in the door."

Professional Profile: Suzanne Patterson, Media Makeup Artist, Hair & Wardrobe Styling, Creative Artistry & FX

"I always had a very creative photographic eye," says Suzanne Patterson. An accomplished costume designer specializing in period clothing, particularly from the Civil War era, she built several authentic

VOICES OF EXPERIENCE

What do you like least about your job?

"For me, it is definitely the long hours in film production (especially on shoots with 16 to 18 hour days and little turnaround time) and the long shooting schedule (sometimes months at a time away from home). It makes a huge difference in how the crew works together, too. The atmosphere can be like family or the 'shoot from hell!' Video and television is MUCH more sane; rarely do I work more than eight hours, and the location work is studio or regional, so I can go home at night."—Suzanne Patterson

"There will always be politicking, and that usually is a function of egos trying to climb the ladder, or own it. But, it's all in the way you handle that, and for me, I just ignore it all and concentrate on more serious things. One thing is for sure: you are only as good as your next booked job."—Suzanne Patterson

What do you love most about your job?

Patterson loves people and makeup affords her the opportunity to meet and work alongside new and interesting individuals. She also loves that her work is never mundane. "There is such a variety in production. I am skilled to do many things, from straight makeup to fantasy alien effects and all the stuff in between, such as glam, period, character, editorial, fashion, stage, etc. I also do hair and wardrobe, so there is a variety to keep me interested and challenged."—Suzanne Patterson

reproduction gowns for various productions: " . . . authentic right down to the smallest details and textile availabilities in that era." While in college, as a lark, she enrolled in a stage makeup class. Excelling quickly, she was soon assisting the instructor in teaching the course.

"I started thinking seriously about makeup as a career after doing some stage productions, but I didn't want to do just straight makeup stuff—it had to be 'push the envelope' type of work, very color-oriented original stuff. I also wanted to work in the film and TV mediums, so early on in my budding career, I did a LOT of work for free—what is known as apprenticing—to learn the inside art of makeup and hone my skills."

CAREER TIPS

★ *"Do something creative every day in your art and always take photos of your work whenever possible. If you are doing FX work, definitely keep a photo catalog of your work. Take advantage of all kinds of makeup venue opportunities. You will learn something valuable from each experience toward building your career. For example, many years ago, before my career, I took a stage makeup class in college and found that I really had an interest and talent in special makeup effects, which led to some serious training later on in my career for FX work. Working for counter cosmetics companies gave me a wealth of diverse faces and skin tones to work on every day, another valuable experience."—Suzanne Patterson*

Patterson took every opportunity that came her way to hone her makeup skills, including work on UCLA and USC student films and deferred pay jobs. "Back in the days before the studio system died out and freelancing took over, apprenticing was a time honored way to learn the craft. I was fortunate to be mentored by some really great makeup artists, such as the Westmores, and Emmy Award [winning] artists like David Dittmar.

"I began to get paid assist jobs and then worked my way to keying independent films and getting onto TV shows and other features. I would have to say that I have had the blessings to work on a wide variety of productions through the years, and that has given me a wealth of knowledge and experience. All, combined, have led to my success as a national makeup artist, respected teacher, and author. I particularly enjoy giving back to my craft, by training and educating the next generation of artists."

Patterson has worked with and designed makeup for some of Hollywood's biggest stars, such as Tim Allen, Melanie Griffith, Jennifer Love Hewitt, Don Johnson, Queen Latifah, Charlie Sheen, Arnold Schwartzenegger, and Jonathan Taylor Thomas, working on productions such as the *Daytime Emmy Awards*, *ABC Monday Night Football*, the *Home*

Improvement television series, and commercials for Coca Cola, Lockheed-Martin Aerospace, and United Parcel Service.

Believing that her talent is a blessing from God, Patterson says she tries to give back by doing "paramedical makeup work for accident victims, cancer patients, burn victims, etc. I also teach workshops and seminars for aspiring makeup artists, and master classes to seasoned artists."

JOB TITLE: COSTUME DESIGNER

Job Overview

After careful study of the script, discussions with the director to understand his vision for the production, and meetings with the production designer, hair, makeup, and art departments, and actors, the costume designer decides on all of the clothing worn by the actors in the production. "All characters reveal things about themselves in the way they dress," explains costume designer Diana Eden. "The primary duty of the costume designer is to tell the story of the script and help the audience understand who the characters are."

Depending on the size and scope of the production, the costume designer may sketch out original designs (or use a sketch artist to render them) and select the fabrics to have them constructed from. Alternately, the designer may rent costumes from a costume shop, or purchase ready-to-wear clothing and have it altered.

"Some days I have fittings with actors, where they're trying on clothes to discover what works for the character, and then I have a production meeting with all the heads of the departments to discuss the production requirements. Then I may go on set to make sure everything is running smoothly, go out shopping, or stop by the workroom where they're making some of the costumes, talk with the pattern makers and tailors, and see my designs coming to life. It's incredibly varied, incredibly peopled, and there is never a dull moment."

Special Skills

In addition to costume design skills, designers must know how to work within a budget, possess basic computer skills, be organized, and have the ability to hire and manage a staff, as well as to work with a variety of personalities. "The actors need to trust you," says Eden.

"You have to earn that trust. You have to be able to coordinate a lot of things. I have a crew of three to eight people, on a feature film it's even larger, and I have to make sure all of those personalities get along well and know their jobs."

Advice for Someone Seeking This Job

Look for work as a production assistant with the wardrobe department, or as a day player, hired to assist on days when there are many extras, so you can meet people and gain some basic experience being on set. Networking is the key to landing a job as a costume designer. Join an organization where you can meet theater people, or volunteer to work for a designer on a stage production where you will have an opportunity to meet people and learn from a working designer.

"I occasionally do theater," says Eden. "I tell people, 'If I'm doing a theater project and you want to come and work with me for free, I'll be happy to teach you what I know.' A lot of designers are very kind. They have been helped by other people, and if they have the time and situation to help someone, many of them will."

VOICES OF EXPERIENCE

What do you like least about your job?

"The thing I like least about the job is the fact that there is no financial security. Even after doing it for a number of years and being well known in the community, when a show gets cancelled or a film ends, you still have to look for the next job. It's quite terrifying. That never seems to go away."—Diana Eden

What do you love most about your job?

"What I love is the interaction with so many people. It's a very collaborative job. From the moment you get hired and read the script, you're meeting with people and working in an interconnected way to realize a common goal. I love working with actors. I love the fact that I get up in the morning and go to the studio."—Diana Eden

Professional Profile: Diana Eden, Costume Designer

Born in England, Diana Eden's family moved to Toronto when she was 10. She knew at the age of five that she wanted to be a dancer, and by 15 had earned a slot with the National Ballet of Canada. When she grew too tall to be a ballerina, she moved to New York and became a dancer and actress on Broadway. "There was never any question that I wanted to be involved in the performing arts."

What began as a hobby soon led to designing and sewing clothes for fellow Broadway dancers. "It never occurred to me that I would be designing costumes, but I obviously loved clothes." Looking to expand her acting career into film and television, Eden relocated to Los Angeles in 1969, and supported herself between acting jobs by designing clothing.

Her first costuming break was a combination of luck and years of honing her sewing and design skills, along with experience as a dancer. Eden was asked by an acquaintance to coordinate the dancers' wardrobe for Ann Margaret's nightclub act. "I was hesitant, because I'd never done that. The person rightfully said, 'Well, you've been a dancer, you've worked with clothes, and you're organized. Of course you can do it.' So I accepted the job and took to it immediately."

Through Ann Margaret, she was introduced to Bob Mackie. Recognizing Eden's talents, Mackie offered her a position at Elizabeth Courtney

CAREER TIPS

★ *"Because of the nature of the work, if you're a negative person who finds the hours too long, the actors too difficult, and the situations too confusing, you won't be able to do good work. You have to really love the work and the challenge."—Diana Eden*

★ *"Want it badly enough that you're willing to hang in there. Want it badly enough to really work at it. It's hard when you're young, because you want it right away, but realize that every step along the way is exciting. Even the process of getting from point A to point B is exciting. Realize that at each step there are things to be learned and things to be enjoyed."—Diana Eden*

Costumes, working as his assistant. At night she took extension courses to improve her skills and knowledge of costume design and filmmaking, but working alongside Mackie was where she really learned the business. "His work ethic, his perfectionism, his attention to detail, and the people he surrounded himself with—there was no better education."

During the five years Eden worked for Mackie, she assisted him on the Las Vegas show *Jubilee* and on the Academy Awards show. "I did just about everything, other than designing. I made sure everything from his sketch was realized on time, and to some degree, on budget. I assisted other people in the organization as well, like Pete Meneffee. Then I realized it was time to become a designer in my own right."

While working at Elizabeth Courtney, Eden worked on outside projects, such as equity waiver theater productions, often for free, to make contacts and gain design credits. "I would do a very, very tiny production and that would lead to a slightly bigger production. Every time I got a good review, I would send out a flyer to everyone I knew. I even took out ads in the trade papers quoting the reviews, just to get my name out there. Eventually it worked."

In 1985, Eden was referred to a producer of *The Facts of Life*. Then in its seventh season, the show's producers were looking for a new designer, and Eden landed the job. "After I interviewed, I learned later that they presented my name to director John Bowab. He had just seen the play *Tamara*, which I had done the costumes for. They used clothing from John Franco Ferre, but I put it all together. John said he noticed that the Commandant was wearing argyle socks, and that he thought it was a brilliant detail." Eden stayed with the show for three seasons.

When *The Facts of Life* ended, she went on to work on other sitcoms and movies of the week, then on to the series *Santa Barbara*.

"One of my favorite jobs, although it was short lived, was the television series *A League of Their Own*. Penny Marshall was producing and directing, and we also had Tom Hanks directing an episode. I loved doing the period clothes. You don't get to do a lot of period clothes in television." Eden's design work on the series earned her an Emmy nomination in 1993.

More pilots, series, and television movies followed. Then she landed the series *Family Law*. "I love to dress people beautifully. I had wonderful, wonderful actors: Kathleen Quinlan, Dixie Carter, and Tony Danza. They're just so professional, so real, and so much fun."

Between jobs, Eden has managed to co-author *RetroChic!*, a guide to vintage clothing stores, and is working on a book titled *How to Break into a Career in Costume Design for Film and Television*.

JOB TITLE: SET COSTUMER OR COSTUMER

Job Overview

Set costumers set up the actors' trailers with appropriate costumes, sometimes serving as a dresser, and take photographs and notes on set during filming to maintain continuity. For example, whether a coat is worn or carried, the placement of a collar, or how a necktie is tied are all part of continuity.

"The set costumers are also in charge of the actors' comfort," says costumer Katrina Migliore. "If you're shooting a scene outside and it's 30 degrees, but it's supposed to be summer, you have to run in between every take and give the actor a coat to wear to keep them warm. The set costumer is in charge of keeping track of handbags and other items that the actor might not want to wear or carry all the time."

Special Skills

Basic sewing abilities are an asset, combined with knowledge of period clothing and styles; also needed are organizational and people skills. "Physical stamina and costuming experience" are necessary skills, advises Kathie L. Pierson. "I personally know how to sew well and have twenty years experience in theater costuming."

Advice for Someone Seeking This Job

Call your local film commission to discover productions coming to your area. Let the film office know you are interested in working as a day player or on low budget productions to gain some experience. A job as a production assistant is another way to make initial contacts. Let those people know you want to work in wardrobe. "When they come across a situation that they're not interested in, they'll pass your name along," says Migliore. "That is how you get your first breaks."

"Go to Fashion Institute of Technology or a similar school for education. Work as a PA in a wardrobe department—get your opportunities from the people you work for. Meet the designers and wardrobe supervisors. They'll help you lots!"

Professional Profile: Katrina Migliore, Costumer

"I've always loved movies," says Katrina Migliore. An art major in graphic design at James Madison University in Harrisonburg, Virginia, she considered architecture and advertising as future careers. "I had freedom in my major to dabble in a bunch of different fields of art. I took photography, I took painting, and I took ceramics." But it was a weaving class that started her on the path to being a costumer.

When Migliore wanted to learn to sew so that she could make something from the fabric she was weaving, a friend suggested she work in the University's costume shop for five or ten hours a week and they would teach her how to sew. "The woman who ran the costume shop became my

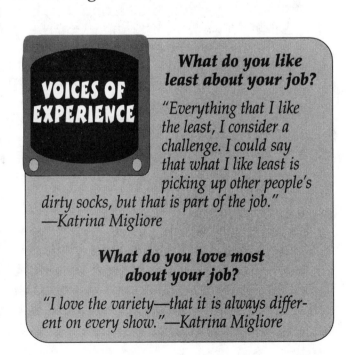

VOICES OF EXPERIENCE

What do you like least about your job?

"Everything that I like the least, I consider a challenge. I could say that what I like least is picking up other people's dirty socks, but that is part of the job." —Katrina Migliore

What do you love most about your job?

"I love the variety—that it is always different on every show." —Katrina Migliore

mentor. When a theater production needed a dresser, she would suggest me. I was always watching her design costumes and sets." In time, Migliore assisted in designing a show and eventually designed costumes for a friend's play. During the summer, she worked for a dinner theater, gaining additional experience.

After graduation, she served a summer apprenticeship in the Santa Fe Opera costume shop. "It was very good training in the right way to sew. It's a very hard-working, strict costume shop. You do it the right way and if it's not right, you do it over until you get it right. They are known for really beautifully made costumes."

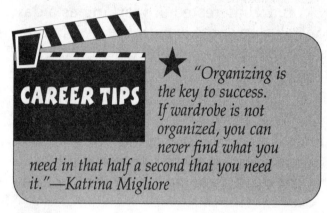

CAREER TIPS ★ *"Organizing is the key to success. If wardrobe is not organized, you can never find what you need in that half a second that you need it."—Katrina Migliore*

Her apprenticeship completed, Migliore remained in New Mexico another year, working for different boutique clothing and accessory designers. Through an employer, she heard of a feature coming to shoot in the area and faxed off a résumé. Late one night she got a call to be on set at 5:30 the following morning to work as a day player on *Speechless*. With another woman, she was sent into a field of 300 extras with Polaroid photographs to maintain continuity. "We had to go around and make sure the extras had the same thing on. It was one of those days where it was cold in the morning and got warm in the afternoon, but if they had their coat on when shooting started, they had to keep it on all day. When they came back the second day, it was a continuation of the scene." Fascinated, Migliore knew she wanted to be part of filmmaking.

She moved to Los Angeles for a short time before returning to Virginia, where she discovered many opportunities to work in film on the East Coast. Through a friend she had met while working on an outdoor drama during college, she landed a job on the television series *Ghost Stories*. "It was grueling and I was working for a lot less than I normally accepted, but the appealing part was that the show was going to turn union and everyone working on it would get into the union free. You'd still have to pay your dues, but you wouldn't have to pay the initiation fee. That is how I got in the union."

From *Ghost Stories*, Migliore went directly to working as a set costumer on the television series *Legacy*. Her next big break was on the miniseries *Sally Hemmings: An American Scandal*, followed by features *Cherry Falls*, *The Patriot*, *Domestic Disturbance*, and *A Walk to Remember*. Proving the importance of maintaining relationships, the supervisor who hired

Migliore for *The Patriot* was the same supervisor she had worked with six years earlier on her first film, *Speechless*.

Although work has not proved to be as consistent as it might have been on the West Coast, Migliore has nonetheless established her name as a costumer with impressive credits. During leaner times, she worked various part-time jobs and formed Glamour Cats to sell purses she designs and creates. She is currently pursuing options to again relocate to Los Angeles.

Professional Profile: Kathie L. Pierson, Costumer, Set Costumer, or Tailor

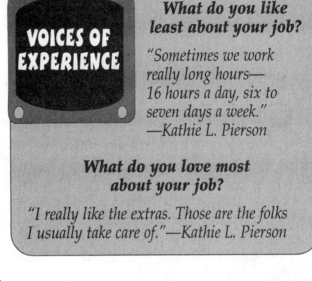

What do you like least about your job?

"Sometimes we work really long hours— 16 hours a day, six to seven days a week."
—Kathie L. Pierson

What do you love most about your job?

"I really like the extras. Those are the folks I usually take care of."—Kathie L. Pierson

"Seeing [my] name in the credits. I love that," says costumer Kathie L. Pierson, who grew up in Delaware. A skilled seamstress, she began working in costuming when she was 20 to earn money for college. Her first costume job was in theater, working at The Grand Opera House in Wilmington, North Carolina. She later graduated with a bachelor's degree in fine arts from the University of Delaware, with distinction in ceramics.

Her entrance into filmmaking came as a result of membership in the IATSE (International Alliance of Theatrical Stage Employees) union through her theater work, which is the same union for film costumers. Pierson's union card enabled her to land work on the movie *Beloved* when the production came to North Carolina. There she met and worked for Cha Blevins, "who is the best wardrobe supervisor from California." Blevins later hired Pierson to work on *The Time Machine*.

Following *Beloved*, Pierson was hired as an assistant costumer for *The Sixth Sense* when it shot in Philadelphia, and as a costumer for *Numbers* when it shot in Harrisburg, Pennsylvania. When not working on a film, Pierson can be found working at the same theater where she originally started out: The Grand Opera House.

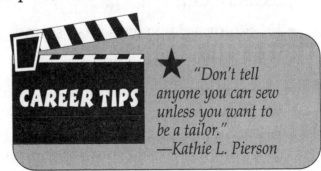

★ *"Don't tell anyone you can sew unless you want to be a tailor."*
—Kathie L. Pierson

●●●●

CHAPTER
9

SOUND AND MUSIC

Sound, in the form of dialogue, background noise, or effects, provides an important means of communicating ideas. Music helps set the tone of a scene and emphasizes the emotions portrayed by the actors. Together, sound and music give dimension to a visual image that would otherwise be mere pantomime.

Those involved in the creation, recording, and mixing of sound and music include:

- Production Sound Mixer: coordinate and monitor the recording of dialogue and ambient sound during filming.

- Boom Operator: handle the overhead boom microphone and concealed wireless microphones.

- Cabler, Cable Man, or Third Man: run cable to the mikes and place body mikes on actors.

- Production Soundman: record onset sound.

- Dialogue Editor: edit the sound recorded during filming.

- Automated Dialogue Replacement (ADR) Supervisor: record lines of dialogue that will be dubbed in (substituted) for unusable passages recorded during filming.

- FX Editor: add or embellish sounds other than dialogue or music.

- Foley Artist: create appropriate sounds for the FX Editor.

- Music Editor: create a temporary score; help sync the final score to the film.

- Playback Operator: play prerecorded music during the filming of a scene.

- Rerecording Mixer: assist the sound editors to adjust recorded sound quality.
- Supervising Rerecording Mixer: combine the dialogue, music, effects, and overdub tracks, and sync them to the film.

Positions involved in creating, selecting, and licensing music for the film or television program's score, sound track, and trailer include:

- Composer and Songwriter: create original music to introduce and underscore the story line.
- President, Senior Vice President, or Vice President of Music: secure music for film, television, and sound track use.
- Music Supervisor: find and license music for film, television, and sound track use.
- Business Affairs or Music Clearance and Licensing: obtain music licenses.

CREATION, RECORDING, AND MIXING OF SOUND AND MUSIC

JOB TITLE: PRODUCTION SOUND MIXER

Job Overview

The production sound mixer is the head of the on set sound department and is responsible for recording the actors' dialogue during the filming of the production.

After reading the script, mixer Tim Cooney determines what microphones and equipment will be needed. During filming, he records room tone and sound ambiance, directs the boom operator, and adjusts sound levels. Later, any unclear dialogue will be rerecorded by the ADR supervisor and replaced. The dialogue track will then have music and effects added to complete the production sound track.

Special Skills

"To work in sound you have to know electronics, simply because you're going to be fixing cables and electronic equipment," says Cooney.

"If you're on location in the Philippines and the machine doesn't work, what are you going to do? I've spent time fixing equipment in the hotel so that I could have it ready for the next day. You've got to have those skills. You have to have a certain amount of people skills and salesmanship—any kind of salesmanship helps, because the hardest part of the job is getting it. The second hardest part is keeping it."

Advice for Someone Seeking This Job

Before embarking on a career in film production, Cooney advises having a year's worth of savings to live on. "Whatever you're doing to pay your bills, save every bloody nickel. You need to have a year's worth of money in the bank all the time, because if you're stressed out about money, you're not going to be focused on what you need to do."

He further advises that anyone desiring to be a production sound mixer should start out working for free. Read the trades to discover what films are in production. Contact the production office and ask if a sound mixer has been hired and who they are. Then contact the union to obtain the person's telephone number and call them to ask if you could work as their PA for free. "In my case, I've had a couple of people say, 'I'm trying to get into sound. I went to college and need some experience.' Or, 'I've always been interested in sound, I don't have the money to go to college, but I want to learn. Can I come and work for free?' I always say, 'Yes, absolutely, come on down.' If somebody is willing to work for free, I'm willing to give them a chance."

Once you've worked a couple of weeks for free for one sound mixer, Cooney advises repeating the process of working free for another sound mixer one or two more times. Go back to the trades and look for nonunion pictures and contact the sound mixer and offer to serve as an assistant to build up some credits. "That's how you get your first paying job. You have to do a few nonpaying jobs first in order to get some kind of credit, some validity. Eventually somebody is going to give you a break. Once you get enough hours, you can join the union."

Professional Profile: Tim Cooney, CAS, Production Sound Mixer

A former rock musician, clown, and elephant trainer, Tim Cooney's journey into the film business is strange and almost unbelievable. From a young age he loved going to the movies. "If I had a spare dime I would put it together with some more dimes until I had enough to go to the movies. When I was a kid, back in the '60s, it cost 50 cents to go to a movie."

An emancipated minor at the age of 15, Cooney soon left home to pursue a career as a musician. He lived with various musicians while putting himself through high school and after graduation, moved from his hometown of Van Nuys, California, to Charleston, West Virginia. There he played in a group that performed music and comedy on a TV program every weekday morning from 7:00 to 8:00. When the group lost its contract and broke up, Cooney found himself flat broke and alone. "I spent Christmas at the Midnight Mission. I said, 'You know, this whole drinking and drug thing just ain't working out.' I was 19 years old. That's when I gave up the drugs. It took me three years more before I gave up the booze."

With nowhere to go, Cooney reconnected with a high school friend who was performing as a clown with Ringling Bros. and Barnum & Bailey Circus. The friend got him a clown job and Cooney got out of Charleston. Circus management liked him so much that they sent him to Ringling Brothers' Clown College. He traveled for another year with the circus following graduation, during which time he began learning to train elephants, "because I really hated being a clown."

VOICES OF EXPERIENCE

What do you like least about your job?

"What I really hate is trying to get the job. It's the worst part of the business. Regardless of what you do in the film business, that would be most people's reaction. It's the hustle I hate, because there is nothing artistic about it and there is nothing technical about it; it's constantly selling yourself."—Tim Cooney

What do you love most about your job?

"What I love most is the actual filmmaking, the actual job itself."—Tim Cooney

Deciding it was time to get off the road, Cooney took a job as an elephant trainer at the St. Louis Zoo, where he remained for three years. On a summer vacation, he returned to California to look up some old friends who were in the animal business. He discovered upon arrival that the business had been sold to actress Tippi Hedren, but went to see the elephants anyway and learned they were in need of a trainer. After verifying that he was indeed an elephant trainer, Cooney was offered twice his zoo salary to train elephants for the movie *Roar*, starring Hedren and Melanie Griffith. It was his first film.

The elephants did not work every day, so Cooney filled the down time by hanging out with the picture's sound mixer. "Having been in music, I knew how to engineer records. I've always been kind of an electronically technical guy. The sound mixer liked me and took me under his wing. He taught me about mixing sound and taught me to be a boom man." When the movie wrapped, Cooney took work on a couple of nonunion movies as a boom man, eventually logging enough hours and experience to get in the union.

His next big break came when he was hired under contract as a boom man at Universal Studios. There he worked year round and was assigned projects by the studio, including feature film *E.T., the Extra-Terrestrial* and television series *Quincy, The Incredible Hulk, Buck Rogers in the 25th Century, Night Rider,* and *Battlestar Galactica.*

CAREER TIPS

★ *"The best advice I could give anyone is one sentence: Do something to further your career every single day. Period. I don't care if you're sick in bed. You get the trades, read them, and redo your résumé so that you can send that out. Do something every single day. Even on Christmas—go to parties where there are people in the business so you can hear about what shows are in production. Find out if they have hired a person for the category you work in. If you do something every day, you will succeed; and if you don't, you won't. I've been working for 26 years, and after 26 years and nine [film award] nominations, it still doesn't even get me the interview. That's the reality of the business."—Tim Cooney*

★ *"It's a people business. I don't care if it's sound, if it's acting, or if it's producing. You have got to know people; you have to make contacts and remember their names and where you worked with them."—Tim Cooney*

Cooney served as a boom man for four or five years before moving up to mixing. The first feature he mixed was *Blue Thunder*, a helicopter film starring Roy Scheider. Afterward, he alternated between boom jobs and mixing, steadily building his reputation until landing the job of mixing the first four seasons of *Murder, She Wrote*, which finally established him as a sound mixer.

"I've been very, very fortunate. I have nine nominations for sound," including three Golden Reels, one of which he won in 2000 for *Noriega: God's Favorite*, three Emmys, two CAS awards, and an Academy Award nomination for *Cliffhanger*.

Filmed in the mountains of Cortina, Italy, "*Cliffhanger* was an unbelievably difficult show—logistically it was a nightmare—but it still remains the most beautiful place I've ever seen. The mountains were just unbelievable. We were there three months. As I was getting in the car to go to Rome, to continue shooting in that location, I kept thinking, 'This place is magnificent. Inspiring.' Receiving the Oscar nomination was like the cherry on the pie."

Cooney continued to work on blockbuster features, including: *Conspiracy Theory, Demolition Man, Die Hard 2, Ford Fairlane, Lethal Weapon 4, Marrying Man, Mighty Ducks 3,* and *We Were Soldiers.*

Many believe Cooney's work on *We Were Soldiers* will win him a second Oscar nomination. "They used 80% of my production track, which is unheard of in a war picture. You're lucky to get 40% as a rule." *We Were Soldiers* was only the second film for director Randall Wallace. "He was such a gentleman. I must say he is probably the best director I have ever worked with. Ever. He was so sound conscious."

The film Cooney is most proud of is the Academy Award winning documentary *The Last Days*, a stirring film detailing the return of Holocaust survivors to Auschwitz. He currently has offers for three features in the upcoming months and is trying to decide which picture to accept. "You either have nothing or you have three projects and you have to turn two down. That's just the way it is in this business."

JOB TITLE: BOOM OPERATOR

Job Overview

The boom operator is responsible for capturing the actors' dialogue by use of the boom microphone or concealed wireless microphones.

Special Skills

Boom operating is a physically demanding job, requiring that the person fulfilling the job be in good physical shape. Boom operators must be strong enough to carry heavy equipment, yet agile enough to slip between lights and other apparatus without knocking them over or casting shadows. They must also be alert, able to memorize dialogue quickly, and possess the ability to get along with a variety of personalities. Being able to maintain a calm temperament under pressure is an asset. Boomer operator Kevin Sorrenson says his early interest in photography was also helpful in understanding lenses and composition.

Cable person/boom operator Bill Shotland improved his boom skills by practicing whenever he could. "In my house, I would take the fishing pole and practice moving through doorways and around chandeliers. On set, when we broke for lunch, I would jump up on the fisher boom and practice doing figure eights, or have people walk while cuing them."

Advice for Someone Seeking This Job

Look for nonunion, low budget productions where you can work for free to gain experience using the equipment. Make connections on those projects with people who may use you again. Volunteer to work for a boom operator for free, so that you can get on set and observe what they do. When the crew breaks for lunch, ask if you can practice with the boom, maneuvering it around the set. "In this business you're always looking for a job," says Sorrenson. "You don't just get a job and you're set; you get the job for as long as the film lasts and when it's over, you're out of work, looking for a job."

Professional Profile: Kevin Sorrenson, Boom Operator

Although his father was a sound recordist for film and television, Kevin Sorrenson did not initially consider following his father into the business. Not knowing what career he wanted to pursue, he studied psychology and mathematics at a junior college for a year and a half, until his father suggested he give audio a try.

"He always made it sound interesting. I didn't have any idea what it was going to entail until I went on a couple of sets and he showed me. You start as a cable man; you're sort of the helper or gofer. I used to watch the walkie-talkies, push the cart around, and run microphone cables."

VOICES OF EXPERIENCE

What do you like least about your job?

"The hours are probably the worst part of my job. On Friday night, we usually work late; sometimes we'll work for 14 or 15 hours. Sometimes you'll come home watching the sun come up; you're drowsy and it's a tough drive. Working conditions can be tough: working in the heat or the real cold and at night when you're exhausted." —Kevin Sorrenson

What do you love most about your job?

"What I like is that you're right up there with the actors, the director, and the camera in the heat of things." —Kevin Sorrenson

Sorrensen quit college at age 19 to pursue the career. One of his first jobs was on producer Aaron Spelling's series *The San Pedro Beach Bums*. The show lasted just long enough for Sorrenson to work the 30 consecutive days necessary to meet the eligibility requirements for joining the union. With just a year's work under his belt, he landed his first movie, *The Driver*. "It was a lot of night shooting in downtown Los Angeles. They used a lot of walkie-talkies and I came down and wrangled them."

He went on to work as a third man (a.k.a. cable man) on the television series *Lou Grant*, where sound mixer Dean Vernon became a mentor, teaching Sorrenson to boom. "He was real insistent that I learn to operate a fisher boom and learn how to do booming and cue."

Little House on the Prairie followed. Sorrensen again served as third man on the sound crew, and again found a mentor, this time in sound-man Frank Meadow. "He let me practice booming, trying shots, and eventually working with the actors." After *Little House*, Sorrensen worked on a variety of projects, steadily making the transition from third man to boom man.

CAREER TIPS

"*Keep your sense of humor or you won't survive.*"
—Kevin Sorrenson

"Your rookie year as a boom operator is really tough, because it's when you make all your mistakes. You dip the microphone into the picture because you don't quite understand framing yet, how a camera operator is going to compose the picture. You have to start learning lens sizes. For instance, 14mm lenses are very wide, so you can't get very close to the actor. You have to learn telephoto lenses; things you can't really learn out of a book. You just learn by observing, getting in trouble, and getting yelled at."

With a couple years' experience working as a boom operator behind him, Sorrensen landed work on the series *Murder, She Wrote*. "I had met the mixer [Tim Cooney] when I was still a third man and he was a boom man. He moved up to sound mixing, remembered me, and thought we could work well together. You tend to work really close with people on the sound crew, so you want to be able to get along with them and be on the same wavelength."

After completing three seasons of *Murder, She Wrote*, Sorrensen left the business for nine years, during which time he worked in construction and manufacturing. Finally realizing that wages and benefits were better working sound, he paid a fee to the union and was admitted back in good standing.

Almost immediately, he landed day work on the series *Party of Five* and worked a couple of nonunion movies in between. Then he started getting calls to work on *Ally McBeal* and *X-Files*, filling in for regulars on their days off.

Sorrensen reunited with sound mixer Tim Cooney, who had given him his first boom job on *Murder, She Wrote*, to work on *We Were Soldiers*, followed by *Joy Ride* and *The Salton Sea*, and television pilots for *Birds of Prey* and *The Lone Ranger*.

JOB TITLE: CABLE MAN, CABLER, SOUND UTILITY

Job Overview

Generally an entry-level position in the sound department (unless there is an apprentice or production assistant working with the crew), the cable man sets up the sound equipment, runs the cable from the microphone to the sound recording equipment, and assists in placing radio mikes on actors when needed. Experienced cablers also operate a second boom when needed or fill in for the boom operator if he needs to leave the set. Cablers assist with maintaining the sound equipment, and may be assigned to handle departmental paperwork.

Special Skills

In addition to having an understanding of the filmmaking process and knowledge of sound equipment, a cable person must be alert and attentive without being intrusive. They should take every opportunity to develop boom operator skills so they can handle a second boom or fill in for the operator when needed.

Advice for Someone Seeking This Job

Working for a sound equipment rental house is a good way to learn about the gear and meet sound mixers and their crew. Once you have some basic understanding of the job, contact working sound mixers and offer to work for free as an apprentice to gain some on set experience and learn more about the job.

Professional Profile: Bill Shotland, Boom Operator and Cable Person

After a year of studying sociology at Palomar College, Bill Shotland's goal was simply to find some type of work that generated enough cash to allow him to ski. Just as disco was about to become a national obsession, he came up with the idea to start a company that would supply live sound reinforcement, lighting, and DJs to nightclubs in the Southern California area. He wrote up a business plan and asked his father to co-sign a bank loan for him to acquire the equipment. Within three months, he had repaid the loan and established a successful business.

A few years later, Shotland was ready for a new challenge. A childhood friend and his father, who owned a transportation company that supplied production companies, suggested that Shotland parlay his sound experience into a career in sound for film and television. They recommended he contact Charlie Knight, owner of a film transfer business and equipment rental house.

"Every morning at 8:00 I knocked on his door and he would say, 'Go away! Go away!'" One day, Knight finally asked what Shotland wanted and he responded, "I want to work as an apprentice and learn to run all this equipment. I don't want to be paid. When I start doing whatever it is that you do here, and I'm able to work on my own, then we can talk about pay." Knight agreed to the proposal and Shotland started the following Monday. A few days into his training, he mastered the transfer gear and was put on the payroll.

In addition to doing transfers, Shotland began prepping and fixing the gear that was rented to sound mixers. During the actors' strike, when gear was not being used, he came up with the idea of renting the company's walkie-talkies to the PGA tour, music concerts, and other live event promoters, earning him a percentage of the profits. He also supplemented his income by renting out equipment left over from his sound reinforcement days, for use in on set music playback.

VOICES OF EXPERIENCE

What do you like least about your job?

"What I like least about my job are the super-long hours. I just want to work 12 hours and go home. Twelve hours is enough for any person. I can't even express how beaten up the body feels when you get into 16- and 18-hour days, day after day after day."—Bill Shotland

What do you love most about your job?

"What I love most about my job is that I do not go to an office. I'm in a different location every day, so I get to see different things."—Bill Shotland

Ready for another challenge and wanting to get out of the office, Shotland started looking for a new job. Through a soundman he had met at the rental company, he received an offer to work as a cable man and second boom operator on *Highway to Heaven*. Committing to work on the show for a season, Shotland stayed until the series ended several years later. "They called it Michael Landon's day care center, because he wanted people to see their families." Instead of a 60-hour work week, Landon usually let the crew go after 40.

"After Michael passed on, I was talking to friends and they asked, 'What are you going to do now?' I said, 'I'll just get another job.' And they said, 'Bill, you have no idea what it's like out here. The business has really changed in the past nine years.' . . . Twelve-hour days had turned into 16-hour days"

Major surgery in the early 1990s kept Shotland from working for nearly two years. He used the time to earn a degree in music and sound engineering, and in 1992 was able to put his name back on the availability roster at the union. That same afternoon, he received a call from Tim Cooney, offering him work on *Die Hard II*. He later learned that Cooney had gotten his name from production sound mixer Darin Knight, son of Charlie Knight, the man whose door Shotland had first knocked on to get into the business.

> **CAREER TIPS** ★ *"If you can dream it up, do it. Go after it. Nothing is too large or too small. Write down your plan and put it into action. Other people won't make it happen for you."—Bill Shotland*

He went on to work on several more features with Cooney, including *Demolition Man, Lethal Weapon 4, The Last Days,* and *Deep Blue Sea.* He turned down Cooney's offer to work with him on *We Were Soldiers*, having recently undergone four months of physical therapy for his knees. "I didn't think running through the brush would be good . . . " Instead, he stayed in Los Angeles to work on *National Security* and the series *Once and Again.* He subsequently reunited with Cooney to work on the feature *The Sultan of the Sea.*

JOB TITLE: SOUNDMAN, PRODUCTION SOUNDMAN, OR SOUND TECHNICIAN

Job Overview

A production soundman records on set sound.

Advice for Someone Seeking This Job

"Don't get caught up in money," says soundman Detdrick McClure. Many refuse the opportunity to work, gain experience, and make contacts, because they will not accept low or no paying jobs. When you're starting out, "It's not about the money; it's about who you are going to be brushing elbows with. You have to be willing to sacrifice. There were times when I couldn't afford to go home to see my folks or friends and family because I chose to be here. You have to stick with it and be willing to suck it up.

"Take anything. I did things for free because the name of the game is meeting people. Work hard and let people see your work ethic, busting your butt. Then they'll call you and say, 'Hey, man, you worked really hard for nothing. I got a show next week and I need a PA'—and you're hired. Do whatever you can to just get in and meet people."

Professional Profile: Detdrick McClure, Soundman (Writer/Director)

Star Wars was the film that made Detdrick McClure want to be a film-maker. He was only eight at the time. As he grew older, movies seemed out of reach for a kid from Georgia with neither contacts in the business nor a bankroll to fund the endeavor.

McClure enrolled at Savannah College of Art and Design (SCAD) as a graphic design student, switched his major to painting and then architecture, before settling in as a film and video major. "It was the mid-to-late '80s, when independent film started to happen with Spike Lee and Jim Jarmusch—filmmakers like that, making movies for about $30,000 to $100,000. No money at all, no stars; just writing a script and making a movie. That was the first time that I saw you could just do it. You could be nobody, from nowhere, and just do it. That was like a light bulb going off. It was the first time I knew I wanted to and could be in this industry."

After graduating in 1990, he returned to his Atlanta home to work for the summer and save money. That Fall he drove out to California, "because Los Angeles is the center of the entertainment industry." He stayed with a college friend who had graduated a year earlier, who gave him five names with telephone numbers to begin his job search.

One of McClure's first jobs was as a runner for a production company that was preparing for an out-of-town shoot. He drove all over Los Angeles, delivering airline tickets to the cast and crew. His next break was working on the *American Music Awards* show: "My job was to answer the phone on the stage. I was there for about four weeks and the phone rang probably four times. That was my job." With many of the awards shows crewing up, he was able to go from one show to another. "You get on one show

VOICES OF EXPERIENCE

What do you love most about your job?

"What I love most about my job is sitting down to do an interview with someone that is interesting to hear talk. They could be a plumber or they could be a president. I've listened to the top and the bottom: Louis Farrakhan to OJ, and every celebrity you can think of—Jesse Jackson—amazing people that I admire. The best thing is, you get to sit and listen to people and learn something about them."—Detdrick McClure

and meet people and when that show ends, those people go to something else and you bug them for work until you're working with

CAREER TIPS

★ *"There is a quote about making bold moves and great forces will come to your aid— I believe that. My first bold move was to get in my car and move from Georgia to Los Angeles, never having left the South. You have to be bold in what you want to do and go directly to it as much as you can."—Detdrick McClure*

★ *"Be willing to work on things that don't pay a lot or don't pay at all because it's all about meeting people. It's all about knowing people that can shape the different aspects of your career."—Detdrick McClure*

them on the next thing. Work begets work." Sometimes he worked for free, just to meet people and gain experience.

After working as a production assistant on various music videos, sometimes for 24 hours straight without a break, McClure decided it was time to refocus his career goals. "That is when I decided to do sound. I knew it paid better and was a lot easier. A lot of this town is all about perception. You have to create whoever you are and so I just said 'I'm a soundman,' even though I'd only done sound a little bit here and there. I really wasn't that good at it and didn't know all the things one should know." He worked for free on his first projects, seizing the opportunity to gain sound experience. "You might not be getting paid, but you're working with the gear, so it's on-the-job training."

McClure gained valuable experience running sound, and as a cameraman when he was hired as a camera assistant for the second year of *Real World*. "After the camera guys or sound guys went into overtime [which the production did not want to pay], they would say 'Okay, camera assistant, you're shooting' or 'You're doing sound.'"

Just as the *Real World* experience came to an end, the OJ Simpson trial was heating up. The media demand for crew members was so great that it created a shortage of cameramen and soundmen. McClure landed work with *American Journal* and *Inside Edition*, working 10-hour days, five days a week. "I went from being a PA, making a very minimum amount of money and just barely scraping by, to full time, doubling my salary in a year."

All along, McClure had been writing a script he hoped to one day direct. The sudden increase in income provided an opportunity to invest in himself and make his first film, *Road Dogs*. He continues to work as a soundman, while writing and developing other projects he plans to direct.

JOB TITLE: ADR SUPERVISOR

Job Overview

The ADR (automatic dialogue replacement) supervisor is responsible for the replacement of production dialogue that is unusable due to poor sound quality, script changes, and so on. For example, an actor's voice may be obscured by the sound of an airplane flying overhead during the filming of a scene, or by speaking too softly for the microphone to pick up. Substitutions also may be necessary to accommodate dialogue changes or to clarify a plot point.

Special Skills

A well-rounded background in film production is an asset. ADR supervisors must possess the ability to work well with a variety of personalities for long hours.

Expanded Job Description

"The supervisor spots the show with the sound supervisor, the director, and the picture editor, making note of dialogue to replace," explains ADR supervisor Jim Borgardt. "Next, the ADR supervisor sits down and goes through the entire movie, writing down the starts and end of footage, or time codes, for each line."

Once all the material has been programmed and broken down for each individual actor, the production office is informed of which actors are needed for looping and for how long. The production office contacts the actors or their agents and arranges for them to come into the studio to record. "Then the supervisor comes in with the film and we rerecord the new dialogue against the picture. Then we prepare it for the mix." The new dialogue is delivered to the mixer with the supervisor's notes. "During the recording, I'm taking notes as to what takes are good and what alternates the director might want. Then the editor follows those notes and prepares the tracks and sends them with my notes to the dialogue editor."

Advice for Someone Seeking This Job

Find an ADR supervisor or equipment rental house that will allow you to apprentice to learn the gear and basics of the job. "There are a lot of houses willing to take on apprentices," says Borgardt, "people who work for nothing, and then after a period of time, the house they are working for gives them a paying gig."

Professional Profile: Jim Borgardt, ADR Supervisor

The flashing on and off of neon signs was the theme for one of the first movies a teenage Jim Borgardt made with his parents' movie camera. His first edit was of a train coming and going. However, it was not until several years later that he would discover filmmaking as a career.

Following his honorable discharge from the military, Borgardt enrolled at College of San Mateo in the San Francisco Bay Area. He wanted to take a photography class, but the only course with an opening was in motion picture production, taught by a former *Candid Camera* cameraman.

VOICES OF EXPERIENCE

What do you like least about your job?

A people person, Jim Borgardt's least favorite part of the job is any work he has to do alone.

What do you love most about your job?

"I really love being onstage. I love working with the director and with the actors. I enjoy doing group [multiple actors looping at the same time]. The most fun I ever had was working two days on a prison movie with ten women screaming and yelling for two days—it was so much fun."—Jim Borgardt

"Basically, all he did was teach us how to load and unload this Auricon camera. I excelled at loading and unloading and thought, 'There's got to be more than this to motion picture production. What about scripts and shooting stuff?'"

Undaunted, Borgardt enrolled in the class a second time and became the instructor's PA. "We had students write short scenes and we would shoot them in the hall-ways with this Auricon camera. It turned out to really be a motion picture class."

Borgardt's introduction to the film industry was as a janitor at Francis Ford Coppola's American Zoetrope. "George Lucas was just beginning to mix *American Graffiti*—Walter Murch was doing the mixing. Francis was in preproduction on *The Conversation*. They needed a janitor, so they hired me. That lasted about a week. Then they realized they needed a cleaning service, so they hired one and put me in charge of rental equipment." Coppola had invested some of his *Godfather* earnings into buying equipment that could be rented to whichever production he was working on, namely *The Conversation*. "That was my beginning."

For Borgardt, being able to watch over the shoulders of these great filmmakers was like going to film school. "I was always looking in and asking questions." Eventually he became involved in sound, sometimes being called upon to go out and record background noises, learning while doing.

Moving to Los Angeles, he first found work as a PA, then became an assistant to picture editor Bill Butler. Borgardt's first job as an assistant picture editor was working for Robert Gordon on *Las Vegas Lady*. Having maintained his contacts at American Zoetrope, he let them know that he wanted to work on *Apocalypse Now* and was hired as ADR editor.

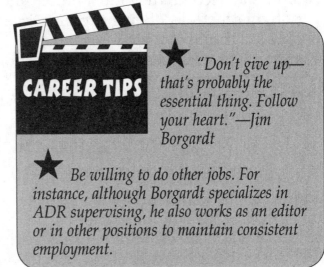

CAREER TIPS

★ *"Don't give up—that's probably the essential thing. Follow your heart."—Jim Borgardt*

★ *Be willing to do other jobs. For instance, although Borgardt specializes in ADR supervising, he also works as an editor or in other positions to maintain consistent employment.*

After going to Cannes with *Apocalypse*, Borgardt took time off from film work to "hang out in Europe." Upon returning to the States, he landed various ADR editor and supervisor gigs, eventually ending up at Cannon Films, where he was reunited with many of the people he had met while working on *Apocalypse*. By the late 1980s, he was working for multiple studios and production companies on film after film, including: *Adventures in Babysitting, Baby Boom, Dominick and Eugene, Flight of the Navigator, Fried Green Tomatoes,* and *Shy People*.

Over the next decade, Borgardt continued to work as an ADR editor or supervisor, for a time working with Dane Tracks on *Bound* and other films. Additional career highlights include *Boogie Nights, Crazy in Alabama, Servicing Sara,* and *Simon Birch*. His work on the television movie *The Crossing* earned him an Emmy nomination. Fueled by his film experiences, he recently returned to school with plans of becoming a psychologist.

JOB TITLE: MUSIC EDITOR

Job Overview

Music editors coordinate the technical aspects of film scoring between the production company and the composer; they create the temporary score and assist in syncing the final score to film.

Special Skills and Education

First, music editors must have musicality and skill using music editing equipment. Second, they must be self-motivated and able to work on a very tight schedule. "Being diplomatic; able to listen carefully to what people are trying to communicate, and then fulfilling their desire without a lot of problems, guess work, or questions back and forth," says music editor Jeff Chabonneau. "It is very important to shut off your mind and listen carefully to what the director is trying to say to you."

A Typical Workday

Chabonneau's schedule is dictated by where he is in the process of adding music to picture for the project he is working on. On a film spotting day, he meets in the studio with the film producers, director, film editor, and composer. Together they review scenes to determine where the music should start and end, discuss any stylistic concerns, and address any other issues. If there is a temporary score already in place, they might discuss whether it works in various scenes. They will talk about specific songs they want to use and address any synchronization problems if there is a live performance. The director may discuss a statement he wants to emphasize with music in a particular scene. "Involvement in the spotting session varies from film to film and project to project. Sometimes the composer and the music editor will spot the film on their own and give their notes or ideas to the producer or the director, although that is very rare. On the series I work on, which is *The X-Files*, I do all the music spotting on my own. I give my notes to the composer and the producers and they give me feedback. The reason we've done it this way is to streamline the process, because we don't have an enormous amount of time to do the score and there is a lot of music in the show. They trust me with knowing, or figuring out, where to put the music in and where to take it out."

After the spotting is complete, Chabonneau will go through the film to time the sequences and create timing notes: a breakdown of the action taking place within in each scene. This is typed out for the composer to see. Within a couple of days, the composer returns with the recorded score, and the music editor and an engineer mix the score. Then, the music editor goes to the rerecording stage and guides the music mixer on how the music should fit into the scene, such as where the music is too loud or too soft, where it should build and fade, and any background source issues. Depending on the project, the rerecording process can take one to three days, or three to four weeks. "On a television show, we're usually on the stage for about two days." Next, the producers and director may suggest changes, such as adding a sound to a scene or switching out a particular piece of music. Those changes are made immediately. The next phase is to document the music. The music editor writes down the timing and order of each piece of music used in the film, adds the author's and publisher's names, and turns it over to the studio legal department to issue contracts and licenses. The last task is to create a backup of all of the materials so they can be placed in the studio vault and a copy of the score sent to the Library of Congress for copyright purposes.

Advice for Someone Seeking This Job

"The way I got established was to work on low budget and no budget films to gain some skills and meet people. When those people ended up working on bigger projects, they took me along with them in a lot of cases," says Chabonneau. "This job takes an investment in material costs, too. You have to essentially own a mini recording studio in order to be viable in the present film economy. No one wants to rent equipment for you, they want you to come fully equipped with state-of-the-art equipment and know how to operate it effectively. When they consider hiring you to do a project, the first questions asked are, 'Do you have a ProTools system? Is it transportable? Can you bring it to a stage? How much are you going to charge us to rent it?'"

Professional Profile: Jeff Chabonneau, Music Editor

Music was Jeff Chabonneau's vehicle into the film and television business. Throughout his teenage years, he played in rock and roll bands and went on to study classical guitar at the University of Wisconsin, but changed his major to biology in his junior year. He enrolled in an anthropology graduate program at University of California at Los Angeles (UCLA). In the fourth year of graduate school, he says, "I ran out of scholarship and grant money and decided I really needed a job."

VOICES OF EXPERIENCE

What do you like least about your job?

"The element I like the least is the egos and personalities involved in the business."
—Jim Chabonneau

What do you love most about your job?

"The work itself. I've got the type of brain where I like doing something very creative. I think I have a real aptitude for combining sound and image together in a way that works. I enjoy that aspect. I like the challenge. I view it as a puzzle that I can solve. I like being able to go through and measure music against a picture and make it work."—Jim Chabonneau

Through a friend, he was introduced to another academic who had returned to music as a composer for New York-based Score Productions, writing music for television soap operas, game shows, and sporting events. Impressed with Chabonneau's musical talent, the composer helped him land a job as music supervisor of the soap opera *Capitol*, filmed in Los Angeles. A year later, he was ready for a bigger challenge.

> ★ *"In this business there is always a deadline. A person has to be able to deal with that pressure and accept that responsibility. Know that you're going to have to set aside your own personal life at times in order to fulfill the job. That can be stressful when you've planned a weekend and that gets dumped because the schedule has changed and you have to get things done by Monday, as opposed to Tuesday or Wednesday. Deadlines are very important. Being punctual is extremely important. These are skills that are necessary."*
> —Jim Chabonneau

Hearing that the major film studios had jobs for music editors, but not knowing exactly what that entailed, Chabonneau boldly called 20th Century Fox to apply. He was told that he needed both experience and union membership to qualify, but he left his phone number anyway. Two days later he got a call asking if he was interested in interviewing for an apprentice music editor position. Hired for his ability to both play and read music, he worked there for two years before the studio closed down the department. The next three years were spent working in television at a small firm in Burbank, frequently with well-known composer Mike Post.

When Post opened Interlock, his own music editing company, Chabonneau was one of four editors hired. Two years later he returned to film work at MGM, then went out on his own as a freelancer, specializing in temporary music scores for film previews.

For several seasons he served as a staff music editor for *The X-Files*, and he has worked on several features, including *Bull*, *Crazy in Alabama*, *Disturbing Behavior*, *It Had to Be You*, and *The X-Files* motion picture.

MUSIC CREATORS AND LICENSORS

JOB TITLE: COMPOSER

Job Overview

Compose music, write lyrics, or both, and often produce the music recording sessions.

Special Skills

Most composers are adept at playing piano, sequencer, synthesizer, or a combination of the three, and most have the ability to produce the music they write. Success requires the ability to compose memorable melodies and lyrics.

"Writing a score is a different skill than songwriting, where you come up with a melody and you either write a lyric yourself or you collaborate with another person to write a song," says composer Steve Dorff. "Writing a score for a film is an integral part of the postproduction process, where you're musical-izing every moment of the movie with orchestral or some kind of music—generally without lyrics—that under-scores the action, whether it is romantic, action-adventure, scary, or excit-ing. The creative process is the same with television as it is with film. The only difference being, there is a much smaller budget for television than for film."

Advice for Someone Seeking This Job

To gain some experience composing songs or scoring for film, contact film schools and make yourself available to student filmmakers.

"Really try to understand the business," says Dorff. "When you read books and manuals, know what the games are and know what the pitfalls are. Know that just writing a song is only half of it. Knowing what to do with a song after you've written it is maybe even more than half of it. You need to know how to demo it, how to pitch it, how to present it. I'm not going to open the hood of a car and try to fix a carburetor without knowing what I'm doing."

What do you like least about your job?

"Having time on my hands, when I'm not busy. That's frustrating for me."—Steve Dorff

What do you love most about your job?

"I love being busy. I love the actual going into the studio and recording with an orchestra, hearing, for the first time, those things that I only heard in my head. When it works, that's my favorite part."—Steve Dorff

Professional Profile: Steve Dorff, Composer, Songwriter

"I always wanted to do music for movies," says award-winning composer Steve Dorff. He began playing piano at age four and was composing little tunes soon after. While in junior high school, he began writing songs and formed a rock and roll band, emulating The Beatles.

To appease his parents, he enrolled at the University of Georgia, earning a degree in journalism, but his real interest remained in songwriting. After graduation, he traveled between Atlanta and Nashville, trying to break into the music business, finally landing his first songwriting contract with Lowry Music in Atlanta. While he dreamed of writing music for films, it took about four and a half years before he made the move to California.

Arriving in Los Angeles in 1974 without any contacts and just enough money to last for two weeks, Dorff began making the rounds. "I just knocked on doors." A demo tape he left for producer Snuff Garrett resulted in an audition and a contract for $250 per week. Dorff cut his musical teeth writing for five of Clint Eastwood's movies (among them, *Every Which Way But Loose* and *Bronco Billy*), producing seven number-one hits in a row.

In 1984, Dorff signed a co-publishing deal with Warner

"There are a lot of people that have a gift, but that don't have the innate common sense and the innate tenacity that it takes to be successful over a long period of time. Anybody can have a hit, but to succeed over and over and over again, over a 20 to 25 year period, requires that intangible thing that allows you to pick yourself up and dust yourself off when you have bitter disappointments."—Steve Dorff

"Stay grounded when you're having a tremendous cycle of success. Always have a couple of balls in the air at the same time. It's hard when you've only got one thing that you're doing—you finish it, and you have to get something else going. It's easier to always try and have something in the wings waiting to segue to." –Steve Dorff

Chapel Music, scoring music for television shows that included *Growing Pains*, *My Sister Sam*, and *Murphy Brown*.

Dorff has written hit songs for artists such as Barbra Streisand, Whitney Houston, and George Strait. He continues to compose for feature films (*Blast from the Past*, *The Cactus Kid*, *Dudley Do-Right*, *Michael*, *Tin Cup*, and many more) and is currently working on the television series *Reba*. Dorff is the father of actor Stephen Dorff.

JOB TITLE: SENIOR VICE PRESIDENT OF MUSIC

Job Overview

At DreamWorks, Todd Homme is responsible for all live action film and television music matters. He works closely with filmmakers to determine music needs and coordinates with his staff to fulfill their requests by contracting a composer, securing a previously recorded or original song, or procuring a sound track deal. He is also involved in the financial aspects of music use.

Special Skills

A broad knowledge of music, music composition, and publishing, and an understanding of how the film industry works, diligence in learning about the industry, who the important players are, staying abreast of new music, and the ability to negotiate are all essential. "You have to be able to get along with people," says Homme "and it helps to have a sense of humor."

A Typical Workday

On any given day, Todd Homme may negotiate a fee to hire a composer for a film, or talk through the logistics of score production with the composer and producers. He meets with directors and producers throughout the filmmaking process to determine their music needs, such as which composer is desired, specific songs they are interested in licensing, artists they may want to record new material for the film, and whether there will be a sound track album. At any given time, he usually will have eight to ten pictures in various stages of production. He may be on the phone talking with a record company representative on sound track issues or arranging for the label to receive artwork and marketing materials. "At any moment I might be called to handle paying a guitar player, hire a world-class composer or a superstar artist, book a studio, or establish a music budget for a film." Throughout the day he may attend a screening of a film, meet with other department employees to ensure they have the information and tools they need, or listen to music for song ideas to pitch to a director.

VOICES OF EXPERIENCE

What do you like least about your job?

"Arguing about money. That is a short sentence about a big subject. I work for very conspicuous people in this business and we're riding the crest of our recent success. We've had Steven [Spielberg]'s picture, Saving Private Ryan, *win several Oscars, including Best Director. Then most recently,* American Beauty, *which was a small film done for a modest budget, with a first-time director and a first-time writer (both of whom won Oscars), together with a young cast. In many respects, it was a small project. The fact that there are three guys that run this company [David Geffen, Jeffrey Katzenberg, Steven Spielberg] that are very big in the industry doesn't mean every project has an enormous budget. Sometimes you get tired of explaining that we have budgets and limits we have to live within."—Todd Homme*

What do you love most about your job?

"Variety—there are all kinds of commingling of people, ideas, attitudes, and challenges. There is always something new. I like working with the people in creative disciplines that are the best in their given field. You get to talk with them and ask questions about their own journey. That is pretty wonderful."—Todd Homme

Advice for Someone Seeking This Job

Become a member of industry organizations and volunteer to work at seminars and other events so that you are in a situation to meet people and develop contacts. Learn all you can about the industry, such as the names of important players. After you have gained a good base of knowledge, apply for an internship or assistant position to get a foot in the door.

Professional Profile: Todd Homme, DreamWorks

Todd Homme grew up in Saskatchewan, Canada, "where everybody freezes and every boy learns to play hockey." Growing up, Homme was torn between a career as a hockey player or as a guitarist. Little did he know that hockey would one day be the key that would open the door to a job in the entertainment business.

Homme attended Berklee College of Music in Boston, and then kicked around in a few bands and gained some recording experience. Heading west in 1989, he quickly discovered that Los Angeles already had too many great studio musicians. He found a job to make ends meet and began coaching and playing amateur hockey. "I ended up on a team with some agents and other entertainment people. I was hating my job and asked if anyone knew anyone in the music or film business." A teammate gave him the name of Bill Schrank, vice president of music production at Warner Brothers Studios, and suggested that he write a letter, since Schrank was too busy to talk on the phone. By this time, Homme was unemployed and beginning to worry about his lack of prospects. About a week after the letter was sent, he decided to try to reach Schrank by telephone. "I was walking downstairs to make the call and the phone rang, and it was him on the other end of the line." Homme was invited to come by the studio to talk, where he learned about jobs he never knew existed, including one he thought he would be perfect for: Schrank's own. "He said, 'Good luck! There are about seven of these jobs in the business, one per studio.'"

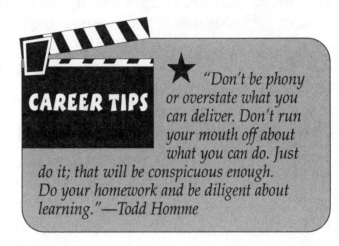

★ *"Don't be phony or overstate what you can deliver. Don't run your mouth off about what you can do. Just do it; that will be conspicuous enough. Do your homework and be diligent about learning."—Todd Homme*

Over the next eight months, Homme was only able to get three or four interviews in unrelated fields. He even offered to work for free, just to gain the experience, but was turned down for insurance reasons. At the point when things looked desperate, he got a message from Schrank that resulted in Homme being hired as manager of music production at Disney Studios. Unaware of his status at his new job, Homme recalls, "I was taken to my office by my assistant (I would have taken the job as my own assistant) and she said, 'You've got a meeting tomorrow morning at eight.' I said, 'Will there be any executives there?' She said, 'Duh. You are an executive.' It was really kind of wacky and unbelievable, because I got the job I dreamt about."

Determined not to lose this opportunity, Homme learned his job duties while working on the 11 films and sound tracks then in production. Over the next four years, he worked on a total of 75 films. A few months after DreamWorks was formed, he came on board as the equivalent of vice president of film music (there are no titles at DreamWorks), working on such box office hits as *Gladiator, Antz, Almost Famous*, and Academy Award winning films *Saving Private Ryan* and *American Beauty*. Homme still plays on a hockey team, which includes some of the industry's most successful actors, agents, producers, and directors, and credits it as being the single most important networking tool he has ever discovered.

JOB TITLE: VICE PRESIDENT OF MUSIC

Job Overview

The vice president of music for a studio or production company is charged with supervising music in both the production and postproduction phases, with an emphasis on pre-existing music. Some also hire composers and producers, and oversee the scoring and mixing process.

Special Skills

"Being organized, responding properly, and keeping my word" are skills film/television music executive Celest Ray cites as keys to her success. "Listening carefully and fulfilling the requests that either Mr. [Aaron] Spelling or the producers have is very important." Knowledge of the music business and a good business sense is important; an understanding of music publishing and how record companies work is essential.

VOICES OF EXPERIENCE

What do you like least about your job?

"What I like least are the politics. I don't like it when deals should happen, but they don't because there is a personal interest in conflict. Or, when one executive won't talk to another executive because they don't want to admit that they have to ask a question."—Celest Ray

What do you love most about your job?

"What I love the most is picking music and seeing that what I've selected tickles the fancy of whoever I'm pitching it to. Then, seeing it on screen—seeing that it really works. That's what I love most about my job."—Celest Ray

Advice for Someone Seeking This Job

Some vice presidents of music are former music supervisors, and most of them are overworked and understaffed. Find someone who needs help and offer to work for them as an intern or apprentice so that you can learn the business. There is much more to the job than just selecting music; you also must know the legalities of music licensing. Once you have an understanding of music licensing, volunteer to work on student films or low budget projects to gain experience.

Professional Profile: Celest Ray, Vice President of Music, Aaron Spelling Productions

A job meant to supplement her income while in college changed Celest Ray's career path from nursery school teacher to film and television music executive. "I always loved music and I really liked the mix of the business aspect with the creative aspect." As a secretary at an independent record label and music publishing company owned by artist Johnny Rivers, Ray gained experience in every conceivable aspect of the business and eventually was promoted to general manager.

After ten years working for Rivers, she was ready for a new challenge. In 1983, Ray accepted an offer from producers Norman Lear and Jerry Perrenchio to be director of music for Embassy Pictures. During her tenure, she supervised such films and sound track albums as *This Is Spinal Tap*, *Stand By Me*, and *A Chorus Line*. When Embassy's theatrical division was sold to Dino De Laurentiis in 1987, Ray stayed on, working on *Crimes of the Heart*, *Backdraft*, and *Bill and Ted's Excellent Adventure*, among others.

Embassy Pictures went bankrupt in 1992, but Ray had been operating her own company, Music in Motion,

CAREER TIPS

★ *"Sometimes we put our fears first, but when there is more trust and more belief, then we can all work together. When we put our fears first, we always loose. I hope that I grow old in the business and that I'll grow to drop my fears, believe in myself, and be a guide for truth. Know that you can be who you are and still succeed."*
—Celest Ray

★ *Work hard and look for opportunities to prove yourself. "When I was working in business affairs and I wanted to do a more creative job, I stood up to the plate and asked for the opportunity. Then, I would stay late to do the work, over and above my business affairs work. Instead of being resentful that nobody was letting me try to be a creative person, I took that on in addition to my other work and people came to rely on me more and more for my creative input."*
—Celest Ray

since 1988. As a contractor, she cleared music rights for *Seinfeld*, numerous projects with MGM and Universal film studios, and a series of film sound track albums for Big Screen Records. Hired part time by Ken Miller to clear music rights for the first season of *Beverly Hills 90210*, she was asked to supervise music for *Melrose Place* the following year.

Ray took a position at Paramount Studios in 1994, but after six months was hired full time by Spelling Entertainment Group as director of music coordination, in addition to supervising music for *Melrose Place*.

Since being promoted to vice president of music, Ray has been involved in numerous Spelling television productions, including *7th Heaven, Any Day Now, Charmed, Kindred,* and *Pasadena.* She also served as music coordinator on the feature *The House of Yes.*

JOB TITLE: MUSIC CLEARANCE

Job Overview

Responsible for obtaining clearances for all music used in film and television projects and trailers produced by the company.

Special Skills

A background in music publishing or knowledge of music licensing is required. "You have to be able to handle multiple tasks at the same time," say music clearance executive Julie Butchco. "Literally, you're talking on the phone, researching a song, making notes as you're going along, and thinking about what your next step is as far as clearing or finding a song. You have to be organized. You have many different projects at different junctures. You're working on movies that are in postproduction and movies that are done, from the initial clearing of songs, to writing up the cue sheets and registering copyrights. You really have to be resourceful, as far as tracking down the owners of songs and the artists that recorded them, and who owns the master rights."

VOICES OF EXPERIENCE

What do you like least about your job?

"All the paperwork that lingers on for months on end, sometimes after a film is done. I wish things could be wrapped up as quickly as they are started."—Julie Butchco

What do you love most about your job?

"I love the feeling you get when you can finally clear a song with an artist or the songwriter. A song that your director really wants and you know it's going to be great for the film, but it's a really hard clearance, or it might be particularly expensive. Just knowing that in the end you got the approval, and you got it at a price that you thought was fair, and you know that everyone was just waiting for that song to clear because they really wanted it in their movie. It's a really great feeling to know you helped."—Julie Butchco

Advice for Someone Seeking This Job

"Don't be embarrassed to start out as an assistant," say Butchco. "Soak up any possible information that you can while you're at that desk. When you're an assistant, you hear a lot more about what's going on, about all kinds of different transactions and pieces of business that you may not necessarily hear if you're just in one specific position in an office. I think when you're an assistant you have a good opportunity to be exposed to a lot of different sides of the business. You can learn how things are done and at what stage they're done."

Professional Profile: Julie Butchco, Music Clearance for DreamWorks

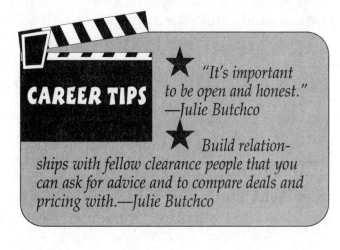

★ *"It's important to be open and honest."* —Julie Butchco

★ *Build relationships with fellow clearance people that you can ask for advice and to compare deals and pricing with.*—Julie Butchco

Julie Butchco's introduction to the entertainment business came as a result of her high school student government activities, when she was assigned to hire bands and organize performers for school dances. Upon entering the University of California at Santa Barbara, she considered going into entertainment law, but wasn't convinced she wanted to be an attorney. "I just decided to get a job in the industry and see if I liked it."

Sending out résumés and going on interviews failed to produce results, until a cousin was able to get Butchco an interview with the producer of *The Young and the Restless* through a contact with one of the show's writers. The interview was purely informational, as the show had no openings, but did result in a referral to a producer at Columbia Pictures Television. That interview got her hired as an assistant in the television licensing department.

After a few years in television licensing, Butchco landed an assistant position in film licensing. Not anticipating another move quite so soon, it came as a surprise when a friend called in 1996 to say he had suggested her for a position at newly-created DreamWorks, and advised her to call Todd Homme for an interview.

Many candidates were anxious to work at the prestigious new studio, but Butchco was a perfect fit for the job of clearing music for film and television. Since joining DreamWorks, she has worked on numerous projects, including box office hits *Almost Famous* and *Gladiator*, and two Best Picture Academy Award winning films: *Saving Private Ryan* and *American Beauty*.

JOB TITLE: MUSIC SUPERVISOR

Job Overview

A music supervisor is hired to oversee all the music that is used in a production, whether for film or television. The supervisor works closely with the director in selecting songs, choosing a composer, if one is used, and acquiring the rights for the production to use the songs. If there is to be a sound track, the supervisor will secure the record deal and work with the appropriate parties involved to bring the album to release.

Special Skills

"The ultimate skill is sensitivity," says music supervisor Barklie Griggs. "When they're looking at a scene in a film, you have to imagine how that character feels, what is happening in their life in this movie, and what song could make that scene better; what music could enhance the feeling. All the while being perceptive about what the director is trying to convey. Also, knowing every kind of music and remembering songs."

Expanded Job Description

Most days, Griggs arrives at his office between 9:30 and 10:00 A.M. His first two to three hours are spent listening to music he has selected for a film he is working on, to ensure that it fits suitably into each scene. "Between, I jump on my computer and check who wrote the song, who has the rights, and how much it will cost to use it." Once Griggs determines that a song works in the scene and will fit the film's budget, he places the appropriate CD in a pile that he will later play for the director.

In the early afternoon, he phones those working with him on current projects—publishers, record company people, and directors. He sometimes meets a director at an editing room to play songs for him. Afterward, he makes calls to find music or to get more specific information about a song he is interested in using. He may be involved in negotiating a composer deal, working to get a new song recorded by a specific artist, or putting together a sound track deal. In the evening, he often attends film screenings.

Advice for Someone Seeking This Job

"Do your homework," says Griggs. "That means you have to know your music. It really helps when you're listening to the radio and you hear a song you like, if you stop and remember how it makes you feel. Did it make you feel sad or happy? What kind of scene could you see it in? Remember feeling, the song title, and the album. Start compiling CDs and make a separate place for songs you love."

Professional Profile: Barklie Griggs, Music Supervisor/Owner, Tilted World Music

It would be hard to decide which Barklie Griggs loves more: films or music. As a teenager, the two consumed all his time and money. "I was always a music fan and a movie buff. I loved going to see movies and I loved listening to music. I paid attention to the music used in films. 'I'm Alright' by Kenny Loggins in *Caddyshack*, Simple Minds' 'Don't You Forget About Me' in *The Breakfast Club*, 'Get Into the Groove' in *Desperately Seeking Susan* by Madonna; the sound track to *Diner* was a favorite. I began to buy sound tracks and just started learning more and more about music."

After high school graduation, Griggs moved from New York to Los Angeles and worked as a waiter while trying to decide what to do with his life. Talking with a regular customer one day, he discovered the man was a film music supervisor. The idea that someone was paid to organize the music for a film had never occurred to Griggs, but now that it had, he realized this was a way to combine his two great loves into a career. Offering to quit his job on the spot and work for free to learn the business, he was politely turned down. Undaunted, he formulated a plan.

Griggs began frequenting record stores daily, reading album covers and making a list of the names and titles of all the music people involved with film sound tracks.

VOICES OF EXPERIENCE

What do you like least about your job?

"There is a certain amount of ego in the movie business, and some of those with bad egos can ruin the business because they make everything so uncomfortable and limiting. You're not inspired by somebody trying to impose their will just because they can, not because that is the best creative choice."—Barklie Griggs

What do you love most about your job?

"Being able to have control over or having a big part of the emotion of a scene that makes people feel a certain way. There is nothing greater than sitting in a screening of a movie and a scene comes on that you know the music is going to start turning people inside out emotionally. They start to feel love or scared or conflicted; that's really the best part of this job. You get to have a creative impact on a movie."—Barklie Griggs

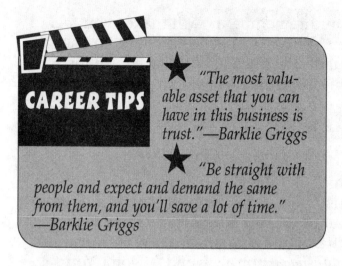

"I started to learn who all the players were." Through a friend who knew a theatrical director, he began supplying music for plays. He studied the *Hollywood Reporter*'s film and television music issue, learning everything he could about the people who held the job he wanted. After four months, he quit waiting tables and began telephoning everyone on his list.

The roommate of a friend telephoned music supervisor Sharon Boyle and secured Griggs an opportunity to send a résumé and cover letter. With a résumé of nothing but restaurant experience, he focused on writing a powerful letter of introduction, stating: "I'm a record junky and I know a lot about music. I have over 800 records and I would die to work for you. And, I make really good coffee." The line about making coffee, he confesses, was a lie: "I couldn't make coffee for the life of me."

After several follow-up calls trying to get a meeting with Boyle, Griggs was given an appointment. "It was Monday, the fourth of March 1990. I threw myself at her. I said, 'Please, I'll do anything. I'll work for free. I'll work from midnight to 6 A.M.'"

With no openings at the company, Griggs left the interview with only the assurance that Boyle would consider his offer. The very next day, one of Boyle's employees announced the need to go part-time, so she decided to give Griggs a chance to come in on a temporary basis and see how things went. He ended up staying for five years, working on a number of big films, including *The Air Up There, Kalifornia, Girl in the Cadillac, The Last Word,* and *Mr. Holland's Opus.*

Ready to test his wings, Griggs opened Tilted World Music in 1995, and under his own company banner has supervised a number of independent films and feature films, most notably *The Associate, Guinevere, Let the Devil Wear Black, Ring of Fire, Scorched, Still Breathing, Thick as Thieves,* and *Wing Commander,* and television series *The Lone Gunmen* and *Pasadena.*

●●●●

CHAPTER
10

PHYSICAL AND VISUAL EFFECTS

When the script calls for a setting too expensive to build, a creature that does not exist, or action that is too dangerous to allow an actor to perform, the special effects team is called in. Runaway vehicles, bullet strikes, and explosions are examples of physical effects: special effects staged during filming without photographic tricks. Snow drifts added to a scene after it has been filmed is an example of computer generated imagery (CGI). The combining of a CGI dinosaur with film footage of an actor running away from it is an example of an optical effect.

The individuals who supervise, design, create, and perform these effects include:

- Stunt Coordinator: devise, plan, choreograph, and oversee execution of stunt sequences.

- Stuntperson: double for actors during dangerous action sequences.

- Aerial Coordinator: supervise usage of aircrafts and pilots.

- Visual Effects Supervisor: plan and oversee the creation of visual effects.

- Visual Effects Producer: oversee budget and production schedule of special effects.

- Visual Effects Art Director: design visual effects.

- Visual Effects Editor: communicates necessary filming information between the visual effects supervisor and the film editor.

- Special Effects Coordinator: organize and oversee on set physical effects.

- Special Effects Crew: those who actually create and execute special effects, whether physical effects, trick photography, or computer generated effects. Includes model builders, matt painters, computer animators, and so on.

- Physical Effects Designer: design and fabricate machinery used to create special effects.

- Physical Effects Technician: create elemental effects, such as rain or wind.

- Pyrotechnician: responsible for special effects involving fire or explosives.

- Special Effects Makeup Artist: design and create more complex makeup, generally involving latex prosthetics.

- Weapons Specialist: provide, maintain, and oversee the use of real weaponry.

- Effects Animator: digitally enhance already filmed effects.

Note: Depending on the size of the production, one individual may fulfill multiple job functions.

JOB TITLE: STUNT COORDINATOR

Job Overview

Working closely with the director to determine his vision for the scene, the stunt coordinator creates and choreographs all stunts and action sequences required for the production. "The stunt coordinator is actually setting up and deciding where the stunt will be done, what will be used, what precautions will be taken, and he's hiring the people that will be doing it," explains action unit director Vic Armstrong.

Special Skills

Proficiency in martial arts, gymnastics, skydiving, motorcycle riding, rappelling, scuba diving, swimming, and the safe and proper use of weapons are skills stunt coordinator/stuntman Steve Gums suggests acquiring. He points out that stunt people must be in excellent physical condition.

He also suggests taking algebra, geometry, and physics courses. "When you're rigging, you've got to have the math [skills] to figure out acceleration. An example of that is: I was rigging a friend's show in the Houston Astrodome. He was doing a 200-foot high fall from the ceiling. We wanted to figure out how hard he was hitting the air bag.

"Strong determination and common sense are also important . . . Another thing stunt people need is perfect timing."

Advice for Someone Seeking This Job

To get started in the business, Gums suggests finding a working stunt-person or coordinator you can learn from. "If you can find somebody that works regularly and is willing to let you train with them, or bring you down to the set and let you hang out, that's a really good way to not only learn, but get in with a group of guys that may hire you in the future."

Action unit director/stunt coordinator Vic Armstrong suggests that prospective stunt people first specialize in one area, such as horseback riding (as he did), fights, gymnastics, and so forth. Then try to land a job based on that special skill, build up film credits, and learn from co-workers. "You have to have a specific ability that somebody wants to use you for, and then you just build on that. Work your butt off and do the rounds and talk to people. Get yourself known and just try to get some credits. It's very, very tough. My daughter is a young stuntwoman and she's finding it hard, even with the contacts I have. You've just got to get a reputation and build on it. I was lucky and took the opportunities I had and made the most of them. I tried to be inventive and original."

Professional Profile: Steve Gums, Stunt Coordinator, Stuntman and Weapons Specialist, President Kontrolled Khaos

Ever since he was a young boy, Steve Gums wanted to be a stuntman. Following high school, Gums graduated from the firefighter's academy, enabling him to understand the basics of creating burns. A self-taught stuntman, he learned by trial and error, performing stunts in his brother's high school film productions. "When the project was complete I would go to class with my brother Jeff, just to watch the teacher's reaction. Imagine being a high school teacher, watching what you expect to be a typical student video project. Then someone on screen gets hit by a moving car and slides up the windshield, or falls down a flight of stairs, or runs across the screen on fire. We definitely got his teacher's attention."

During his first year at George Mason University, Gums took a makeup class, which his brother audited. Perfecting their technique together, they landed work doing special effects and aging makeup for a children's television video production company. Over the next several years, they continued to work for the company whenever needed.

Gums also worked as a systems operator/programmer for the IRS while studying computer science at GMU. "They required this incredibly high level math and crazy amounts of calculus. My math isn't that strong, so it was difficult for me. It was really frustrating because I was doing the job I was supposedly going to school for, and I didn't need all the math they were trying to teach me." He finally determined to change his major to individual studies, which allowed him to devise his own course of study: film and video production.

Still attending GMU, Gums earned certification as an emergency medical technician from Northern Virginia Community College, enabling him to land work as a medic on the feature *Born Yesterday*. Continuing to progress toward his goal of becoming a stuntman, he also perfected skills in rock climbing and weaponry, and earned a black belt in American sport karate and geng-lung-do. Through his martial arts instructor, he gained stunt experience performing a fight sequence in the made-for-video sci-fi film *Invader*.

Gums' first paying stunt job was on an industrial video about rock climbing safety. "I was hired to do some falls. The stunts were pretty minor, but it didn't matter; I was pretty ecstatic because this was my first professional gig. I was actually going to get paid for something that my brother and I had done on our video projects. Everything went perfectly; there were no injuries. The reason I won't forget it, though, is the stunt coordinator kept my money. I never got paid anything for that job. It wasn't an encouraging introduction to the business."

When not working stunts, Gums served as a grip, electrician, and Steadicam assistant. To make ends meet, he also worked as a bouncer, as a rigger for rock and roll concerts and theatrical shows, and he ran security for a club owned by Mick Fleetwood.

Gums' next feature was *Pelican Brief*, working special effects and stunt safety team. "I didn't get any credit for it. If you look at the credits, it

VOICES OF EXPERIENCE

What do you like least about your job?

"At times, this business is completely selfish. It doesn't matter how good you are or what you know, a person usually gets hired because of who they know. You can be better for the job and repeatedly not get it."—Steve Gums

What do you love most about your job?

"What I like most about the job is the ever-changing mental and physical challenges. I like the incredible feeling of teamwork when you're lucky enough to work with a truly good group of stunt people."—Steve Gums

looks like the coordinator did all the work himself. He's the only special effects guy listed; he couldn't be bothered to list any of us." Watching the coordinator prepare for an explosion, Gums learned how to prep for a burn.

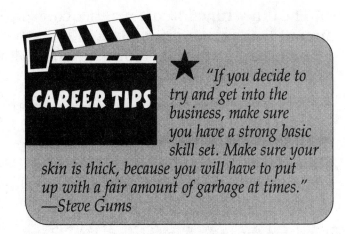

CAREER TIPS

★ *"If you decide to try and get into the business, make sure you have a strong basic skill set. Make sure your skin is thick, because you will have to put up with a fair amount of garbage at times."*
—*Steve Gums*

Over the next few years, Gums landed stunt work on *Deep Impact* and *Cherry Falls*, and television series *7 Days*, *America's Most Wanted*, and *Safe Harbor*. Late in 2001, he and brother Jeff formed Kontrolled Khaos in partnership with other area stuntmen to raise the awareness of East Coast based stunt people.

JOB TITLE: AERIAL DIRECTOR/COORDINATOR

Job Overview

The aerial director is responsible for all functions of airplanes and helicopters as they pertain to motion pictures, television, and commercials.

Expanded Job Description

"I take it from inception to wrap," explains aerial coordinator Steven Wright. The aerial director begins by reading the script to determine what aircraft are required on camera (picture ship or story helicopter) and/or are needed to film certain shots. "I start working on a budget for how many days we're going to need them and any extra costs: if an aircraft needs to be painted, we need to put search lights on them, or guns or rockets, or whatever some writer and/or director has dreamed up. I'll contract the aircraft, source out suppliers and do the contracts on behalf of the production company, and handle insurance. I usually handpick the crew, as well. It depends on what the production manager wants me to handle from an administrative point of view."

"From a flying point of view, I put a camera on a helicopter and I fly around and chase things. That's what you do as a function of a camera pilot. That's part of the whole package—if you're chasing cars down the street, helicopters, boats, or trains. I've chased commercial jets and military jets. You name it, I've chased it."

The other function of an aerial coordinator and his crew is to fly the aircraft that appear on camera. "I'll do the wardrobe thing and double whomever. I just finished doubling for Morgan Freeman in *Dreamcatcher*. I played Morgan flying a helicopter."

When multiple aircraft are used, Wright may remain on the ground. Standing next to the director and first AD, he directs the aircraft by telling the pilots how he wants them to maneuver. "I kind of translate from filmology to helicopter-ese." The aerial director must be able to envision what effect the director wants to achieve and translate that to the pilots.

The aerial director may also be charged with a second unit. "They'll hand me the storyboards and say, 'Here's what we want—go get it.' So I'll jump in with a cameraman and we'll thunder off into the skies or the mountains and shoot it."

Special Skills

In addition to being an expert pilot, Wright says, "Being a good listener really helps. Having passion for your work. Everybody says you have to love what you do because then it's not like work—you just love it and do it."

Advice for Someone Seeking This Job

Once a pilot has earned an aviation license, one way to break into film, television, or commercial work is to land a job with an existing company that does a lot of film work. Then you can gain experience and make contacts for future jobs. "You have to learn about the different camera mount systems and what their capabilities are, what they can do and their limitations," says Wright. "The limitations of your aircraft are critical . . . There are so many guys, especially the young ones, that get their licenses and have visions of Air Wolf dancing in their heads."

Professional Profile: Steven J. Wright, Aerial Director/Coordinator

Steven J. Wright discovered his love for flying while serving in the Royal Canadian Mounted Police (RCMP). One winter, some hunters were missing in central British Columbia and a helicopter was brought in to assist the Mounties in the search. Chosen to go up in the helicopter, Wright jumped in behind the pilot and the two set off. "We flew around for about 45 minutes or an hour. When we landed, he landed in the exact skid marks in the snow—he put it down in the exact same spot."

Always mechanically inclined—"I started riding motorcycles when I was eight years old and I drag raced when I was a teenager. I've always been good with motor vehicles, boats, and cars"—Wright was instantly fascinated with helicopters and began visiting the local hanger whenever he could. An RCMP transfer took him to Vancouver, where he put himself through a commercial helicopter school. He completed his training in Calgary and worked as a pilot in northern Canada for a couple of seasons to build up flying hours.

Returning to Vancouver, he formed Wright Brothers Aviation (later changed to Vancouver Helicopters, Inc.), purchasing his first helicopter in 1981. Wright quickly built up his business by committing to stay in the city during the summer months when others left to fight forest fires or to pick up charter work. His clients responded by awarding him the winter contracts that his competitors were vying for. His early jobs included traffic reporting for a Vancouver radio station, and he formed Calgary Helicopters to cover that market as well. Over time, he picked up work with the local police department, television stations, and some video work, expanding into feature films as production companies began coming to Vancouver to shoot.

"I cut my teeth working in television, doing news. From there I started working with a lot of the local cameramen and was recommended by the news guys. A lot of ex-news camera guys become film cameramen. I started on little local films, then commercials, and went right into film."

VOICES OF EXPERIENCE

What do you like least about your job?

"What I like least is the ego. Film is full of ego. You have to deal with it, understand it. Your own ego, as well."
—Steven Wright

What do you love most about your job?

"I love being given the freedom to go out and shoot. That's when my creativity comes out and I can put my input into it, design shots and go and execute them. Come back the next day and in dailies they go 'Oooo . . . aaahhhh . . . ' That's the most rewarding."
—Steven Wright

One of the early feature films in Wright's career was *Narrow Margin*. "We blew up a Jet Ranger on that show. There were a lot of shots with guys crawling all over the train, while going through canyons. It was great working with Peter Hyams because I learned a lot from him about light, color of light, temperatures, and things like that. It was great working with some of the L.A. stunt guys." Another highlight was the feature film *Alaska*.

In the late 1990s, Wright began selling off his various company holdings and relocated to Palm Springs, California. "It can get really crazy

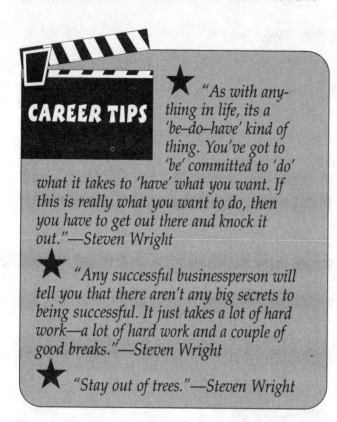

when you've got three or four different jobs on the go and you're scrambling here and there. At one point, I remember we had eight films on the go simultaneously. Each film required about a thousand phone calls, so our phones never stopped ringing. In the film industry they change everything—so you have to nail them down. For every hour of flying, we maybe had to put in an hour and half of telephone work."

Wright purposefully took a year and a half off from film work, but was eventually drawn back into the business by offers he could not refuse. He accepted work on the television series *Atomic Train*, and feature films *Lake Placid* and *Reindeer Games*. "I don't really chase work. I keep my ear to the railroad track a little, but I look for the more interesting jobs and work with people that I've worked with before."

JOB TITLE: VISUAL EFFECTS SUPERVISOR

Job Overview

The visual effects supervisor is responsible for designing those visual effects that cannot be produced on set due to practical, budgetary, or safety constraints. For example: a stunt involving two cars narrowly avoiding head-on collision is dangerous and expensive to create. A safer and more cost-effective way of accomplishing the stunt might be to shoot each of the cars individually and combine the footage using computer generated effects to ensure the maximum action value. Visual effects people are also responsible for correcting shots. For the movie *Bounce*, visual effects supervisor Al Magliochetti was called upon to alter the background footage to make it appear that there was more snow. Visual effects may also be required to remove unwanted elements from shots, such as telephone wires.

Expanded Job Description

Ideally, Magliochetti is involved with a project while the script is still being written. Because of his training in writing and directing, in addition to visual effects, he is often able to make suggestions to the writer that will maximize the visual effects budget.

Generally, he reads the script and makes notes about possible effects. He meets with the director and/or producer to discuss the director's vision for various effects. Often, he reviews the storyboard to identify particular sequences that involve effects. Then he, the director, and other department heads, such as art director, stunts, and makeup effects, meet to discuss who will handle the various aspects of the effect: "If it's a transformation, makeup effects can handle the altering of the person's body structure up to a certain point. After that, a digital effect might take over to blend, or morph, to the next stage of the makeup. In the case of stunts, the stunt people will outline what they can safely do. Let's say they are going to perform a high fall off a building, but need to be tethered by some type of safety wire. We will discuss the best angle to shoot from and what it will cost to remove the wire using visual effects."

Next, Magliochetti submits a budget that outlines what the various effects will cost. In some instances, the effects job will be presented to several effects companies and it becomes the producer's job to decide who is the most cost-effective person to deliver the quality desired.

Once filming begins, Magliochetti prefers to be on set as often as possible when scenes involving effects are shot. This enables him to do damage control, correcting potential problems and continuity errors. He also takes photographs, measurements, and notes to use when the effect is put together. Although some prep work can be done at this stage, generally he must wait until the locked picture cut of the film is available before he begins creating the effects.

Once the picture is locked, Magliochetti can begin ordering the original negative to be pulled and scanned to the specific lengths required to complete the shot. Once the footage is scanned, it can be loaded into the computer as a series of sequential files. "We don't work on it as a movie, we work on it as a group of stills. If you were to see this data in the computer, there would be the shot number, with a number after it, like 001, 002, 003. Each of these individual frames is loaded sequentially as a separate photograph." Similar to animators working on cells, the work is broken down into single frames.

Temporary shots are completed first to ensure the visual effect is proceeding in the manner the director and producer envision. For many directors and producers, committing their film and financial resources to the visual effects department is a leap of faith. Temporary versions of the shots allow them to see they have hired the right person to deliver the effect. "We give them a lower resolution version on video so they can see the direction the effect is going in. It is a lot easier to implement any changes they have at this stage. Once everything is locked down perfectly, a change could send us back to square one. Keeping the lines of communication open is important."

Once temps have been approved, the final render is made. "Basically, we have the computer complete the shot at film resolution. The sequential files are then transferred to a data tape and delivered to a service bureau, where the sequences are read into a laser film printer, which creates a new negative for the film—essentially a duplicate negative with the newly created visual effects in place. Then hopefully you get paid and get a credit!"

Special Skills

Visual effects artists must have advanced computer skills and an understanding of cutting edge technology as it applies to the creation of visual effects. A well-rounded background in filmmaking is a must.

Advice for Someone Seeking This Job

"Learn filmmaking," says Magliochetti. "Don't just learn computers. Film is a very collaborative medium; you need to be aware of other people's jobs. More importantly, you need to know film itself: you need to know a little about the chemical structure of film—how it works and how it reacts to light. Creating the effect is only part of the equation. Ultimately, you must make the effect look like it was shot on film. Many computer people forget this. That is why a lot of effects are digital looking. The average viewer can't really tell what is wrong with a shot, but it doesn't look right. The visual effects person's job is to integrate the digital effect into the film seamlessly, so that it looks like it was always a part of the film."

"Learn to draw, which teaches you how to see, and then go out and make a little movie—a little short. Make as many of them as you can because the process teaches you almost everything you need to know to go out and do a visual effects supervising job . . . Learn how to be a film-maker," advises visual effects supervisor Jeffrey Okun. From the short films you create, put together a reel of your best work to show potential employers. "I recommend that you go to work at a little visual effects house where they will give you an opportunity to grow, as opposed to a big visual effects house where you'll be a runner or the guy logging stuff, and it takes years to move up . . . There are a billion little companies that desperately need people who want to learn and are willing to sleep on the floor or whatever it takes for their opportunity."

Professional Profile: Al Magliochetti,
Visual Effects Supervisor and Owner, Eye Candy

"I was always interested in movies," says Al Magliochetti. "I have been making my own films since the age of ten." The small-town Connecticut native was captivated by classic monster movies from a young age. "I didn't find them scary, I found them fascinating: when I saw the invisible man unwrap these bandages and there was no head underneath, or when I saw this man standing in the light of a full moon and then turn into a wolf—these images to a child of 7 or 8 years old were completely fascinating. I wanted to know how those effects were done."

At the time, not much was written about how effects were created, but Magliochetti searched for answers. Along the way he learned more and more about film, developed a passion for it, and decided to make his own movies. He soon discovered that effects were a way to make his movies stand out.

After high school, Magliochetti attended film school at Columbia College in Chicago. Midway through his studies he decided to take a year off from filmmaking. "I had to decide whether it was something I wanted to pursue as a profession or if it was just a hobby. I was still locked into the small-town Connecticut mentality and didn't know for sure if it was something I could do. Hollywood seemed so far away and unapproachable; it was kind of intimidating."

During the year break from film school, Magliochetti attended a state college, taking general education classes and discovering that he missed filmmaking. With much of his general course work behind him, he was able to concentrate on film for the remainder of his college education, enrolling at the University of Bridgeport in Connecticut. "At the time, it was the number four film school in the country. They used teachers from NYU, the number three film school in the country."

While other Bridgeport film students made several short films, Magliochetti opted for another approach, channeling all his resources into one film with numerous visual effects. "It was eight minutes long and there were 128 shots in it. Of the 128 shots, 65 of them had some form of visual effect. The most complicated one had 43 layers of film." The film earned a Student Academy Award nomination.

After graduating from Bridgeport, Magliochetti began to look for a job. Living about an hour and a half outside of New York City, he spent his days papering Manhattan production companies with his résumé. "Anyone who would let me through the door!" When the phone didn't ring with an offer, he made cold calls, following any lead he could find. He discovered an ad in a horror magazine that had been placed by a woman in Canada who was seeking a makeup effects artist. Magliochetti called: "I learned some makeup effects while studying animation and visual effects." Although the telephone call did not immediately lead to work, the two traded makeup techniques and eventually met. He agreed to pass out some of the woman's business cards at a horror film convention, where he managed to network his way into his first couple of jobs.

Another break came through reading an article in the same horror magazine, about a low budget independent filmmaker who had released a film that was heavily censored. "I was curious about what was cut out of the film, so I located his phone number and called the guy." A few months later, the director's producer called Magliochetti and asked him to come to New York for a meeting. He was hired and put in charge of effects for the director's next movie, *Brain Damage*, which went on to become a cult horror favorite.

VOICES OF EXPERIENCE

What do you like least about your job?

"My least favorite thing is trying to clean up someone else's mess."
—Al Magliochetti

What do you love most about your job?

"My very favorite thing is sitting very quiet and unassuming in a movie theater with a paying audience, watching the final result of my work, and hearing the reactions around me; the satisfaction of knowing that my work is being seen and appreciated."
—Al Magliochetti

Through his earlier connection with the woman in Canada, Magliochetti was asked to speak at a horror convention in Toronto, where he made contacts that led to his first television job, working on the *Friday the 13th* series. Work continued to come sporadically. He moved to North Carolina for a year and worked in makeup and miniatures at De Laurentiis Studios. In 1991, he decided to give Los Angeles a try.

"I heard *Terminator 2* was employing every effects person they could find—even those with minimal experience. At that point, I had a pretty good résumé, so I thought it might be worth a shot. I didn't know that Los Angeles effects companies are very geographically prejudiced. Meaning, if you're not in Los Angeles, they won't import you for work. They don't want to tell you to come from out of state, because they don't want that responsibility if the work dries up. To get a feel for what work was available, I got a Los Angeles voice mail number for $10 a month. I put that number on all of my résumés and mailed them out while I was still on the East Coast. Basically, I faked my geography." Once he received enough job leads that he felt confident about making a living in Los Angeles, Magliochetti relocated.

Thinking he was moving to work on *Terminator 2: Judgment Day*, Magliochetti arrived in Los Angeles to discover that the production was stalled for a few weeks. Stranded, he printed up résumés and began taking them to production companies around town. "I had been out here three weeks and a day, when I got a call from a company that needed help on a film called *The Dark Half*, which became a complicated film to complete." The company's other projects were pushed to the back burner while everyone worked on *The Dark Half*. Magliochetti went in after hours, on his own time, to work on the other movies, so that the company would not get too far behind schedule. "The one I did the most work on was *The Addams Family*."

Although Magliochetti created most of the visual effects for *The Addams Family* himself, the film's success found many others taking credit for his work. "I was shocked one night to turn on a documentary show on special effects. One of the makeup artists for *The Addams Family* was showing my footage of the hand running across the street and claiming it was a robot hand that he built. I couldn't believe it!"

Eventually, Magliochetti did work on *Terminator 2* for a couple of weeks, but continued to devote his free time to *The Addams Family*. His next break was being hired as supervisor of animation on *Star Trek VI: The Undiscovered Country*. Although he was taking on more responsibility, the effects facility he was working for did not give him a raise. "When I had the audacity to ask for a raise, they let me go, saying they couldn't afford me."

The effects load for *Star Trek VI* was shared with another house, Industrial Light and Magic (ILM)—the world's premiere effects facility. When Magliochetti telephoned his colleagues at ILM to let them know he was no longer involved with the project, they invited him to come work with them. At ILM, he not only continued his work on *Star Trek VI*, but worked on *Hook*, as well.

Having worked steadily for more than six months, Magliochetti decided to permanently move from the East Coast to the West. "I threw all my belongings in a truck and drove out to stay. Suddenly, all the effects splurge dried up and I didn't have any work for the next six months."

Terminator 2 proved to be a groundbreaking film for computer generated visual effects. Once it hit screens, traditional animation was outdated. Up until this time, effects were created by traditional animation and graphics; the only computers were motion control cameras.

Magliochetti knew he would not only have to learn to use a computer, but also figure out how to integrate his experience into this new technology. A break in his learning curve came through *Waterworld*.

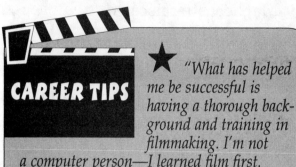

CAREER TIPS

★ *"What has helped me be successful is having a thorough background and training in filmmaking. I'm not a computer person—I learned film first. I have held down almost every conceivable job possible on a film set, at one time: from cameraman, to running sound, to being a production manager. I know what everyone's job is and how those jobs overlap. That enables me to give more to the production."—Al Magliochetti*

Similar to what had happened when *Terminator 2* had gone into production, *Waterworld* employed anyone who had even rudimentary knowledge of effects, training them to complete the project. Working on *Waterworld*, Magliochetti mastered computers and discovered the potential they had for creating visual effects.

After *Waterworld* wrapped, he went to work for an optical facility whose primary services were titles and simple visual effects. When he landed the job of visual effects supervisor on *Jason Goes to Hell: The Final Friday*, Magliochetti struck a deal wherein the facility would provide support, in terms of equipment and personnel to put the effects together, and he would create all the animation. "I did every frame of animation for *Jason Goes to Hell* myself. I had a crew of three people: one person running an optical printer; one person running my animation camera to shoot my artwork, because it was a union shop; and one person to transcribe my notes into optical printer terms, so they could be composited on the film properly."

Through a connection made in a film chat room, Magliochetti discovered that Columbia College, where he first went to film school, had a support group in Los Angeles. Serendipitously, the association was having a get-together the following week, very close to where he lived. Magliochetti was able to reconnect with people from his film classes 20 years earlier, one of them being a writer/director who was putting together a remake of the 70s cult film *Vanishing Point*, for Fox Television. "He asked me what was possible with visual effects and computer graphics. At this point I had a 486 computer with a whopping 16 megs of RAM that I purchased for the very good price of $5,000! I wanted to get into computer graphics, but RAM was hideously expensive. With 16 megs, I was limited in what I could do."

Hired as the effects supervisor for *Vanishing Point*, Magliochetti planned to farm out the more complicated effects to shops around town, and handle the basic effects with his own equipment. When three-quarters of the filming was completed, the crew, pushed to the breaking point by the production manager, decided to unionize. To handle the union conversion, money had to be taken from postproduction: editing, music, and visual effects. Left with less than one-third of the original visual effects budget, the director and producer met with Magliochetti to discuss concentrating on just the effects he was working on, or cutting them all. Although he had only an early version of Photoshop and a morphing program to work with, he convinced them to let him see what he could do.

"With only 16 megs of RAM, I had to be resourceful. I was trying to make these programs do things they weren't designed to do. I figured out a way to make the morphing program do motion tracking—which I still can't believe I did. Fortunately, there was just enough versatility in these programs that I was able to squeak by and create all the effects required, and even do a few fix-its.

"At this point, I thought, 'If I can do this with a machine that is just limping along, what happens if I get a couple of machines that have some real firepower?' That was the next step."

In 1996, Magliochetti formed his own effects company, Eye Candy. His first projects were a couple of children's films for Kushner-Locke Company and Full Moon. From there it was onward and upward, with work on the miniseries *Dune*, and features *Bounce*, *Miss Congeniality*, and *The Cider House Rules*.

Interestingly, the producer of *Vanishing Point*, Alan Blomquist, who had been so impressed that Magliochetti was able to create visual effects with his bargain-basement computer, was one of the producers of *The Cider House Rules*, proving the clichés: "What goes around, comes around," and "It is not only *what* you know, but *who* you know." Magliochetti is currently finishing up work on *Ghost World*.

Professional Profile: Jeffrey A. Okun, Visual Effects Supervisor

A former comedian, musician, and record producer, it was probably Jeffrey Okun's work as a magician that best prepared him to be a visual effects supervisor. He earned an advanced degree in international marketing and management from the United States University in England, and gained entertainment experience in a variety of areas before discovering his talent for filmmaking.

At one point, Okun drove a tow truck by day and worked nights as a standup musician, performing a comedic musical act and touring with a band called The Cross. The group caught the attention of Jimi Hendrix, who signed the act with the intention of producing them. Hendrix jammed with the group, took them to a concert, and then flew off to England and died.

A brief fling with record producing followed. "I dropped out of that and went to the unemployment office and picked up magic. In those days you had to sit in the unemployment office for days. It wasn't like it is today, where you fill out a form and they mail you a check. You had to actually go there, fill out the form, be interviewed, and sit there until they found a job for you . . . My job was to convince people that they didn't want to hire me.

"I used to sit down in the unemployment department and read books on magic and bore all the people by trying magic tricks out on them . . . 'Pick a card . . . ' I learned a lot of things about visual effects through magic. It's all about illusion and misdirection."

At the time, Okun's next-door neighbor was a film music composer. He introduced Okun to a friend named Saul Bass, who needed a gofer. "Saul was one of the leading graphic designers in the world, the guy who reinvented the title sequence for movies. He won an Academy Award for a short film called *Why Man Creates*. He was quite influential and knew everybody under the sun. He was George Lucas's student adviser when Lucas was at USC."

Because Bass didn't drive, Okun's job was to pick him up and drive him to meetings and work locations. The first Saturday, he drove Bass to USC: "They had rented somebody's apartment and were shooting out the window to the USC football field, where the marching band was standing by to march and form the word 'And' for a title sequence for *That's Entertainment II*. The DP offered me a doughnut, which was phenomenal, and let me look through the lens. It was a brand new lens that had just been invented, called an 11:1 zoom. From where

VOICES OF EXPERIENCE

What do you like least about your job?

"What I like least about the job is that there is a great deal of talk and waving your hands around, trying to get people to understand what it is that you can do for them . . . People come to you asking for something nobody has ever seen before. You present them with an idea and they say they have no idea what you're talking about—that's because nobody has ever seen it before!"—Jeffrey Okun

What do you love most about your job?

"What I love the most about the job is that it is never boring . . . You never know what new and exciting challenge you're going to have to solve."—Jeffrey Okun

we were, I could zoom back and see the entire stadium or zoom in and get just one person on the field. From that moment on I was totally hooked . . . The doughnut and looking through the lens was the thing that hooked me."

Bass was simultaneously working on two major projects at the time: NBC's Fiftieth Anniversary Special and an industrial film for Warner Communications, which gave Okun the opportunity to observe the editors of each. He begged them to teach him about the process. The assistant editor on one project abused Okun's offer to work for free by assigning him to take out the trash, pick up food, drop off and collect his dry cleaning, and have his car gassed up, washed, and detailed, but taught him nothing about filmmaking. The other editor, Gary Rocklen, not only taught Okun about film editing, but allowed him to practice using the equipment.

"I would get in at 8:30 and make the coffee for everybody in the building, go out and get the pastries, open up all of the offices, turn on the lights and get the air conditioning set. Then I would go pick up Saul and bring him in, and then do gofer work all day long. At 5:30 I'd take Saul home, and then go back to the office and edit from 6:30 until 3:00 in the morning. I would sleep on the floor of the editing room until about seven or eight, then get up and go into the bathroom and scrub myself down with paper towels. I did that for six weeks. At the end of the six weeks, Gary [Rocklen] came to me and said they had very bad news: they had decided to reinstall the segment I was editing. I'd have to take the whole segment apart and put it back into its original roll so they could work on it. I begged him to look at the segment. He did, then ran out of the room and came back with Saul. They looked at it and then ran out of the room and came back with the producers of the piece and looked at it. Then everybody left the room. Saul came back in and said, 'Well, my boy, we're going to air your piece.' So the first thing I cut was shown on national television."

The assistant editor who had treated him poorly was fired and Bass made Okun his editor. "Saul said, 'I'm not going to pay you very much,' and I still had to do my gofer job, but at night I cut the Warner's piece . . . Eventually, Saul added slide library to my title. He was paying me $500 a month. I was editing all night and every weekend, and doing gofer work all day long." After a year, Bass allowed Okun to hire someone else to do the gofer work, giving him more time to edit. Okun worked with Bass on a variety of commercials, television specials, and a 30-minute film over the next few years, becoming his postproduction supervisor, line producer, location manager, and assistant director. Over time, he gained expertise in effects, working with the optical houses on Bass's footage.

After explaining the effect Bass wanted to achieve, Okun would sit with the technicians while they worked, eventually learning the technology. "I didn't know I wasn't supposed to do that. I was a very entertaining fellow, telling them jokes and getting them coffee . . . " In time, when he brought in footage and they told him the effect was impossible, he was able to offer creative suggestions for accomplishing it. "Eventually, these optical houses would get phone calls from movies that were in trouble and they would tell them to talk to me—I became known as 'the fix it guy.'"

The first feature Okun was called in to fix was *The Last Starfighter*, directed by Nick Castle. "It was really the first movie that ever used 3-D computer created graphics—not *Tron*, as everyone thinks. It turned out to be a small success and my name got around. That's how I became 'the visual effects guy': I got drafted into it."

Working on films like *Die Hard 2* and *Shocker*, Okun established himself as the optical king. On *Shocker*, he replaced a supervisor who had made promises to director Wes Craven that he could not fulfill. "I had to unravel everything, down to finding out where the negative was . . . and figure out how to accomplish a ridiculous number of shots in a ridiculously short amount of time, for no money." With technology rapidly changing in the early 1990s, he began mastering the digital effects world.

For *Sleepwalkers*, Okun employed the use of morphs in a new way. "Nick Garris is the nicest director in the world. He actually understood [visual effects] and gave us the proper amount of time to do them. We did half of the film optically and half of the film digitally. It was another transition stage. We did morphs like nobody had seen before . . . the camera was moving all the time instead of locked off."

Working with director Renny Harlin on *Cutthroat Island* required yet another set of skills. Okun had to create the illusion of two ships doing battle with one another, having only one ship to work with. When the director dangled people over an ocean that wasn't there, Okun had to create it. A big yellow crane was left behind the actors in a sequence of shots, which Okun had to remove in post. Having seen Okun perform magic in the repair of *Cutthroat Island*, Harlin expected even bigger tricks when he directed *The Long Kiss Goodnight*.

"Renny, being a quick learner, figured he didn't really have to shoot anything on the right set or in the right places. He would say to me, 'That building that is behind the actors won't be there. Instead, there will be a giant lake. All these trees on the left side will be office buildings about 20 or 30 stories tall. In front of the railroad tracks we'll have a four lane freeway.' I'd say, 'Renny, something in the shot needs to be real. Couldn't we shoot in front of a lake?' He'd say, 'You can do it.' Over his loudspeaker system he would say, 'If anybody has seen anything in the shot that they do not like, don't worry about it because Jeff Okun will fix it.' That just freezes your heart. I learned not to panic and that I could do anything, given enough time and money."

Okun's next big break came when he was offered the visual effects coordinating job for *Tomorrow Never Dies*. He would be the first American to handle the visual effects for a Bond film. At about the same time, he got a call from Barry Levinson to work on *Sphere*. Deciding he needed to do a "serious" picture over another action movie, and knowing there

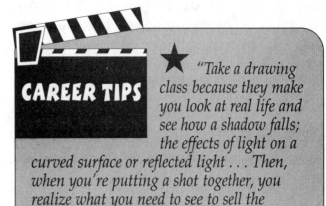

CAREER TIPS

"Take a drawing class because they make you look at real life and see how a shadow falls; the effects of light on a curved surface or reflected light . . . Then, when you're putting a shot together, you realize what you need to see to sell the illusion."—Jeffrey Okun

would always be another Bond film, Okun took the Levinson film. "How did I know it would turn out to be a terrible movie?"

After repeatedly turning down the invitation to work with Renny Harlin again on *Deep Blue Sea*, Okun was "blackmailed" into taking the job. "It was the first film where I got to create CG co-stars [the sharks]." He went on to work on *Delivering Milo*, directed by Nick Castle, who had also directed *The Last Starfighter*, Okun's first feature. *Red Planet, Death to Smoochy*, and the pilot for the television series *Birds of Prey* followed. Okun is currently at work on *The Last Samurai*.

JOB TITLE: PHYSICAL EFFECTS

Job Overview

"Physical effects designers are called upon by the production company when they cannot find a vendor that can do what it is they want to do, in a standard way," explains physical effects coordinator Jim Gill. "We come in and build or fabricate custom equipment for the shoot. A physical effects person also deals with elemental effects such as wind and rain, and other offshoots like pyrotechnics—where we blow things up and create fire and things like that."

Special Skills and Education

"For me," says Gill, "petroleum engineering was a good study because it deals with electronics, hydraulics, and pneumatics—all the subspecies of engineering, whereas most engineering courses are focused into electrical." He also sites a background in "still photography and color darkroom" as being assets. "There are a lot of things that make an effects person: they're on, they're alert, they're awake. If you're in a key position where you're trying to sell the job—trying to schmooze people—you have to be a little more of a salesperson and, obviously, have the skills and talents to do the job quickly."

Advice for Someone Seeking This Job

As the industry shifts more and more toward computer generated effects, the demand for physical effects will also change. "We don't have to take a lot of pain to fly somebody with thin wires. We can slap a couple of big cables on them and fly across the room and let the wires be removed in post." In some ways the computer has made Gill's job easier, but he foresees a time down the road where jobs are few and far between because of it. He suggests learning a variety of effects skills.

VOICES OF EXPERIENCE

What do you like least about your job?

"The best and worst is that it's quick and different. What comes in the door isn't the same boring thing again and again. It usually requires some thought and effort. Vice versa, you're always having to think and come up with new stuff, so you can't relax . . . "—Jim Gill

What do you love most about your job?

"It is probably the best hands-on engineering job I could find. I start [by] meeting with someone who has an idea or concept they want to transmit via film, and I help with the development of that idea. I will then come back and figure out how to make it happen in the physical world—build or fabricate something. Then I get to take it to the set and perform whatever it needs to do."—Jim Gill

Professional Profile: Jim Gill, Physical Effects and Co-Owner of Reel EFX, Inc.

Although Jim Gill took a few film classes in high school and even made a 45-minute movie, he did not consider filmmaking as a career option until a few years after college. Majoring in physics at Marietta College in Ohio, he later switched to petroleum engineering, but eventually earned a bachelor's degree in philosophy: "I could get out a semester early and didn't have to take all the math." After graduation he settled into a job trading commodities: "I started out as a runner on the [exchange] floor taking orders, and eventually moved up to where I had a seat . . . and traded."

A vacation with a cousin living in Studio City brought Gill the opportunity to visit a film set, where he met a man who owned an effects company. Suddenly, Gill realized how his engineering skills and talents could be utilized in filmmaking. Having always wanted to be an inventor, he saw the opportunity to fulfill that dream through inventing machines that would create special effects.

A couple of months later when his seat at the Exchange expired, Gill put everything he owned in a trailer, moved to Los Angeles, and said, "Hire me." He had no experience, but his earlier contact, the owner of Reel EFX, allowed him to hang around and learn. When an extra set of hands was needed for a job a week and a half later, Gill was hired. A year later, he was running the shop.

Today, Gill is a co-owner of Reel EFX and has been with the company for more than 15 years. The company has worked on numerous commercials for Honda Motorcycles, Lexus and Mazda, music videos for 98 Degrees, Bon Jovi, and Puff Daddy, and features such as *Clock Stoppers, Minority Report, The Outing, Skinned Deep,* and *Swordfish.* Gill invented the original frozen moment camera rig system that was later used in filming *The Matrix,* and designed the industry standard DF-50 haze machine and Diffusion Spray fogger.

JOB TITLE: PYROTECHNICIAN OR SPECIAL EFFECTS

Job Overview

Pyrotechnicians devise and orchestrate effects involving fire and explosives, and build the electronic devices used to create those effects. Examples of pyrotechnic effects include blowing up a building or vehicle, burning down a building, setting a person on fire, creating smoke effects, or staging fireworks.

Special Skills

In addition to his skills in pyrotechnics, special effects supervisor/pyrotechnician Robert Hutchins's background in theater proved an asset to understanding the theatrics of creating effects. An understanding of the filmmaking process is also important.

Advice for Someone Seeking This Job

The best way to get into this field is to apprentice under a skilled pyrotechnician. California law requires that pyrotechnicians be licensed by the state. "It's an apprentice program in California," explains Jim Gill. "You get a 3 card and work under other people. After you've done that for a couple of years and shown you have safely handled a number of kinds of work, they will vouch for you and you advance to the 2 card, then the 1 card. Then you can run off and blow things up yourself.

"I recommend people learn as much as possible about computer and digital effects, because that's the future." Contact pyrotechnicians to ask if you can observe them at work, and see if you can get an apprenticeship. Another option is to contact companies that stage fireworks displays.

Professional Profile: Robert Hutchins, Special Effects Supervisor and Pyrotechnician

From the time he was in junior high school, Robert Hutchins was involved in theatrics. He took drama classes, acted in productions, and worked on stage crews in high school. After graduating from high school in 1972, he took a few courses in radio and television production at Pasadena City College, then went to work full time at Magic Mountain in the entertainment department, "running sound, lights, and pushing chairs," from 1974 to 1976. Thereafter, he periodically returned on a freelance basis to work on special promotional events.

VOICES OF EXPERIENCE

What do you like least about your job?

"What I like least is lifting heavy objects."
—Robert Hutchins

What do you love most about your job?

"What I like most is the variety. No two jobs are the same . . . it's always a different location, working with different people."
—Robert Hutchins

"The big thing [at Magic Mountain] was Halloween. We dressed the park to be spooky and hired actors to run around as ghouls or whatever." Hutchins was part of the crew charged with staging an alien attack on the train that ran through the park and surrounding pastureland, using pyrotechnics to create special effects. The park employed several technicians who normally worked in the film industry to orchestrate these effects. By working with them, Hutchins learned some basic techniques in pyrotechnics and fireworks displays, and made contacts in the film industry. One of those contacts was Joe Viskocil, who later won an Academy Award for his work on *Independence Day*.

Viskocil became a mentor, helping Hutchins refine his skills and referring him for film work. He went on to stage manage the "Kingdom of

Dancing Stallions," before going to work at Cinnebar, a set construction and special effects house in Los Angeles. Starting out in construction, he moved into the electronics show, staying with the company for eight years. Having only a class 3 card for pyrotechnics, Hutchins hired Viskocil to help him on jobs requiring a higher classification. In turn, Viskocil hired him to work on *Terminator 2: Judgment Day* and other productions.

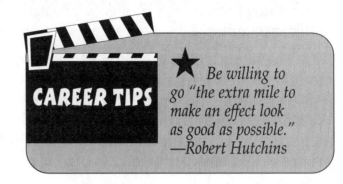

CAREER TIPS

★ *Be willing to go "the extra mile to make an effect look as good as possible."*
—*Robert Hutchins*

Hutchins left Cinnebar in 1993 and picked up freelance work, creating effects for commercials, designing programs for computer games, staging fireworks displays at Magic Mountain, and working as a pyrotechnician on feature films that included *Apollo 13* and *Free Willy 2: The Adventure Home*. His first special effects coordinating job was on the straight to video production *Mercenary*, the result of a recommendation from a friend he had worked with at Cinnebar. Hutchins also coordinated *Virus*, and moved up to special effects supervisor on *Pavilion of Women*. When not involved with a feature, he continued working on commercials and staging fireworks displays.

The relationship with Viskocil also continued. Hutchins was hired to work with him on *True Lies*, *Independence Day*, *Alien: Resurrection*, *Dante's Peak*, and *Godzilla*.

JOB TITLE: SPECIAL MAKEUP EFFECTS ARTIST OR EFFECTS MAKEUP ARTIST

Job Overview

When a cosmetic effect is required for a motion picture, television program, or print ad, that goes beyond what the straight makeup artist would do cosmetically, a special makeup effects artist is called in. "Whether it is the addition of a prosthetic or the reproduction of an actor in the form of a puppet or mechanical monster, it falls under the category of special makeup effects," say makeup effects artist Gabe Bartalos, who specializes in the design, sculpture, fabrication, and application of animatronics and prosthetics makeup effects.

"Generally, a job begins with meeting the director to discuss his vision and special effects needs. I'll get a copy of the script, read it through and make notations, and then I begin breaking it down scene-by-scene and making a list of requirements. Next, I sketch out initial ideas to show the director and ensure we're on the same wavelength. Sometimes I'll make what is called a mock-ette, like a clay illustration."

Bartalos then develops a cost projection to submit or "to see what is realistic to achieve."

"Once a budget and sketches are approved, I often sculpt another model before we begin on the full-size work. Then, we set about sculpting the life-size monsters over armatures and mechanical frameworks. We bring the actors to the studio early on in the process to take measurements and cast their face and body, and may have them return as work progresses to ensure pieces fit correctly and work as desired."

Once the sculpture of a face is completed, it is segmented: face, cheeks, nose, chin, and forehead are separated to make the finished prosthetics easier to apply. "The sculpture could take up to a week or more, depending on the complexity of the design; when you segment it, you have about another week of mold making. After the molds are finished, you get into running the foam rubber—the foam rubber has four components that are mixed together in a temperature controlled room and poured into the high temperature molds. Then the molds are stuck in an oven for three hours at like 250 degrees. When you open the mold, out come soft spongy foam rubber pieces. These are the actual prosthetics that will travel to the set to be applied to the actor. You run as many of these pieces as you need for shooting days. (Pieces are used once and thrown away at the end of the day.) If we're shooting three days, we'll run an extra set as a safety."

Bartalos must arrive on set a couple of hours before shooting begins to glue the foam rubber prosthetics to the actor's face. "Usually I'm there the entire day, keeping an eye on the makeup, knowing that the wear and tear of a day, the actor's facial movements, and heat of the lights takes a toll on it. You keep your colors and adhesive standing by and you touch it up, as it needs it.

"You're kind of a pep squad for the actor—this poor guy, buried in all this rubber for the whole day—you encourage him, or maybe offer a thumbs up/thumbs down to the different expressions he is trying.

"It is fun to see the actor bring your work to life. It's kind of the punch line to the whole process."

At the end of the shooting day, it is no small task to remove the special makeup effect. "A heavy prosthetic makeup can take up to 30 to 40 minutes to be removed. You go in with a skin sensitive oil that breaks down the adhesive and you slowly work it off the face, so that after a whole day of shooting, when their skin is a little more sensitive, it's not going to get beaten up. The prosthetic goes in the trash, you put some cold cream on the actor and send them off to take a shower. And get ready to do it all over the next day."

Shooting days are long for makeup effects artists. If the production were shooting 14 hours, from 7:00 A.M. until 9:00 P.M., special effects might arrive around 4:00 A.M. to begin applying makeup, so that the actor can walk on set by 7:00. At the end of the day, another hour or two may be required to remove the makeup and prepare for the following day. "The hours can be grueling," Bartalos says. "The way I look at it is, I think makeup effects is one of the fun-est forms of the arts for cinema, so I figure the long hours are the trade off. If you're getting to do something this cool, they're going to make you earn it."

Special Skills

Makeup effects artists should be skilled in sculpting and have the ability to sketch their ideas. They should possess an understanding of cosmetic chemistry, makeup application, lighting, anatomy, and color theory.

Advice for Someone Seeking This Job

"Get your hands on a camera and start creating effects for your own movies. It's a great way to see what works and doesn't work, at your own expense. Take risks and try anything, just to see what you can do. Then, put your name up on the board at film schools and volunteer to work on independent student films to gain more experience. Once you have footage of some work you've done, start applying to work at a big effects shop to gain professional experience, or try to land work on an independent film. Look for a mentor—someone who has been in the business for a while that you can learn from and go to for advice.

"This job is all about your sculpting and painting talents. Get a block of clay from an art store and start modeling a face, a hand, a character, trying to get what's in your head through your hands into the clay. Take a pad and a nice pencil and start doodling and doodling. Start practicing; tighten those skills. Spend hours making some cool drawings and some sculptures. Take pictures of your work or a color copy. Then take the images and photos you've created and start banging on some doors because everyone, including me, is always keeping their eyes open for new talent to surround themselves with—to be inspired by, to be supported by. You never know what the next job needs. It may need a bunch of new people to crew up to get through the job."

Professional Profile: Gabe Bartalos,
Makeup Effects Artist and Owner, Atlantic West Effects

"I have always loved movies, especially fantasy films," explains Gabe Bartalos. From a very young age he was captivated by the fantastic creatures and special effects he saw on the big screen. Recognizing their son's burgeoning passion, his parents gave him a Super-8 camera for his twelfth birthday. With neighborhood friends, Bartalos began to make his first movies. "Our films always had special effects in them and I started to zero in on that aspect. As I became more involved, I realized that artwork was the driving force behind the effects. When you see a decapitated head or a skinned body, if you look at it, there is a lot of artwork that lies behind the gruesome sight. I began to realize this was a great way for me to take all the painting and drawing that was my second love and channel it into my first love—movies." Throughout junior and senior high school, Bartalos took every art class and worked to develop his artistic talents.

While attending a horror/fantasy/sci-fi convention, "a gathering of filmmakers, film fans, and merchandisers," Bartalos heard that a film called *The Deadly Spawn* was being shot in New Jersey. Visiting the set, he was offered the opportunity to be an extra for a scene, and more importantly, he met Arnold Gargiullo, the man responsible for the film's special makeup effects. "He was very approachable and friendly, and lived two towns away from me in Westchester, New York. He said, 'Come on out to my studio, punk, and let's see your stuff.' I went out and showed him my humble, but ever-growing and enthusiastic portfolio."

Gargiullo told Bartalos he could "come and clean some buckets and the floor for no money" and get a chance to see that the work was not as "romantic" as he might suspect. "I was more than happy to do it. I was basically

VOICES OF EXPERIENCE

What do you like least about your job?

"Budget restraints. I hate when you have a great idea and the director loves it, but it has to be scaled back considerably because there isn't enough money."
—Gabe Bartalos

What do you love most about your job?

"I love sculpting and painting. I'm fascinated by faces and their expressions. I love getting my hands dirty with cement, clay, plaster, rubber, and blood. I love movies, especially genre fantasy films . . . I love coming up with a bizarre idea, sketching it out, sculpting up a model, and having the director say, 'That's exactly what I visualized. How soon can you build it?'"
—Gabe Bartalos

a sponge, soaking up information. It was a pivotal point for me, of hitting another level, where suddenly I could see what I called 'real' materials being used: resin, plaster, urethane, and foam being mixed properly. It was amazing."

Over time, Bartalos was added to the payroll. He was invited to visit the sets of films Gargiullo was working on and entrusted with more responsibility in the shop, as a mold maker and fabricator. "I was probably 15 or 16 years old, going out on the film sets and learning set etiquette very quickly: when to shut up and stay out of the way, and how to be a professional in sometimes difficult situations."

After high school graduation, Bartalos entered art school at Syracuse University. He continued to receive offers of work from Gargiullo, and returned to the workforce after completing one semester, spending the next year and a half working on a wide array of films, doing straight makeup, beards, wigs, and prosthetic work. "It was really a crash course, a wonderful education: hands-on in the makeup effects industry."

While Bartalos was honing his craft, gaining experience, and making contacts, the industry was evolving. Makeup effects artists were becoming film superstars. "People like Tom Savini became my idol. He was responsible for the ultra-violent splatter films of the early '80s. At the same time, Rick Baker emerged. Because of his outstanding work on *American Werewolf in London*, makeup effects was acknowledged by the Academy and made an award category." Baker took home the Oscar, the first for makeup effects, aside from a special award for *Planet of the Apes* in 1966. "It was a groundbreaking time. Rick Baker really took the art aspect of effects and brought it to the forefront, where the better your artwork, the better your gags will look. That became a whole new rush for me.

"It also marked the end of what is often criticized as the easy fix of blood effects. It opened up the door for nicely crafted creatures, elegant sculptures, cool demons, and graceful monsters. It really fueled the flame of, 'Hey, I could actually make money doing this!'"

Bartalos began looking through local trades for opportunities to branch out on his own. When Gargiullo turned down work on a film called *Spookies*, he suggested Bartalos. "Arnold had done some gags, but gracefully left and let me tackle some of the others. That was exciting, seeing my own creations on screen." The job led to work on *Killer Dead*, "a massive zombie film," shot in Connecticut and upstate New York. Bartalos designed the effects and managed a team of workers, using his apartment as a studio. "We had up to 40 zombies going, three-quarters of them actors in makeup and masks."

In 1986, a 20-year-old Bartalos and his dog relocated to Los Angeles with "a list of three or four effects shops." Within his first week, he landed a job at MMI studio, working on effects for a film called *The Dolls*. A month later he was on a plane to Italy with a crew of two others, assigned to supervise the film's effects.

Upon returning to the States, he took a job as a sculptor and mold maker with Reel Effects, then crewing up for *Friday the 13th Part VI: Jason Lives*. The company later sent him to Houston, to work on *The Lamp*. While there, he received a telephone call from Tom Savini, who was in Austin working on *Texas Chain Massacre Part II*, inviting him to join his crew when *The Lamp* finished. "Working with Tom was a real thrill. It was his work on *Friday the 13th* that began my fascination with horror in films and the execution of executions."

Once back home in Los Angeles, Baralos continued to see the value of working for studios, constantly refining his craft, but began to also look for projects he could do on his own. One that came his way was *Brain Damage*, shot in New York. Directed by Frank Hennelotter, *Brain Damage* quickly became a horror favorite and began a collaboration between Bartalos and Hennenlotter that spanned many years and genre classics such as *Frankenhooker, Basket Case 2*, and *Basket Case 3*.

> ⭐ **CAREER TIPS**
>
> *"Take every art class you can, from drawing to crafts and sculpting. Rent movies and study the special effects and try to recreate some of what you see on the screen. Be constantly working on the design of something. Each time you build a mask or monster, whether life-size or a model, even if it doesn't work, you learn something."—Gabe Bartalos*

Soon afterward, he received a call from idol Rick Baker, who was crewing up for *Gorillas in the Mist*. "I was so happy and honored to join that team. I spent a couple of months working on what he was hoping would be—and I think he accomplished—the ultimate gorilla suits that could cut in with footage of live gorillas—a really hard thing to do. It was amazing: idolizing him in the past and then working closely with him. I realized he was a real gentleman and fantastically talented. Though he had a large crew supporting him, he was the driving force behind everyone."

Bartalos later worked with Baker on a number of projects, including *The Beauty & the Beast* television series, *Coming to America, Gremlins 2: The New Batch, Something Is Out There*, and Michael Jackson's "Moonwalker" video.

Having gained a reputation for creativity, dedication, and dependability, effects shops began to call on Bartalos when they had tight deadlines to meet or needed additional workers to complete a project. In 1988, he opened Atlantic West FX, initially working out of his apartment. With more and more work coming his way, Bartalos rented studio space, later hiring additional effects artist to work for him.

This led to more film projects such as *Dead Space, Fright Night Part 2, Timemaster, Blookrush,* and the massive dinosaur construction for Douglas Trumball's *Back to the Future, the Ride,* shot in IMAX for Universal Pictures. "I long admired Doug's work. He was always resurfacing with an industry advancing process. As I sculpted T-Rex, I was impressed as to how specific he was about some of the details, while other aspects he let me run with."

In 1991, he met video artist Matthew Barney, who needed some satyrs built for his film *Drawing Restraint.* Happy with Bartalos's work, Barney hired him for five films shot over eight years that involved amazing locations from Budapest, Isle of Man, and Canadian Glacier fields, to deep underwater locales off the coast of Florida, and the extreme tip of the Chrysler Tower in New York City. The films were layered with heavy metaphors, bizarre sets, and to keep Bartalos busy, a wide variety of beautifully executed mythological character makeups.

Between film projects Bartalos honed his makeup effects skills by working on a series of covers for *Rolling Stone,* shot by high profile celebrity photographer Mark Seliger. Highlights included turning David Spade into a Pan-like character and the now infamous Marilyn Manson "naked feather shot."

Bartalos was recently contacted by Los Angeles-based Imaginary Forces to create the disturbing anatomical disintegrating effects for the current antismoking campaign.

Specializing in design, sculpture, and application of prosthetics makeup effects, Bartalos's Atlantic West Effects' additional credits include *Freejack, Playing God,* the *Leprechaun* series, *Side Show, Sometimes They Come Back, Genii, Slaughter of the Innocents,* and *Skinned Deep.*

JOB TITLE: EFFECTS ANIMATOR

Job Overview

The effects animator is responsible for creating noncharacter elements that enhance the shot and cannot be produced during filming. This includes tones and highlights, shadows, fire, sparks, stars, and the general enhancement of special effects, such as explosions, monsters, cloud formations, weaponry fire, and so on. For example: if footage of a spaceship and a blank sky have been shot separately and combined, the effects animator might be called upon to create the ship's shadows, or to add stars to a night sky.

Special Skills and Education:

The ability to draw, coupled with knowledge and skill with computer animation programs.

Advice for Someone Seeking This Job

An internship at places like Class-Key Chew-Po Commercials and other animation houses is a good way to get into the business. Find a freelance effects animator who is willing to teach you in exchange for your free services. "Branch out and get a couple of different skills down—don't limit yourself just to animation," says effects animator Harry Moreau. "Learn some software packages and be versatile."

VOICES OF EXPERIENCE

What do you love most about your job?

"I love it all. I really do. I've gotten into doing a lot of compositing and I really, really like that—it's a lot of computer work. I'm still into the traditional type animation, but the computer is kind of new for me. Animation has been my first love, but now I can combine the computer, which is a nice little addition."—Harry Moreau

Professional Profile: Harry Moreau, Animator and Effect Animator

"I always wanted to draw cartoons. I loved the Disney stuff. Warner Bros. was great too, but Disney was my favorite," says Harry Moreau, who grew up in Alhambra, California, not far from Disney Studios. Fresh out of high school at age 19, he landed a job as a driver, delivering film for the Haboush Company.

Owner Victor Haboush had worked as an animator on such Disney classics as *Pinocchio* and *Fantasia*. One of his animators, John Kimball, was the son of Ward Kimball, another legendary Disney animator. Moreau felt inspired just being around these men whose work he admired.

One day when extra help was needed to hand paint cels, Moreau volunteered. When it was discovered he could draw, he was hired as John Kimball's assistant, where he continued to hone his timing and technical skills. He enrolled at University of Southern California (USC), but eventually quit when he realized that he was learning more on the job.

During his five years at Haboush Company, Moreau worked on numerous television commercials and the film *K-9000*. "It was all traditional animation, at that point. We animated on paper, then painted on the cels in color. It was a wonderful time. There were all these boutique houses and ladies that would paint the cels."

After leaving Haboush, he freelanced for a time, working mostly on commercials and some film shorts. Doug Trumbull, a former director for Haboush, landed a job on *Close Encounters of the Third Kind* and hired Moreau as an animator on the

CAREER TIPS

★ *Practice on your home computer and hone your animation skills. Constantly try out new techniques.*

film. "Stars don't show up on film, so we had to actually paint them. We spit them out of an airbrush on black paper and then shot them. The comets and little meteors, shooting stars, were all done by animation. We animated the belly of the mother ship . . . " Many now-common animation techniques were devised on that film.

After *Close Encounters* wrapped, Moreau went to work at Apogee (which later became Industrial Light and Magic) working on *Battlestar Galactica* and its spin-off television series. "Unlike traditional animation, these effects had to look real because people knew what fire, explosions, and even lasers looked like . . . I fondly remember my time at Apogee, being surrounded by really, really talented people—the most talented crew of people."

Subsequently, Moreau spent two years doing camera work at Cinema Research, moved on to compositing and effects animation at Perpetual Motion Pictures, before returning to freelance work, which he continues to do. Some of his film credits include *Cats Don't Dance*, *Firefox*, *Little Mermaid*, *Never Say Never Again*, *Rover Dangerfield*, *Spirit: Stallion of Cimarron*, *Star Trek: The Motion Picture*, and *Titanic*.

● ● ● ●

CHAPTER
11
EDITORIAL

There is the story that the screenwriter wrote, the story that the director filmed, and the story that the editor assembled. Ideally, each is the same story.

Even before a production wraps, the editor is busy assembling the film footage into a rough version of the story known as an editor's cut. Working with the director, the editor refines the story through several stages until it is deemed ready to be shown to the producer or studio. Once approved, further changes may be necessary based upon screening audience reaction, before the final cut is made.

Those involved in the editorial process include:

- Editor
- First Assistant Editor
- Second Assistant Editor
- Apprentice Editor
- Negative Cutter
- Projectionist

JOB TITLE: EDITOR, FILM EDITOR, OR PICTURE EDITOR

Job Overview

In consultation with the director, the editor is responsible for the complex process of assembling the film or video footage in a cohesive sequence to ensure continuity. Some editors perform magic, repairing damaged elements, solving story problems, and turning poor performances into good ones.

Although generally hired before shooting begins to assemble their editorial crew and handle other preparation, the editor's most important job of cutting the film begins the day photography begins. Dailies are synchronized with the sound track and viewed each day with the director. The editor makes note of the best performances, particularly those the director prefers, and begins assembling the film scene by scene. An editor's cut is delivered shortly after the picture has wrapped.

"It's sort of like constructing a house," explains editor Edward Salier. "You have plans or a script; you have materials, which is everything that has been filmed; and you follow the script to construct the show out of the materials you've been given."

Special Skills

An editor must be a good listener and collaborator, and still have the ability to work long hours alone. "You can't allow your own ego to get in the way . . . it's not what I want to see, it's what the director wants to see. I really have to be able to sit and listen to him, get a sense of what he wants to accomplish, and deliver that as quickly and efficiently as possible. If he wants to see something different, I try it that way. I have to have ideas, but ultimately be able and willing to go along with whatever his vision is . . . It's an intense job. It's a long workday. You have to be able to work on your own. You have to have people skills and you have to have the technical skills. If you're lacking one of those, you're going to have a really difficult time."

Advice for Someone Seeking This Job

Salier cautions students coming out of film school that, even though they have earned a degree and gotten some experience, they are not going to land a job as an editor or even an editor's assistant. "The business doesn't work that way. You have to earn your stripes and pay your dues. You have to be willing to start at the bottom. My advice is to get an internship, where you can meet people and build relationships. Then be willing to work really, really hard. You have to be in a place and position where you can learn the skills and meet the right people. I can't emphasize enough it's a relationship business. Keep your eyes and ears open and your mouth shut. "

There are many avenues for finding a production assistant or apprenticeship job, where you can observe and eventually get some hands-on experience. Look into local television stations, commercial production houses, or postproduction facilities. Don't limit yourself to features or series television when looking for an internship.

Professional Profile: M. Edward Salier, Editor

It's hard to believe that editing was an accidental career choice for Edward Salier. As a young boy, he loved putting puzzles together to see the finished picture. Interested in visual arts, photography, and graphic design, the New Jersey native attended college before taking a postproduction assistant job at a small New York film company. Eventually he became an apprentice editor, although he was still undecided on a career. "To be honest, it was a job: money. I was in the business for probably five or six years before I decided it might be a career."

Having put in two years as an apprentice, Salier moved up to first assistant, working on a film called *Little Murders*. He landed a sound editor position on his next picture. "Supervising the sound editing of that movie, I got a real solid insight into how you put a movie together, how you construct the sound effects, and the whole process from beginning to end, as far as postproduction and editorial is concerned."

VOICES OF EXPERIENCE

What do you like least about your job?

"The negative part of it is the insecurity of finding your next job when the [current] job is over. And occasionally, working with very unpleasant people."
—Edward Salier

What do you love most about your job?

"Every show is its own little puzzle. You get to see the picture when you're done. That's what I love about it. I [also] love the collaboration, the people I work with, and the environment and atmosphere."—Edward Salier

In his early twenties, Salier began editing promotional pieces for upcoming movie releases. His first project was a behind-the-scenes making of the movie piece for *Song of Norway*. While working on it, he discovered his love of editing. "I decided this was intriguing, because you really get to construct something. I got to do the kind of things I enjoyed . . . the structural aspect of making puzzles."

As work opportunities dwindled in New York, Salier relocated to Los Angeles in 1978. Although he had worked in the industry for a number of years, he still faced difficulties getting into the union in Los Angeles. Without union membership, he was unable to work on features and television series, which were almost all union controlled. To subsidize his income between nonunion productions, he got involved in the computer industry, doing programming.

Salier's first break came soon after, editing the horror film *Silent Scream*. He found more work on low budget independent features and then got involved in videotape editing. "What I saw happening was, the future of television was going away from film and toward videotape, so I made the decision to get involved at an early date . . . In terms of editing, they were looking for people that could learn the new computerized editing system. I was in a position to do that. I had the dramatic editing background and the computer background, so I could learn these new systems that were replacing the traditional film editing equipment, that very few people knew how to run."

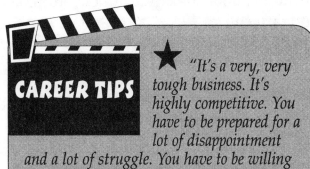

CAREER TIPS

★ *"It's a very, very tough business. It's highly competitive. You have to be prepared for a lot of disappointment and a lot of struggle. You have to be willing to put in years to get to the point where you have opportunities. It's not going to happen overnight."—Edward Salier*

Salier mastered the new technology and was admitted into the union, and work began coming in a steady stream. Over the next decade he worked on a variety of television series, including *Beverly Hills 90210*, *The Client*, *The Division*, *Lois & Clark: The New Adventures of Superman*, *Quantum Leap*, and *Sliders*.

JOB TITLE: POSTPRODUCTION FACILITY MANAGER OR DIRECTOR OF POSTPRODUCTION

Job Overview

The manager or director of a postproduction facility helps achieve the client's postproduction goals, from taking the initial phone call that asks "How do we do this?" to offering suggestions and explaining what can be achieved with different effects, to creating the master tapes that meet the technical specifications of the end user.

As senior editor at Scene Three Media Works, Joe Askin's responsibilities also include hands-on editing of material that Scene Three produces, as well as being hired to edit for outside clients.

Special Skills and Education:

In addition to editing skills and a thorough understanding of the film-making process, a successful film editor must possess a strong work ethic.

Whether knowledge is gained in school or working on the job as an intern, Askin believes it is important to understand the history of the film industry, its traditions and special lingo. "It helps you fit in and feel comfortable about the environment. It makes people realize you've tried hard to learn things."

Advice for Someone Seeking This Job

Working as a runner, PA, or grip are good ways to get on set, where you can gain exposure to all aspects of production.

"Internships are a good way to decide if you're going to like working in the business," says Askin. "People in the TV business have a certain personality, just like theater people have a certain personality and musicians have a certain personality. You've got to make sure you're going to like being around those people.

"If you're in a small town working at the cable TV station, you're not going to get too many opportunities. So you might have to pick up and move to a bigger city. Just be aggressive: knock on doors and hope that somebody, a mentor, takes you under their wing."

Professional Profile: Joe Askin, Director of Postproduction, Scene Three Media Works

Joe Askin has been fascinated with television since he was 10 years old. The Louisville native avidly watched news programs, not to keep up on current affairs, but because he found the production aspect interesting. By the time he was 15, he had acquired an 8mm camera and a simple editing splicer, and began filming shorts. He continued to make movies in high school and would sometimes gather his family together, set up the projector and screen, and stage a little premiere. "When those were received favorably and I wasn't embarrassing myself, that people seemed to like them, I realized it was worth pursuing as a career."

Askin's first lucky break came during high school. His mother worked for the board of education in the audiovisual department, giving him access to all of their equipment. "They had just gotten some black and white cameras and tape recorders—this was '72. These were relatively inexpensive. Nobody at the school board knew how to use them, or cared about using them. I'd go in and hook it all up and learn how to make stuff work. That was my first taste into the technical side." Soon he was teaching adults how the equipment worked, how to make dubs, and edit.

In his senior year of high school, Askin's mother got him an interview at the local public television station, also owned by the school board, which led to an apprenticeship. "I would go over to the TV station in the afternoons and just hang out and learn how to light, run camera, and use professional gear. They had opened a brand new facility. It was state-of-the-art."

Askin enrolled at Western Kentucky University in the fall of 1973. "They had spent several million dollars on a brand new facility. The professors were excellent. Some came from the outside world; they were producers for CBS. On Thursday they would leave and go do NFL Football [broadcasts] and come back to teach on Monday." Unlike some schools, where students were only allowed to watch the staff operate the equipment, the students at Western played an integral part in the programming the school produced.

"They would get a federal contract to create programming and try to make money with the productions. So it was real work; it wasn't just student projects. Out of the senior class, they would hand-pick five or six of the top students to be part-time employees."

Askin was already acquainted with some recent graduates of the school, who made calls on his behalf. When he went for an introduction interview with the faculty, he was offered a student employee position normally reserved for seniors. By the end of the first semester he had earned the same rights and privileges. "It was the first time that had ever happened, and was a pretty substantial break in my career." During that semester, one of the faculty members alerted Askin to an opening at the local television station, which he applied for and was offered. "I had two jobs and was a first semester

VOICES OF EXPERIENCE

What do you like least about your job?

"The worst part is the creativity, when it's not there. When what's handed to me is not very good and my own ambition and work ethic feels compromised because I can't make it good. That is very frustrating . . . Unfortunately, people that view it (the footage) a year from now may not know these situations existed, and are going to judge the product they're watching. Sometimes you really have to grit your teeth and trudge through it."—Joe Askin

What do you love most about your job?

"The creative aspect is certainly the best part of my job. It's really fun to work with other creative people. It's like the old saying, 'I can't believe they are paying me to do this.' That's really true when someone hands you great work and you're just taking it and doing your part. All the elements are there in the right order: the actors did a great job, the cast did a great job, and the wardrobe looks great. Then it's really a lot of fun."
—Joe Askin

★ *Some editors are 'jacks of all trades,' skilled at editing a variety of formats, but many specialize in one genre. Comedy editors are proficient at timing and making a joke work. They know how to cut the reaction shot to generate the best laugh and really play out the joke to its fullest extent. The same goes for cutting together a romantic love scene or a big action sequence. "When a producer is looking for someone to work on their project, they're probably going to gravitate toward someone who has a lot of credits doing that [genre]."—Joe Askin*

★ *"In our company, there is not a single clock in the building and there is a reason for that: you can't worry about going home. That's the work ethic thing; you're so wrapped up in the job that not just minutes slip by, but literally seasons slip by. We don't have windows. Not for any good reason other than it would probably be disheartening to see the sun rise and go down and the seasons change, and realize you're just pounding away on the same piece of work. If you're sheltered from that, it keeps your concentration. It's like when sports figures says they're 'in the zone.' You want to focus entirely on this one moment that you're trying to get across to the audience."—Joe Askin*

★ *Get your hands on a video camera and begin editing your own footage on your home PC, and discover whether you have a talent for editing.*

freshman carrying 18 hours, which was way too much. So I chose not to stick with the TV station job, and concentrated on the university job—I lived and worked there year round for four years. I never went home. I loved the work and was having a great experience learning more than I could possibly imagine." In his senior year, he was hired as a full time staff member.

Situated just over the border from Tennessee, Western students were frequently hired whenever Nashville productions needed extra help. "Generally it was carrying wardrobe, props, and sets; that sort of job. They'd call the university and a bunch of us would drive down and make union wages, rubbing elbows with the Hollywood types."

Initially interested in directing, he gravitated toward post-production once in college. When the staff editor quit during Askin's sophomore year, he was offered the full time position. "It was the closest thing to directing without directing, because you're deciding what shots go where and in what order."

After graduating in 1977, Askin went to work for WDCN, the Nashville public television station. He was there only four months when a college friend who was working in Los Angeles on *Hee Haw* called to offer him a job. He started the job in January 1978, but after two years realized that Los Angeles was not where he wanted to raise a family. So, he returned to

Nashville and his former job at WDCN. He was there only a short time when Scene Three opened. Askin joined their staff in the spring of 1981.

"We've done over 300 music videos, and I stopped counting at about 4,000 commercials that I've done." Other credits include *A Day in the Life of Country Music* for CBS, the NASCAR film *Thunder Theater, Music City U.S.A.*, and the series *CeCe's Place* starring CeCe Winans.

JOB TITLE: FIRST ASSISTANT EDITOR, ASSISTANT EDITOR, OR ASSOCIATE EDITOR

Job Overview

The assistant editor manages the editing department, maintaining an environment that allows the editor to devote his time and energy to the creative process of editing the film. With the assistance of the second assistant(s) and the apprentice(s), the first assistant editor is responsible for logging and organizing footage; maintaining all department reports and paperwork; interfacing with outside vendors, such as the film lab and sound transfer facility; taking notes during dailies and throughout the editing process, and whatever else is needed to keep the department running smoothly. After the picture is locked, the first assistant editor oversees the film through postproduction until the final print is completed. Some editors permit their assistants to gain hands-on experience editing a scene.

Special Skills

Assistant editors must be good communicators, extremely organized, and detail oriented.

Advice for Someone Seeking This Job

Obtain whatever experience you can by volunteering to work for free on student and low budget films, commercials, or videos. Then try to find a position as a production assistant assigned to editorial, or as an apprentice. Working for a

VOICES OF EXPERIENCE

What do you like least about your job?

"I least like when personalities become more important than the project itself."
—Michael Reynolds

What do you love most about your job?

"What I love most about my job is spinning plates. I love the fact that there is so much to learn and that every job is different . . . I also love working with Ridley [Scott] and Pietro [Scalia]. There is a level of excellence with them that they bring to each project."
—Michael Reynolds

postproduction facility or a local television station is another potential inroad.

Professional Profile: Michael Reynolds, First Assistant Editor

Raised in Southern California, Michael Reynolds initially planned a career as a theatrical director. He studied at UCLA, earning a bachelor's degree in theater, film, and television in 1989. While in school, his direction of department productions received acclaim. But it was when he directed a short film that he realized his eye was better suited for film than stage, and began pursing editing.

CAREER TIPS

"Put aside your ego and realize that people are hiring you to work for them. They're not looking for you to be the most brilliant editor. You work for them. Normally you're not going to be cutting picture right away; you're going to be making cappuccino."—Michael Reynolds

Reynolds' first post-college job was working as a production assistant on the television series *Parenthood*. Producer Sascha Schneider was so pleased with Reynolds's work that when he expressed a desire to get into editing, Schneider facilitated his hiring as an apprentice editor on the series *Veronica Clare*. Reynolds did some work for National Geographic before landing his first film, the low budget feature *Pontiac Moon*, as an apprentice for editor Anne Coate.

Impressed with Reynolds's work ethic, Coate hired him as an assistant editor on the next three features she worked on: *Congo, Striptease,* and *Out to Sea*. He picked up some additional work between those projects, including a month on *The Jackal*, before going on to *The Horse Whisperer*.

When renowned film editor Pietro Scalia mentioned to friend Anne Coate that he was looking for a first assistant, she recommended Reynolds. He was hired for *Playing by Heart* and went on to work on *Gladiator* and *Black Hawk Down*.

JOB TITLE: SECOND ASSISTANT EDITOR

Job Overview

The second assistant editor supports the first assistant in all his duties. Although delegated assignments may vary, second assistant editor Steve Sacks explains that generally "My job is to conform picture. I get a list from the editor and go to the shelves where all the film is kept, all the daily reels. My goal is to cut through all the reels, get the needed shots, and put them together."

Special Skills

Computer aptitude and a basic understanding of film editing are assets to becoming a second assistant editor.

Advice for Someone Seeking This Job

One way to become a second assistant editor is by starting out as a production assistant, preferably assigned to the editing department. Let it be known that you want to work in editing. Offer to work for free, assisting an editor, in exchange for observing.

Professional Profile: Steve Sacks, Second Assistant Editor

Los Angeles native Steve Sacks studied broadcast journalism at Arizona State University with the intention of working in sports. He served several internships working in newsrooms during semester breaks, where eventually he was allowed to edit sports highlight reels. "I got to pick which clips were used and write notes. The sports producer or the sports anchor would take my notes and he'd put his own style into it and use the footage I picked."

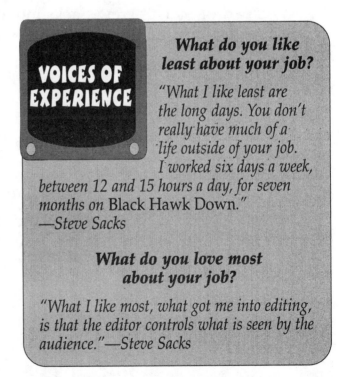

VOICES OF EXPERIENCE

What do you like least about your job?

"What I like least are the long days. You don't really have much of a life outside of your job. I worked six days a week, between 12 and 15 hours a day, for seven months on Black Hawk Down.*"*
—Steve Sacks

What do you love most about your job?

"What I like most, what got me into editing, is that the editor controls what is seen by the audience."—Steve Sacks

After graduating with a bachelor's degree in 1991, Sacks moved back to Los Angeles and landed a production assistant job on a live morning talk program called *The Home Show*. "I was a day player. They called me in whenever they needed me."

When a permanent production assistant job opened up in editing, he was offered the position. In time, he was selecting and editing the music for teasers and promos, and recording celebrity voice-overs, while continuing to assist the editors.

Two and a half years later, Sacks was out of work when the show was cancelled. Finding it difficult to locate another job in the film industry, he got out of the business for a couple of years and worked at a restaurant.

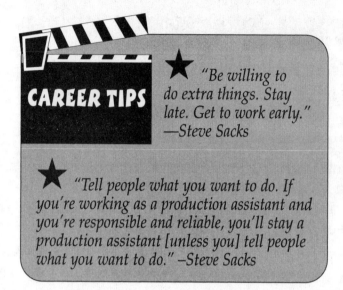

CAREER TIPS

★ *"Be willing to do extra things. Stay late. Get to work early."*
—Steve Sacks

★ *"Tell people what you want to do. If you're working as a production assistant and you're responsible and reliable, you'll stay a production assistant [unless you] tell people what you want to do."* –Steve Sacks

Through a friend, Sacks got back in the business as a day player on the feature *Dante's Peak*. Production assistant work on a few television movies and series followed. He served as writer's PA on the second season of the series *Clueless*, followed by a stint as postproduction PA on the pilot for *Love, American Style*.

Sacks' work as a PA in several different areas made him realize that he wanted to return to editing. Soon after making the decision, he was offered work as a production assistant to editor Pietro Scalia on *Playing by Heart*. It proved a pivotal point in his career. As part of Scalia's crew, Sacks moved up to apprentice editor on the features *Gladiator* and *Hannibal*, then second assistant editor on *Black Hawk Down*.

JOB TITLE: APPRENTICE EDITOR, APPRENTICE FILM EDITOR

Job Overview

Apprentice editor is an entry-level union position within the editorial department. They assist the assistant editor and editor as instructed, usually handling the cataloging of film and shuttling it between the film lab and sound transfer facility, and the editor and projectionist. "An apprentice editor is a combination of production assistant and assistant editor," explains apprentice editor Rex Teese. "We help log film and help load everything into the Avid [or Lightworks] editing machine. We run back and forth between developing houses, dropping off and picking up film. When it comes time to start cutting the picture together, we're there splicing the film for the preview cut. It's pretty much all digital now, but when they start previewing the picture, they go back to film. I'm like an overpaid librarian. I keep track of everything that comes in from production—every frame."

Advice for Someone Seeking This Job

Teese suggests landing a position as an office PA for a production or, as he did, with the area film office, as a good place to break into the business. His rise to success came quickly because he started his career in Richmond, Virginia, a considerably smaller filmmaking market than Los Angeles, where there was less competition for jobs. Another option is making connections with classmates in film school, editing their school projects. As they go on to work on other projects, they will already know you and your reputation.

Professional Profile: Rex Teese, Apprentice Editor

"I am just a long string of lucky breaks," says Rex Teese of his swift rise to success. He began editing movies while in high school. "In art class we had to make commercials for one of our projects. And for Spanish class we had to do these skits where we spoke Spanish. I usually wrote them." To get out of doing some of the work, Teese took on the responsibility for editing the pieces, which turned out to be more work. "This was back before you could do anything on computer." Using footage shot on VHS with a handheld camcorder, he rigged two VCRs to use for editing, stopping and starting and rerecording to make the edits.

After high school, Teese set his interest in filmmaking aside to attend Virginia Commonwealth University in Richmond, Virginia, where he studied to become a teacher and football coach. In his last year of college, while doing student teaching, he discovered that "I'm a pretty decent coach, but I'm a terrible teacher."

Inspired to contact the Virginia Film Office for an internship, he started work at the end of the 1997 school year, just as other students were leaving. Being the only intern in a small office afforded Teese a wealth of opportunities to gain experience and make industry contacts. "One day the Film Office loaned me out to a video shoot for the Dave Matthews Band. It was my first film job: working with this band I had been listening to for a couple of years. It was great!"

In the summer of 1998 he was hired as office PA on the *Legacy* pilot. Whenever he wasn't working, he could be found looking over the shoulders of the show's editors, watching and learning the craft. "The production manager and I didn't get along too well—we had a clash of personalities. She was about half a second away from firing me." Luckily for Teese, the editors were swamped and hired him on as an apprentice. When the *Legacy* editors weren't using the editing equipment, they allowed Teese to use it. "I was spending weekends and nights—all this time working on the machine. Toward the end of the show, they had to kick me off so they could work." By the end of the production, he had become accomplished at using a Lightworks machine and spliced a two and a half minute segment that remained in the released version.

Legacy was canceled early in 1999. Although Teese had gained editing experience and skill, his knowledge was based on the Lightworks system, whereas most editors use Avid. His next jobs were as an office and set PA on such projects as *Cherry Falls* and *The Contender*. While working on the TV movie *Cupid and Cate,* Teese received a call from Martin Jones, who runs Tim Reid's New Millennium studio, where a film called *Nothin' 2 Lose* was being edited. "They hired a guy named George Kelly, who cut commercials locally. He knew how to use an Avid, but fortunately for me, the machine at New Millennium was Lightworks. I got the job because I knew how to use the machine." Teese spent the next four months cutting the movie, finishing up in February 2000.

While working on *Nothin' 2 Lose*, Ridley Scott and some of his crew were in town scouting locations for *Hannibal* and visited New Millennium. Teese seized the opportunity to introduce himself to executive producer Branko Lustig and they talked briefly. He submitted his résumé to work on the film and two months later he received a call from Wesley Sewell, the associate editor. "I talked with him for about 20 minutes and he asked me to come down to the office. I did and we talked about 45 minutes. At the end, he just looked at me and said, 'Okay.' I asked, 'Do I have the job?' He said, 'Yeah, that's why I had you come down here.'"

One day he asked Sewell why he had hired him, and was told that people had said "we have this guy in town and you've got to hire him." Teese assumed it was because he was a good apprentice. He later learned "they didn't want to bring an apprentice from out of town and have to pay per diem and housing. I was the only one in the union, so they said, 'You've got to hire him.' That's how I got the job: I was the only guy in town."

Working on *Hannibal*, he got to watch the great editor Pietro Scalia at work. "It was like film school. Every day I'm sitting there in dailies with Ridley Scott and Pietro Scalia.

VOICES OF EXPERIENCE

What do you like least about your job?

"There is nothing that I don't like about my job."—Rex Teese

What do you love most about your job?

"What I like most about my job is that I've been fortunate to work for several legends of filmmaking: Ridley Scott, and the editor I now work for, Pietro Scalia. I've met and worked with some of the greatest guys in film."—Rex Teese

They're telling me everything I ever wanted to know. It was amazing. I learned a lot on that show."

His next film was *Hearts in Atlantis*, directed by Scott Hicks. The Australian crew did not bring in an apprentice editor, putting Teese in the right place at the right time. Once again, "I was the only guy in town, so I got the job." When the film wrapped, with no other project on the horizon, Teese filled his time editing a short movie for a friend and putting together highlight reels for local football coaches. He also directed, shot, and edited a DVD of performances for a local band.

Hearing that Ridley Scott was set to direct *Black Hawk Down*, with Scalia serving as editor and Sewell as associate editor, Teese lobbied for the apprentice position. While the film was shooting in Morocco, Scalia used an apprentice out of London whom he had previously worked with. When the film returned to Los Angeles, Teese was offered the job. Beginning in August 2001, he worked 6-day, 75-hour work weeks until the end of December. He drove home to Virginia for Christmas, and had been in town only five

CAREER TIPS

★ *"Take advantage of the opportunities that arise. I've known a couple assistant editors who, when the show is over, won't have anything more to do with it. Every once in a while, they'll be asked to come back and [do additional work on the film] and they'll say, 'No, no, I really can't do it.' You have to make yourself available to help whenever you can."—Rex Teese*

★ *Set goals: "I set goals for myself. When I started working at the Film Office, I said, 'Within seven or eight months I want to get a job working on a film or television show.' I did it within four. When I was hired on Legacy, I set a goal to be working editorial within seven months. Within three months, I was working editorial. When I first started editing, I set a goal to edit a movie or TV show by the time I was 29. I turned 26 and had already edited a movie. Again, I beat my deadline by half."—Rex Teese*

★ *Find a good mentor: "I have been lucky in that I've had extremely good teachers. George Kelly, who was the editor on* Nothin' 2 Lose, *taught me a lot. The two Canadians, Robin Russell and Don Cassidy, who were the editors on* Legacy, *were kind enough to let me just sit behind them and watch them work for three or four hours every night. When I'd ask them questions, they'd always answer them for me. I was lucky to work with Wes Sewell. He designed a lot of the classes that Avid used to teach other editors, because he was one of the first people to use it.*

days before receiving an offer to work as the projectionist for the DreamWorks feature *Ring*. Finishing up in early summer 2002, Teese returned to Virginia to edit some low budget films for friends, hoping to soon work again with Scott, Scalia, and Sewell.

JOB TITLE: PROJECTIONIST (EDITING DEPARTMENT)

Job Overview

Projectionists are responsible for obtaining the previous day's sound and film footage, syncing them together, showing them during dailies, and maintaining the projection equipment. On location, they move the equipment, set it up, and break it down each day.

> **CAREER TIPS** ★ *"A lot of editors are what I call 'closed door editors,' meaning they never want anybody walking in. But on* Hannibal, *every day Pietro [Scalia] would bring us in and show us what he was doing and ask us what we thought. We were bouncing around ideas. He'd tell me what I needed to know. He was a very open guy and a very good teacher."—Rex Teese*

"It takes about an hour and a half to set up and about an hour to break down," explains Rex Teese. "I'm usually set up an hour before dailies, just in case anything happens." Because all the footage cannot be viewed at lunchtime, a second round of dailies may be shown at the end of the day. "Plus, you've got second unit going and they may have a different schedule than the first unit. It's a good job. I get to sit there with the producer, the director, and the editor, and listen to them talk back and forth about how the movie will be cut together."

●●●●

CHAPTER
12

PUBLICITY AND MARKETING

For every big budget blockbuster that has viewers lining up outside theaters, there are hundreds of otherwise excellent productions that potential audiences never hear about. Sometimes all that separates the blockbuster from the sleeper is the money to advertise. Some of those responsible for getting the word out include:

- Personal Publicist: generate press coverage for a specific client or clients.

- Studio Publicist: generate press coverage for the studio's finished productions.

- Unit Publicist: generate press coverage during the filming of a production.

- Unit or Still Photographer: photograph the production process for publicity use.

JOB TITLE: UNIT PUBLICIST

Job Overview

The unit publicist is the marketing coordinator for a film that is in production. "The unit publicist's job is to be with the movie as it is being made," says unit publicist Cid Swank. During that time, they create materials that will help sell the movie to distributors and to the public. This includes building a press kit with talent-approved stills shot during the filming of the movie, artist biographies, press releases, and other marketing materials. "Basically, you're the one providing information to the studio, the financier, as well as to the outside world, anything that is going on with the film at the location spot."

Specials Skills and Education

Unit publicists must possess strong verbal and written communication skills. Their job is to excite others about the movie they are working on, through written materials and verbal communication. "Because communication is such a big part of the unit publicist's job," says Swank, "you want to get a degree in a subject where you are forced to write a lot of papers. My degree is in English literature. History is a good degree to get because you have to analyze the past and write about it—which is a big part of what a unit publicist does. A political science degree or any of the liberal arts are good." People skills and adaptability are other important talents of a successful unit publicist.

Advice for Someone Seeking This Job

Swank suggests reading Steve Rubin's book *Reel Exposure.* Serving as a production assistant is a good way to gain practical experience on set. Offer to work for free with another unit publicist on a small independent film.

Life experience has prepared Swank for her job as unit publicist. An example she points to is a shoot that took her to Morocco. Having previously spent time in a Muslim country, she understood the cultural differences. "When I arrived off the plane, I was wearing a dress. My upper arms were covered and my knees were covered and I wore this stupid hat . . . It made the Moroccans respect me all the more because I didn't get off the plane in my Banana Republic safari shorts and tank top. I knew I was going to a Muslim country and I came prepared for it. Being a woman, in a very male dominated society, they respected me all the more because I played it by their rules and was very respectful of their customs. A unit publicist is someone who has got to be a jack-of-all-trades, and understand that the movie is the first and number one priority."

Professional Profile: Cid L. Swank, Unit Publicist

"I have always loved movies. They were a big part of my life growing up," says Swank, who was raised in Asia in the '70s. American television programming was very limited in Asia at the time; movies quenched her thirst for American culture. "My parents were always taking us to the movies. It was like a family night: on Sunday we would go to a movie and out to dinner . . . it was such a positive childhood memory."

Swank returned to the United States and enrolled at University of California Los Angeles (UCLA). Although she considered a degree in motion pictures and television, she lacked the confidence to attack the extensive application process and instead opted to major in English literature. After graduation, she accepted a marketing position at a firm in the Los Angeles area. Noticing film sets popping up around her, she wondered if there was a marketing person associated with movies.

Twenty-eight years old and unhappy with her job, Swank finally quit. For the next nine months she satisfied her longing to travel around the world. During those months, she became aware of movies being shot in foreign locations and began to wonder if there was a position in the film industry she could fill that would pay her to travel. While picking wine grapes in Australia, she had an epiphany and decided to return

VOICES OF EXPERIENCE

What do you like least about your job?

"It is the task of identifying all the stills that are taken on a movie set. Everyone knows the main stars and the director, but people at the studio don't necessarily know the director of photography or the first AD. Because you take behind-the-scenes pictures, they need to know who exactly is in the picture they get. It is a very tedious task to identify everyone. It takes a lot of time."—Cid Swank

What do you love most about your job?

"Some unit publicists just love the writing aspect of the job—it's like writing a big term paper . . . For me, the big love is the fact that I'm paid to travel. I get to go into totally new cultures and learn how to work in that environment. That's what I love most."—Cid Swank

to Los Angeles to enroll at UCLA Extension, where she could learn how to make movies and try to land a job in the film business. With no financial aid from family or friends, Swank recalls, "I took my credit cards and got myself into debt enrolling at UCLA Extension, taking two classes at the beginning, because that is all I could afford. I held down a job as a waitress and a limo driver to make money to pay for rent and food."

Swank took advantage of the internship program, applying to work 10 hours a week for college credit (no salary) as a production assistant on *Guncrazy*, starring Drew Barrymore. As an office PA, her primary job was to make photocopies of scripts and whatever else was needed. On her second day, she was called into the producer's office; he had her résumé on his desk. Recognizing her experience in marketing, he offered her the job of unit publicist for the film. Instead of college credit, she would earn $500 for eight weeks of work. "Since there was money involved, I said yes. I haven't looked back since."

Swank worked hard and generated a lot of press for the film, building industry relationships along the way that got her recommended as unit publicist for another film. "The producer was so impressed with what I did for *Guncrazy*, she offered me $2,000 for eight weeks." The film was a low budget independent with a relatively unknown cast and no distribution. Struggling to generate any publicity at all, she became frustrated at the lack of press interest in covering the film. A friend suggested she contact Steve Rubin, a successful unit publicist. Rubin suggested she buy his book on unit publicity, *Reel Exposure*.

CAREER TIPS

★ *It is important that the unit publicist has a good working relationship with the still photographer, since they work very closely. One of the functions of the unit publicist is to alert the still photographer to potential candid shots that are important for telling the story. "Let's say there is a great moment where my director and my producer and my stars are all having a good time—I need to make sure that picture is taken. Or let's say I find out the local newspaper wants to do a story on one of my supporting actors. I have to alert the still photographer to make sure a picture is taken of the supporting actor with the lead actor, to supplement the story."—Cid Swank*

★ *"Treat everyone—everyone—not just your lead actors, not just your director, not just your producer, but everyone: your key grip, your grip, your craft services person— treat each person like they are important to the movie, because they are important. Treat them with respect. Always say 'thank you' and 'please.' Manners go a long way when you're working on a film"—Cid Swank*

★ *"Be open to last minute change. Don't ever take it personally when something has to change, because it's never about you; it's about what is going on with the movie as a whole."—Cid Swank*

"I went out and bought the book and read it cover to cover. It talked about all the different tasks and chores, as well as the politics of being the unit publicist on a movie set, but he never wrote about how you take a movie that has no distributor and no known actors, and get press for it; he didn't have that chapter." Two days later, after reading the book, she called Rubin again and explained her dilemma. "He laughed and said, 'Well, that's tough. You got a problem.'" Rubin advised she write the best press notes possible, which included biographies, synopsis, and quotes, and use it as her calling card. Over the next few years, Rubin would continue to be a mentor, answering questions and offering encouraging advice.

Before the film wrapped, Swank received a call from Nikki Palmer, the person selling the international rights to *Guncrazy*. Impressed with the press materials Swank had created for the film, Palmer offered her six months work on four different films for a salary of $500 a week. "That's when I quit the waitress job and I quit the limo driving job."

Her next big break came when she was recommended to Raffaella De Laurentiis to serve as unit publicist on *Trading Mom*, where she worked with Academy Award winning actress Sissy Spacek. Swank continued going from project to project. Through her connection with Steve Rubin, she landed a job with Showtime in the summer of 1993 to work on *The Birds II: Land's End*. She continued to work various projects for Showtime, at one point accepting a three-month contract to work four different movies.

Swank's ability to maneuver the set, her understanding of industry politics, and the fact that she was a good writer, earned her respect within the film industry. Raffaella De Laurentiis recommended her to director Dino De Laurentiis and daughter Martha, who hired Swank to come to Morocco to work on two Bible stories they were filming there. Impressed with her work, the De Laurentiises promised to hire her for their next feature. Over the next few years she worked on several made for television movies, and features such as *Breakdown* and *Stir of Echoes*.

After *Stir of Echoes*, the De Laurentiises hired Swank for *U-571*. "That was a huge movie—a $95 million budget—that was shot in Rome and Malta." Even though Matthew McConaughey was well known in the United States, he was an unknown commodity overseas, an important market for the film. It fell to Swank to educate the international press, proving she could handle big stars and an expensive movie.

Over the next two years she worked on several projects, including features *Warden of Red Rock*, *Blast*, *Proof of Life*, *Serving Sara*, and *Beyond Borders*. Swank has successfully combined her love of movies and travel into a career, while building a reputation for handling difficult shoots in exotic locations with ease.

JOB TITLE: UNIT PHOTOGRAPHER, STILL PHOTOGRAPHER, OR SPECIAL ASSIGNMENT PHOTOGRAPHER

Job Overview

Unit photographers photograph the making of the movie. They are responsible for capturing dramatic moments in scenes, photographing the cast, director, producers, and crew members while working and in candid moments off camera, and shooting portraits of actors and key personnel. "I tell the story of the making of a movie by shooting behind-the-scenes photos," says photographer Brian Hamill. "Sometimes motion pictures are tense, because there is a lot of money riding on it. Others, like Woody [Allen]'s are a more relaxed atmosphere. Either way, you have to make sure that you come away with good photos that capture the dramatic point of each scene, that tell the story. Good portraits of all the main people, especially the actors. I always try to shoot a poster, too . . . A lot of times they'll hire a special to come in, just to shoot the poster. Having been on that side of the fence, as a special, I kind of know what they want, so I always set up a little portrait session and try to capture the motif of the movie so they'll use it as a poster. You get paid extra when you get a poster."

Special Skills

"First of all, you have to be a good photographer," says Hamill. "You have to have a good eye. You have to be very perceptive and alert when you're a still photographer. You have to have eyes in the back of your head. You also have to know when to get in and get your photographs, when to get close enough to get good ones, but at the same time be unobtrusive. You almost have to be invisible. You have to not be afraid to get in there and get the pictures—you can't be intimidated by actors—you have to cover the scene. The people at studios don't want to know what happens in the trenches, they want results. It's up to you to work at the top of your talent as a professional and do whatever that requires."

Advice for Someone Seeking This Job

Hamill advises aspiring unit photographers to find someone who works on movies that can get you on a set to observe what goes on and watch the still photographer at work. To gain some experience, he says, "Try to find a low budget, nonunion production and volunteer to do some pictures for free. If I was doing it all over, I would work for free to get on a movie set and get some experience. Shooting pictures in a fashion studio is so much different than shooting movies. There are so many people. You can be in the way, especially with delicate love scenes or scenes involving anger or tension. You have to tiptoe, but at the same time, you have to get the work done."

Professional Profile: Brian Hamill, Still Photographer

For Brian Hamill, filmmaking was not the outcome of a designed plan. "I wanted to be a photographer. When I was 16, my older brother bought me a little brownie snapshot-type camera and I started taking pictures of my friends that I hung out with in Brooklyn. They were kind of graphic and design-looking pictures."

Prior to leaving New York to study art at the University of Arizona, Hamill decided to see if any colleges offered a degree in photography. He discovered Rochester Institute of Technology, not far from his home.

"Originally, I really wanted to be an artist, but I wasn't that good. When I picked up the camera, I was able to put elements of design into my photographs."

Hamill earned an associate's degree from RIT, but was drafted before he could finish his bachelor's. He served in the army from 1966 to 1968, then finished his schooling at City University in New York City. "I started working right away. I worked for about two years as an assistant for a couple of fashion photographers."

When Harvey Matofsky, a public relations friend of Hamill's older brother, came to New York, he changed the direction of Hamill's career. Matofsky needed a photographer and Hamill's brother recommended him. The introduction turned into an offer of work on a picture (never released) that was shot in Rome, Tanzania, and Sicily. When filming wrapped, he immediately went to work on *Doc*, shot in Spain.

VOICES OF EXPERIENCE

What do you like least about your job?

"There is no down side. I always wish that it paid more money. I think I'm underpaid, although other people in the business think I'm overpaid, because I get more money than most people. But compared to actors and directors and so forth, what they make, it's like a drop in the bucket."—Brian Hamill

What do you love most about your job?

"What I love the most is that I get to work in a business that I like. I've loved movies since I was a kid, so I couldn't think of a better subject to shoot than actors and the personnel involved with making movies."—Brian Hamill

After five months' work in Europe, Hamill returned to the United States and, with the help of cinematographer Gerald Hirschfeld and assistant cameraman Alec Hirschfeld, applied for membership into IATSE (International Alliance of Theatrical Stage Employees) Local 600. He was admitted two years later.

With two pictures to his credit, Hamill "got the bug" to pursue additional film work. Until he was admitted into the union, he worked on several nonunion films and began to pick up work as a special on an impressive list of features, including *The Conversation*, *The Gambler*, *Gator*, *Three Days of the Condor*, *Women Under the Influence*, and *Zandy's Bride*. "The movie company wanted additional coverage of different scenes. Having seen my portfolio, they hired me as a special. Whereas a unit photographer works from day one, until the end of the movie, a special comes in and only covers certain scenes. They may be scenes that are two days a week for ten weeks, or every day for three weeks."

In the mid-1970s, Hamill met Woody Allen at the famous New York eatery Elaine's. The two struck up a friendship and working relationship, begun on *Annie Hall*, that has spanned nearly 25 years and 22 pictures, including *Alice, Bullets Over Broadway, Broadway Danny Rose, Crimes and Misdemeanors, Hannah and Her Sisters, Manhattan Murder Mystery, Mighty Aphrodite, New York Stories*, and *The Purple Rose of Cairo*.

CAREER TIPS

★ *"Always work at the top of your talent. Never settle for less. The best picture is always yet to be taken. You do a good job and say, 'I'm going to do a better job on my next movie.' Always, always feel in your head that the best work is yet to come."*—Brian Hamill

When not working with Allen, Hamill worked with other great directors, including Martin Scorsese on *Raging Bull* ("I loved working on *Raging Bull* because I'm a big boxing fan. Getting to work with [Robert] De Niro was great."); Sydney Pollack on *Sabrina* and *Tootsie* ("Every day was a new adventure with Dustin [Hoffman] dressed as a woman. We'd go around and try to see if we could fool people. I'd take him to restaurants or into a friend's office and he'd pretend to be Dorothy Michaels, a soap opera actress."); Penny Marshall on *Big*; and Nora Ephron on *You've Got Mail*. "*You've Got Mail* was great, because it was the second time I worked with Tom Hanks. I did *Big* with him. Hanks is such a wonderful guy. It was nice to see that he is still the same guy, years later, after he became this big, huge star."

Hamill first worked with Barry Levinson on *The Natural*. Ten years later they reunited on *Jimmy Hollywood*, and have since worked on *Disclosure, Sleepers, Donnie Brasco, Sphere, Liberty Heights, An Everlasting Piece*, and *Bandits*. "The Barry Levinson movies were great to work on, because he's such a gifted director. He and Woody have been my North Stars in the business."

For Hamill's success, he still considers that "[the] best work is yet to come."

● ● ● ●

CHAPTER
13
SPECIALISTS

There is a small army of talented individuals whose specialized services are essential to many productions, but whose jobs are not generally known outside film and television circles. A few of these include:

- Agent: solicit and procure work for clients.

- Animal Wrangler: provide and train animals to perform specific actions.

- Casting Director: select actors to portray the characters in a production.

- Catering: prepare and serve hot meals cooked to order at meal breaks.

- Craft Services: provide snacks and beverages between meals; general clean up.

- Script Supervisor: maintain continuity of plot, speaking lines, movement, and so on, during filming.

JOB TITLE: AGENT

Job Overview

The primary function of an agent is to secure work for, and develop the careers of, their clients. Many agents carve out a niche by specializing in representing only above-the-line or below-the-line clients. Some concentrate further by representing only writers and directors, producers, or actors. Agents are actively involved in soliciting work for their clients, making it necessary to have strong relationships throughout the industry, and to stay abreast of which deals are being made and which productions are getting the green light. Agents also negotiate fees and contractual obligations for their clients.

Special Skills

Since most entry-level office jobs in the film industry are assistant positions that require secretarial skills, agent Jonathan Furie suggests cultivating strong typing and computer skills. After graduating from college and before going to work in the William Morris Agency mail room, Furie says, "I took a six week intensive shorthand and typing course. I really prepared myself for when I did make it out of the mail room onto an agent's desk." Agents and their assistants must be good communicators, have strong organizational skills, and always follow through.

Advice for Someone Seeking This Job

While a few obtain work as an assistant or secretary to an agent at a smaller talent agency, most agents begin in the mail room at one of the major agencies. While it may seem demoralizing for a college graduate to be delivering mail and running errands, the mail room is a rite of passage and provides an opportunity to learn the names of studio executives, directors, writers, producers, and others in influential positions in the industry. As an assistant, you'll have the opportunity to see how deals are negotiated and structured, and to make personal contacts. Many agencies require a bachelor's degree to get into the mail room or agent's training program.

Professional Profile: Jonathan Furie, President of Montana Artists Agency

Although he grew up in Beverly Hills with the film industry all around him, Jon Furie did not consider a job in the business until after college. He was first introduced to the possibility while working summers in a clothing store. Each year, William Morris Agency chairman Norman Brokow would bring his children to the store to purchase back-to-school clothing. One time, he asked if Furie had ever considered working in the film industry. Brokow handed him a business card and suggested that after he finished college, Furie might interview with the agency to start in the mail room.

"I put his card away and I really didn't think that much of it. I was going to school and studying psychology, child development, and abnormal behavior." Furie had nearly graduated from UCLA when he realized that he did not want to continue on to get his Ph.D. in psychology. Uncertain as to what he wanted to do, he remembered the earlier conversation, found the card, and wrote Brokow a letter saying that he would be honored to interview with the William Morris Agency. He started in the mail room in 1984.

Furie was eventually promoted out of the mail room and onto a desk as an assistant to an agent. He left William Morris a year later to take an assistant position with the Jay Michael Bloom Agency, in the department that handled writers, where he remained for 13 months. Then it was on to United Artists for a year to work in the studio's film acquisition department, where he watched movies and made recommendations about films the studio should purchase and distribute. Furie's next move was to Twentieth Century Fox Films to work for then-president of production, Scott Rudin. Three months later he transferred to work for another production executive, serving as a combination executive assistant and development

VOICES OF EXPERIENCE

What do you like least about your job?

"The part I like least is having to make the call saying, 'You came very close.' Oftentimes, clients will interview for three or four jobs and not get one. The other part I like least is when clients are not working as much as they'd like to and you know that they've got a wife, kids, a mortgage, and they're having trouble making their monthly nut."—Jonathan Furie

What do you love most about your job?

"What I love the most is the phone call from a buyer, meaning a studio executive, producer, or director, who says, 'We want to hire your client.' Then making the call to that client and saying, 'I have good news for you today.' That's the most rewarding."—Jonathan Furie

executive, charged with reading and making recommendations about which scripts the studio should purchase and put into development.

Fourteen months into his time at Fox, Furie was offered a job with independent film company Mainline Pictures, to acquire and develop screenplays. Eighteen months later, Mainline lost their funding and Furie was out of a job.

Furie had possession of a screenplay written by Noah Stern, which the writer wanted to direct. Deciding to produce the $3 million project himself, Furie enlisted Norman Lear's Act III Productions to back the first-time producer and writer/director. Thirteen months later *Pyrates*, starring Kevin Bacon and Kyra Sedgewick, was released.

The next project was *Tainted Blood*, a $2.5 million made-for-television movie, starring Raquel Welch. Furie's third film, *True Crime* with Alicia Silverstone, had only a $1.6 million budget.

"I did not have a true office; I worked out of my home. I did not have a secretary. I did not have a computer—I had an old IBM Selectric typewriter. I answered my own phone and typed my own letters. I did not have a development fund of money to option scripts or purchase material. All the projects I got were by convincing the writers I could get their movies made."

Furie's producing fees were commensurate with the declining budgets of his films. He found himself at a crossroad four and a half years later, where he could either align himself with a bigger producer or become an agent. When he realized that what he liked most about making movies was putting the crew together, it became clear to him that agenting below-the-line artists was the right job for him to pursue.

★ *"The job requires a lot of sensitivity to dealing with not just people's career success, but people's career lows, as well . . . I represent people who have chosen to be freelance artists. They don't know where their next job is. They could work for a year and then they could be sitting for three or six months without a job . . . Last year with the impending strikes—the potential writers' and actors' strike—they made a lot of films in the first half of the year, and they made very little product in the second half of the year. So it was a lot of conversations with clients, letting them know it was nothing they were doing wrong; the work wasn't there."—Jonathan Furie*

Unable to find a position with an agency representing below-the-line clients, Furie took a job with a firm that wanted to expand into handling writers and directors, with the hope that he could later transition into the area he really wanted. After nine months, he was not only representing writers and directors, but also was participating in the below-the-line business. When he asked if he could move into that area, his boss informed him that there were no openings. So he put out the word that he was looking to move to another agency.

After being introduced to Montana Artists owner Carl Bressler, Furie was hired as a below-the-line agent, representing clients in those categories for film and television. Now with the firm for six years, Furie serves as president, overseeing a staff of 12 that includes other agents, assistants, and a business affairs executive, in addition to working as an agent.

JOB TITLE: ANIMAL TRAINER OR FILM ANIMAL TRAINER

Job Overview

Maintain, train, and provide animals of all types for movies, television programs, commercials, and still photography.

Special Skills

Basic dog obedience skills are an asset. Although schooling is not necessary, any study of animal care and behavior are also assets.

Expanded Job Description:

Film animal trainers have three typical days: prep days, days on the set, and days when there is no current job. On a typical prep day, the trainer is on payroll to work certain animals for a specific trick or project. "Right now I'm prepping for the new Benji movie," says trainer Anne Gordon. "There are two Benji dogs and two of us trainers. We start about 9:00 in the morning and train all day long. We take turns with the dogs and work different behaviors and actions. We try to anticipate what we're going to need. We give them lots of breaks during the day, walks, and naptime. We work many, many short little sessions."

On days when the animal will be acting, the trainer receives a call time, which can vary anywhere from 6:00 in the morning to 3:00 in the afternoon. "You check in with the first AD and let them know you're there and find out what time you're going to be needed. Ideally, you like some time on the exact set where the animal is going to work. If the animal is not going to work for a couple of hours and they aren't shooting on the set you're going to use, you go in with the animal and run him through what the action is going to be so the animal is prepared. There is also a lot of down time, just sitting around waiting and keeping the animal happy, comfortable, and exercised. When the animal is called to work, you work with the director and the first AD to set up what you need. If you're working with a tiger, then everybody that doesn't need to be there clears the set. If you're working a house pet, you tell everybody when they say 'cut' that the grips need to wait until we get the cat or dog out and safe before they start moving equipment." Once all the logistics are worked out, the animal performs its role however many times are necessary to get the shot. The animal is then either released or waits for an additional scene. Although there are no time limits on hours an animal can work, the Humane Society governs the welfare of actor animals to ensure they are not abused.

When Gordon is not working on a specific project, she volunteers at Silver Screen or other animal facilities. "I help take care of the animals. I've got some wild animals I brought down from my old company [Anne's Animal Actors] and I do the cleaning, feeding, and care. I do some basic training with animals that need to be brought up to a higher level so they will be more marketable when a job does come around."

Advice for Someone Seeking This Job

"The best way to learn this job is by doing it," says Gordon. "Every single animal training company that I know of takes volunteers and welcomes volunteer help. That's the way you get started. When I'm not on the payroll, I still go out and volunteer my time at Silver Screen Animals. The more time you volunteer, the more likely you're going to be the one who goes out the door when there is a paying job." To obtain names and telephone numbers for film animal trainers in your area, contact your state film office or commission.

VOICES OF EXPERIENCE

What do you like least about your job?

"Ofttimes the animal will be put on the back burner, if it's not a major starring role." At the end of the day, after the actors are released, the animal is brought in and expected to quickly do its scene with no rehearsal. "Sometimes, there is not a lot of respect given to animals. They expect them to be a little robot and come out and work instantly, even though they've been made to sit around for 16 hours. That can be very frustrating."—Anne Gordon

What do you love most about your job?

"It's very, very satisfying when you take a dog or animal that knows almost nothing, bring it to the point where it can be a lead role in a feature film, and they pull it off." —Anne Gordon

Professional Profile: Anne Gordon, Film Animal Trainer

"I knew from a very, very young age that I wanted to work with animals," says Anne Gordon. "I just didn't know how that would manifest itself." The Washington state native attended Western Washington University, where she earned a bachelor's degree in biology with a minor in animal behavior.

While still in school, Gordon volunteered at the Seattle Zoo, where she was hired on after graduation and worked her way up to being a zookeeper. Three years later, she wanted a job with more animal interaction, so she spent eight months working for free with a trainer in Riverside, California, who taught people how to train wild animals.

Once back in Seattle, she acquired a few wild animals (wolf, tiger, fox, deer, raccoon, and so forth) and started an educational program to teach local school children respect for wildlife and endangered species. Recognizing that there was no one in the Northwest providing animals for film work, she began networking to let people know that she and her animals were available.

After five years with the school program, Gordon decided to let it go and devote her efforts to film work. Realizing that dogs and cats were in greater demand than wild animals, she focused more in that direction, forming Anne's Animal Actors. Her first feature job was providing forest animals and a dog pack for *Harry & the Hendersons*. For her first television series, Disney's *Danger Bay*, she trained skunk, otter, bear, raccoon, and dogs.

Gordon has since amassed an impressive resume that includes providing animals for feature films *A River Runs Through It*, *The Hand That Rocks the Cradle*, *Legends of the Fall*, *Practical Magic*, *Vanilla Sky*, and for television movies and series *Stephen King's Rose Red*, *The Fugitive*, *Northern Exposure*, *Sliders*, and *Twin Peaks*.

When the film business in the Northwest began drying up in 2001, Gordon decided to relocate to Los Angeles. She sold her animals to Silver Screen Animals in November and took a job with the company. One month later she landed the job of co-trainer for the two dogs that will share the starring role in the upcoming Benji movie.

JOB TITLE: CASTING DIRECTOR, CASTING AGENT, OR CASTING ASSISTANT

Job Overview

Generally hired by the producer, the casting director works closely with the director to find the appropriate people to perform the various acting roles in the production.

Special Skills

A casting director must possess the ability to recognize acting potential and ability. People skills are a fundamental requirement for the job. A casting director must be able to communicate with the film director to gain a clear understanding of his vision for the production's characters, and be able to make those who are auditioning feel at ease in what is often a stressful situation.

Advice for Someone Seeking This Job

A casting director must have the confidence of a producer and director to land the job. To build that confidence, most have interned or apprenticed with other casting directors. Contact casting directors and offer to work for free so you can observe the process. You might answer an open audition call so you can experience the casting process from the actor's perspective. Experience and relationships are necessary.

Professional Profile: Kim Petrosky, Casting Director, Kim Petrosky Casting

Kim Petrosky is a self-described people person. She loves working with people, especially actors. Before heading for Broadway, the Nashville native earned a bachelor of fine arts degree in 1985 from the School of the Arts in North Carolina. Her first break in New York was as an assistant stage manager of an off-Broadway play.

VOICES OF EXPERIENCE

What do you like least about your job?

"I least like people that don't understand how important casting is for a picture; they take the job lightly."—Kim Petrosky

What do you love most about your job?

"I love most finding that perfect person that is just so right for the role, and the director is ecstatic—I'm ecstatic. It just feels right and it fits right and things come together. The other thing I like is being able to call an actor at their day job, at a restaurant, and tell them they got the part."—Kim Petrosky

Hooking up with a family friend who is a cinematographer, Petrosky began assisting him with grant research and other production assistant duties on a documentary he was making. Eventually she learned to cut the 16mm film and edit it. But it was when a friend who was a casting director needed some help, that Petrosky found her niche in the industry.

"I jumped into it and realized it was what I wanted to do. I love actors. And, you get to sit and audition people and work with the director. I found it really exciting . . . Susan [Shopmaker] did little, tiny films, crazy things where we were looking for prostitutes down on Tenth Avenue in the middle of the night and wrangling them for different scenes."

Attracted by the "crazy hours" and "nutty people," Petrosky reveled in casting. She worked for Shopmaker for a couple of years before moving back to Nashville in the early 1990s. After a brief return to New

York, she relocated permanently to Nashville in 1992 to build her own casting business. "I adore New York, but I wanted to be a person with a house and a car; I wanted to use my driver's license again.

"I knew that films occasionally came to the area and there was some production, so I basically reinvented myself." Petrosky first held an open casting call so that she could meet the Nashville talent. "Basically I said, 'Casting Director relocating to Nashville.'"

CAREER TIPS

★ *"You should love film and know as much about actors as possible."* —Kim Petrosky

★ *Taking acting classes can help a casting director better understand the process of acting, recognize potential talent, and put actors at ease so they can give a good audition performance.*

Through a New York friend, who was serving as production coordinator on the CBS pilot *X's and O's*, Petrosky landed her first casting job. The Reba McIntyre series *Is There Life Out There* followed, and gradually Petrosky began building a solid résumé that includes *Ghosts of Mississippi*, *The Green Mile*, *Last Dance*, *The Legend of Bagger Vance*, *Midnight in the Garden of Good and Evil*, *October Sky*, *Patch Adams*, *Run Ronnie Run!*, and *We Were Soldiers*.

"I love to work. I love the whole process, from trying to get a job, all the way through it."

JOB TITLE: CATERING

Job Overview

Catering provides substantial hot meals for the cast and crew, every six hours, as unions require. These individuals are responsible for planning meals, purchasing food and preparation materials, cooking, set-up and presentation, preparing any make-to-order items, breakdown, and clean-up. Catering is a separate union from craft services. Catering is under the transportation department. "My union is 399 Local," explains caterer Joe Hanna. "My title is chef/driver. I go on production as a special equipment handler because I am the chef and I drive a truck."

Special Skills

Beyond being a "marvelous chef," Hanna credits his success to the fact that he enjoys eating and cooking food, is very clean, and takes great pride in his presentation of food. Catering people must be very service-oriented. "My day is always changing: 'Set up here, be ready at this time; no, we have to move, now you have to be ready at this time; now you need to do a dinner, or we have an extra 100 people to feed.' It's always changing. You have to take that well. I'm a very take-charge guy and I like to coordinate. I'm very good with my client, very local."

Expanded Job Description

On a shooting day, Joe Hanna typically begins work around 3 A.M. for a 6 A.M. call time. "I have to be ready to feed 175 people breakfast at 6 A.M. Breakfast is usually a walking meal. They come up to the truck where I'm cooking a made-to-order breakfast." Crew members may order items off of a menu like omelets, burritos, pancakes, French toast, rancheros, eggs, steak, bacon, and so forth. While Hanna cooks up their requests, the crew helps themselves to coffee, juice, and other beverages from the truck. Hanna will have already set up a buffet table filled with an array of fresh baked muffins, pastries, croissants, bagels, Danish, fruits ("whatever is fresh at the time in that region"), hot and cold cereals, smoked fish, and other items. He must have everything organized so that the crew can finish eating and be ready for shooting to begin by 7 A.M.

Lunch is served six hours after shooting begins, with the transportation department eating one half hour earlier. "Lunch is a magnificent spread. It's about 30 feet of fresh salad bars, fruits, grains, and breads. Then you have your entrees each day, whether it is a barbecued filet mignon or a grilled lamb chop. You have a seafood item every day that is generally regional. Then you have a poultry item each day, which can be anything from free-range turkeys to chicken breast prepared any way you like it. Then you have baked potato bars, rice; and pasta bars are very common. And light and healthy desserts, and some real fattening ones too." Catering must be very organized so that everyone can be fed and get back to work in one hour.

Many times the catering truck will have to move location during the day. "It is extremely vigorous work. Half of my day is just making sure everything is clean and handled properly and stored at the right temperature: hot food served hot and cold food served crisp and cold. You may have a whole kitchen to move once a day, serving 175 people. That means you're setting up everything from tables and chairs, beverage stations, buffets; sometimes you're setting up an outside kitchen for barbecue and saute stations, sundae bars, pasta bars, and so forth."

Dinner is never planned. Ideally, a shooting day lasts 12 hours, so another meal is not required by the union if the shoot breaks on time. However, if a shooting day runs long, the caterer may be called upon at the last minute to feed the cast, crew, and even extras.

Advice for Someone Seeking This Job

Catering is a tough field to break into. Hanna advises that the first step is to "participate." He suggests, "Take production assistant work just to get around filmmaking. If you want to go the catering end, culinary school is a wonderful way, but I also believe in real world work ethics. I would encourage you to spend time working at one of your favorite restaurants. I would certainly suggest going to work for another motion picture catering firm. There are a lot out there, more so in California. The catering done on location out of these trucks is extremely specific. It's not something you're going to learn in school or at your favorite restaurant. However, those two places will give you the skills needed when you get the opportunity to go on a movie set."

VOICES OF EXPERIENCE

What do you like least about your job?

"What I like least about catering is that you'll go to some foreign desert sometimes for 15, 16, or 17 weeks and work 100 hours a week and never slow down." —Joe Hanna

What do you love most about your job?

"What I love most about my job is being able to travel and being exposed to so much culture. I also like the personalities you get to meet and work with on a daily basis. People in film are usually glowing, radiant, and wonderful, special people. They usually feel they are very blessed to be in their position and in turn treat you very kindly. It's a very family feeling on a movie set. That's what I like most about it."—Joe Hanna

Professional Profile: Joe Hanna, President/Executive Chef, Hanna Brothers

"I got into filmmaking through culinary arts," says Joe Hanna. Growing up in southern Florida, he discovered his love for food preparation at an early age. "My grandmothers were wonderful chefs in their own right. My dad's mother was a very traditional Lebanese cook and had 20 people eating in her home every night. My mom's mom was a very southern Irish chef, a very traditional pot roast type of cook. I like both of my grandmothers a lot and enjoyed spending time with them. When I spent time with them, we cooked."

Working in restaurants as a teenager, Hanna began washing dishes and worked his way up. He studied at Palm Beach Culinary Institute, served a 2,000-hour internship at the five-star Breakers restaurant in Palm Beach, and earned an associate degree in restaurant management from Palm Beach Junior College. At age 20, he opened Two Cousins Gourmet Delicatessen, Bakery & Catering Company in Jupiter, Florida. He was soon hired to cater for Burt Reynolds Dinner Theater and Burt Reynolds Ranch.

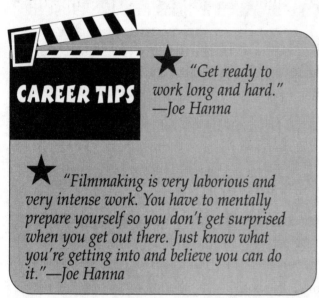

CAREER TIPS

★ *"Get ready to work long and hard."*
—Joe Hanna

★ *"Filmmaking is very laborious and very intense work. You have to mentally prepare yourself so you don't get surprised when you get out there. Just know what you're getting into and believe you can do it."—Joe Hanna*

When the *B. L. Stryker* series began production not far from Hanna's restaurant, the catering company handling the job frequented his establishment, purchasing items from him. "I developed a relationship with them and became involved in the catering of the movie. Six months later I sold my business and began catering only for movies."

The 23-year-old relocated to New York to work for Coast-to-Coast Catering, working on productions in New York and Chicago. Some of the early features he worked on were *Ace Ventura: Pet Detective, Ace Ventura: When Nature Calls, Folks!, Home Alone 3, Straight Talk,* and *Virus.* He remained with the company for nine years before forming Hanna Brothers. Some of the company's credits include: *Ali, The Contender, Gods and Generals, High Fidelity,* and *Welcome to Collinwood.*

JOB TITLE: CRAFT SERVICES

Job Overview

Craft Services are the individual(s) responsible for providing between-meal snacks and beverages for the cast and crew throughout the course of a filming day. Meals are provided by catering, a different union than craft services.

JOB TITLE: SCRIPT SUPERVISOR

Job Overview

The script supervisor keeps a record of the scenes that have been shot, ensuring continuity with regard to the set, lighting, props and costumes; notes any deviations in the script and dialogue; and records the director's instructions to the editor.

"A script supervisor has three main responsibilities," explains script supervisor Susan Youngman Hoen. "One: they communicate to the editor the director's vision through notes. Two: they watch over continuity, which may be the most important thing, and they assist all the departments with continuity. Three: I am there for the director, making sure we don't forget a shot.

"All script supervisors take notes in almost the same way. It's a universal language that editors understand. There are lines that go down the script and you write what the shot is called, how many takes and which takes were the favorite."

Special Skills

A script supervisor must be detail oriented, able to recognize any deviations in the placement of furniture and props, changes in wardrobe and dialogue, and must record those differences. Good verbal and written communication skills are necessary; a calm temperament under pressure is an asset. "No one wants to spend 15 hours a day on a set with someone who is high strung or gets anxious and crazy," says Hoen. "You've got to be friendly and easy to get along with."

Script supervisor Thomas Johnston points out the necessity of having a strong work ethic: "It's a business of incredibly long hours. You have to stick in there every hour of a 14-hour day.

Advice for Someone Seeking This Job

Before you can become a script supervisor, you must know the mechanics of the job. There are several schools that teach script supervision, particularly in the Los Angeles area. There are also books that explain what notations are necessary, and how and where to make them in the script. Once you have an understanding of the basics, Hoen suggests contacting a working script supervisor and asking if you can come watch them work. Volunteer to work for free on student and nonunion projects to gain some experience. "You learn from experience."

Johnston says you have to be willing to work for nothing under sometimes terrible conditions. "Eventually what happens, if you do this enough, is the people you work with tend to move up, remember you, and refer you to other people. You work with them and they move up and you.

"You have to seek out your own work," he adds. "You can't wait for people to call you. You have to make yourself available. It's sending a lot of résumés out and making a lot of phone calls to production offices. Half the time, or more, you'll call and they'll say, 'We've already hired somebody.' Or, you send a résumé and you never hear back. You just have to keep doing it and keep doing it, and sooner or later, somebody will remember you and give you an opportunity."

Professional Profile: Thomas Johnston, Script Supervisor

Being in the right place at the right time and making the most of the opportunity is how Thomas Johnston became a successful script supervisor. He became interested in movies in his teens, met other high school students who shared his interest, and with them formed a film club to make 8mm movies for school assemblies.

Unable to decide on a career, Johnston completed general education courses at a community college and Arizona State University. In his second year, he took an interest in film classes, later transferring to San Francisco State University where he earned a bachelor's degree in filmmaking. While still in school, he began working as a production assistant at area film companies.

After graduating, Johnston returned to his Arizona home and worked on a freelance basis, primarily as a camera assistant, for a local commercial production company. Hearing that a movie called *Raising Arizona* was coming to shoot in the area, he contacted the production company and expressed his desire to work on the film. In the early stages of production, Johnston was offered a position as production assistant, working with brothers Joel and Ethan Coen and cinematographer Barry Sonnenfeld while they shot camera tests. For a few weeks, Johnston drove the equipment van, loaded the cameras, and assisted as requested. Once the film was organized and the production office open, the Coens asked Johnston to be their script supervisor. "I had never done it before, but they weren't finding anyone they were happy with. They felt they could teach me how they wanted me to do it better than if they hired someone who had been doing it."

Johnston had never considered working as a script supervisor, but soon realized, "It was a job that put me in the middle of the action.

I would be there when they were shooting every shot in the movie. I would be working closely with the directors, the cinematographer, editors and actors . . . It was a great learning experience."

As *Campus Man* prepared to shoot in Arizona, the producers got a copy of the crew list for *Raising Arizona* and contacted Johnston about handling the script supervision. About six months after the picture wrapped, Johnson was again contacted to script supervise, this time for the feature *Prison*, shot in Wyoming. Upon returning to Arizona, he was hired to script supervise the television series *The Highwayman*.

"That was the job I truly learned to be a script supervisor on. Television is a really, really demanding way to work. On a feature, you may shoot two or three pages a day. On [*The Highwayman*] we averaged 12 pages a day. It's a lot more work for everyone, including myself. The difficult part for the script supervisor is that not only do you have to keep track of the current episode, but you're shooting inserts and pickups from previous episodes that you may have shot three or four weeks ago as well. It was a very demanding job, maintaining continuity from scene to scene . . . I really had to find ways to refine what I did."

At the time, the Coen brothers were directing a film every two or three years. Whenever they went into production, they called Johnston. During the next several years he worked with them on *Miller's Crossing, Barton Fink, The Hudsucker Proxy,* and *O Brother, Where Art Thou?*

"[The Coens] became more popular and successful. Doing their movies and having them on my résumé got me in the door to people, and a lot of people sought me out because of them. You tend to get judged by the people you work with rather than the work you do in this business."

VOICES OF EXPERIENCE

What do you like least about your job?

"Sometimes you end up working in horrible conditions that are very cold or very hot, very dusty and very cramped."
—*Thomas Johnston*

What do you love most about your job?

"The thing I like most is taking something that is totally artificial and giving it the illusion [that] it is happening in real time." Johnston also enjoys the fact that his job puts him in close proximity to the director, and sometimes affords him an opportunity to have some creative input.—*Thomas Johnston*

Until 1988, all of the productions Johnston worked on were shot in his home state or nearby locations, so he remained based in Arizona. Script supervising *Barton Fink* was his first experience working in Los Angeles.

At one point, in the early 1990s, he lived a nomadic lifestyle, shuttling from one location to another.

Johnston first met cinematographer Barry Sonnenfeld while working on *Raising Arizona*. When Sonnenfeld got the chance to direct his first feature, *The Addams Family*, he hired Johnston as script supervisor. Shortly after production began, Johnston sought out the film's editor and introduced himself. "I told [Dede Allen] how I got into script supervising . . . She took a liking to me and took me under her wing. She really, really taught me a lot about filmmaking, editing, and about my job as a script supervisor. It was like a dream experience, because she was somebody I really respected. I learned a tremendous amount about filmmaking . . . Dede allowed me to come into the editing room and watch her cut. She would explain to me why certain things worked and why she preferred certain angles; how to make things go together, not only in technical terms, but in story terms."

★ **CAREER TIPS** *"Be willing to jump in and do whatever needs to be done."* —Thomas Johnston

Johnston's admittance into the union while working on *The Addams Family* opened additional doors, brought more choice of projects, and enabled him to pursue work with other filmmakers he admired. He came to know producer Patrick Markey while working on *The Tie That Binds* and *Bogus*, and shared his desire to work with Robert Redford. A couple of years later, when Markey was producing *The Horse Whisperer*, he arranged for Johnston to meet Redford. Johnston was hired for the project and also script supervised Redford's next picture, *The Legend of Bagger Vance*. "Once you have a good relationship with a director, usually you'll end up working with that same person over and over again."

From the time he first entered film school, Johnston's goal was to eventually make his own movies. Together with David Elton and Eric Tignini, friends since high school and film school days, the three managed to carve out time between their individual projects to write, produce, and direct an independent film called *Jerome*. Several years in the making, the film successfully toured film festivals and aired on the Sundance Channel and Showtime.

Although always busy, Johnston managed to squeeze in four days off after wrapping *Analyze That*, before reuniting with the Coen brothers to script supervise *Intolerable Cruelty*.

Professional Profile: Susan Youngman Hoen, Script Supervisor

Undecided about what she wanted to do after high school, Susan Youngman Hoen enrolled at Questa College, near her home in San Luis Obisbo, California, to study journalism. She quickly discovered it wasn't for her, but found that the school's radio and television stations did pique her interest. Initially working on news programming, conducting interviews, and producing shows, she came to realize that telling fictional stories was more appealing. Once she decided that she wanted to work in film or television production, she enrolled in the film department at Cal-State Long Beach.

"That was a great experience for me, because that school is hands-on: you're the director, the sound mixer, the editor, or you write the story. You do everything." While in school, she landed her first internship working on *American Bandstand*. The production taped four shows on Saturdays. Hoen's assignment was to guard the female dressing rooms during the taping, to ensure that the dancers didn't sneak back and steal one another's clothes.

Her next internship was on the television series *Secrets and Mysteries*, assisting the writing staff with research. After graduation, she landed a job in the mail room at Fox Television, later moving to 20th Century Fox.

With no friends or family in the film industry, Hoen began the arduous process of looking for a production assistant job. After looking through *TV Guide* to discover which shows were on air, she sent résumés to the production companies that produced the shows. She also searched *The Hollywood Reporter* and *Variety* for films in production and sent out more résumés. Eventually, one landed on the desk of a producer for *The Gary Shandling Show* on the very day he fired his receptionist. He called Hoen and offered her the job.

VOICES OF EXPERIENCE

What do you like least about your job?

"What I like the least is that it's a very hard job. You always have to be on. Every single take, you have to be paying attention to every detail. It's exhausting."
—Susan Youngman Hoen

What do you love most about your job?

"I like helping everybody on the set. Being the right-hand man, so to speak, to the director. It's a fun position because the director counts on you in so many ways to not miss anything. Sometimes they ask your opinion, so you have some creative input."
—Susan Youngman Hoen

Later, she became a writer's assistant on *Night Court*. "You sit around a table with the writers and they pitch jokes and lines and come up with story ideas. You write down what they say, then you type it up, and put

★ *Whether you're working on a small independent film, a series, or a feature, "it's just as important that things match and shots cut together. The job is the same, the only difference is how much you get paid."—Susan Youngman Hoen*

★ *"Some directors are really verbal and tell you what their plan is and how they want to cover everything. With them, it's easy to make sure you don't miss anything. But some directors keep it all in their head, so you just have to go with the flow and make sure that you pay attention to what they talk about. Some directors will just tell their director of photography, and some will tell their AD. You just need to be around and pay attention, without being annoying."* —Susan Youngman Hoen

out the scripts." During this time, Hoen decided that she wanted to be a director, and that the best route to becoming one was through script supervision because, "they work side-by-side with the director."

She enrolled in a script supervision course and contacted a couple of working supervisors to ask if she could observe them at work. "I would script supervise quietly in the background, and then we would talk and compare what I did with the notes she took. I just learned from being on set."

While continuing to work as a production assistant or writers' assistant on sitcoms, Hoen gained experience handling script supervision for the show's splinter units. "No one really wants to give a script supervisor their first chance, because there is so much responsibility in the job. The mistakes show on film. Shots won't cut together because they don't match. Your notes are important to an editor; it saves them a lot of time if they don't have to sit and watch every little take." Experience working with the splinter units enabled her to move permanently into supervision.

Hoen's early jobs were on television specials and variety shows, then came series work, and her first feature, *Forsaken*. She script supervised a number of children's television series, including *The Secret World of Alex Mack*, *The Journey of Allen Strange*, and *100 Deeds for Eddie McDowd*. It was one of the executive producers of *The Journey of Allen Strange* who discovered Hoen's goal to direct and gave her a break. "It was an episode of a half-hour, single camera film. That, by far, was a highlight of my career, to know that people trusted me so much that they gave me a chance to direct." While she enjoyed the experience, it taught her that she no longer wanted to pursue directing as a career.

Hoen subsequently worked on the Tim Burton special *Lost in Oz*, and the television series *C.S.I.: Crime Scene Investigations*, *Pasadena*, and *That's Life*.

●●●●

CHAPTER
14

REGIONAL OPPORTUNITIES

If you are serious about pursuing a career working on feature films or series television you generally need to live, or frequent, Los Angeles or New York City, where the industry is based, or other cities, such as Richmond, Virginia, Wilmington, North Carolina, or Austin, Texas, where a great deal of production takes place.

However, not everyone has the means or desire to relocate to an industry hub. Many have carved out a successful career working in film, television, commercial, and music video production in other regions of the country. This chapter is dedicated to presenting some of those opportunities.

JOB TITLE: FILM COMMISSION OR FILM OFFICE AND LOCATION MANAGER

Job Overview

There are approximately 250 film commissions around the world that represent locations and interests under their jurisdiction. Each state has a film office with additional offices in counties or regions of the state. There is a film commission for Australia and even one for Bosnia. "Everyone is vying for film production activity on behalf of their community," explains Virginia Film Office location manager Andy Edmunds, "for the obvious economic impact it brings to the region in terms of jobs and dollars. It's the type of industry that comes into an area and doesn't require you to build more schools or roads. Kind of like tourist dollars."

Although offices vary, most film commissions have a director or manager who oversees all the office activities and strives to promote the area they represent to filmmakers. The commission director also works with government agencies to ensure their support in allowing filmmakers to work in the area with maximum ease. The marketing and communications managers are charged with publicizing the area and advertising why it is a great place to make movies, television series, or commercials. They create brochures and press materials, and service them to filmmakers and the media. Often, the design and maintenance of a web site falls under their management. The location manager is responsible for maintaining photographs and information about various locations around the state, for assisting filmmakers in finding appropriate locations, and for obtaining the necessary permission, permits, and licenses to shoot in that location. The Film Office serves as a liaison between the production company and various government entities.

Edmunds obtains copies of scripts or storyboards for commercials, television, and feature films that are considering shooting in Virginia. He formulates ideas for potential shooting locations by going through the office files of nearly 14,000 photographs from around the state. "They are separated by categories and subcategories, so if I'm looking for barns or a plantation home, I can go to the various categories and pull those files." The office is in the process of converting files of photographs to digital images that can be accessed and searched on the Internet. Sometimes Edmunds might go out, or send a scout, to look for specific sites and to shoot photographs for the specific project they are pitching, which will later become part of the permanent files.

"It's a lot of detective work. If you're looking for pools for a movie, you look for a big mansion that might have a pool, or you might call pool companies and ask where they service pools. Then you have to convince them to tell you who has a nice pool."

The package of potential locations is assembled and sent off to the production company. Often they will narrow their selection of potential sites to a particular region and then scout that area in person. "We rent cars, a suburban or helicopters, whatever it takes, depending on the level of the production and what we feel would be justified to spend on this client. We show them the locations and turn on our charm. We'll wine and dine them and develop a relationship, because it's totally a relationship business."

When a production has chosen to shoot in Virginia, the Film Office provides logistical support, including access to a database with local support services and potential crew members. "Once they start shooting, inevitably there are public relations issues that pop up: 'Why are these trucks parking on my street and disrupting my life?' We help solve those issues by educating people to the economic development . . . why this temporary inconvenience is worth the trouble."

When not working on a specific project, Edmunds makes calls to line producers and other filmmakers to discover what they are working on, hoping to convince them to film in Virginia.

Special Skills

Location managers must possess social skills that enable them to work well with a variety of personalities, the ability to convey trust to the property owners and production crew, a talent for problem solving, and tenacity. "You don't really have to be that great of a photographer," says Edmunds. "The job is about 35% photography, 50% detective work, and the rest is sales skills to convince someone to let you go on their property and shoot pictures of it."

Advice for Someone Seeking This Job

Visit the film office in your area and let them know you would like to work for them. Offer to serve as an intern. Look through their photo files and study the presentation, then offer to go out and shoot some location for free, to show them what you can do. "Work for free," says Edmunds. "just to get in there and meet people. All the information about productions coming to the state funnels through the film office."

Professional Profile: Andrew Edmunds, Location Manager, Virginia Film Office

At the age of 13, Andy Edmunds was a professional musician, writing songs and dreaming of becoming a rock and roll star. He developed his musical talent growing up in a small Virginia town of 1,200 people. While studying music at Virginia Commonwealth University, he became interested in filmmaking. Taking classes in the mass communications

VOICES OF EXPERIENCE

What do you like least about your job?

"What I like the least is the politics. Because we are a government entity, there are political issues that you have to be sensitive to that may not seem logical in the big picture. Fortunately, Virginia is very supportive of the industry. Sometimes things take longer than they should in terms of making decisions."—Andy Edmunds

What do you love most about your job?

"What I love most is being involved in the creative process, getting involved in telling the story with the locations and images we can provide. I also like the sales part of it: 'What are we going to do to position ourselves to get this project?' I like the detective portion of finding solutions to unique location challenges."—Andy Edmunds

department allowed him access to their camera gear, which he used to make music videos of his band.

Devising a unique idea for a music video, he convinced a bank officer to loan him $20,000 to make it. "I ended up having to basically make BMW payments for the next seven years." Although the video did not land the band a record deal, it received critical acclaim at the Houston International Film Festival. "It was the pursuit of the dream. You get this vision in your mind and you pursue it doggedly until you get there."

Edmunds' break into the film business came through a roommate who offered him some construction work on a television movie titled *Lincoln* that was coming to town. While Edmunds was building wardrobe racks in a warehouse, location manager Charlie Baxter spotted him working hard and asked if he would like to be the assistant to special effects person Russell Hessey. "I said, 'Well, what does that mean?' He said, '$750 a week.' I said, 'Okay, I'm you're man.'"

When the production wrapped, Baxter asked Edmunds to scout locations and shoot some photographs for him. "I said, 'What does that mean, location scout?' He said, '$750 a week.' And I said, 'I'll do that.' He sent me looking for a gas station that looked like 1950s and gave me a list of what he was looking for."

For the next few years, Edmunds continued to pick up work scouting locations, often serving as assistant to the location managers of the productions coming to the area, including *First Kid, The Monroes, My Name Is Bill W., Sinbad, True Colors,* and other projects.

Due to become a father, Edmunds decided to give up his entrepreneurial self-employed lifestyle for a permanent position. Having gotten to know the staff of the Virginia Film Office, he called director Rita McClenny and offered to come in and do anything, including working for free. "She threw me a few dollars and I started working freelance

> ★ **CAREER TIPS**
>
> ★ *"The people who do a job and give up when it's done or do something halfway are the ones that won't succeed. People who are relentless and always come up with a creative solution for a problem are successful."—Andy Edmunds*
>
> ★ *"Location managers are the most unrespected and unrecognized part of a production. You never hear about them, but they are such a key component to a production. If it had not been for the location scout going out and finding these cool locations and options for the production designer and the director, a lot of movies you see wouldn't have looked that cool."—Andy Edmunds*

as a scout for the film office." When the office created a communications position, Mary Nelson moved from locations manager into the new slot, leaving a vacancy in her former job. About 110 individuals applied for the position, with Edmunds landing the job. Since being hired in 1997, he has worked on numerous productions, including *The Contender, Forces of Nature, Hannibal, Hearts in Atlantis, Major Pain, Minority Report, Random Hearts, The Replacements, Rules of Engagement,* and *The West Wing.*

JOB TITLE: EXECUTIVE DIRECTOR, AMERICAN FEDERATION OF TELEVISION AND RADIO ARTISTS (AFTRA)

Job Overview

Manage and direct day-to-day administration, public relations, and promotional activities, including contract negotiation, enforcement interpretation, budgets, and staff supervision.

Special Skills

"People skills are the most important above everything else," says executive director Randy Himes, "because we work with the good, the bad, and the ugly. There are people who default on payments, people who are good payers, and people who are irate because they don't like unions. You've got to be able to think quickly on your feet and you need strong negotiating skills."

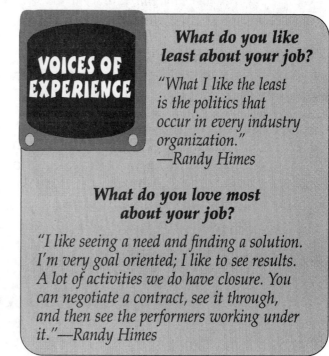

What do you like least about your job?

"What I like the least is the politics that occur in every industry organization."
—Randy Himes

What do you love most about your job?

"I like seeing a need and finding a solution. I'm very goal oriented; I like to see results. A lot of activities we do have closure. You can negotiate a contract, see it through, and then see the performers working under it."—Randy Himes

Advice for Someone Seeking This Job

Volunteering to work on a committee or help with an event will allow you to learn more about the organization, and for the organization to become familiar with your work habits and abilities. Previous experience in the music industry is helpful.

Professional Profile: Randy Himes, Executive Director, American Federation of Television and Radio Artists (AFTRA) and Screen Actors Guild (SAG)

Raised in Rockford, Illinois, Randy Himes's journey to working in the film and television industry began with his love of music. In his youth, he played in rock bands and devoted eight years to the French horn. After high school, he enrolled in the recording industry management program at Middle Tennessee State University with the intention of becoming a recording engineer. Upon graduating, he sent out résumés and worked at a gas station in Murfreesboro, Tennessee, while trying to get a music industry job. A local deejay, who was a regular customer, found out about Himes's interest and recommended him for an interview with the head of the Nashville AFTRA and SAG office.

CAREER TIPS

★ *"You've got to be able to do whatever it takes to get the job done."—Randy Himes*

★ *"You've got to be versatile and flexible. With AFTRA and SAG, there are no black and white lines in many areas. You have to be flexible enough to deal with that and not become frustrated."—Randy Himes*

Following a marathon three-hour interview to be sure that he did not want to pursue a performing career, Himes was hired as a local field representative in 1978.

Later promoted to a national representative position, Himes remained stationed in Nashville, but traveled extensively. He found a mentor in an AFTRA attorney who taught him negotiation skills, which proved invaluable as he negotiated contracts at radio and television stations and became involved in troubleshooting operations around the country. When the chapter director left the organization in 1986, Himes was appointed to fill the post of executive director, where he remains today.

JOB TITLE: GENERAL MANAGER, TELEVISION STATION

Job Overview

General managers are responsible for the physical management and operation of the television station. They set and implement policy and may also be involved in programming and production decisions.

Skills for Success

"Skills are important: can you direct and shoot? Do you have a good eye? Are you a good writer?" asks KBYU Television's general manager Duane Roberts. "Those kinds of things are important, but I think my ability to survive—even flourish—in the broadcasting environment is directly related to the fact that I like people. I like working with them, I like problem solving; that has made all the difference. I love telling stories and using media to tell stories. Those are skills that I have learned and been able to gather that have been really helpful. Over all, I think it's really about understanding and caring about people, because that's who your audience is. It's not about making the product; it's about helping people who are on the receiving end of that product. That sounds kind of philosophical, but I really believe it. That's the way I operate."

Advice for Someone Seeking This Job

To obtain a management position, candidates generally need advanced education. Experience will be gained while getting that education. Though it is much more difficult, another avenue is to make an independent film that someone might see and then offer you a job. It is important to define what you want to achieve and then set your course to obtain it.

Professional Profile: Duane Roberts, General Manager of KBYU Television

A high school English teacher's writing assignment led Duane Roberts to discover

VOICES OF EXPERIENCE

What do you like least about your job?

"I like least, I think, the challenges of trying to reach your vision with resource issues that are constantly upon you. You spend more time trying to find resources to do things than actually doing things."
—Duane Roberts

What do you love most about your job?

"I think what I like most is the opportunity to be involved in creating and delivering content that can change people's lives. To help people be better, to really enrich their experience. I like that at KBYU . . . we really have a focus on enriching people's lives and their experience. I like that the best because I'm involved in something that is good."
—Duane Roberts

his passion for media production. Students were instructed to write about what they wanted to be when they grew up. Roberts wrote about being a policeman, even though he had no desire to be one. "I wrote my theme, turned it in, and she gave me an 'F'. I'm an 'A' student; I was pretty upset about it." The teacher asked Roberts what he did want to be, to which he had no answer. "She said, 'I've got an announcement for a job opening at the local radio station and I want you to go down there and apply for it. Whether you get the job or not, you write a paper on your experiences applying for this job.'" Roberts applied and got the job.

For the next two years, while in high school, Roberts worked as a DJ for the 250-watt radio station in his hometown of Worland, Wyoming. "I got a paid position to work weekends, run the board, and play the records, read the news, and do the announcements." He later learned what set him apart from the other applicants was his ability to cold read copy aloud. "I attribute that to my mother, because in our family we read stories to each other out loud from the time I was knee high."

Roberts went on to study broadcasting at Brigham Young University, where he became the first student announcer for KBYU-FM. "I had some good mentors at BYU, in terms of how to do good creative work and the technical, operational things. But one teacher kind of opened the world of instructional and educational television to me. I was a freshman and had grandiose plans about being in broadcasting." Through this teacher, Roberts got involved in instructional television: delivering video instruction from a central location to other places on campus. "It was the first vestiges of distributed learning, I suppose. This one teacher really lit my fire about media being more valuable."

> **CAREER TIPS**
>
> ★ "Define what your vision is. What do you really want to do? I encourage anyone that's interested in media to think about what kind of story they want to tell and what's the purpose of those stories. When they've defined that, then they can find a path to get there."—Duane Roberts
>
> ★ "I think broadcasting media is a great business. I really enjoy it and I think it's more powerful now than ever. I think the opportunity to do good is enhanced, as well as the opportunity to do things that aren't so good. It's a time where you can use your talents to tell stories that uplift and enrich, or that will destroy; or at least push people down into the bottom of the pit, rather than lift them up. I think you have a choice."
> —Duane Roberts

Roberts earned a bachelor's degree in communication arts in 1967, prior to joining the United States Air Force to fight in Vietnam. Initially enlisting for four years, he stayed on for 24, working in motion picture production, audio/visual production and management, public relations, and media relations. "I made a career of it, all in communications. I learned a lot about media and how it can instruct, inform, and persuade."

During his military tenure, he attended the University of North Carolina to earn his master's degree in radio, television, and motion picture production.

Retiring from the military in 1991, Roberts returned to BYU to work on his Ph.D. and to teach. He was immediately offered an associate news director position and has since become the general manager of KBYU television station. He completed his doctorate degree in instructional psychology and technology. "I guess I had interest in enrichment for a long time. I'm in a perfect position now, because I get to apply what I know about instructional psychology, technology, and creative media with BYU television channel. It's pretty exciting."

JOB TITLE: NEWS CORRESPONDENT, CORRESPONDENT OVERSEAS, OR CORRESPONDENT

Job Overview

Correspondents are individuals employed by news agencies to contribute regular news stories from locations around the world. A former CNN Correspondent Overseas, stationed in Seoul, Jeanne Ringe was charged with reporting from Korea three times a week on business, economics, political, military, and other areas of interest. Sometimes an on-air reporter works with a producer who edits their script, or the script may be sent in to the assignment desk, where an assignment editor checks it for accuracy and so forth. In Ringe's case, she was responsible for writing and producing her own segments.

JOB TITLE: NEWS PRODUCER

Job Overview

Assignments vary, but some of a news producer's functions include: searching out potential guests, conducting pre-interviews and writing them up, making arrangements for interviews to be taped, and producing segments. After filming, the news producer may work with an editor to edit the story, and arrange for the correspondent to do a voice-over. Some producers may also be charged with writing segments or editing copy.

Special Skills

News producer/correspondent Jeanne Ringe recommends majoring in English, history, or liberal arts. "You have to be able to think clearly and write clearly. Writing for television is different than writing for print. You can learn the lingo and restrictions of writing for timed pieces once you get into television. If you're a good writer to start with, you can refine those skills."

Advice for Someone Seeking This Job

After obtaining a bachelor's degree, some recommend going on to journalism school. Others, like Ringe, advise going directly to a job in a newsroom. A college internship is a good way to get into a newsroom, learn the various job functions, prove your work ethic, and make contacts that might lead to future employment.

Professional Profile: Jeanne Ringe, News Producer and Correspondent

"In the right place at the right time" is the theme of Jeanne Ringe's career. The Virginia native originally enrolled in high school Spanish because she wanted to communicate with her Latin American boyfriend. Excelling in the language, she went on to major in Spanish at the University of Texas with the intention of working as an interpreter at the UN until marriage and children came her way.

To support herself during her last two years of college, Ringe worked at the state legislature. She got involved with the Jimmy Carter presidential campaign, but did not survive the transition into the White House. On her way to apply for a job in a think tank, she got off the elevator on the wrong floor and stumbled into the offices of the Mutual Radio Network. Ringe decided to put in an application, was interviewed by the news director, and was hired on the spot with the promise to make her the next Connie Chung. Until then, she was to serve as the newsroom secretary and learn the business of news. When the news director was fired a couple months later, Ringe learned the first rule of broadcasting: "Never believe anything anybody promises you."

Ringe worked for Mutual from 1977 to 1980, earning a meager $200 a week. When the company put the *Larry King Show* on the air, they offered Ringe an extra $10 a week to help book guests. She was later promoted to producer of the show for another $15 a week. "That was probably the toughest schedule of any job I ever had. I would go into work at 10:30 or 11:00 at night. The show started at midnight and we were on the air live for five and a half hours. I would go home and unplug my phone and sleep from 6 A.M. to about 2 P.M., and then get up and try to book guests for that afternoon. At the time, nobody knew who Larry was. Guests had to pay their own cab fare, find their way into this confusing building in Crystal City [Washington, D.C., area], and there was a complicated elevator security system. We were losing guests all the time—it was a nightmare." After a time, Ringe asked for an additional $15 a week and quit when she was refused. "I was making so little money at the *Larry King Show* that I had to sell my car to pay my rent one month. Yet, we were taking the show on the road 12 weeks a year, staying in great hotels, riding in limousines. I'd come home and have no food in my refrigerator. My parents and everyone else thought I was nuts for killing myself for this job, but I loved it. It was in my blood by then."

While working on the King program, Ringe would sometimes pitch ideas to the *Tomorrow Show*. "I was a big fan of Tom Snyder. I just called up one day and said, 'Look, we've had these guests on and I think you should have them on.'" She continued to call and became friendly with one of the producers, who got her an interview with the executive producer when she quit King's show. Hired to work for five weeks on a temporary basis, "I sold everything I had and moved to New York." At the end of the five weeks she was invited to stay on. There she worked with Robert Morton, who later went on to produce *Late Show with David Letterman*.

By the time Snyder's show was cancelled two and a half years later, Ringe was being represented by agent Alfred Geller, who sent her on an interview with an upstart cable channel in Atlanta: CNN. Unimpressed by the fledgling operation, she happened to pick up a trade magazine while waiting for her interview and discovered that CBS was launching a new program. She immediately phoned from the lobby of CNN to set up an interview for when she returned to New York. Hired on as an associate producer for *CBS Morning News*, Ringe was

VOICES OF EXPERIENCE

What do you like least about your job?

"The negative side of things is that the job gives you a knowledge of the world that is miles wide and sometimes only an inch deep. You never become a real expert at anything unless you specialize as a reporter."—Jeanne Ringe

What do you love most about your job?

"If you are a curious person, journalism is the most wonderful career to have because it allows you to explore every aspect of life: the good, the bad, and the ugly; the extremes of wonder and grandeur to the depths of depravity and everything in between."—Jeanne Ringe

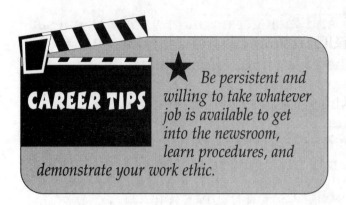

CAREER TIPS

★ *Be persistent and willing to take whatever job is available to get into the newsroom, learn procedures, and demonstrate your work ethic.*

responsible for booking guests and working on segments for hosts Diane Sawyer and Bill Curtis. She even got the opportunity to utilize her Spanish skills when the foreign desk sent her to Central America on assignment with Sawyer.

Ringe left CBS late in 1984 to start up her own company, Idea Factory, to produce television promos, videos, and radio projects. She returned to CBS six months later as producer of *Face the Nation* with Leslie Stahl. In that role, Ringe preinterviewed potential guests, wrote up the interview notes, helped determine what hot news topics the show would cover each week, and booked guests based on the preinterviews. "On Saturdays we would sit around and put the questions together with Leslie. Basically, we had a brainstorming session where we would sit around and compile information, and then come up with a road map of questions for the interviews. Then, sometimes I would cut the taped piece that introduced the day's stories."

After leaving CBS, Ringe briefly produced segments for *Travel & Adventure*, a nationally syndicated travel program, and with TVAM, British Independent Television, traveling around the U.S. with their correspondents. She put together funding to make a documentary for PBS, then spent two years at the Library of Congress as director of the Global Library Project, where she was charged with producing television documentaries about the Library of Congress and its collections.

Ringe married a foreign service officer in 1987 and moved with him to Seoul, Korea. There, she landed a job reporting for CNN, producing two to three stories each week for the next few years, and also acted in six episodes of a Korean soap opera. Following a nine month return to Washington, D.C., for her husband to undergo language training, the pair was assigned to Kiev. Originally slated to open a field office there for CNN, things did not pan out and Ringe accepted a position as vice president of production for a television direct marketing company, requiring a monthly commute between Kiev and Los Angeles. When the company folded in the late 1990s, Ringe retired from the business to raise a family.

JOB TITLE: PRODUCER, COMPANY OWNER

Job Overview

Along with partner Kitty Moon Emery, Scene Three Media Works co-owner Marc Ball is charged with developing a vision for the company and overseeing expansion into various media areas. He is involved in creating and facilitating the projects that the company produces.

Special Skills

Marc Ball cites the company's dedication to customer service as being a key to their success. "Our customers want to come back once we've worked with them. We genuinely want them to succeed. When we finish a project, we didn't let the client sit it on the shelf. We make them send it to whomever they were supposed to, and make them show it. We beat on them in a friendly way. We care about what happens to that product after we finish it. In a sense, we make an investment in our clients." Ball also feels that the quality of the company's staff is essential to its success.

Advice for Someone Seeking This Job

"If I was just getting out of high school and I knew that I wanted to be in the film business, I would go to a television station and I would offer to be their janitor for the summer if they would let me go with the news crews," says Ball. "Find someone who can make that decision; it's going to cost them to put you on their insurance. You're not going to make any money, but you're going to be around the business and you're going to learn about it . . . Then go to school and study. I'd suggest studying writing. There is no basis for doing anything in the world that doesn't start with being able to write well. Even if you're not that good at it, struggle through and learn to get an idea down on paper . . . Next I'd find somebody that would let me work for free, just to be around and watch. Then I'd take that experience to the next level and ask to run the vault or work as a production assistant, a position where I could impress somebody with my commitment, and at the same time be around the business. I'd try to do that while I was in school. Once you've got your degree, then not only do you have a degree, but you've been around the business and have some experience. Typically, and certainly at Scene Three, the people that get hired are the people that impress someone: 'I think this person can do it.' 'I think we ought to give this person a shot.' That's who gets the job: the person who has shown their commitment and zeal. At the same time, you have to be able to demonstrate that you're bright and intelligent. That's the kind of people that excel."

Professional Profile: Marc Ball, Producer, Co-Owner, Scene Three Media Works

Interested in the arts from an early age, Marc Ball did not discover filmmaking until he was studying to be a music conductor at Western Kentucky University in Bowling Green, his hometown. "I dabbled in theater and really enjoyed it. I did a bit of writing. I played the piano and saxophone. I directed some choirs. That's what led me to theater. They had a musical they needed somebody to be in charge of music for."

While working on theatrical projects, it occurred to Ball that television production utilized many of the same skills. Upon graduating with a bachelor's degree in music, he began pursuing work in the film business. Not wanting to relocate to New York or California, he found work at an advertising agency in Indiana. Within the agency, he formed a small audiovisual company to produce slides, audiotapes, and still photographs.

Obsessed with the filmmaking aspect of the job, Ball worked into the night and early morning on projects. "In the morning, people would come in and I'd get a shower and go back to work. Maybe sleep some; sometimes I didn't sleep at all." Before long, the film company had eclipsed the agency and the two parted. Ball went on to produce and direct commercials in the Chicago area before deciding to form his own production company.

Wanting to remain in the South, Ball considered several cities as home base for his company. Word of his search reached the ears of the bank president of Nashville City Bank, who began courting Ball to consider Nashville. "I didn't have two dollars, but for some reason he said, 'We want you to move here.'" In 1974, just three years out of college, Ball opened Scene Three.

VOICES OF EXPERIENCE

What do you like least about your job?

"The least enjoyable part of my job is the meetings. There is a lot of time spent on little decisions that, frankly, you could go either way and it wouldn't matter one-thousandth of a percent to the finished product."—Marc Ball

What do you love most about your job?

"What I love the most about my job is seeing things come together in unusual ways. Or seeing people that I work with make things happen in a fluid and smooth way."
—Marc Ball

Shortly after forming the company, Ball became the national director of advertising for Ronald Reagan's presidential campaign, affording him the opportunity to shoot commercials, town meetings, and documentaries. While working on the campaign, Ball met Kitty Moon, who handled film production for the Republican Party. When the project ended, Ball invited Moon to become a partner in Scene Three. One of the pair's first clients was Tennessee's Department of Tourism, for which they produced the phenomenally successful "Elrod and Elvira" television spots.

"We created these very funny rural folks named Elrod and Elvira. They were in their 50s or 60s, living in the country. We had several things happen to them: a spaceship landed in their yard; a shark came after them. It became really, really well known throughout the state and kind of put us on the map; we became known by it. We didn't have any marketing; the work was our marketing. We just answered the phone."

In the early 1980s, Ball got interested in video and became the first company in the area to expand into video postproduction. "You could come in and edit, and leave with your finished product. That was incredibly exciting to me. We would bring video people together with film people and try to use the best of both technologies." A block of buildings was purchased to house the company's growing concern, including a former movie theater that was renovated into a television studio.

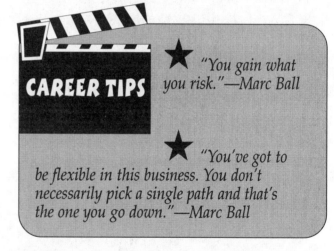

CAREER TIPS

★ "You gain what you risk."—Marc Ball

★ "You've got to be flexible in this business. You don't necessarily pick a single path and that's the one you go down."—Marc Ball

Finding it inconvenient to rent equipment out of Atlanta or other cities, the company began acquiring cameras, dollies, cranes, trucks, lights, and other gear, out of necessity. The company continued to grow their commercial client base, while expanding into music video production. Ball directed projects for Garth Brooks, Billy Ray Cyrus, Amy Grant, Vince Gill, Goo Goo Dolls, George Jones, Toby Keith, Trisha Yearwood, and many others, totaling more than 200 to date. Ball also produced and directed *A Day in the Life of Country Music* for CBS, the series *CeCe's Place, Celebrity Homes & Hideaways, Class of 2000,* and *Gospel Today.*

Over the next several years, Scene Three Media Works expanded to become a digital media center, combining video and audio editing technologies. The company formed an alliance with television producer Mitchell Galin's On the Lam, Inc., to produce television programming.

Recently, Ball created and produced the film *Thunder Theater* for R. J. Reynolds, a traveling exhibition that toured NASCAR tracks, with a 50-foot screen and seating to accommodate an audience of 200 people. "It was on Winston Cup racing, shot in 65mm and projected in 70mm, like IMAX . . . We were at the races, in the racing pits. We rented a track and reenacted some of the close-ups that you couldn't get during a race. It all came together seamlessly and was just about as exciting a NASCAR experience as you can get.

"This company is just a big accident," says Ball of his success, "but that's what drove it."

● ● ● ●

APPENDIX I – GUILDS, ORGANIZATIONS, AND UNIONS

Guilds

Key to Acronyms

AFL: American Federation of Labor
AFM: American Federation of Musicians
CIO: Congress of Industrial Organizations
IATSE: International Alliance of Theatrical Stage Employees
IBEW: International Brotherhood of Electrical Workers
IBT: International Brotherhood of Teamsters
MPMO: Motion Picture Machine Operators

Academy of Motion Picture Arts & Sciences (AMPAS)
8949 Wilshire Blvd.
Beverly Hills, CA 90211-1972
Phone: (310) 247-3000
Fax: (310) 859-9351
web site: *www.oscars.org*

Academy of Television Arts & Sciences (ATAS)
5220 Landershim Blvd.
North Hollywood, CA 91601
Phone: (818) 754-2800
Fax: (818) 761-2827
web site: *www.emmys.org*

Affiliated Property Craftsmen (IATSE, AFL, Local 44)
11500 Burbank Blvd.
North Hollywood, CA 91601
Phone: (818) 769-2500

Alliance of Motion Picture & Television Producers (AMPTP)
15503 Ventura Blvd.
Sherman Oaks, CA 91436
Phone: (818) 995-3600
Fax: (818) 382-1793

American Academy of Independent Film Producers
2067 S. Atlantic Ave.
Los Angeles, CA 90040
Phone: (213) 264-1422

American Association of Producers (AAP)
10850 Wilshire Blvd., Ninth Floor
Los Angeles, CA 90024
Phone: (310) 446-1000
Fax: (310) 446-1600
web site: *www.tvproducers.com*

American Cinema Editors, Inc.
100 Universal City Plaza
Building 2282, Room 234
Universal City, CA 91608
Phone: (818) 777-2900
Fax: (818) 733-5023
web site: *www.ace-filmeditors.org*

American Federation of Film Producers
Warner Hollywood Studios
Pickford Building, Suite 204
The Lot Studios
West Los Angeles, CA 90046
E-mail: info@filmfederation.com
web site: *www.filmfederation.com*

American Federation of Musicians (AFM Local 47)
1777 N. Vine St.
Hollywood, CA 90038
Phone: (323) 462-2161
Fax: (323) 461-3090
web site: *www.promusic47.org*

American Federation of Musicians (AFM Local 802)
322 West 48th Street
New York, NY 10036
Phone: (212) 245-4802
Fax: (212) 293-0002
web site: *www.local802afm.org*

American Federation of Television and Radio Artists (AFTRA)
5757 Wilshire Blvd., Suite 900
Los Angeles, CA 90036
Phone: (323) 634-8100
Fax: (323) 634-8246
web site: *www.aftra.org*

260 Madison Ave., Seventh Floor
New York, NY 10016
Phone: (212) 532-0800
Fax: (212) 545-1238
web site: *www.aftra.org*

American Film Institute (AFI)
2021 N. Western Ave.
Los Angeles, CA 90027
Phone: (323) 856-7600
Fax: (323) 467-4578
web site: *www.afionline.org*

American Society of Cinematographers (ASC)
P.O. Box 2230
Hollywood, CA 90078
Phone: (323) 969-4333
Fax: (323) 882-6391
web site: *www.cinematographer.com*

American Society of Composers, Authors & Publishers (ASCAP)
7920 Sunset Blvd., Third Floor
Los Angeles, CA 90046
Phone: (323) 883-1000
Fax: (323) 883-1049
web site: *www.ascap.com*

1 Lincoln Plaza
New York, NY 10023
Phone: (212) 621-6000
Fax: (212) 724-9064
web site: *www.ascap.com*

The Art Directors Club of Los Angeles
7080 Hollywood Blvd., Suite #410
Los Angeles, CA 90028
Phone: (213) 465-1787

Assistant Directors Training Program
Directors Guild - Producer Training Plan
14724 Ventura Blvd., Suite 775
Sherman Oaks, CA 91403
E-mail: trainingprogram@dgptp.org
web site: *www.dgptp.org*

**Association of Film
   Commissioners International
   (AFCI)**
314 North Main, Suite 307
Helena, MT 59601
Phone: (406) 495-8040
Fax: (406) 495-8039
web site: *www.sfci.org/index2.asp*

7060 Hollywood Blvd.
Los Angeles, CA 90028
Phone: (323) 462-6092
Fax: (323) 462-6091
web site: *www.sfci.org/index2.asp*

650 North Bronson Ave., Suite 223B
Los Angeles, CA 90004
Phone: (323) 960-4763
Fax: (323) 960-4766
web site: *www.aicp.com*

3 West 18th St., Fifth Floor
New York, NY 10011
Phone: (212) 929-3000
Fax: (212) 929-3359
web site: *www.aicp.com*

Broadcast Music Inc. (BMI)
8730 Sunset Blvd., Third Floor West
Los Angeles, CA 90069
Phone: (310) 659-9109
Fax: (310) 657-6947
web site: *www.bmi.com*

Broadcast Music Inc. (BMI)
320 West 57th St.
New York, NY 10019
Phone: (212) 586-2000
Fax: (212) 489-2368
web site: *www.bmi.com*

**Broadcast TV Recording Engineers
   and Communications
   Technicians (IBEW, Local 45)**
6255 Sunset Blvd., Suite #721
Los Angeles, CA 90028
Phone: (323) 851-5515

Casting Society of America
606 N. Larchmont Blvd., Suite 4-B
Los Angeles, CA 90004-1309
Phone: (323) 463-1925
Fax: (323) 462-5753
web site: *www.castingsociety.com*

Casting Society of America
2565 Broadway, Suite 185
New York, NY 10025
Phone: (212) 868-1260 x22
web site: *www.castingsociety.com*

**Costume Designers Guild (IATSE,
   Local 892)**
14724 Ventura Blvd., Penthouse C
Sherman Oaks, CA 91403
Phone: (818) 905-1557

Directors Guild of America (DGA)
7950 Sunset Blvd.
Los Angeles, CA 90046
Phone: (310) 289-2000
Fax: (310) 289-2024
web site: *www.dga.org*

110 West 57th St.
New York, NY 10019
Phone: (212) 581-0370
Fax: (212) 581-1441
web site: *www.dga.org*

Hollywood Foreign Press Association
292 La Cienega Blvd., Suite 316
Beverly Hills, CA 90211
Phone: (310) 657-1731
web site: *www.thegoldenglobes.com*

Independent Feature Project (IFP)
18750 Wilshire Blvd., Second Floor
Beverly Hills, CA 90211
Phone: (310) 432-1200
Fax: (310) 432-1203
web site: *www.ifp.org*

Industrial Designers Society of America (IDSA)
1142 Walker Rd.
Great Falls, VA 22066
Phone: (703) 759-0100
Fax: (703) 759-7679

International Brotherhood of Electrical Workers (IBEW, AFL-CIO, Local 40)
5643 Vineland Ave.
North Hollywood, CA 91601
Phone: (818) 762-4239
web site: *www.ibew.org*

International Documentary Association
1201 W. Fifth St., Suite M320
Los Angeles, CA 90017-1461
Phone: (213) 534-3600
Fax: (213) 534-3610
web site: *www.documentary.org*

International Photographers Guild (Cameramen) (IATSE, Local 659)
7715 Sunset Blvd., Suite #300
Los Angeles, CA 90046
Phone: (213) 876-0160
web site: *www.cameraguild.com*

International Sound Technicians, Cinetechnicians, Studio Projectionists and Video Projection Technicians (IATSE, MPMO, AFL, Local 695)
11331 Ventura Blvd., Suite #201
Studio City, CA 91604
Phone: (818) 985-9204

Los Angeles Press Club
6363 Sunset Blvd., Suite 530
Los Angeles, CA 90028
Phone: (323) 469-8180
Fax: (323) 469-8183
web site: *www.lapressclub.org*

Makeup Artists and Hairstylists (IATSE, Local 706)
11519 Chandler Blvd.
North Hollywood, CA 91601
Phone: (818) 984-1700

Motion Picture Association of America (MPAA)
15503 Ventura Blvd.
Encino, CA 91436
Phone: (818) 995-6600
Fax: (818) 382-1799
web site: *www.mpaa.org*

Motion Picture Costumers (IATSE, MPMO, AFL, Local 705)
1427 N. La Brea Ave.
Los Angeles, CA 90028
Phone: (323) 851-0220

Motion Picture Editors Guild (IATSE, Local 700)
West Coast Office
7715 Sunset Blvd., Suite 200
Hollywood, CA 90046
Phone: (323) 876-4770
Fax: (323) 876-0861
web site: *www.editorsguild.com/index.shtml*

East Coast Office
165 W. 46th St., Suite 900
New York, NY 10036
Phone: (212) 302-0700
Fax: (212) 302-1091
web site: *www.editorsguild.com/
index.shtml*

**Motion Picture Illustrators
and Matte Artists (IATSE,
Local 790)**
13245 Riverside Dr., Suite 300A
Sherman Oaks, CA 91423
Phone: (818) 784-6555

**Motion Picture Screen Cartoonists
(IATSE, Local 839)**
4729 Lankershim Blvd.
North Hollywood, CA 91602
Phone: (818) 766-7151

**Motion Picture Set Painters and
Sign Writers (IATSE, AFL,
Local 729)**
11365 Ventura Blvd., Suite 202
Studio City, CA 91604
Phone: (818) 842-7729

**Motion Picture Sound Editors
(MPSE)**
P.O. Box 8306
Universal City, CA 91606
(818) 762-2816

**Motion Picture Studio Grips
(ATSE, AFL, Local 80)**
6926 Melrose Ave.
Los Angeles, CA 90038
Phone: (323) 931-1419

**Motion Picture and Video
Projectionists (IATSE, Local 150)**
2600 Victory Blvd.
Burbank, CA 91505
Phone: (818) 842-8900

**Music Video Production
Association**
940 N. Orange Dr., #104
Hollywood, CA 90038
Phone: (323) 469-9494
Fax: (323) 469-9445
web site: *www.mvpa.com*

**National Academy of Recording
Arts & Sciences (NARAS)**
3402 Pico Blvd.
Santa Monica, CA 90405
Phone: (310) 392-3777
Fax: (310) 392-2306
web site: *www.grammy.com*

**National Association of Television
Program Executives (NATPE)**
2525 Olympic Blvd., Suite 600E
Santa Monica, CA 90404
Phone: (310) 435-4440
Fax: (310) 453-5258
web site: *www.natpe.org*

**Producers Guild of America
(PGA)**
400 S. Beverly Dr., Suite 211
Beverly Hills, CA 90212
Phone: (310) 557-0807
Fax: (310) 557-0436

Production Assistants Association
8644 Wilshire Blvd., Suite #202
Beverly Hills, CA 90211
Phone: (310) 659-7416
Fax: (310) 659-5838

**Production Office Coordinators
and Accountants Guild (IATSE,
Local 717)**
14724 Ventura Blvd., Penthouse
Suite
Sherman Oaks, CA 91403
Phone: (818) 906-9986

**Publicists Guild of America
(IATSE and MPMO, AFL,
Local 818)**
14724 Ventura Blvd., Penthouse
Suite
Sherman Oaks, CA 91403
Phone: (818) 905-1541

**Scenic, Title, and Graphic Artists
(IATSE, AFL-CIO, Local 816)**
14724 Ventura Blvd., Penthouse 5
Sherman Oaks, CA 91403
Phone: (818) 906-7822

**Screen Story Analysts (IATSE
Local 854)**
14724 Ventura Blvd., Penthouse B
Sherman Oaks, CA 91403
Phone: (818) 784-6555

The Scriptwriters Network
11684 Ventura Blvd., Suite #508
Studio City, CA 91604
Phone: (323) 848-9477
web site: *www.scriptwritersnetwork.
com*

Set Decorators Society of America
Los Angeles Center Studios
1201 West Fifth St., Suite M340
Los Angeles, CA 90017
Phone: (310) 289-1959
web site: *www.setdecorators.org*

**Set Designers and Model Makers
(IATSE, Local 847)**
14724 Ventura Blvd., Penthouse B
Sherman Oaks, CA 91403
Phone: (818) 784-6555

**Society of Motion Picture and TV
Art Directors (IATSE, Local 876)**
14724 Ventura Blvd., Penthouse
Suite
Sherman Oaks, CA 91403
Phone: (818) 762-9995

**Sound Construction Installation
and Maintenance Technicians
(IBEW, AFL-CIO, Local 40)**
5643 Vineland Ave.
North Hollywood, CA 91601
Phone: (818) 762-4239
web site: *www.ibewlocal40.com*

**Studio Electrical Lighting
Technicians (IATSE, MPMO,
AFL-CIO, Local 728)**
14629 Nordhoff Blvd.
Panorama City, CA 91402
(818) 891-0728

**Studio Transportation Drivers
(IBT, Local 399)**
4747 Vineland Ave., Suite E
North Hollywood, CA 91602
Phone: (818) 985-7374
Fax: (818) 985-8305

Theatrical Wardrobe Attendants (IATSE, Local 768)
13245 Riverside Dr., Suite 300
Sherman Oaks, CA 91423
Phone: (818) 789-8735

Women in Film (WIF)
6464 Sunset Blvd., Suite 1018
Los Angeles, CA 90028
Phone: (323) 463-6040
Fax: (323) 463-0963
web site: *www.wif.org*

Writers Guild of America, East (WGA)
555 West 57th St., Suite 1230
New York, NY 10019
Phone: (212) 767-7800
Fax: (212) 582-1909
web site: *www.wgaeast.org*

Writers Guild of America, West (WGA)
7000 W. Third St.
Los Angeles, CA 90048
Phone: (323) 951-4000
Fax: (323) 952-4800
web site: *www.wga.org*

APPENDIX II—FILM SCHOOLS

ARIZONA
Arizona State University
P.O. Box 870112
Tempe, AZ 85287-0112
Phone: (480) 965-7788
web site: *www.asu.edu*

CALIFORNIA
**Academy of Entertainment and
  Technology**
Santa Monica Community College
1900 Pico Blvd.
Santa Monica, CA 90405-1628
Phone: (310) 452-9277

American Film Institute (AFI)
2021 Western Ave.
Los Angeles, CA 90027-1657
Phone: (323) 856-7600
Fax: (323) 467-4578
web site: *www.afionline.org*

**Assistant Directors Training
  Program**
15260 Ventura Blvd., Suite 1200-A
Sherman Oaks, CA 91403-5347
Phone: (818) 386-2545
web site: *www.dgptp.org*

**California College of Arts &
  Crafts**
1111 Eighth St.
San Francisco, CA 94107-2247
Phone: (800) 447-1ART
web site: *www.ccac-art.edu*

**California Institute of the Arts
  "Cal Arts"**
24700 McBean Pkwy.
Valencia, CA 91355-2397
Phone: (805) 255-1050

Loyola Marymount University
One LMU Dr.
Los Angeles, CA 90045
Phone: (310) 338-2750
web site: *www.lmu.edu*

Sundance Institute
225 Santa Monica Blvd., 8th Floor
Santa Monica, CA 90401
Phone: (310) 394-4662
web site: *www.sundance.org*

**University of California, Santa
  Barbara**
Santa Barbara, CA 93106
Phone: (805) 893-2485
E-mail: appinfo@sa.ucsb

UCLA Extension
**Department of Entertainment
  Studies and Performing Arts,
  or The Writer's Program**
10995 Le Conte Ave.
Los Angeles, CA 90024-2883
Phone: (310) 206-1542 or
  (800) 825-8252
web site: *www.unex.ucla.edu/*

**University of Southern California
  (UCLA)**
School of Film and Television
P.O. Box 951622
Los Angeles, CA 90095-1622
Phone: (310) 825-5761
web site: *www.ucla.edu*

University of Southern California (USC)
School of Cinema/Television
Garden Terrace 106, University Park
Los Angeles, CA 90089-2211
Phone: (213) 740-8353
web site: *www-cntv.usc.edu/*

DISTRICT OF COLUMBIA
American University
4400 Massachusetts Ave., NW
Washington, DC 20016-8001
Phone: (202) 885-6000
web site:
   http://admissions.american.edu

FLORIDA
Florida State University
Tallahassee, FL 32306-2400
Phone: (850) 644-6200
web site: *http://admissions.fsu.edu*

Valencia Community College
P.O. Box 3028
Orlando, Florida 32802-3028
Phone: (407) 299-5000
web site: *www.valencia.cc.fl.us/*

GEORGIA
Savannah College of Art & Design
P.O. Box 2072
Savannah, GA 31402-2072
Phone: (800) 869-7223
web site: *www.scad.edu*

ILLINOIS
Columbia College Chicago
600 S. Michigan Ave.
Chicago, IL 60605
Phone: (312) 344-7130
web site: *www.colum.edu*

Northwestern University
Department of Radio, Television, and Film
Evanston, IL 60201
Phone: (847) 491-7315
web site: *www.northwestern.edu/*

MASSACHUSETTS
Emerson College
120 Boylston St.
Boston, MA 02116-4624
Phone: (617) 824-8600
web site: *www.emerson.edu*

NEW YORK
Columbia University/Columbia College
212 Hamilton Mall, Mail Code 2807
1130 Amsterdam Ave.
New York, NY 10027
Phone: (212) 854-2522
web site: *www.columbia.edu*

Long Island University
C.W. Post Campus
720 Northern Blvd.
Brookville, NY 11548-1300
Phone: (516) 299-2900
web site: *www.liu.edu*

New York University (NYU)
Tisch School of the Arts
721 Broadway, 8th Floor
New York, NY 10003-6807
Phone: (212) 988-1918
web site: *www.nyu.edu*

School of Visual Arts
209 East 23rd St.
New York, NY 10010-3994
Phone: (800) 436-4204
web site: *www.schoolofvisualarts.edu*

NORTH CAROLINA
North Carolina School of the Arts
1533 South Main St.
P.O. Box 12189
Winston-Salem, NC 27127-2188
Phone: (336) 770-3290
E-mail: *admissions@ncarts.edu*

University of North Carolina at Wilmington
601 South College Rd.
Wilmington, NC 28403-3297
E-mail: admissions@uncwil.edu

UTAH
Brigham Young University
A183 ASB
Provo, UT 84602
Phone: (801) 378-2507
web site: *www.byu.edu*

Sundance Institute
P.O. Box 16450
Salt Lake City, UT 84116
Phone: (801) 328-3456
web site: *www.sundance.org*

APPENDIX III—DIRECTORIES AND DATABASES

Directors Guild Directory
Directors Guild of America
7920 Sunset Blvd.
Los Angeles, CA 90046
Phone: (310) 289-2000

Hollywood Agents & Managers
  Directory
Hollywood Creative Directory: The
  Film and Television Industry Bible
Hollywood Interactive Entertainment
  Directory
Hollywood Creative Directory
3000 W. Olympic Blvd., Suite 2525
Santa Monica, CA 90404
Phone: (310) 315-4815
Fax: (310) 315-4816
web site: *www.hcdonline.com*

Hollywood Reporter Blu-Book, The
The Hollywood Reporter
5055 Wilshire Blvd.
Los Angeles, CA 90036
Phone: (323) 525-2150
web site:
  secure.telescan.com/blubook.asp

The Industry Labor Guide
Phone: (818) 995-4008
web site: *www.entertainment*
  publisher.com

International Documentary
  Association Membership Directory
  and Survival Guide
International Documentary
  Association
1551 S. Robertson Blvd., Suite #201
Los Angeles, CA 90035
Phone: (310) 284-8422

Internet Movie Database
web site: *www.imdb.com*

LA 411
NY 411
411 Digital
411 Animals
Entertainment Executives 411
Producers 411
Agents, Managers & Casting
  Directors 411
LA 411 Publishing
5700 Wilshire Blvd., Suite 120
Los Angeles, CA 90036
Phone: (323) 965-2020
Fax: (323) 965-5052
web site: *www.la411.com*

Cinematographers, Production
  Designers, Costume Designers and
  Film Editors Guide
Film Composers Guide
Film Producers, Studios, Agents and
  Casting Directors Guide
Film Writers Guide
Special Effects and Stunts Guide
Television Film Writers Guide
Lone Eagle Publishing:
  Entertainment Industry Resource
2337 Roscomare Rd., Suite #9
Los Angeles, CA 90077-1815
Phone: (310) 471-8066
web site: *www.loneeagle.com*

Moviebuff Online
web site: *www.moviebuffonline.com*

Pacific Coast Studio Directory
Phone: (800) 722-5667
web site: *www.studio-directory.com*

Paymaster
Phone: (818) 955-6000
web site: *www.ep-service.com*

Writers Guild of America Directory
Writers Guild of America
7000 W. Third St.
Los Angeles, CA 90048
Phone: (213) 951-4000

APPENDIX IV—FILM FESTIVALS

AFI Los Angeles International Film Festival
2021 N. Western Ave.
Los Angeles, CA 90027-1657
Phone: (323) 856-7707
Fax: (323) 462-4049
web site: *www.afifest.com*

Austin Film Festival
1600 Nueces, Suite 101
Austin, TX 78701
Phone: (512) 478-4795
web site: *www.Instar.com/austinfilm/ filmorder.htm*

Los Angeles Independent Film Festival
5455 Wilshire Blvd., Suite 1500
Los Angeles, CA 90010
Phone: (213) 937-4155
Fax: (213) 937-7770
web site: *www.laiff.com*

New York Film Festival
Film Society of Lincoln Center
70 Lincoln Center Plaza
New York, NY 10023-6595
Phone: (212) 875-5610
Fax: (212) 875-5636
E-mail: filmlinc@dti.net

Slamdance Film Festival
6281 Hollywood Blvd., Suite 520
Los Angeles, CA 90028-6311
Phone: (323) 466-1786
Fax: (323) 466-1784
web site: *www.slamdance.com*

Sundance Film Festival
307 W. 200 South, Suite 5002
Salt Lake City, UT 84101-1268
Phone: (801) 322-4033
Fax: (801) 575-5175
web site: *www.sundance.org*

Telluride Film Festival
53 South Main St., Suite 212
Hanover, NH 03755
Phone: (603) 643-1255
Fax: (603) 643-5938
E-mail: Tellufilm@aol.com

APPENDIX V—MAGAZINES

American Cinematographer
Phone: (323) 969-4344
web site: *www.cinematographer.com*

Back Stage West
Phone: (323) 525-2356
web site: *www.backstage.com*

Cinefex
Phone: (909) 781-1917
web site: *www.cinefex.com*

Creative Screenwriting
Phone: (323) 957-1405
web site: *www.creativescreenwriting. com*

Daily Variety
Phone: (818) 487-4554
web site: *www.variety.com*

DGA Magazine
Phone: (310) 289-2000
web site: *www.dga.org*

Entertainment Employment Journal
Phone: (818) 920-0060
web site: *www.eej.com*

Fade In
Phone: (310) 275-0287
web site: *www.fadeinmag.com*

Film & Video
Phone: (800) 777-5006
web site: *www.kipinet.com/film*

Film Comment
Phone: (800) 783-4903

Film Music Magazine
Phone: (818) 729-9500
web site: *www.filmmusicmag.com*

Hollywood Reporter
Phone: (323) 525-2150
web site: *www.hollywoodreporter.com*

International Photographer
Phone: (323) 876-0160
E-mail: cameramag@aol.com

Location Update
Phone: (818) 785-6362
web site: *www.cineweb.com*

Locations
Association of Film Commissioners
    International
Phone: (323) 462-6092
web site: *www.afci.org*

Millimeter
Phone: (800) 441-0294
web site: *www.millimeter.com*

Movieline
Phone: (800) 521-1966
web site: *www.movielinemag.com*

Moviemaker Magazine
Phone: (310) 234-9234
web site: *www.moviemaker.com*

Premiere
Phone: (800) 289-2489
web site: *www.premiere.com*

Scenario
Phone: (800) 222-2654
web site: *www.scenariomag.com*

Written By
Phone: (323) 782-4522
web site: *www.wga.org/WrittenBY*

APPENDIX VI—BOOKS

Brown, Blain. *Motion Picture and Video Lighting*. Newton, MA: Focal Press, 1996.

Buzzell, Linda. *How to Make It in Hollywood: All the Right Moves*. New York: HarperPerennial, 1996.

Dunne, John Gregory. *Monster: Living Off the Big Screen*. Vintage Books, 1998.

_____. *The Studio*. Vintage Books, 1998.

Ensign, Lynne Naylor and Robyn Eileen Knapton. *The Complete Dictionary of Television and Film*. New York: Stein and Day Publishers, 1985.

Fitzsimmons, April. *Breaking & Entering*. Los Angeles: Lone Eagle Publishing Company, 1997.

Goldman, William. *Adventures in the Screen Trade: A Personal View of Hollywood and Screenwriting*. Warner Books, 1989.

_____. *Which Lie Did I Tell?: More Adventures in the Screen Trade*. Vintage Books, 2001.

_____. *William Goldman: Four Screenplays With Essays: Marathon Man, Butch Cassidy and the Sundance Kid, The Princess Bride, Misery*. Applause Theatre Book Publishers, 1997.

Gottlieb-Walker, Kim, ed. *Setiquette*. Los Angeles: International Photographers Guild, 1997.

Harmon, Renee, James Lawrence, and Jim Lawrence (Contributor). *The Beginning Filmmaker's Guide to a Successful First Film*. Walker & Co., 1997

Harmon, Renee. *Film Directing: Killer Style & Cutting Edge Technique*. Los Angeles: Lone Eagle Publishing Company, 1997.

Houghton, Buck. *What a Producer Does: The Art of Moviemaking (Not the Business)*. Silman-James Press, 1992.

Levy, Frederick. *Hollywood 101: The Film Industry, (How to Succeed in Hollywood Without Connections)*. Los Angeles: Renaissance Books, 2000.

Litwak, Mark. *Reel Power*. New York: Plume, 1986.

Lumet, Sidney. *Making Movies*. New York: Vintage, 1996.

McAlister, Michael J. *The Language of Visual Effects*. Los Angeles: Lone Eagle Publishing Company, 1993.

Merritt, Greg. *Film Production: The Complete Uncensored Guide to Filmmaking*. Los Angeles: Lone Eagle Publishing Company, 1998.

Phillips, Julia. *You'll Never Eat Lunch in This Town Again*. New American Library Trade, 2002.

Resnik, Gail and Scott Trost. *All You Need to Know About the Movie and TV Business.* New York: Simon & Schuster, Inc., 1996.

Seger, Linda and Edward Jay Whetmore. *From Script to Screen: The Collaborative Art of Filmmaking.* Owlet, 1994.

Seger, Linda. *Making a Good Script Great, 2nd Edition.* Samuel French Trade, 1994.

_____. *When Women Call the Shots: The Developing Power and Influence of Women in Television and Film.* Henry Holt, 1997.

Squire, Jason E., ed. *The Movie Business Book.* New York: Simon & Schuster, 1983.

Taub, Eric. *Gaffers, Grips, and Best Boys.* New York: St. Martin's Press, 1987.

Taylor, Hugh. *The Hollywood Job-Hunter's Survival Guide/An Insider's Winning Strategies for Getting That (All-Important First Job and Keeping It).* Los Angeles: Lone Eagle Publishing Company, 1992.

Uva, Michael G., and Sabrina Uva. *The Grip Book.* Woburn, MA: Focal Press, 1997.

Wilson, John Morgan. *Inside Hollywood: A Writer's Guide to Researching the World of Movies and TV.* Cincinnati, OH: Writer's Digest Books, 1998.

_____, Introduction by Peter Bart, Editor in Chief, *Variety. Variety Power Players 2000.* New York: A Perigee Book, 1999.

GLOSSARY

A-list The very best; the highest quality. Usually describes top talent.

above-the-line or **above-the-line expenses/costs** Expenses incurred before production begins, including acquisition of the story rights or a project from another company; fees paid to the creative talent: actors, directors, producers, and writer(s); and travel.

above the title Contractual billing of an actor's name above the film's title.

acquisition The purchase of distribution rights to a packaged or finished project by a production company, studio, or distributor.

attached talent Generally, the actors, director, producer, or writer who have agreed to participate in a specific project prior to it being sold.

action 1) The command given by the director, or another, to begin shooting a take; 2) the movement and business going on within the camera's view.

adapt or **adaptation** To rewrite a story from one medium to another, such as from a book to a movie screenplay.

ADR (Automatic Dialogue Replacement) Rerecording of production dialogue on a sound stage, against picture, to replace dialogue that is unusable for reasons such as a change in words, poor sound quality, or other problems.

aerial cinematography Film shot from a helicopter, airplane, or other airborne machine, with a camera hand-held by a cinematographer or mounted on the aircraft.

agent The person or firm that promotes, solicits work, and negotiates contracts for an above-the-line or below-the-line talent or property.

animator Generally, the animator is responsible for creating cartoon characters, the most common form of animation, but the process can also include silhouettes, props, and other objects. An animator determines the amount of change needed in each cel or individual frame of film to create the illusion of movement.

apple boxes Boxes, usually constructed from wood, used to raise the height of an actor, piece of furniture, light, or prop, during a shot. In the early days of filmmaking, an actual apple box was used.

apprentice A person who learns job functions and gains experience by working under the direction of a skilled technician.

art department Crew members charged with creating and maintaining the visual look of the production. Individual positions include: art director, assistant art director, carpenter, draftsman, greensperson, leadman, production buyer, production designer, set decorator, set dresser, property assistant, property master, special effects supervisor, swing gang.

atmosphere The mood or emotional tone of a scene as communicated by lighting, music, camera angles, and so on.

Avid Brand name of the Macintosh computer-based nonlinear digital film editing system.

B-roll Secondary background footage that will be cut into the film's primary story line to help establish atmosphere, location, and so on.

back end Percentages and fees paid to individuals or companies after a production has turned a profit.

back lot An out-of-the-way area of studio property where permanent outdoor settings or "streets" are erected, each depicting a different geographical location or time, whose look can be altered as needed.

below-the-line or **below-the-line expenses/costs** Budgeted expenses assigned to crew and production costs such as art department, camera, electrical, film and film processing, hair dressing, location fees, makeup, music licensing and recording, production staff, props, retakes, set construction, set dressing, sound recording, special effects, studio rental, transportation, visual effects, and wardrobe. Those fees not associated with above-the-line expenses.

bible The compilation of all information pertaining to story lines and locations, and the complete history of each character. Used as a reference guide to maintain continuity and consistency from one episode to the next in an ongoing film or television series.

billing The ranking of actors' names in credits, advertising, and so on.

blocking The planned movement or position of the performers and cameras for a shot. "Marks" are taped to the floor or "chalked" to ensure accuracy and consistency.

blue screen A blue backdrop against which an actor is filmed, which will be digitally replaced with background footage in postproduction.

boom The pole that holds the microphone above the performers' heads and out of the shot, so the sound mixer can record their dialogue.

breakdown The process of analyzing a script to discover critical information needed by each department. For example, a shot-by-shot description of action to be photographed; specific props called for in the script; costume changes for each character; and visual effects to be created.

callback Any additional interview(s) or reading(s) with an actor after the initial audition.

call sheet Daily schedule of times for actors and crew to report to the set.

camera package All equipment related to the camera used on a shoot.

cast 1) The actors in a production; 2) The process of selecting actors to portray characters in a production.

CG Computer generated.

clip A short excerpt of film footage used for promotional purposes.

continuity The consistency of dialogue, physical movement, clothing, hairstyles, makeup, furniture, props, and other elements, within a shot or scene.

coverage The filming of a scene with multiple cameras and camera angles to provide sufficient choice of footage for later editing.

crane A piece of heavy equipment with a mobile arm upon which the camera is mounted, enabling sweeping camera movement and high angle shots.

credits The names and titles of cast and crew involved with a production.

cutting The process of selecting, editing, and splicing film footage together.

dailies Footage from the previous day's shoot, screened at the end of the workday.

day player A day player is a performer or crew member hired on a daily basis. For instance, a production might be shooting an outdoor scene with hundreds of extras, and hire a day player in the wardrobe department or grip department to assist with the added volume of work. Serving as a day player is a good way to get on set, learn how things operate, and make contacts for future jobs.

deal memo The legally binding preliminary outline of a contract.

development The process of readying a screenplay to the point where filming can begin.

digital effects Computer generated special effects.

director's cut The version of a film edited to the director's specification.

dissolve The optical effect of one shot or scene fading into the next.

dolly A piece of wheeled equipment set on a track and upon which a camera is mounted, enabling smooth camera movement.

dubbing The addition of sound to film footage in postproduction. See *looping*.

dupe A duplicate copy of a negative made from the original negative. See *print*.

effects Sounds or images created to heighten the action or mood of a scene.

electronic press kit (EPK) Videotaped cast and crew interviews and behind the scenes footage used to generate free publicity from the media.

episodic television An ongoing weekly television series.

extras Background actors with nonspeaking parts.

feature A full-length motion picture.

film commission Organizations set up to invite and assist filming within a particular city, state, or country.

film stock The unexposed material used to capture photographic images.

final cut The edited version of a film that is released to theaters.

financier The organization or individual(s) who provide the funding for a production.

first-look deal An arrangement whereby a studio pays a production company's overhead costs in return for the first option on their product.

flag A cloth or metal covering used to soften a light's effect.

foley The postproduction process of adding sound effects to match the action taking place on-screen.

footage Exposed film containing a photographic image.

green light A project approved for production is said to have been given the "green light."

gofer The lowest level production assistant, often unpaid, who performs menial tasks and errands. Literally, to "go for." See *runner*.

guild An organization set up to protect the rights of and set the standards for its member craftsmen. See *union*.

honey wagon The chain of personal trailers, dressing rooms, and portable toilets brought to a location shoot.

independent film, indie A film produced without the funding or input of a major studio.

in the can A production that has finished shooting, but is not yet edited for release.

(the) industry The motion picture industry, in general.

infomercial Television advertising presented in the format of regular programming.

Lightworks Brand name of the DOS-based nonlinear digital film editing system.

literary A category term for writers, directors, and some producers.

location The setting where a scene is filmed, which is usually pre-existing and away from the studio or soundstage.

looping The postproduction recording and replacement of actor dialogue within filmed footage. See *dubbing*.

made-for-video; direct-to-video A full-length feature made specifically for the video market, rather than for theatrical release.

mail room The department of an agency or studio responsible for sorting and delivering incoming mail. The entry-level training ground for future agents and studio executives.

marketing campaign The planned promotion and publicity of an upcoming film.

material A category term for screenplays and manuscripts.

matte painting A painted background inserted into the filmed footage during postproduction.

merchandising Licensed products whose design is based on a film or television show.

mix The compilation of various sound tracks into one.

montage A rapid sequence of filmed images used to suggest the passage of time.

networking Social contacts made within an industry with the aim of advancing one's career.

nonpro An individual who does not work in the film industry.

notes A brief written notation of inconsistencies or problems in a screenplay or during filming that need to be addressed and fixed.

novelization A fictional literary work based upon a film or screenplay.

on location Filming that takes place away from the studio or soundstage.

on set The immediate area where a scene is filmed.

one-sheet A standard size movie advertising poster, usually about 2 × 3 feet.

opening The debut of a film to general release.

option A deal to pay a deposit toward the potential future purchase of a project.

overhead The cost of operating a business, including rent, equipment, salaries, utilities, and so on.

package A term describing a script with a key cast or crew member committed to participating in its production.

perk An additional, nonmonetary privilege given to a key cast or crew member to "sweeten" the deal.

picked up A film or television project or series which is purchased, approved for production, or renewed is said to have been "picked up."

pitch The verbal presentation of an idea or story line to those entities who might purchase it.

point of view (POV) The subjective perception from which a story is told.

polish A minor rewrite to refine a screenplay.

postproduction Every process that goes into finishing a film after the principal photography is completed.

preproduction The process of readying a project for production that occurs between the development and filming phases.

press junket A post-screening one-on-one publicity interview marathon between the media and a production's director and lead actors.

press kit A publicity package of photographs, cast and crew biographies, production synopsis, and so on, sent out to the print media.

principal photography The period of time allotted to complete filming.

print The positive image printed from a film negative, or a duplicate copy of that image. See *dupe.*

production A term describing the filmmaking process or the project itself.

production assistant (PA) An entry level position, production assistants are generally assigned menial tasks such as making photocopies, fetching coffee and lunch, and running errands. Production assistants are attached to a department, such as camera department, costume department, the production office, art department, and so forth.

production board A board with a series of strips representing master scenes used to visually organize the production into the actual sequence of scenes in which they will be shot. Strips vary in color to distinguish day from night shooting.

production company A firm that develops and produces film or television projects.

production report A daily accounting of hours worked, footage shot, and other production information used to monitor budgets and schedules.

production sound Dialogue and ambient sound recorded during filming.

prop Any item that is used or handled by an actor, or is otherwise identified in the script.

publicity The generation of free media coverage and advertising.

pulling focus The process whereby the assistant camera operator maintains consistent focus by adjusting the lens to compensate for the movement of the camera.

query letter An unsolicited letter sent to a producer or agent to elicit interest in a writer's product.

reel A video résumé containing samples of a director's, cinematographer's, or crew member's best work.

rough cut The intermediate edited version of a film made subsequent to the initial assembly of footage, but prior to the refining process of the fine cut.

runner Sometimes referred to as a production assistant, the runner's primary function is to run errands such as picking up and delivering packages, videotape, scripts, contracts, and lunch. See *gofer.*

sample A script or screenplay used as an example of a writer's work, to obtain a writing assignment or commission.

scene A section of a script taking place in a single location, or focused on a specific character or group of characters, that ends with the movement to another location.

score A film's musical sound track.

screenplay The script for a film production. See *teleplay*.

script The written story line that the director and actors work from; contains plot development, characters, dialogue, and situations.

set The immediate area where filmed action takes place, often constructed on a soundstage.

set up The arrangement of camera and lighting for a particular scene or shot.

shoot The act of filming with a camera; the location where filming is taking place.

shooting schedule A detailed listing of filming days and times, cast and crew members required, location changes, and transportation needs.

shooting script The version of the script that has been approved for production.

shop To present or "pitch" a project to those entities capable of financing it.

shot A brief, unedited section of film devoted to a single item or view.

slate The clapboard filmed at the start of each take, identifying the shot and take by number for the editor.

sound effects Sound other than music, narration, or dialogue that is added in postproduction.

soundstage A hangar-like building where filming takes place under controlled conditions on specially constructed sets.

spec script A completed script that has not been contracted from a writer, that is offered for sale; literally, on speculation.

stand-in A person who substitutes for an actor during the long process of blocking and lighting.

Steadicam A movie camera that is mounted to the body of its operator and maneuvered by him.

storyboard A sequence of drawings that depict the story line as a guide for filming.

studio A company formed to acquire, finance, produce, and distribute films or television programming.

sync; synchronization The exact matching of sound to filmed action.

syndication Generally, describes television programming licensed for reruns after its original network contract has expired.

take One filmed version of a particular scene.

talent A category term for a writer, director, or actor.

teleplay The script for a television program. See *screenplay*.

time code The sequential reference code attached to each frame of film that aids the editor in cutting the footage together.

trades Entertainment industry publications like *Hollywood Reporter* and *Daily Variety*.

trailer A compilation of film clips taken from a soon-to-be released feature and used for promotional purposes.

trainee An entry-level position similar to a production assistant, the difference being a trainee is generally being groomed for a specific job within a company.

treatment The written synopsis of a screenplay, giving an overview of the characters and story line.

turnaround The period of time between when a studio decides not to proceed with a project, and the project is resold to another buyer to recoup production costs.

union An organization that protects the rights of and sets the standards for its members. See *guild*.

union scale The minimum pay rate approved by a union for its members.

wrap A shot, shoot, or production that is completed is said to be "wrapped."

video playback The videotape that is available for immediate viewing before the film is processed.

voiceover Narration delivered by an off-screen voice, added to the on-screen footage.

ACKNOWLEDGMENTS

I feel honored and privileged to have interviewed and heard the stories of the individuals profiled in this book: Arthur Anderson; Vic Armstrong; Joe Askin; Marc Ball; Carlos Barbosa; Gabe Bartalos; Charles Thomas Baxter; Alan C. Blomquist; Donna E. Bloom; Jim Borgardt; Julie Butchco; Russell Caldwell; Dwight Campbell; A. Anthony Cappello; Jeff Charbonneau; Todd Cherniawsky; Tim Clawson; Tim Cooney; Richard Crudo; Mel Damski; Allen Daviau; Laura J. DeRosa; Steve Dorff; Gary Duncan; Peter Dunne; Diana Eden; Andy Edmunds; David Emmerichs; Brian Erzen; Bob Foster; Jonathan Furie; Clarke Gallivan; Mike Gentile; Jim Gill; Peter Giuliano; Kim Golasheksy; Steven Goldmann; Anne Gordon; Anne Grace; Barklie Griggs; Steve Gums; Brian Hamill; Joe Hanna; Mike Harris; Duncan Henderson; Randy Himes; Susan Youngman Hoen; Todd Homme; Robert Hutchin; Jason Ivey; Patrick Read Johnson; Thomas Johnston; Bobby Jones; Jay Kemp; David Lazan; Neil A. Machlis; Al Magliochetti; Jeff Mann; Clark Mathis; Detdrick McClure; Katrine Migliore; Harry Monreau; Bob Munoz; Jeffrey A. Okun; Suzanne Patterson; Kim Petrosky; Kathie Pierson; Justin Raleigh; Jane Raimondi; Celest Ray; Michael Reynolds; Diana C. Richardson; Jeane Ringe; Duane Roberts; Ernest H. Roth; Steve Sacks; M. Edward Salier; Duke Sandefur; John Schwartzman; Russell Senato; Bill Shotland; Kevin Sorrensen; Cid L. Swank; Beth Szymkowski; Rex Teese; Eric Tignini; Rick Toone; Daniel Turrett; Mark Walpole; Stuart Wilson; and Steven J. Wright.

Thank you Art Ford, Richard J. Gelfand, Julie Houlihan, Will Jennings, Brian Loucks, Mary Jo Mennella, Kathleen Merrill, Jacquie Perryman, Mary Beth Phelps, Harry Stinson, and Vinny Tabone, who were interviewed, but due to time constraints and other technical issues their stories were not included. I am also grateful for the many others who agreed to be interviewed, but scheduling conflicts conspired to keep us apart. I hope there will be an opportunity in the future.

Special thanks to my new friends Charlie Baxter, Andy Edmunds, and Bob Foster, and long-time pals Gabe Bartalos and Al Megliochetti, for introducing me to some of your friends who are profiled in this book. A very, very special thanks to my dear friend Daniel Turrett, who went above and beyond to connect me with many, many of his friends— I cannot find strong enough words to express my gratitude.

Thank you to the young men and young women I have had the privilege of teaching and working with in Sunday school, Young Women, and Seminary, particularly: Ashley Brickle, Chesarae Collier, Deborah

Collins, Kevin Collins, Katharine Dinwiddie, Devon Dixon, Diane Dixon, Eric Ellsworth, Carly Frazier, Rachel Frazier, Randi Harris, Scott Hotard, Steven Hotard, Wren Hunter, Hollie Johnson, Amy Linder, Sarah Linder, Mindy Nabrotzky, Ricky Parris, Brad Peterson, Kristin Peterson, Alexis Price, Keri Reed, Vickie Rosa, Mark Sanderson, Ashley Savarda, Rachel Settle, Todd Soderquist, Diana Stucki, Eric Thomas, Travis Thurman, Sierra Westfall, David Williamson, Diane Williamson, Kiel Wilson, Christie Winborn, Jessica Winborn. And to the missionaries currently serving whom I am so proud to know: Elder Scott Allen, Elder Scott Collins, Elder Chris Harris, Elder Jon Hekking, Elder Clint Proctor, and Elder Jesse Welsh. Thank you Susan and Jay Yates for your love and prayers.

Special thanks to my agent Diedre Knight of The Knight Agency, for your continued love, support, and prayers (I've said it before, but you are a gift from God and I treasure you in my life); to my wonderful editor at Barron's Educational Series, Wendy Sleppin, for her encouragement and enthusiasm; to Steve Matteo, Barron's publicity manager, for his energy and excitement, and to Lou Vasquez and Bill Kuchler for the beautiful design and layout of this book.

Thank you to my family for their continued love and support: Luana Peck, Jim and Linda Peck, Dustin, Stacy, and Braden Peck, Dennis and Carolyn Peck and family, Earlene Crouch, Jody and Stephen Williams, Rob and Georgia Crouch, Kevin, Danielle, Bryan, and Camille Crouch, Julie and David Ashby, Amanda, Michael, and Lindsey Ashby, and Delores Sanders. I could not have completed this book without my husband, best friend, and love, Kevin (The Kev), who is a gifted writer, editor, and cheerleader. Above all, I must acknowledge Jesus Christ for his example and love, and my Heavenly Father for his blessings and love.

This book is dedicated in loving memory of:

Charles W. Peck, October 20, 1918–February 25, 1997

and

Robert B. Crouch, July 23, 1925–April 14, 2002

●●●●

INDEX